EVALUATING DEVELOPMENT ASSISTANCE: POLICIES AND PERFORMANCE

EADI BOOK SERIES 12: SERIES ON EVALUATION OF AID
edited by Olav Stokke (This volume is also No. 75 in the series
Norwegian Foreign Policy Studies, Norwegian Institute of
International Affairs, Oslo.)

EVALUATING DEVELOPMENT ASSISTANCE
Policies and Performance

edited by

OLAV STOKKE

FRANK CASS • LONDON
Published in collaboration with
The European Association of Development Research and
Training Institutes (EADI), Geneva

First published in 1991 in Great Britain by
FRANK CASS & CO. LTD.
Gainsborough House, Gainsborough Road,
London E11 1RS, England

and in the United States of America by
FRANK CASS
c/o International Specialized Book Services, Inc.
5602 N.E. Hassalo Street
Portland, Oregon 97213

Copyright © 1991 EADI and authors

British Library Cataloguing in Publication Data
Stokke, Olav
 Evaluating development assistance : policies
 and performance. – (EADI book series; 12)
 I. Title II. Series
 338.91

ISBN 0714634468

Library of Congress Cataloging-in-Publication Data
Evaluating development assistance : policies and performance / edited
by Olav Stokke.
   p.   cm. — (EADI book series ; 12)
 ISBN 0-7146-3446-8
 1. Economic assistance—Developing countries—Evaluation.
 I. Stokke, Olav, 1934— . II. Series.
 HC60.E798   1991
 338.9′1′068—dc20   91–29762
                                                            CIP

All rights reserved. No part of this publication may be reproduced in any form or by any means, electronic, mechanical, photocopying, recording or otherwise, without the prior permission of Frank Cass and Company Limited.

Typeset by Regent Typesetting, London
Printed in Great Britain by
Antony Rowe Ltd, Chippenham, Wilts

Contents

Foreword	vi
Acronyms and Abbreviations	ix
1. Policies, Performance, Trends and Challenges in Aid Evaluation *Olav Stokke*	1
2. Evaluation Policy and Performance: The State of the Art *Helge Kjekshus*	60
3. The Evaluation Policy and Performance of Britain *Basil E. Cracknell*	71
4. The Evaluation Policy and Performance of Denmark *Henrik Schaumburg-Müller*	100
5. Evaluation Policy and Performance in the Federal Republic of Germany *Stefan A. Musto*	127
6. Aid Evaluation in the Netherlands *Enno W. Hommes*	149
7. The Evaluation Policy and Performance of Norway *Olav Stokke*	163
8. The Evaluation Policy and Performance of Sweden *Kim Forss*	208
9. The Evaluation Policy and Performance of the United Nations Population Fund (UNFPA) *Kerstin Trone*	227
10. The Role of an Evaluation Unit: Functions, Constraints and Feedback *Basil E. Cracknell*	248
Index	272
Notes on Contributors	297

Foreword

The present volume belongs to a series focusing on the evaluation of development assistance. This series is part of a research and publishing programme under the auspices of the Working Group on Aid Policy and Performance of the European Association of Development Research and Training Institutes (EADI). An earlier volume focuses on the performance and economic impact of food aid and a forthcoming volume on evaluation methods.

The decision to make evaluation of development assistance its major task was reached in Madrid in 1984 when the Working Group on Aid Policy and Performance responded favourably to a position paper by the Convenor. That year, the Working Group had fulfilled its first major task with the publication of *European Development Assistance*, Volumes 1 (Policies and Performance) and 2 (Third World Perspectives on Policies and Performance) as No. 4 in the EADI Book Series, published by Tilburg. Three years later, at the EADI 5th General Conference in Amsterdam, the evaluation programme was formally launched. At that point, funding had been secured for the first project, and the planning and design of the projects could enter a new phase.

The three volumes are emerging from a similar process. For each project, a design is worked out by the organisers. Outstanding researchers or experts in the relevant field are asked for comments on the design. These consultations are followed by invitations to provide a component study. The draft studies for each project are presented at a workshop to which, in addition to the authors, a selected group of experts, representing the immediate environment of the chosen theme (researchers, top administrators and others in the specific field), are personally invited. It is the matured versions of drafts which have been scrutinised through this process and then edited that are presented in this series.

The series starts with a volume on a high-profile and controversial aspect of aid policy, food aid (Edward Clay and Olav Stokke (eds.), *Food Aid Reconsidered: Assessing the Impact on Third World Countries*). The present volume on evaluation policies and performance will be followed by a third on evaluation methods. That project is now in the editorial phase – the draft papers were discussed at a workshop in March this year.

Evaluation of development assistance became increasingly important during the early 1980s for several – and very often contradictory –

FOREWORD

reasons. Basically, however, the stagnation in economic growth among the donors and pressures on their internal and foreign economy brought their aid programmes under strain. Critics of aid saw in evaluation an instrument to justify cuts in the ODA programme – as the outcome was taken for granted: aid did not work or at best very badly. Proponents of development assistance – and the aid agencies – came under pressure to prove that aid, after all, did work. Evaluation was seen as an instrument to this end, too. The Cassen Report (Robert Cassen and Associates, *Does Aid Work?*, Oxford University Press, 1986) – being commissioned by the Task Force on Concessional Flows set up by the Joint Ministerial Committee of the Boards of Governors of the World Bank and the International Monetary Fund – is just another expression of this need to prove that aid does work.

However, perspectives on evaluation vary with positions. An aid agency may perceive the needs and priorities differently from those responsible for overall policy (minister, government, parliament) – and even within an aid agency, priorities and needs may be conceived differently from the (country or sectoral) desk level than from the top management. The evaluation policy and performance may therefore differ from one country to another, depending on the balance struck between the different perspectives. This balance has more than an academic interest – in the end it affects the effectiveness and efficiency of national aid programmes.

This was the major concern when the EADI project was conceived. Evaluation may serve both as a management tool and as a policy instrument in the control and direction of aid implementation. It was felt that a review of the evaluation policies and performance of a selection of European countries – including some of the major aid providers and countries with different evaluation systems – might bring an important policy tool out in the open, to be discussed within a comparative framework. Outstanding researchers in the field and top administrators of aid evaluation with a distinct analytical leaning were invited to contribute the component studies involved.

The papers were presented at a workshop in June 1988 organised by the Norwegian Institute of International Affairs at Lysebu, on the outskirts of Oslo. Aid administrators outside the core group were also involved. That fertile interaction of administrators and researchers resulted in a significant strengthening of almost all the papers that are now presented in this volume.

No research and publishing programme on this ambitious scale could proceed without much help and goodwill. The overall programme received, at an early stage, a funding commitment from the Ministry of

Development Cooperation, Oslo, that made it possible to proceed with the planning. The Ministry has generously contributed to the particular project on evaluation policies and performance by funding the major costs involved in organising the Lysebu workshop. We acknowledge this grant with pleasure and appreciation.

From the very beginning, the programme has had the privilege of being integrated in the research programme of the Norwegian Institute of International Affairs in Oslo and has benefited from its institutional support. The project on evaluation policies and performance has, in particular, benefited from the efficient secretarial support of Ms Tone Strand Muss, especially during the workshop at Lysebu. Warm thanks also go to Ms Wendy Davies for her assistance in editing the present volume, and to Mr Neil Tomkinson who has provided the volume with an Index.

Olav Stokke
Convenor, EADI Working Group
on Aid Policy and Performance
Oslo, October 1990   Director, Evaluation Programme

Acronyms and Abbreviations

ACP	African, Caribbean and Pacific countries, signatories of the Lomé Conventions
ATP	Aid Trade Provision (the UK)
BCB	British Consultants Bureau
BITS	Beredningen för Internationellt och Tekniskt Samarbete (Swedish Agency for International Technical and Economic Cooperation)
BMZ	Bundesministerium für Wirtschaftliche Zusammenarbeit (Federal Ministry for Economic Cooperation, FRG)
CDG	Carl Duisberg Gesellschaft (Carl Duisberg Society)
CIDA	Canadian International Development Agency
CIP	Commodity Import Programme
CK	Centralkommittén (Central Committee, Sweden)
CR	Country Review
DAC	Development Assistance Committee (OECD)
DANIDA	Danish International Development Agency
DED	Deutscher Entwicklungsdienst (German Volunteers' Service)
DGIS	Directorate-General for Development Cooperation
DKK	Danish Kroner (currency)
DM	Deutsche Mark (currency)
DSE	Deutsche Stiftung für Internationale Entwicklung (German Foundation for International Development)
DTI	Department of Trade and Industry (the UK)
EADI	European Association of Development Research and Training Institutes
EC	European Community
ECOSOC	Economic and Social Council (UN)
EVSUM	Evaluation Summary (ODA)
FAO	Food and Agriculture Organisation (UN)
FES	Friedrich Ebert Stiftung
FMI	Financial Management Initiative (the UK)
FMU	Financial Management Unit (the UK)
FNS	Friedrich Naumann Stiftung
FRG	Federal Republic of Germany

GDP	Gross Domestic Product
GNP	Gross National Product
GTZ	(Deutsche) Gesellschaft für Technische Zusammenarbeit (German Agency for Technical Cooperation)
IBRD	International Bank for Reconstruction and Development/World Bank
IDA	International Development Association (IBRD)
IER	Internal Evaluation Report
IGBA	Independent Group on British Aid (the UK)
ILO	International Labour Organisation
IMF	International Monetary Fund
IMPOD	Importkontoret för u-landsprodukter (Import Promotion Office for Products from Developing Countries, Sweden)
IOV	Inspectie Ontwikkelingssamenwerking te Velde (Inspection Unit, the Netherlands)
IRDP	Integrated Rural Development Project
IRV	Insats- och resultatvärdering (Assessment of activities and results, Sweden)
JIU	Joint Inspection Unit (UN)
JMU	Joint Management Unit (the UK)
KfW	Kreditanstalt für Wiederaufbau (Bank for Reconstruction, FRG)
LO	Landsorganisasjonen i Norge (Norwegian Trade Union Federation)
MAFF	Ministry of Agriculture, Fisheries and Food (the UK)
MC	Mixed Credits
MDC	Ministry for Development Cooperation (Norway)
MIS	Management Information System (ODA)
MP	Member of Parliament
NGO	Non-Governmental Organisation
NOK	Norwegian Kroner (currency)
NORAD	Norwegian Agency for International Development
NOVIB	Nederlandse Organisatie voor Internationale Samenwerking (Dutch Organisation for International Cooperation)
NTUF	Norwegian Trade Union Federation
NUPI	Norsk Utenrikspolitisk Institutt (Norwegian Institute of International Affairs)
ODA	Overseas Development Administration (United

ACRONYMS AND ABBREVIATIONS

	Kingdom)
ODA	Official Development Assistance
ODI	Overseas Development Institute (London)
ODM	Ministry of Overseas Development (United Kingdom)
OECD	Organisation for Economic Cooperation and Development
PAC	Public Accounts Committee (the UK)
PAR	Programme Analysis and Review (ODA)
PC	Programme Committee
PCR	Project Completion Report
PEC	Projects and Evaluation Committee (ODA)
PF	Parallel Financing
PGN	Policy Guidance Note (ODA)
PPR	Project Progress Report
SADCC	Southern African Development Coordination Conference
SAREC	Swedish Agency for Research Cooperation with Developing Countries
SEK	Swedish Kronor (currency)
SIDA	Swedish International Development Authority
SWEDFUND	Swedish Fund for Industrial Cooperation with Developing Countries
TC	Technical Cooperation
TOOL	(Dutch NGO)
TOR	Terms of Reference
TPR	Tripartite Project Review
UK	United Kingdom
UN	United Nations
UNDP	United Nations Development Program
UNESCO	United Nations Educational, Scientific and Cultural Organisation
UNICEF	United Nations (International) Children's (Emergency) Fund
UNIFEM	United Nations Development Fund for Women
UNFPA	United Nations Fund for Population Activities/ United Nations Population Fund (renamed 1988)
UNIDO	United Nations Industrial Development Organisation
USAID	United States Agency for International Development
VSO	Voluntary Service Organisation (the UK)
WHO	World Health Organisation
WID	Women in Development

1

Policies, Performance, Trends and Challenges in Aid Evaluation

OLAV STOKKE

'The ideal organization would be self-evaluating. It would continuously monitor its own activities so as to determine whether it was meeting its goals or even whether these goals should continue to prevail.'

Aaron Wildavsky [1972]

In the 1980s, evaluation of development assistance came increasingly to the fore. It became the universal remedy around which actors with highly conflicting attitudes towards aid could rally. Politicians wanting to do away with public spending on development assistance – or looking for arguments for reducing aid in a strained budget situation – saw evaluation as an instrument for legitimising such policy positions. Proponents of increased aid – although in the 1980s the main concern has rather been to maintain aid at its established level [*Stokke (ed.), 1989*] – saw it as a means of proving that aid worked. Governments and aid agencies with responsibility for aid programmes saw evaluation as an instrument to legitimise aid-spending *vis-à-vis* both its critics and the public at large.

Although monitoring and evaluation, in one form or another, have always been an integral part of governance in most, if not all, types of political systems, the way these public activities are conceived of and organised today is fairly new. In Europe, evaluation, as a tool in public administration, was first introduced in the field of development assistance. In its infancy in the 1970s, it gradually became generally recognised and institutionalised in the late 1970s and early 1980s, when most European aid agencies established evaluation units within their organisations. However, the contexts in which the evaluation and monitoring functions were organised varied from one country to another, as did the foci chosen.

Evaluation has the potential to influence aid performance. The foci chosen, the direction of attention, the questions asked, all signal to the aid agencies' operative units what really matters at the end of the day. The strength of such signals depends of course on how recommendations are followed up. Evaluation policy and performance, therefore, go beyond the immediate outcome of individual evaluations.

In this study of the aid evaluation policies and performance a comparative approach adds to the insights gained from studying the policy within the confines of one country. Although the component studies focus on single countries, the approach to the subject matter follows a common research design. In this chapter, the policies and performances of these countries are analysed from a comparative perspective.

The main purpose of this study is to take stock of the evaluation policies that were evolving in Europe during the 1980s. Since we are covering new ground, the emphasis is on descriptive analysis, the main objectives being

(1) to examine the institutional models chosen by a selection of west European donor countries and the priority given to evaluation in terms of the resources (personnel and finance) allocated and the amount of evaluation work being carried out;
(2) to identify and discuss the main orientation of the evaluation policies and performance of these countries, especially the priority given to competing concerns and in particular the balance between 'control' and 'management' functions.

There are competing norms involved, too, adapted to the functions referred to in (2) above and, by the same token, also reflecting such policy choices. One (i) relates to whether evaluation should be *independent* – carried out by *external* evaluators – or *internal* – carried out by the aid agency itself. Another (ii) relates to the question of openness – whether evaluation reports should be open and available to all or restricted to the aid agency and those with a direct responsibility for aid implementation.

Yet another dimension of the policy relates to the participation, within evaluations, of the recipients of aid. This applies, in the first place, to the authorities of the host country (for bilateral state-to-state aid) but may involve other actors on the recipient side as well – ultimately the beneficiaries and other stakeholders. To what extent and in what manner are recipients involved in the evaluation efforts of the countries chosen for the component studies?

Basically, evaluation is supposed to produce and disseminate information. The key questions, accordingly, are *who* are producing *what kind* of information, *how*, to *whom*, for *what purpose* and with *what effects*? In this study, the emphasis is on who, what kind, to whom and for what purpose.

Both large and small European countries have been selected for separate studies, the United Kingdom (UK) and the Federal Republic of Germany (FRG) among the larger and, from the smaller, the so-called front-runners – the four countries which have provided most official development assistance (ODA) as a percentage of gross national product (GNP), namely Denmark, the Netherlands, Norway and Sweden. For years these four countries have provided aid above the target of 0.7 per cent of GNP. An international agency – the United Nations Population Fund (UNFPA) – is included, for two reasons in particular: the UNFPA works through other agencies to implement aid, and its monitoring and evaluation system has recently been the subject of a thorough review in which the experiences of previous approaches were discussed and conclusions drawn for the future.

This volume starts with a presentation, in Chapter 2, of the state of the art of evaluation, with particular reference to the co-operation within the Development Assistance Committee (DAC) of the Organisation for Economic Development and Cooperation (OECD). The author, Dr Helge Kjekshus, has participated in the process as a member of the Expert Group on Aid Evaluation established by the DAC, in the early 1980s, to coordinate the evaluation of aid among its members. The volume ends (Chapter 10) with a study of the role of an evaluation unit within an aid agency, its functions and constraints, with particular reference to the feedback of evaluation findings. Its author, Dr Basil Cracknell, formerly Head of the Evaluation Department of the (UK) Overseas Development Administration (ODA), draws on his experiences in the ODA.

I. WHAT DOES EVALUATION MEAN?

Towards a General Definition

Evaluation may be designed and used for many different purposes. As noted, actors with different, even contradictory, attitudes to aid may see different potentials in the use of evaluation. The cultural and political environments can also vary quite extensively. Such variations may have a bearing on the kind of evaluation that is contemplated or indeed possible to carry out. Administrative traditions vary, too, with similar effects. Basically, however, evaluation may be defined as a process in which, at a certain point in time, the result of a defined input into a system is systematically assessed and reported.[1]

This general definition gives room for a variety of activities. *The input* refers to the resources (of different kinds) and activities which are mobilised in order to produce a defined output. *The result* refers to the effects of this input, intended as well as unintended; such effects may relate to material as well as less material factors related to the quality of life. In the early period of aid evaluation, economic dimensions were in the forefront; in the 1970s, the socio-economic dimension came increasingly to the fore, related, *inter alia*, to social target groups (the poorest, women, children); and in the 1980s, attention was also focused on the ecological dimension and the effects of aid on the environment.

The outcome may be identified by different *techniques* – varying from the tools of different scientific disciplines to impressionistic observations. This applies to *assessments*, too. Assessments relate, in the first place, to the causality between input and output. In a social setting, the outcome often results from a wide range of inputs and interactions. The validity of an assessment may, therefore, depend on the ability of the approach and method used to isolate and measure the effects stemming from the specific input focused on; in this respect, needless to say, the quality of assessments may vary extensively, depending on the appropriateness and sharpness of the approach and the tools. The outcome will also be affected by environmental factors, such as systemic characteristics (related, *inter alia*, to culture, economy and politics) and resources, including the natural environments. The effect of a given aid intervention ('input') may, accordingly, differ extensively from one environment to another and, as an environment may change over time, the effect may also vary along this dimension within a given social system. The various *methods* of assessment are not equally well adapted to the different environments; methods do not possess cross-cultural generality, nor are they politically and ideologically neutral and theoretically unambiguous – they may reflect different concerns, values and perceptions of what matters in life.

The format and modes of *reporting* can also vary extensively – from scientific theses to news reports or an informal chat. As far as *timing* is concerned, the assessment may be undertaken before the 'input' is actually made (namely during the preparatory or planning stage of an aid intervention), during the period in which it is provided or after it has been finalised. The main concerns of an evaluation would vary with the point in time, in the cycle of an aid activity, at which it is carried out.

Given this broad spectrum of combinations, many activities will be defined as evaluation. However, the concept is often narrowed down in various ways – in particular by excluding the less formal variations. The term is often reserved for fact-finding processes in which professionally accepted methods are used to identify the results and assess or measure the outcome and the causalities involved. Although competent journalism – and informed, informal chats over a glass of beer – may provide feedback of a similar kind and equal quality, in an even more efficient way and with greater impact, only investigation processes that are formally reported are usually included in the concept. In actual practice, however, both the degree of sophistication with regard to the methodology and the degree of formality in the reporting may vary extensively from one country to another and also, within countries, from one field to another – and may, *inter alia*, reflect the predominant culture and technology. Even so, there is a trend towards internationally agreed concepts nurtured by the need to share experiences across borders and to improve meaningful communication.

Evaluation: A Recent Phenomenon in Europe

Evaluation, as broadly defined above, has, in one form or another, been part of governance within most social, economic and political systems. In a more systematic and formal sense, however, evaluation is a rather recent phenomenon, originating in the United States (US) in the early 1950s as a tool in public administration [*Kjekshus, 1991*].[2] Cracknell [*1988*] distinguishes, with particular reference to the evaluation of development assistance, between three phases of development; the early developments (1960s and 1970s), the explosion of interest (1979–84), and the coming of age (1985 to the present). Guba and Lincoln [*1987, 1989*], however, trace the roots of what is today recognised as evaluation even further back, identifying the emergence of the first generation in the early 1920s, the second in the early 1940s and the third in the mid-1960s – each with their distinct characteristics[3] – and with the emerging fourth generation knocking ever more loudly on the door since the early 1980s.[4] Among Third World countries, India was an early starter. A Programme Evaluation Organisation was established in the Indian Planning Commission in 1952, and evaluation has been evolving at the central and state levels there ever since.[5] Within the UN system, evaluation was introduced in the early 1950s – and in 1959 UNESCO produced a field manual for evaluating development projects [*JIU, 1982*].

In its more mature form (second and third generation), evaluation arrived in Europe relatively late – mainly as an administrative tool related to development assistance. The main carriers were the example provided by the bilateral US aid agency (USAID) and those of the international agencies, in particular the World Bank, with a top leadership drawn from the US administrative tradition. In Europe, evaluation of aid was, in some countries, taken up in the early 1960s and expanded in the late 1970s and early 1980s. It has gradually spread to other fields of public administration.

However, if success is measured by the degree of institutionalisation [*Cook, 1978*], evaluation of aid has an impressive record to show for the late 1970s and early 1980s; most bilateral European aid agencies built up separate evaluation units during that period and they have gradually been strengthened. Research institutes have gradually oriented themselves towards commissioned research and evaluation assignments and consultancy firms have been established for this purpose. Professional organisations – and journals – have yet to appear, however. For research institutes and consultancy firms alike, the main driving force for the involvement so far has been to bring in funds, not to increase professionalism within evaluation and improve both approaches and tools. In the early 1990s, to encourage a young faculty member to put all his or her energy into evaluation would most probably have been a shaky advice if academic promotion was the ultimate objective.

Towards a Common Language?

Within the field of development assistance, a conceptual framework was developed during the early 1980s. The OECD's Development Assistance Committee has taken a leading role in an effort to arrive at an internationally standardised language in this field, although it should be emphasised that this process is still at an early stage.

Given the context of development assistance, the OECD [*1986: 65*] defines evaluation as 'an examination as systematic and objective as possible of an on-going or completed project or programme, its design, implementation and results, with the aim of determining its efficiency, effectiveness, impact, sustainability and the relevance of the objectives ...'.[6]

This definition also gives room for many different activities. Other definitions, including the general definition given earlier, are even broader and may even include *appraisals* – investigations of the conditions and possible results of an intended input as part of the planning process or even before the planning starts.

As already noted, the major concerns of an evaluation depend to a large extent on when in the project cycle it is carried out – beforehand (as an appraisal), during its implementation phase or after the project (or the outside intervention) has been completed. The distinction between different types of evaluation is, therefore, related to this timing, but other aspects are also involved, such as organisational matters – in the first place, who are involved in the evaluation, insiders or outsiders, and who are the immediate users, the aid managers or the decision-makers, ultimately the electorate (for political systems that involve an electorate). Distinctions may be drawn between the following categories:

(1) *Auditing* – carried out by the State Auditor, an independent agency – implies a control of whether the financial resources are being used properly and in accordance with the established objectives. Such reviews are not always included under the evaluation umbrella.[7]

(2) *Monitoring* is part of the administrative follow-up of an aid activity (project, programme) during its implementation phase and, typically, focuses on operational activities such as management and the implementation of project-related objectives. Monitoring, accordingly, is mainly the responsibility of the implementing agency and is to a large extent carried out by the operative units themselves through regular reporting – including a final report on completion (*internal*).[8]

(3) *Reviews* are *internal* evaluations (although outside expertise may be drawn upon), carried out by the implementing agency. These may take place once or at regular intervals during the lifetime of a project (programme), for instance, as a *mid-term review*. Reviews and internal evaluations may be distinguished from monitoring both in terms of scope (they are more ambitious and also involve the objectives set) and organisation (a separate task force is used, not a reporting system involving the operative units).

(4) The core concept of *evaluation* is related to a professional assessment of the effectiveness and efficiency of an aid activity – which may involve the additional task of coming up with proposals for improvements. Evaluation of the *effectiveness* of aid is generally associated with the assessment of the extent to which the resources used (the 'input') have succeeded in achieving the agreed objectives set for the intervention – or, even broader, the general aims of aid as (if) defined. *Efficiency* is generally associated with the more narrow relation between costs and results (cost effectiveness) – *inter alia*, the management performance. Evaluation of the *impact* of an aid intervention is associated with effects on the recipient side in terms of economic, socio-cultural, environmental, institutional and technical factors.

Evaluation of the effectiveness, efficiency and impact of an aid intervention may take place during the project or programme cycle but is often associated with *ex post* investigations – undertaken at some point in time after a project or programme has been completed (that is, when the transfer of ODA resources has ended).

Evaluations of this kind are mainly carried out by *external* evaluators (which, in part, explains the distinction between (3) and (4)) – or by a combination of external and *internal* evaluators – although, in practice, not all aid agencies will necessarily be in line on this.

The main distinction, appraisals aside, is between monitoring and the other forms of evaluation. The distinctions matter, not least in improving the clarity of language. However, monitoring and evaluation may well be conceived of as a continuum along several dimensions, as suggested by Binnendijk [*1989*], which makes it less urgent to distinguish the two as separate functions and easier to recognise the multiple levels of objectives, the variations in data-collection techniques and timing, the structural and organisational mixes, and the levels of management users that may be appropriate in the related assessment processes.[9]

The Definition Revisited: Ideals vs Present Reality

As the demand for more evaluation of aid gained momentum in the 1970s and early 1980s, small evaluation units were established within most European development assistance agencies in order to administer – in some instances even to carry out – the evaluation function. The units were set up in many different institutional environments. The overall administrative cultures differed as well – with implications for the direction of their activities. Although efforts have been made to arrive at an internationally agreed language – which, if successful, might have an impact on evaluation far beyond just improving the communication process and might even affect evaluation policy and practice – a rather varied picture emerges of the European scene.

With reference to this scene, therefore, the most valid definition that can be offered will still be the following. Evaluation of aid is the range of activities administered, financed or carried out by the evaluation unit of the administrative body responsible for development assistance! Although the net was cast with a wider perspective in mind, this operational definition – with its country/agency-specific and time-related implications – will, to some extent, implicitly guide even the authors of the country studies in this volume, as the focus for each study will be the evaluation policy and performance within the confines of a given country. Given the fact that the administrative structures with the responsibility for monitoring and evaluation vary from one country to another, which I shall return to in the following section, this affects the coherence of the definition and therefore the activities which are presented and discussed in the component studies.

II. THE INSTITUTIONALISATION OF AID EVALUATION

During the 1970s and early 1980s, several European countries (and most international aid agencies) established evaluation units, usually as an integral part of aid administration. However, the administrative systems responsible for the implementation of aid differed from country to country, as did the models chosen for the institutionalisation of the evaluation function. The choice of model may reflect evaluation concerns, priorities and norms within the various political systems and administrative cultures.

The main *problématique* involved relates to the multiple functions to be achieved through evaluation, *inter alia*, *improving aid delivery* and *controlling whether aid is working according to the objectives set*. The first of these functions is assumed to be of primary concern for the institutions responsible for the implementation of aid – *the management*; the second for the policy-makers – the Government, Parliament, ultimately *the voters and tax-payers*.[10] These functions do not necessarily conflict with each other, though they may do; however, they do reflect competing concerns. The various actors in the arena have different, even conflicting, major concerns related to these functions. The way evaluation is organised, in particular the norms (guidelines) that define its framework, but also where the evaluation unit is situated in the administrative structure, may well indicate its primary function.

Several dilemmas are involved. Thus, formal and informal links with the aid implementing agency (or agencies), with both decision-makers and operative units, are important if evaluation is to serve as an effective tool in the administration of aid. On the other hand, in order to give credibility and legitimacy to the findings *outside* the implementing agency and to ensure the integrity of the process as an objective and *critical* scrutiny of aid, it is important that evaluation is delinked from the implementing agency or at least that there is a certain distance *vis-à-vis* the operative units. Linked to this *problématique* is the question of how *centralised* or decentralised the organisation of the evaluation function should be, that is, where the responsibility for evaluation (including both monitoring and *ex post* evaluation) is vested within the aid administration.

Although the administrative systems in which the evaluation unit became integrated vary quite extensively from one country to another, we may distinguish between the policy level and the implementing level of the aid administration; at times, however, this borderline may be arbitrary and rather blurred.

The political responsibility for aid is usually vested in a ministry (and a Minister), although, in some cases, it is split between several ministries. In most countries, the Ministry of Foreign Affairs is responsible for all or most of the development assistance, with political responsibility vested in the Minister of Foreign Affairs. However, models vary between countries and – over time – also within countries. In a few countries, a separate Ministry for Development Cooperation has been established, with political responsibility vested in a Minister. In others, political responsibility is vested in a Minister for Development Cooperation within the Ministry of Foreign Affairs, or a Deputy Minister looks after aid issues.

In some administrative structures, the Ministry (or a department within the Ministry) serves as a secretariat to the Minister for issues involving aid policy – which makes it quite easy to identify 'the political level' within the administration. In other structures, however, the Ministry also takes on an aid-implementing function for all or part of the aid programme – which makes the distinction between the policy level and the implementing level more blurred. In several systems, however, the implementation of the aid programme or part of it is delegated to administrative organisations outside the Ministry, mainly to governmental organisations (aid agencies) with a varying degree of independence *vis-à-vis* the Ministry; in other cases implementation may be delegated to semi-public organisations or even to NGOs or the private sector.

Thus, aid administration differs quite substantially from one European country to another. These systems were first established in the 1950s and 1960s, as an integral part of very different administrative systems – quite apart from the differences in administrative culture. When the evaluation function became institutionalised during the 1970s and early 1980s, the institutional models therefore differed. In the mid-1980s, the DAC Expert Group [*OECD, 1986*] distinguished between three different patterns – centralised, integrated and dual systems – adding that, in actual practice, various combinations of these organisational patterns were used.

(1) In the first (*centralised* and independent) system, the evaluation unit is answerable directly to top management (a board of directors, the Director-General, the Minister) and is responsible for coordinating evaluation throughout the agency, formulating evaluation guidelines, carrying out sample or special evaluations directly and drafting proposals for follow-up action.
(2) In the second (centralised and *integrated*) system, the evaluation unit is located in a separate body but it is controlled by and reports directly to a policy committee within the administration.
(3) In the third (*dual system*) model, the responsibility for evaluation is shared by the central staff and the staff of the field missions. The central evaluation unit is independent of the operating units, carries out special evaluation studies, reports to top management and sets standards for evaluation. In some aid agencies, a third layer is established – between the (decentralised) operational units and the central evaluation unit – on a regional or recipient country basis (related to resident representatives).

The countries included in the present study have established administrative systems that differ somewhat from each other, but also show similarities. The systems established by the Netherlands and the Scandinavian countries come close to the pattern described in (1), although with variations and with components close to those of (2) and (3) as well. The system established by the United Kingdom (ODA) fits, broadly speaking, into (2) and in the former Federal Republic of Germany (FRG), a system has evolved that combines components of (1)–(3) – although it comes closest to (3).

These various evaluation units are all rather small, with limited resources both in terms of staff and operational budget. Most units *administer* evaluations, and their staff is only occasionally engaged in actual evaluation work. In this regard, the ODA (UK) evaluation department and the Dutch inspection unit represent the main exceptions.

In the *Netherlands*, a dual evaluation system emerged in the 1970s. In order to strengthen the control function, an inspection unit was established within the ministry but independent of the operative units of the aid administration. During the initial phase, it also had a forward warning function *vis-à-vis* the Minister with regard to projects and issues with a potential to create political crises. Its main orientation, therefore, was towards the decision-making level of the ministry. Evaluation and monitoring oriented to the needs of the managerial level of the aid administration are organised by the country and functional desks. Although the inspection unit is supposed to advise the desks, for instance, on terms of reference, this does not always happen. In addition to this dual evaluation system within the ministry, a third system has evolved; NGOs have increasingly built up evaluation systems of their own in order to ensure ODA financing of development activities [*Hommes, 1991*].

In the Scandinavian countries, evaluation units evolved within the aid agencies (whose structures differ somewhat from each other); in all three countries, the evaluation function was closely related to research within the agencies. Evaluation was institutionalised at a late stage in *Denmark*, where the evaluation unit is located in the secretariat of the aid agency (DANIDA, which is part of the Ministry of Foreign Affairs) within the division for evaluation, research and documentation and therefore close to the top management of aid within the agency [*Schaumburg-Müller, 1991*]. In the case of *Norway*, the unit was transferred, in 1984, from the aid agency (NORAD) to the Ministry of Development Cooperation and situated in the department of planning. In 1989, this ministry merged with the Ministry of Foreign Affairs. Throughout its existence, however, the unit has been independent of the operational departments of the aid administration. A parallel evaluation system emerged during the second half of the 1980s. The aid agency (NORAD) established a monitoring and evaluation system of its own, characterised by a high degree of decentralisation and oriented towards the managerial level of the aid administration. The activities of the two systems are not coordinated with each other [*Stokke, 1991*]. In *Sweden*, the evaluation unit is situated within the planning secretariat of the Director-General of the main aid agency (SIDA). However, the institutionalisation of the evaluation function is highly fragmented with the compartmentalised aid administration; the specialised aid agencies operate evaluation systems of their own, adapted to their particular needs the Ministry of Foreign Affairs also frequently conduct; evaluations, focusing particularly on the aid-delivery systems, including the aid agencies. Within the SIDA, something close to a dual evaluation system exists, as the operative units have resources for monitoring and evaluation at their disposal [*Forss, 1991*].[11]

In the *United Kingdom*, the evaluation function is more closely integrated in the decision-making and implementing units of the aid administration (ODA). The evaluation department reports directly to the Projects and Evaluation Committee (PEC), which is in charge of both project approval and evaluations, and the PEC also influences the evaluation priorities. The department, accordingly, is mainly oriented towards the decision-making level of the aid agency. However, it also maintains close liaison with the geographical desks and functional divisions of the ODA. These desks are responsible for monitoring, so even here a dual system exists; this dualism grew in the second half of the 1980s, when the work on project completion reports was improved and taken over by the desks. Although the aim is a system where evaluation can build upon monitoring, the evaluation department is not closely involved when the plan for monitoring is prepared and evaluation and monitoring tend, in practice, to be kept separate [*Cracknell, 1991a, 1991b*].

In the *FRG*, an evaluation unit is located in the Federal Ministry of Economic Cooperation, where the ultimate responsibility for most aid is vested. The unit is placed outside the regular, administrative hierarchy, with direct access to the policy-making levels of the ministry and an emphasis on the control function. However, the evaluation function is also decentralised to the many agencies under private law, including the private foundations aligned with the main political parties, through which a large part of German aid is channelled. These all monitor and evaluate their own activities [*Musto, 1991*].

In no case has the evaluation function been situated outside the aid administration; strangely enough, such a solution has apparently not even been contemplated, although evaluation models which are independent of the implementing authorities do exist in the various types of

POLICIES, PERFORMANCE, TRENDS AND CHALLENGES

State Auditors. In Norway, this institution is appointed by and reports to Parliament, in Sweden and the UK it is appointed by and reports to the government. Dual systems also exist, as in Denmark, where both Parliament and the government (Ministry of Economic Affairs) appoint auditors. A similar status would probably be ideal, even the norm, for an evaluation unit if the control function was to be achieved in a fully neutral and independent way. One would assume that such an independent position *vis-à-vis* the aid-implementing authorities would also make it better suited to demonstrate, *vis-à-vis* the general public (the electorate), that aid works.

These concerns have been attributed to the political level (Parliament, government – ultimately the electorate). Among those included in this study, the unit which has probably been most independent of the implementing agencies, and therefore most closely reflects such concerns, is the inspection unit of the Dutch aid administration during most of the 1970s; the evaluation department of the ODA is probably closest to the opposite end of this spectrum. However, all evaluation units have been placed at some distance from the operative units of the aid administration.

Even so, the other major concern alluded to above, namely to improve the delivery system (managerial concerns), has been addressed in all of the systems. On the basis of the inclusion of the evaluation function in the administrative structure, the main emphasis in most systems is given to this concern. The core question – if posed at all – has been related to the *degree* of independence of the evaluation unit *vis-à-vis* the *operative* units of the aid agency, seldom *vis-à-vis* the planning units and the general management of these agencies, on the contrary. Thus, typically, the ODA evaluation department (in the UK) is specifically designed to serve a management function.

The degree to which the evaluation unit is independent of the operative units of the aid administration is an important – but not the only – indicator in any assessment of the balance struck between the two concerns identified. In the following sections, this balance will be discussed on the basis of other indicators. Before that, however, I will discuss some characteristics related to aid, namely the objectives set, which have an impact on the implementation of aid and in turn on its evaluation.

III. AID OBJECTIVES AND EVALUATION: A TRICKY MARRIAGE

Evaluation of aid is not an end in itself; as noted, it is an instrument in public administration which is given two main functions, to *control* (and demonstrate) that aid works according to the objectives set and to *improve* the delivery system. Within the confines of a donor country, the main stakeholders as far as the control function is concerned are the politicians (ultimately the electorate); politicians also have a stake in the second function, but here the aid administrators have the largest stake. Development assistance, therefore, is what matters, including the aid policy in terms of aims, strategies, guidelines and delivery systems. Dealing with evaluation exclusively in technical terms, therefore, removes it from the reality of which it is an integral part.

The administration of development assistance has certain features particular to this field of public activity [*Stokke, 1987*]. The administration, to a large extent, is *indirect*; ultimately, it is up to other administrative systems (international agencies, recipient countries, NGOs) to implement the aid policy through the administration of the resources. Still, the aid administration is part of the public administration of the donor country and is influenced by its established administrative traditions.

The aid policy area also has some features of its own [*Stokke, 1984a, 1984b; 1989a, 1989b, 1989c*]. The aid policy of a donor country is moulded in a setting that includes both external (international) and internal (domestic) environments; within both, it is influenced by, *inter alia*, systemic interest and values as well as those of the private sector. The resource basis limits the room for manoeuvre; changes in the resource basis and in the prevailing economic situation also affect the outcome. The policy which emerges, therefore, tends to differ from one country to another. Thus, a superpower government with global interests and commitments may be expected to pursue different aims from those pursued by the governments of smaller countries. Whereas superpowers tend to use aid as an instrument in a foreign policy which may best be analysed within paradigms of international realism, the aid policy of some Western middle powers may be better analysed within paradigms of humane internationalism [*Stokke, 1989a*].

For evaluation, the *objectives* set for the ODA become the most crucial point of departure, particularly *vis-à-vis* stakeholders at the political level whose main concern is assumed to be whether aid works (involving the control function). This does not imply that the objectives themselves, even overall objectives, should be exempted from scrutiny.[12] However, an evaluation which is to take objectives set for aid at the policy level, as the ideal against which aid implementation is to be assessed, may be confronted with problems which are not easily overcome, including the following:

* The more fundamental development aims set for aid may be elusive, competing – even conflicting – with no clear priority established between the various objectives.

* To be effective, aims must be operationalised and adapted to different environments and aid activities.
* A compartmentalised aid programme may lead to the compartmentalisation of objectives.
* There are also unstated aims which compete with development aims.

The Predominant Aims: Too Elusive as a Basis for Evaluation?

At the policy level, aims are often formulated at a high level of generalisation. In some donor countries, aid policy is formulated in great detail, in terms of general aims, strategies and guidelines, and characterised by a large degree of stability, regardless of changes in government (Norway and Sweden are cases in point); in others, aims are less visible, formalised and stable and emerge from general policy statements that may vary from one government to another or even from one minister with the responsibility for foreign aid to the succeeding one with different perspectives and priorities [*Stokke, 1984a, 1989b*].

However, although there exist great variations both with regard to explicitness and emphasis, most donor countries have economic growth and poverty alleviation as stated objectives for their development assistance. In their policy declarations, European governments have hummed the tunes of the day – and these tunes have changed over the years, though some have become evergreens which compete with the newest hits even among the young generation. During the 1960s, typically, *economic growth* was the overall objective for aid. In the mid 1970s, after the International Labour Organisation (ILO) had coined the *basic needs* strategy – and particularly after the strategy had been recommended to its member governments by the OECD – the aims of this approach to development, or fragments of such aims, were included in policy declarations by most European governments. The strategy was, however, open to different interpretations. Many donor countries have a host of other objectives for their aid, too – including the promotion of social justice, democracy, human rights, environmental concerns both local and global and, in general, *sustainable development*. During the 1980s, crisis management has increasingly come to the fore as a high-priority objective for aid, related, in particular, to the desperate debt situation of many Third World countries, with *structural adjustment* topping the hit list.

These objectives are all rather general and may be open to different interpretations. This is why – in the arena of domestic and international politics – consensus can be reached among actors with widely different interests and values. Aims at this level, therefore, tend to be elusive as a basis for evaluation. This also applies in cases where the general aims for aid have been formalised and demonstrate a great capacity for continuity, surviving changes in government. The problem becomes even more difficult in cases where the aims are less formalised – for instance, when they are based on a statement made by the minister of the day rather than on a government White Paper which has been approved by Parliament.

The political authorities (the government, Parliament) have seldom, if ever, established a clear priority between the different aims; different political actors (political parties), being parties to a consensus, may hold different priorities.[13] Even various general aims may be in competition with each other, or conflicting. The absence of priority, therefore, becomes a problem when such aims are to be taken as the point of departure for evaluation.

The discussion above has been limited to the general aims of the *donor*. If development aims on the *recipient* side are added, the *problematique* alluded to will be even more complex and difficult to relate to; these aims – and priorities – will not necessarily be similar to those of the donor, and they may be markedly different from them.

Operationalised Objectives: The Missing Link

At the level of aid implementation – and for evaluation – aims at a high level of generalisation have to be operationalised in order to be effective, and this has nowhere been considered a priority task by the aid administration. Some political declarations of intent (aid objectives) have not even been intended for this kind of exercise. However, developmental objectives of the kind indicated above not only stand out as the main justification for aid, they also constitute the primary motive for providing development assistance, particularly for the champions of aid but even for some governments. They should, accordingly, constitute a point of departure for aid evaluation in order to answer the key question (at the political level): does aid work?

The general development objectives have to be operationalised at the level at which aid is implemented in order to serve as a point of departure for evaluation. A shift of level – from overall aims set for aid to the objectives set for a small project supported by foreign aid – may involve different worlds. At all levels, however, the performance should be assessed against the objectives set; even at the project level, however, the stated *overall objectives* for aid may be taken as a point of departure. A basic problem involved relates to the translation process: to what extent are the objectives set for the particular project derived from the general aims set for the development assistance?

Usually, evaluators have to relate to an established reality, namely a development project or programme as implemented. The extent to which objectives for this programme have been derived from the general aims set for aid (by the authorities of the donor), or established at all in operational terms, varies from one aid agency to another and, within agencies, from one sector or field to another. However, objectives at the project level have seldom been derived from the overall aims; within several areas, such an exercise is admittedly difficult. Formalised objectives for aid activities have, for many agencies, been weakly developed. As observed by Kerstin Trone with reference to the UNFPA, few projects have been designed well enough to allow measurement of impact [*Trone, 1991*]. Recently, however, many aid agencies have put more energy into the formulation of objectives for aid interventions in terms that can be operationalised and measured as an effect of the increased emphasis on evaluation [*Kjekshus, 1991*].

Poorly developed aid objectives create problems for evaluation. For the aid agencies, the obvious answer to such problems would be to put more effort into the formulation of operational objectives where this is feasible or possible. But what should be done when objectives, at the project or programme level, have been poorly developed, if at all, or in situations where their link to the overall aims is weak or rather indirect, if it exists at all? Should whatever objectives are set be taken as the point of departure or should, for the purpose of the evaluation, objectives at the programme level, derived from the overall aims, be established? Few aid agencies have issued policy directives relating to this question, although some have urged that the overriding aid aims should be addressed by the evaluators, as in the case of Norway [*Stokke, 1991*]. Or should the evaluators, as suggested by Kim Forss [*1991*], even transcend the objectives set and depart from external criteria, such as criteria for development established by development theory?[14]

Compartmentalisation of Aid May Lead to Compartmentalisation of Objectives

Another feature of aid programmes may partly explain why objectives are so seldom derived from the overall aims set for aid. A development assistance programme is to a large extent compartmentalised. Part of the programme is channelled into *multilateral* systems; the UN and the World Bank constitute the major ones. Within these, and particularly within the UN system, a host of sub-systems exists, namely the various specialised agencies and special funds. The *bilateral* aid of a donor country is also compartmentalised, being channelled to different recipient systems (governments, NGOs) and provided to different sectors, for different purposes and in different forms, administered by specialised administrative units of the aid agency.

This compartmentalisation affects the implementation of aid in terms of its orientation. The general orientation of an institution, or of a specialised, administrative unit, and its specific culture, that is, the predominant 'world-view', values and interests of the unit, tend to govern the formulation of both general aims and more particular, project-related objectives set for aid being channelled through the system. The aims emerging within the various compartments of an aid agency will not necessarily or primarily reflect the general aims set for aid by the political authorities of the donor country. Exorcism in the form of policy statements insisting that the general aims set for aid should apply to all development assistance (as in the case of Norway) cannot mask the fact that the compartmentalisation of aid may also involve a compart-mentalisation of objectives. The various compartments often represent different worlds. For instance, the World Bank (which receives a fairly high proportion of the ODA of most donor countries through the International Development Association (IDA)) represents a totally different setting – in terms of predominant 'world-view', culture and organisation – than that of, for instance, a local NGO engaged in a vocational training programme for women; and the confines of non-project aid are usually quite different from those of project aid. Thus, objectives set for aid within a structural adjustment programme seldom relate to the alleviation of poverty; at best the links are indirect [*Addison and Demery, 1987; Cornia, Jolly and Stewart, 1987*].

The compartmentalisation of aid may imply a delinking of objectives from the overall aims set for aid by the political authorities. This applies, in particular, for aid being channelled through organisations outside the aid agency, both multilaterally and bilaterally; however, it applies even to aid being administered by the different departments of the aid agency itself, provided for different purposes and in different forms. However, it applies more to some types and forms of aid than to others. The linkage with the overall aims is probably stronger for some of the bilateral aid forms at a middle level, being situated somewhere between programme aid and traditional project aid, namely sectoral or area-oriented programmes (sector programmes for rural drinking water, women and child care, etc.). At the project level, the link between the overall aims set and project objectives may be rather diffuse and indirect even in cases where efforts actually have been made to derive the objectives from the general aims. However, even here a distinction should be made between the different compartments – for projects within some sectors or areas, the link may be quite direct (aid targeted for specific purposes or social groups).

However, the recognition of such effects would probably not affect established structures; the probability is that aid would continue to be split and also to be channelled through systems and institutions with aims different from those set for aid by the political authorities of the donor. After all, like statements of norms, the established distribution emerges, in most cases, from decisions by the government and Parliament, too, namely from the annual budget proposals by the government as accepted by Parliament. Norms and practice may differ even when the responsibility is vested in the same authorities. The established patterns are reinforced by structural factors. An established distribution pattern is more often than not continued through the budgetary routines – a deviation may necessitate a justification. Policy planning and budgetary processes, coordinated by an administrative structure (the Ministry of Finance) with a leaning towards a holistic perspective on development may constitute an additional factor; it may be assumed that this perspective would have spin-offs for the administration of aid as well, resulting in a relaxed attitude towards demands for a rigid application of the overall aims to the whole spectrum of aid-supported activities. Nor does an aid agency operate in splendid isolation; it has, for instance, to adapt its aid programme to a recipient country (for state-to-state aid), to the prevailing needs (as defined by the recipient's political authorities), and also to the composition of the aid provided by other donors to the particular recipient. From the overall perspective of a ministry of finance, on both sides in an aid relationship, it may well seem more important to improve the infrastructure than supplying clean drinking water for poor people living in remote areas, even with poverty alleviation as the stated, overriding objective set for the aid programme.

These features also affect evaluation, and especially evaluation of whether aid works, departing from the overriding aims set. The *problématique* related to general aims above applies here, too. Where objectives are not derived from the general aims set for aid, the consequence of the most convenient choice (to depart from whatever objectives have been established) may well be that for projects/programmes and compartmentalised aid, the most important questions from the perspective of the policy level of the donor country may remain unaddressed by evaluation.

What About the Unstated Objectives?

The administration of aid is almost everywhere the responsibility of the Ministry of Foreign Affairs. Aid policy, almost by definition, is part of the foreign policy of the donor country – and moulded in external and domestic environments that vary from one country to another. Although there are manifest variations, all donor governments tend to pursue (selfish) interests and values in addition to the stated (mainly idealistic) development aims when forming and implementing the aid programme. This applies, in particular, to objectives related to employment and business interests at home; the main powers tend to give priority to global, strategic concerns as well. As a policy often emerges as the result of alliances, a government may structure the aid programme in such a way as to ensure broad support from a multitude of (primarily domestic) stake-holders. Private sector economic interests in the donor country may, therefore, even be woven into the structure of the aid programme – as in the case of Denmark from the very start [*Svendsen, 1989*]. However, in some countries, notably the UK, the usually unstated objectives have been stated; the political, industrial and commercial concerns of the donor are established as expressed objectives for aid along with the development objective [*Cracknell, 1991a*].

A most fundamental question, therefore, might well be whether the stated development aims are the real ones. Some unstated objectives compete with the stated development aims and may influence the allocation of aid monies. Such objectives result, in particular, from the interests and values of the domestic environment in which the aid policy is formed [*Stokke, 1989c*].

How should evaluation of aid relate to such unstated objectives? Should they be treated as if they were non-existent? Or should they be brought out into the open and taken as a point of departure for evaluation; that is, should the terms of reference ask for an assessment – or an evaluation mission, independently of this assignment, to make an assessment of the extent to which these expectations have been satisfied through ODA? Should the effect of such unstated, competing objectives on the attainment of the stated development objectives of aid, and their follow-up by the aid agency, be part of the evaluation? It is assumed that some competing objectives may impede an efficient fulfilment of the stated development aims by influencing and distorting the choice of inputs (type of resources, forms and channels of aid). The effects of tied aid may illustrate the point [*Kamphuis and Jepma, 1990*].

The most crucial question that emerges, therefore, is what kind of information will be in demand – and what kind of questions may as well be left alone? The answer will depend on who the stakeholders are and on the relative influences on evaluation policy of the various stakeholders. There is a practical side to this, too. Not all programmes, nor all questions, can be addressed. And as noted by Raizen and Rossi [*1982*], when a programme has vague or diverse goals, evaluators and those who commission an evaluation must be able to agree on which goals should be assessed.

This applies to the scope and the orientation of evaluation, too. It is generally accepted that evaluation should produce information conducive to improving the effectiveness and efficiency of aid. But how far does this agreement hold? It will usually include the operative units of aid management, on both the donor and the recipient side, but how far up the ladder does it go in the administration responsible for aid imple-mentation? Should it also include the policy, even the politicians with responsibility for the policy, on both sides? In recent practice, evaluation has actually focused on policies on the recipient side, at least for some types of aid (including structural adjustment loans), but what about the donor side? Would the revelation of constraints on the donor side of the kind indicated above, that is, the possibility of a negative impact on the effectiveness of declared development objectives stemming from the donor's competing, even contradictory, policy objectives, be considered a priority task for evaluation?

The institutional setting of the evaluation function matters in this regard; it is not common for government policies to be systematically questioned by the central administration, certainly not openly. In most countries, even Parliament might be uninterested in, or hostile to, this kind of query, though the opposition – and even the recipient (provided there were no negative effects on aid volume or aid relations) – might be interested.

The strategies, guidelines and instruments of aid policy (involving the aid channels and the various forms of aid) are of crucial importance for how aid works. It follows that even these aspects should be scrutinised. The core question would, again, be to what extent these features in the implementation of aid were conducive to achieve the stated, overriding objectives set for the development assistance, and – correspondingly – how far those designs established with the purpose of serving objectives different from (or even contradictory to) the stated ones have had a negative impact.

As a management tool in the administration of development assistance, evaluation has from the very start been initiated and pursued by the donor countries. Although a reassessment may be under way [*Kjekshus, 1991*], demands for evaluation have met with little enthusiasm from the recipients of aid, though accepted as part of the conditions involved. Policy constraints of a kind similar to those referred to above on the donor side also apply on the recipient side – with even greater force, one may assume, since the aid intervention is, more often than not, designed and proposed from the outside and seldom emerges as the result of domestic political processes. From the perspective of the policy level of the donor, the impact on aid effectiveness and efficiency of such constraints would pose an interesting task to be addressed through evaluation.

IV. THE DIRECTION OF THE EVALUATION EFFORTS: CONFLICTING PERSPECTIVES

Some features of aid policy, discussed in section III above, may reinforce effects resulting from the institutional setting of the evaluation function, described in section II. Here institutional patterns were used as indicators for assessing the outcome of conflicting concerns attributed to actors with major interests involved in evaluation – with particular reference to the political and management levels. It may be assumed that, once established, the administrative setting of an evaluation unit matters for the future orientation of its work, too. Thus, if situated in an administrative structure with managerial functions, this location may reinforce management concerns within the unit, in particular, through expectations arising from the immediate environments, which in turn may have an impact on the orientation of its attention.

However, although some actors carry more weight than others – and actors in the administrative environments may be in a position to exert a particularly strong influence in most bureaucratic structures – outside actors may also be in a position to influence the evaluation policy and its implementation; such stakeholders may be found on both the donor and the recipient side. Conflicting interests and varying perceived needs will be at work in moulding the evaluation policy. The balance struck between the 'policy' and 'management' levels is, therefore, best assessed on the basis of the declared policy and the actual performance.

The objectives and priorities, emerging from policy statements and the actual evaluation performance, would indicate the relative emphasis given to the two concerns. If the focus is on aid aims at a high level of generalisation, this is assumed to reflect the policy level concerns. It is assumed that the main concern at this level will be related to the *control* function and, in particular, to the crucial question: does aid work? Does aid have the impact expected of it? The question relates, in particular, to the overriding aims set for development assistance (for example, the improvement of economic or social growth, human rights, poverty alleviation – where such aims apply). If, on the other hand, the main focus is on aid objectives at the project level, this is assumed to reflect managerial concerns. It is assumed that the main concern at this level would be to find ways and means to improve the effectiveness and efficiency of aid. The most pressing questions to be addressed by evaluation will, accordingly, relate to the more immediate needs of the management of aid projects and programmes; the closer to the operational level, the more specifically related to project management. The balance struck becomes manifest in the direction of evaluation efforts, too – whether directed towards the major issues and overall concerns (policy) or towards the more limited, single projects (management).

However, as noted, the distinction between the two levels is not always easily drawn, for several reasons. Thus, within an aid-implementing agency, the top leadership and some units with a responsibility for overall implementation (planning, evaluation, liaison with other donors, etc.) are concerned with policy issues, too – and need feedback on the overall impact of aid for (policy) management decisions. At the policy level, on the other hand, there will also be a concern for efficient management and, therefore, an appreciation of the need for the kind of feedback that would be conducive to this end. At all levels, there will be general agreement on several of the functions which evaluation may fulfil. And there will be a shared distaste for bad news, too, especially if splashed out in the open. This applies, in particular, to those who carry the political and administrative responsibility for aid (and less to the political opposition).

Although these indicators are therefore not the sharpest tools for identifying the dominant determinants, the distinction is interesting in its own right, as it describes an important feature of the evaluation policy. What kind of picture emerges from the component studies?

Most aid agencies have established a *planning system* for evaluation assignments, though with a short planning horizon – usually two years (the FRG operates a yearly plan, Denmark and Sweden a three-year revolving plan). Several evaluation units have budgets of their own varying between two and three million US$, which limits their activities; in some agencies, however, the budget for evaluation is not specified (Denmark, Sweden). In most agencies, the evaluation plan is prepared in close consultation with the aid-implementing units of the administration (the geographical and functional desks and, where applicable, the resident representatives in the main recipient countries). This coordination is particularly close in the case of the United Kingdom. The plan is presented for approval to higher levels in the aid administration, and in a few cases to a (civil service) decision-making body. In the UK, the decision-making body of the ODA (PEC) provides active guidance.

The involvement has almost everywhere been restricted to the civil-service level, with two exceptions. In *Denmark*, the plan is presented to the Board of the DANIDA – an advisory body external to the ministry. However, at the policy level (government, Parliament), interest in evaluation has been lacking. The other exception is *Norway*, where Parliament and successive governments have given quite detailed directions for evaluation by setting the objectives, the strategy and the guidelines. The strategy also includes directives for planning: all aid channels, aid forms and sectors should be subject to evaluation over time. Parliament has even requested that specific themes and programmes should be evaluated.

Most evaluation units have focused on the delivery system rather than addressing the more fundamental question: does aid work? The DAC Expert Group noted that two factors are paramount in the donor's selection of projects: first, decisions related to the specific project and, second, the programme planning and review needs of the donor agency. Because most evaluations deal with problems in the field, they are often like expanded monitoring reports on project status and the steps necessary to solve operational problems. There is a tendency to plan on a project-to-project basis, which implies that some contextual, strategic, macro-economic and cross-cutting issues escape systematic review [*OECD, 1986*]. In his broad overview, Roger Riddell concluded that evaluation reports were not satisfactory as a basis to answer the question of whether aid works [*Riddell, 1987*]. The major study by Robert Cassen, commissioned by the Task Force on Concessionary Transfers set up by the joint Development Committee of the IMF and the IBRD to answer just that core question, concluded in the same vein: evaluation reports tended to be inadequate to answer this question as their preoccupation was with delivery issues and themes rather than impact [*Cassen, 1986*]. Reporting on the central systems for monitoring and evaluation set up or strengthened during the 1980s by the South Asian countries, Michael Bamberger relates a similar story: the emphasis has been on the monitoring of project implementation rather than on the evaluation of project operation and sustainability and the assessment of project impacts [*Bamberger, 1989*]. These assessments coincide with the observation by Helge Kjekshus that, in most instances, the potential of evaluation 'was limited to the bare needs of aid managers and rarely put to use to explore the wider consequences of aid, its success or failure in achieving its goals and its impact in recipient settings' [*Kjekshus, 1991*].

Although these observations portray the overall picture, some nuances may be discerned. Several agencies have also increasingly addressed the more fundamental questions related to the impact of aid, particularly towards the end of the 1980s. Attention has increasingly been directed towards the broader objectives of aid. Thus, in the guidelines set for evaluation by most DAC members, it is requested that the reports deal with such important aspects as sustainability and the effects on women and the environment. In addition, there has been a trend towards a sectoral and thematic approach and towards synthesising lessons learned, based on a series of evaluation reports. Even controversial policy issues have more frequently been addressed. However, there are differences in approach and performance.

The profile of the evaluation systems dealt with in the component studies – as assessed on the basis of the indicators discussed, namely the major orientation of their evaluations – differs slightly. Even here, the British system seems to be most consistently adapted to managerial concerns, though mainly at the decision-making level, while the Norwegian and Dutch systems seem to be most oriented to policy-level concerns; however, the spectrum is not a particularly wide one.

Within the *ODA*, the preoccupation is to improving aid delivery. Impact studies and *ex post* studies are almost non-existent. However, within these confines, a reorientation has taken place during the 1980s towards more emphasis on synthesising wider lessons learned from monitoring and evaluation reports. In the late 1980s, it became obligatory to address the issues of sustainability, the role of women and environments. Priority has been given to the provision of information which might be useful for the civil service decision-making level of the aid administration [*Cracknell, 1991a, 1991b*].

The German and Danish systems come closest to the British in this respect. In the *FRG*, however, there is also a stated intention to address the question of accountability. During the 1980s, cross-sectoral evaluations of projects have been increasingly undertaken and country studies have also been commissioned [*Musto, 1991*]. In *Denmark*, the main purpose of evaluation, up to the early 1980s, was to assess operations and the effects of single projects in order to improve performance. During recent years, however, more emphasis has been given to the assessment of the efficiency, effectiveness, impact and sustainability of projects and the relevance of their objectives. Even if there has been an increasing interest in cross-cutting issues, multi-bi aid and general development issues, the TORs have not asked for an assessment of poverty alleviation, a major objective of Danish aid. Although there was a reluctance at the political level to use evaluation as a management tool up to the early 1980s, evaluations have basically been oriented to serve managerial concerns. In 1982, however, when Danish aid was subjected to a major review, a majority recommended that accountability *vis-à-vis* the overall aims set for Danish aid should also be evaluated. However, it took the aid administration another six years to commit itself to this task [*Schaumburg-Müller, 1991*].

In the case of *Sweden*, Kim Forss [*1991*] identifies the primary function of evaluation as a means of persuasion, namely to mobilise support for some management decision, with particular reference to the decentralised evaluations carried out by the operative units. This applies less to the evaluations being administered by the evaluation unit of the SIDA; these serve to legitimate the SIDA in the eyes of the general public.[15] However, the delivery system of the SIDA and the specialised aid agencies are themselves subject to government-commissioned evaluation; this also applies to aid forms (for instance, disaster relief), aid channelled through NGOs and some country programmes after the countries concerned had ceased to be major recipients of Swedish aid. The National Audit Board has also been active in scrutinising the SIDA in particular and some critical aid areas (such as the aid agencies' use of consultants, and the use of aid for import support).

In the dual *Dutch* system, a division of labour has evolved where the so-called internal evaluations (which may use external evaluators) are mainly oriented to serve day-to-day management needs, while the external evaluations (the inspection unit, where one of the seven inspectors is the core person in evaluation teams recruited from outside) have been oriented towards policy and management needs. The inspection unit has recently concentrated less on inspections and more on policy development, including sectoral aid and policy issues, such as the commercialisation of aid. Country studies have also occasionally been conducted [*Hommes, 1991*].

In the case of *Norway*, Parliament and government were, as noted, active in moulding evaluation policy. In the declared policy, the overriding aims set for Norwegian aid belonged to the centre court; projects and programmes, as well as the policy orientation of the systems through which aid was channelled (multilateral aid agencies, NGOs and even the governments of recipient countries), were to be assessed against these aims. Thus, there was an emphasis on accountability; for Parliament, the main emphasis has been on the 'does aid work?' question, while the government has laid more stress on managerial concerns. This policy has to a large extent been followed up in practice, too – though in varying degree, with regard to the overall objectives. All main aid channels have been scrutinised, including the aid agency itself. The programmes to all main recipients of bilateral aid have also been evaluated (10 country studies). Aid channelled through NGOs and bilateral aid through international agencies ('multi-bi') have been evaluated; the multilateral aid component, however, has almost totally escaped the scrutiny of evaluation. Since the mid-1980s, policy issues have been increasingly addressed [*Stokke, 1991*].

The main distinction between these evaluation systems lies perhaps in their attitude towards policy issues. Describing the British system, Basil Cracknell points out that, whereas the USAID regards evaluation of policy as a crucial aspect, in the ODA policy-making is viewed as the responsibility of senior management and not a primary purpose for evaluation. He seems to detect a general trend towards this position, maintaining that probably most evaluation units are increasingly reluctant to get involved in directly evaluating highly sensitive aspects of aid policy but rather prefer to evaluate selected individual instances of the result of such policies. Even at the project level the tendency is for evaluators to side-step policy-type value judgements [*Cracknell, 1991b*]. However, as noted above, other systems have recently given increased emphasis to policy issues. This is reflected, in particular, in the stated Norwegian evaluation policy and even in the follow-up, where policy issues are given high priority [*Stokke, 1991*].

However, some aspects of aid are neglected by almost all European evaluation systems. This applies, in particular, to one large ODA component, namely *multilateral aid* through the international aid agencies. Participation in the governing bodies of the international agencies seems to be considered, by most donor countries, a satisfactory vehicle to take care of the control function, in addition to their self-evaluation. However, additional information has increasingly been collected through evaluations of multi-bi aid activities. The international agencies and their aid delivery systems have only exceptionally been subject to evaluation by any of the donor countries, separately or jointly.

Evaluation has almost exclusively focused on bilateral aid, including the systems through which bilateral aid has been channelled. Some agencies (in the FRG, the Netherlands, Sweden and – most systematically – in Norway) have conducted country studies of some of the main recipient countries. Such major reviews are resource-demanding operations and could probably best be undertaken as joint enterprises. As argued by Enno Hommes, like-minded countries should join together in carrying out such studies, rather than leaving them to the World Bank with its limited and ideologically biased perspectives [*Hommes, 1991*].

The impact of aid on *poverty alleviation* has received little attention by most agencies, if it has not been completely neglected. Impact studies are, on the whole, few and far between. The reluctance of aid agencies to undertake impact studies or, more generally, to address the accountability question (does aid work?) is explained, with particular reference to the UK (ODA), partly by the technical difficulty of assessing whether or not a project has been a success shortly after its completion, and partly by financial constraints – costs are considered prohibitive for budgetary reasons [*Cracknell, 1991a*].

The aid programmes of most donors have increasingly taken on new forms, which differ from that of traditional project aid. To assess the effects of sector or cross-sectoral programmes and the various forms of non-project aid usually needs more involvement and a longer time-framework than that allotted to the evaluation of projects, carried out by teams set up to inspect and report within a tight time-schedule. It also calls for different tools from those in common use in project evaluation, more in line with those in common use within scientific research. This applies, in particular, when the bigger issues, such as the effect of aid on poverty alleviation, participation, sustainability, the situation of women and institutional development, are to be properly addressed. Evaluation of the effects of aid as related to overall aid objectives – and impact studies in general – are certainly more demanding in terms of time, skills and finances than the evaluation of projects. And yet another challenge becomes more transparent: the political aspects involved in evaluation will be more visible, particularly when the major programmes are evaluated.[16] But, given the new forms of aid, there is probably no alternative to meeting these new challenges. By concentrating evaluation on projects, the effect may well be that the focus is narrowed down to an assessment of effects at a low level in the hierarchy of objectives – leaving the most important ones aside. There is a growing awareness of the need for more evaluation of these aspects, which is to some extent reflected in the reorientation which has taken place recently within some evaluation systems, though not necessarily within aid agencies, impressed by the problems involved and preoccupied with the more immediate task of preparing and implementing new aid assignments.

V. INDEPENDENCE: EXTERNAL vs. INTERNAL EVALUATION

Earlier, a distinction was drawn between *internal* and *external* evaluations. One aspect related to this distinction is the question of independence. It is widely assumed that external evaluation will be more independent,[17] and therefore more reliable, than internal evaluation, where the evaluators are drawn from the aid agency itself, which may involve loyalties to colleagues in the aid-implementing units or, for that matter, to the leadership.[18]

The arguments for using internal evaluators are mainly related to managerial concerns, although costs may also be involved. Insiders may know better than outsiders what kind of information would be most relevant to the agency; the feedback to the aid administration would be more effective and the internal learning from evaluation better served by using staff members instead of engaging outsiders for the task; and the follow-up might also be more effective.[19] According to the DAC Expert Group, with reference to mixed teams, donors have found from experience that 'participation by a qualified member of the agency's staff is necessary to bring to the work of the other evaluators an understanding of the agency's internal operations and regulations' [*OECD, 1986: 46*].

The balance struck between external and internal evaluation constitutes another indicator of the relative weights given to policy and implementation. At the policy level, the primary concern would be to obtain independent and reliable information on what is going wrong or right, that is, external evaluation. This is all the more important because independent evaluation serves the function of legitimating aid (if it conveys good news, that aid works) or at least the good behaviour of politicians *vis-à-vis* aid (who demonstrate a willingness to look critically into what is taking place if the news is bad). The primary concern of the aid agency would, in contrast, be to obtain insights which could be of immediate use in order to adjust current activities and improve future plans and which might contribute to the internal learning of the agency. For these purposes, internal evaluation might be sufficient, and even considered more effective and efficient than external evaluation.

The country studies reveal some differences in the approach and performance of the evaluation systems included on this account, too. For most of the agencies, however, the emphasis is increasingly on the use of external evaluators. This applies, in particular, to the *Scandinavian* evaluation units. In Denmark, evaluation was the responsibility of the operational units of the aid agency up to 1982; during recent years, however, external independent researchers and consultancy firms have been relied upon. The DANIDA staff has participated in evaluation teams as resource persons [*Schaumburg-Müller, 1991*]. In the case of Norway, Parliament has insisted that evaluation should be independent *vis-à-vis* the aid agency and those evaluated and has requested the same independence *vis-à-vis* the authorities of their home countries for recipient country participants in these teams. Although mixed teams were used in the 1970s and early 1980s, since then team members have been almost exclusively externally recruited [*Stokke, 1991*]. In Sweden, *ex post* evaluations are usually carried out by external consultants, although the staff of the evaluation unit participates, for professional reasons, in one or two evaluations every year [*Forss, 1991*].

The prevailing view in the *FRG* is that evaluation teams should be independent and neutral. Usually, external evaluators are commissioned by the ministry for this task. However, mixed teams are also relied upon – but the ultimate responsibility is then vested in the external evaluators [*Musto, 1991*]. In the dual *Dutch* system, external evaluators are commissioned even for the evaluations carried out by the operational desks, although desk officers may sometimes participate in teams as resource persons. For evaluation carried out by the inspection unit, evaluators are recruited externally. However, the core person in an evaluation team is one of the seven inspectors. The self-evaluation carried out by NGOs may also rely on external evaluators [*Hommes, 1991*].

In the *UNFPA*, too, the distinction is between internal and external monitoring and evaluation. Internal evaluation, which is the responsibility of the programme staff, may also draw on external consultants. In-depth evaluation, run by the evaluation unit, relies on external consultants. However, the unit itself takes on an important role both in the preparatory phase, when a background paper is prepared and the questions to be addressed are identified, and in the fieldwork, where an evaluation officer is a full member of the team and acts as the co-ordinator. More recently, technical officers have also taken part in some evaluations [*Trone, 1991*].

In the *United Kingdom* (ODA), the evaluation function is closely integrated in the administration. The general approach is mixed evaluation teams. The teams consist mostly of persons from outside the ODA – academics or retired senior members of the ODA, occasionally commercial consultants. However, the geographical and functional desks of the ODA play important roles in the selection of projects to be evaluated and give advice on the terms of reference and the selection of evaluators; staff members may also take part in an 'associate' capacity, though not if they have been directly involved in the project. The desks involved will, for large evaluations, be represented on a steering committee and their views are also sought after the report is produced, particularly on any recommendations emerging from the report, before the evaluation department comes up with its recommendations for follow-up. Basil Cracknell argues that 'most aid agencies have found that mixed teams are the most satisfactory, and that the evaluation report is more likely to be geared to specific action appropriate to the agency's needs if one of its in-house staff members has had a major part in its formulation' [*Cracknell, 1991b*].

VI. OPEN VS CLOSED EVALUATION: A TREND TOWARDS GREATER OPENNESS

In public administration, traditions differ substantially from one country to another along the closed–openness spectrum. Such differences also apply, within a country, from one sector or policy area to another – restrictions on insights into public affairs are not necessarily limited to those sectors which every government surrounds with secrecy for reasons of security. Matters involving relations with foreign governments – or private firms, when business secrets are invoked – tend to belong to the closed end of the spectrum, even in administrative systems which are relatively open. Development assistance belongs, by its very nature, to this end of the spectrum.

However, other concerns apply, too. Restricting information and insights can have a negative effect on feedback, in particular, *vis-à-vis* the political level (Parliament) and the public at large, including research milieus and other milieus outside the aid agency which have an interest – or a stake – in aid policy or aid in general. This may influence the public debate on aid and even the position of aid with the public. Since 'bad news' is so attractive to the media, such news tends to leak – and gains in attraction if it is restricted information. The balance struck may serve as yet another indicator of the relative weight given to implementation and policy level concerns.

The way evaluation became institutionalised tended to result in internal documents, not in independent assessment for public scrutiny, according to an assessment by DAC evaluators in the early 1980s [*Kjekshus, 1991*]. However, even on this account, the various European evaluation systems differ. In the late 1980s, the Scandinavian countries and the Netherlands followed an open line, with the UK in a middle position and the FRG following a restrictive line. However, the main trend has been towards increased openness.

In the *Scandinavian countries*, evaluation reports are open and available to all. In Sweden, this is established by law. In the case of Norway, it used to be left to the Director of the NORAD to decide whether an evaluation report should be open or not. In 1983, however, Parliament insisted that evaluation reports should be open and accessible, and the government agreed the following year. This has been followed up, although evaluations carried out by the aid agency have not been published. In Denmark, evaluation reports were previously restricted to the aid agency (DANIDA). They are now freely accessible upon request, provided the recipient country has agreed. In the *Netherlands*, the reports from the inspection unit were, in the 1970s, confidential, restricted to the top management and the Minister, but they are now open to everybody. This applies even to the reports of the NGOs [*Hommes, 1991*].

In the *UK*, the trend has been towards increased openness, although it is still up to the ODA to decide in each case whether a report should be public or not. In the 1980s, the ODA has been exposed to strong pressure to make evaluation reports freely available. About two-thirds of all evaluation reports by the evaluation department have been made public and more recently almost all have been made accessible [*Cracknell, 1991*]. By contrast, in the *FRG*, evaluation reports are not published. Reasons given are consideration for the Third World partners ('developing countries are generally keen to ensure that the evaluation findings remain confidential') and concern for the integrity of the evaluators (publication 'may erode the evaluator's courage to speak out openly') [*Musto, 1991*].

Evaluation reports may well be used as a tool for decision-making, particularly by the aid-implementing agency but also at the political level, even if they are not open and available except to the managers and political decision-makers. If the reports are not open and available, however, the public debate cannot to the same extent utilise the information provided. What really matters, even in systems where evaluation reports are open and accessible, is that the information produced is brought to the attention of those who have an interest (or a stake) involved, whether at the managerial or political level – ultimately the general public. This involves communications systems, techniques and procedures for feedback which I shall return to in the following two sections. As observed by Kim Forss, with reference to Sweden, the problem is that evaluation reports are not widely read; they are read only by those closely involved, namely the programme officers, the project staff and the authorities of the recipient countries [*Forss, 1991*]. This observation probably has a general bearing, and it may apply even in other countries that practice openness.

VII. FEEDBACK: THE SINE QUA NON OF EVALUATION

Feedback is the *sine qua non* of all evaluation. The information produced in the process has to be brought to the attention of its potential users in order to be effective. This brings up two crucial questions: who are the potential users? and how is the information best brought across to these users? There is, however, an additional question of equal importance which needs to be raised becauce it is often neglected, namely who has the responsibility for the feedback? Is this the responsibility of the evaluators? With the exception of providing the report, probably not. Is it then the responsibility of the evaluation unit? Probably to some extent, but not necessarily – although several evaluation units have taken on some or all the responsibility even for feedback. To my mind, however, feedback of information emerging from evaluation is part of the aid implementation. The main responsibility for bringing the information home to its potential users (stakeholders) and making effective use of it should therefore be carried by the aid administration. This applies to the feedback to stakeholders outside the aid agency as well.

The stakeholders – in and out of the aid administration, in the donor and recipient countries and elsewhere, depending on the issue – have different concerns at stake. Feedback needs to be organised according to the purpose it is to serve and adapted to the relevant audience. This is a necessary but not always sufficient precondition for an evaluation to be effective. The recipients of feedback from an evaluation are the users – or the assumed or potential stakeholders – as perceived by those who commissioned the evaluation.[20]

The way feedback is organised – how the various kinds of information are reported back and to whom – may also serve as an indicator on the question addressed in the previous sections: whether the objective is primarily to serve the concerns of the implemention or the policy level. With this indicator the question can be broadened to include the two levels on the recipient side too.

The most crucial question is: who are the recipients of feedback from evaluation? After all, the information provided tends to be adapted to the particular demands of the recipients. In the above discussion, the distinction has been between the political and the aid implementing level. Although this remains the most important one, further differentiation within the two levels may be necessary when feedback is discussed.

At the *aid-implementing level*, several units stand out as natural recipients of information emerging from evaluation. On the donor side, these may be grouped in three categories, (a)–(c), as follows:

(a) *The operative units* with a direct responsibility for the activities under evaluation – in the field and at the home base of the aid agency. These units would be natural recipients of feedback from evaluation of all kinds of aid-financed activities and all kinds of evaluation because of the learning aspect involved. However, certain types of evaluation would be of more direct interest than others. This applies especially to information emerging from monitoring (if included in the evaluation concept) and from evaluations of a type that is close to monitoring and carried out during the implementing phase (such as annual reviews, mid-term reviews and internal evaluations), where the conclusions may have a bearing on the future course of an activity.

Feedback of this kind may be organised in many different ways – the most obvious one being that the units obtain a direct access to the evaluation report. Procedures involving direct communication and exchange may enhance effectiveness – for instance, at the field level, by including a summary report by the evaluation team at the end of its field work, where the main conclusions are reported to those immediately in charge of operations.

(b) *The planning units.* Evaluation is often referred to as belonging to the end phase of one aid activity and having the purpose of providing information of value to the first phase of a new one – the planning of new activities of a similar kind. In actual practice, this ideal seldom materialises. Even in administrative structures where aid planning is centralised in one unit (the planning department), it may be more or less restricted to macro-level decisions, such as the distribution of resources to the various recipients and sectors. The planning of ongoing and future aid-financed activities usually involves operational units along geographical and/or functional dividing lines and the administrative hierarchies to which they belong. To be effective, therefore, information has to be fed into the relevant operational units of the implementing agency as well.

(c) *Decision-makers* at the implementation level are most important potential recipients of feedback. Who the decision-makers are varies from one administrative setting to another and even, within the same aid agency, according to the type of aid. A typical distinction is between bilateral and multilateral aid and, within both, aid may be compartmentalised; for instance, bilateral *financial* aid is typically decided by a completely different set of decision-makers than is *poverty-oriented* aid.

The structure of the aid administration differs from one country to another, as noted. In countries where a more or less integrated aid administration has the responsibility for most of the bilateral aid programme – and even the multilateral one, too – decision-making and some degree of coordination are vested in a body consisting of the heads of departments; in others this authority is shared with yet another layer – an executive board. The executive board may belong to the political level through delegated authority from the government. The secretariat of the Minister fulfils such a function in other administrative structures. As noted above, the administrative units at this level, even when composed solely of civil servants, belong to a grey zone where the same type of questions tend to be raised as those raised at the political level.

At the *political level*, a distinction should be made between the government and Parliament (including its specialised committees).

(d) *The government* – which, in most cases, refers to the political leadership of the Ministry responsible for development cooperation – needs information that serves as a basis for drawing up guidelines for future aid implementation and for the allocation of resources within a short and medium-range, time perspective. It also needs a system which maintains a control function. *Vis-à-vis* Parliament – and even more *vis-à-vis* the mass media – it even needs an early warning system, in particular, to protect itself against surprises in the form of 'bad news'. Feedback from evaluation may be an important input for several of these purposes, although clearly not all types of feedback would capture the same attention.

So far, reference has been made to potential users within the more or less closed administrative system with a direct responsibility for the planning and implementing of aid. It is assumed that the government, particularly in systems characterised by a more closed administrative tradition, will be inclined to share the predominant preference at the implementing level, namely to keep what may turn out to be critical information restricted and for internal use.

(e) The primary function and, accordingly, the concerns of *Parliament* are different. Parliament decides on policy and funds. While the control function of evaluation, therefore, certainly becomes important, the main questions would relate to whether aid works according to the aims set. However, the efficiency of aid is also seen as important. To the extent that these questions are addressed, feedback from evaluation would be of interest also at this level. As noted, evaluation also serves the additional function of legitimating the aid spending – or at least Parliament's handling of aid – provided the evaluation is open and accessible, independent and critical.

However, there are also stakeholders outside the formal policy-making structures of the donor country. This applies, in particular, to the following:

(f) The legitimising function relates to the feedback to *the general public* – with a bearing on the relation between the electors and the elected; for most practical purposes it is a question of feedback to *the mass media*. Milieus of particular interest would also include *research institutes* orientated towards development and relations with the Third World and others with an interest in aid issues, including *NGOs* and *business*.

(g) Potential stakeholders on the donor side have been identified above. According to its basic justification, however, the main concern of ODA is to assist in creating development on the recipient side. Activities financed through ODA are to a large extent administered by systems closer to the end use of the resources than the donor's administration, even in cases where this is extended to the recipient country (with decentralised authority vested in the office of the resident representative). From a development perspective, therefore, it would be even more important to feed information derived from evaluation into the administrative and policy systems of the recipient than those of the donor. To what extent have insights emerging from evaluation been fed into the recipient's administrative and political systems? And to the extent this has been done, to whom has the information been directed?

The latter questions relate to the same categories which have been identified in (a)–(f) above. However, the prime responsibility of a donor agency, given the formal aid relationship, is towards its partner; for state-to-state aid, these are the authorities of the recipient country identified in (c)–(d).

What about the other stakeholders? In a formal sense, the responsibility for transmitting the information to those who might benefit from it or have an interest in receiving it – and indeed the decision whether to transmit it or not – is vested in the authorities on the recipient side. However, such a constraint on the part of the donor is indeed a strange bird in the aid relationship, although it may be interpreted as a tribute to the sovereignty of the recipient government. If the development perspective is maintained, and the aid relationship also in this respect includes elements of (even agreed) intervention – it would be equally important to bring insights emerging from evaluation to the attention of both the planning and implementing levels of the relevant administration and – if pertinent – even to the highest policy-making level.

Although prevailing conditions for the mass media vary extensively in the Third World – as indeed the environments for critical public debate – the performance of aid, and aid issues generally, call for public attention in view of the crucial role foreign aid is playing in many Third World countries. Universities and research institutes within these countries have an even more important role to play in this regard than their opposite numbers in the North since, in many Third World countries, they are among the very few producers of independent, or semi-independent, critical insights and alternatives to those of the government administration; in some Third World countries, they are, to some extent, even allowed to play a watch-dog role. They offer themselves, from the value perspective of pluralism, participation, even democracy, as obvious recipients of insights emerging from evaluation.

How do the evaluation systems dealt with in the country studies fit into this framework? The general observation is that the patterns emerging from the previous indicators are reinforced. This indicator tends to further clarify, in particular, the picture provided in the previous section. Even in systems where evaluation reports are open and accessible, entry may still be narrow: access often depends on a specific request and initiative. Few systems have given emphasis to the dissemination of

POLICIES, PERFORMANCE, TRENDS AND CHALLENGES

relevant information to the various categories of stakeholders. As Basil Cracknell comments, it is ironic that the most important phase of the evaluation process has hitherto been given the least attention [*Cracknell, 1991b*]. This applies particularly to stakeholders outside the aid administration.

The *Scandinavian* countries follow somewhat similar patterns. The normal practice is to make the reports available for those who request copies and to announce the evaluation and its main findings. There is a press release – in the case of Norway, a press conference is arranged too. Norway and Sweden make particular efforts to publish the evaluation reports. The SIDA publishes two series of booklets, in Swedish and English respectively, and annual summaries of all SIDA projects; in Norway, a similar series of evaluation reports is published, mostly in English, and a series of country studies (books) in both English and Norwegian. This general feedback is directed to all categories identified above.

In addition, more specialised feedback is provided to the political level and the implementation level. Thus, in the case of *Norway*, summaries of the main findings are presented to Parliament in the government's annual report on aid and North–South relations. The evaluation report and a proposal for follow-up – also based on comments from all parties involved in the implementation, including the authorities of the recipient country – are presented to the main decision-making body of the Ministry, the staff meeting of all heads of departments and often also the political leadership. A synthesis of the evaluation report is provided to all sectoral offices and, occasionally, seminars are run for the staff, too. For the country studies there has been a two-day seminar attended (more or less compulsorily) by representatives from the top leadership of the ministry and the NORAD, all relevant desks, as well as the resident representative of the country concerned and the core evaluators. The monitoring and evalua-tion reports of the aid agency, however, have not been published and they have only occasionally been reported outside the NORAD [*Stokke, 1991*]. In *Denmark*, the findings have been included in the DANIDA annual report to the Board. After fieldwork, the evaluation teams report to the DANIDA resident representative and the draft report is discussed with the involved desks in the DANIDA. Reports are also used in internal staff training courses [*Schaumburg-Müller, 1991*].

In the dual *Dutch* system, evaluation reports of the operational desks are not published and feedback is mainly restricted to the desks involved; they do not reach the higher levels of the Ministry. Although the inspection unit's evaluation reports are usually written in international languages and are open to all, they are not widely distributed. These reports have an impact on the policy units of the ministry and are also of

37

interest to members of Parliament. However, feedback to the political level and to the development community in the Netherlands could be improved, according to Enno Hommes: the inspection unit has no direct access to the Minister, there is little contact between the unit and key MPs involved in aid questions and the reports are not forwarded to the advisory council on aid [*Hommes, 1991*].

For the more closed systems, feedback is almost exclusively oriented towards the managerial and decision-making levels of the civil service. Thus, in the case of the *FRG*, the reports are accessible for inspection by the bodies in which responsibility is vested (Parliament, its budget committee, the cabinet, auditors). Emphasis, however, is on the feedback to the operational units – the recommendations are discussed in detail with the implementing agencies concerned and there is an annual review to find out if they have been followed up [*Musto, 1991*].

This applies also to the *United Kingdom* (ODA), where systematic efforts have been made in tailoring feedback to the particular needs of civil service decision-making and planning. Most emphasis is given to the senior management level; the decision-making body (PEC) sets aside a number of meetings yearly to consider evaluation reports which are given a cover note in which action is recommended. A cover note is prepared by the evaluation department in close cooperation with the operational units concerned, which at an early stage have received the report for comments. Summaries are provided to the middle- and upper-level staff of the ODA. It is mandatory for a new aid project proposal to confirm that all relevant evaluations within the same sector have been taken account of. As there is advance notice of new projects, the evaluation department feeds into the operational units summaries of relevant evaluation reports already during the preparatory stage of a new project. The findings emerging from evaluations are integrated in managerial vehicles, such as the Policy Guidance Note, the Sector Planning Manual and the Office Procedure. Feedback to the outside, however, has been somewhat restrictive; evaluation reports have, by and large, been accessible upon request [*Cracknell, 1991a, 1991b*].

In the *UNFPA*, evaluation reports are printed and freely distributed after the government's permission has been granted. Before this, all involved parties have a chance to comment on the draft, and the programme committee of the UNFPA takes a stand on the recommendations. One year later, the evaluation unit makes a follow-up assessment of the use made of the evaluation. Syntheses of the results of selected evaluations within the same area are disseminated for use in the preparation of new projects and programmes and for policy purposes. The emphasis is on bringing feedback to the decision-makers as fast as possible. As pointed out by Kerstin Trone [*1991*], it is not possible to please all audiences with one report, nor is there time to prepare many versions.

The performance of the evaluation systems also varies with regard to feedback to the recipients. It is common practice to hand over the evaluation report to the authorities of the developing country concerned. These are also invited, by most agencies, to comment on the draft or the final report. In a few cases (the FRG, the Netherlands, the UNFPA), the evaluation teams are expected, at the end of the field visit, to report and discuss the main findings with the responsible authorities on the recipient side. Thus, even *vis-à-vis* the *authorities* of the recipient countries, the feedback is of limited scope. However, information emerging from major evaluations serves as important input in the yearly dialogue on future cooperation between donor and recipient authorities (such as for the revolving, multi-year country programmes of the Scandinavian countries with some major recipient countries). There have been no systematic efforts to provide feedback to others than the central and occasionally also the local authorities. For the open evaluation systems, the published evaluation reports (in international languages) are, of course, available for all categories of stakeholders in the recipient countries, provided they are informed about their existence and find their way to the publisher. However, as noted by Henrik Schaumburg-Müller with reference to Danish evaluation reports, the circulation is usually very limited and often the reports do not even reach the local project authorities. Little information is available either on the distribution of the reports or on the degree to which the information provided penetrates the recipient government's own evaluation and feedback systems [*Schaumburg-Müller, 1991*].

VIII. THE CASE FOR A DATA BANK

The previous section focused on the efforts to convey information emerging from evaluation directly to potential users, addressing the question: who are the recipients? A follow-up question is *how* – in what forms – the feedback is transmitted. Evaluation reports are not usually among the most exciting literature around and, for most potential recipients, time is a scarce resource. In order to attract attention, therefore, the information provided must be relevant (as perceived by the receiver) and in an accessible form. Different stakeholders will look for different aspects of the aid performance, a fact that has implications for the presentation. It is therefore important for the outcome of an evaluation that the assessments and recommendations are presented in forms which are adapted to differentiated target groups.

This question is also addressed in the country studies. The general picture that emerges is that only a few efforts have been made in differentiating feedback to different audiences. The main exception has been the information provided to the decision-making bodies of the aid administration. The learning aspect becomes of crucial importance, too. As noted, this has been neglected, although increased emphasis has been directed, by some agencies, to synthesising experiences from several evaluation reports within the scope of a geographical area or a sector, and summaries of evaluation reports have been circulated to the staff, most systematically by the SIDA and the ODA. Staff seminars on evaluation reports have occasionally been organised and some agencies have used the reports in staff training courses.

An additional aspect has increasingly come to the fore, namely the organisation of *information systems*. This is of crucial importance both because of the large turnover of personnel in the aid administration, particularly in systems where the personnel rotates (especially where the aid administration is an integral part of the foreign service), and because of the increasing number of evaluations, nationally and internationally. By 1985, the DAC Expert Group on evaluation estimated that over 9,000 evaluation reports had been prepared by the bilateral donors participating in the group and the European Commission, together with the World Bank and the regional banks [*OECD, 1986*]; by 1991 this number may have increased to about 16,000 if produced at the same rate (1,100 per year). The evaluations carried out by the UN system and other agencies were not included and would have increased the number substantially. Some international agencies and bilateral agencies (the World Bank, USAID, CIDA) have established computerised information systems (information banks). This task has recently been given priority within the DAC co-operation. Starting in 1987, the Canadian aid agency (CIDA) offered to work out a register for the DAC group, based on its own system and standardised reports from the other agencies, to be operational in 1990. However, Third World governments are not expected to share the information computerised in this register [*Kjekshus, 1991*]. To what extent have the agencies included in this study themselves established information systems – and who has access to these?

Few agencies have built up systems of their own, as the costs involved have been considered prohibitive. However, the UNFPA have established a low-cost computerised system for lessons learned from evaluation, including both in-depth evaluations and more elaborate internal evaluations. The system is for internal use, including the participating UN agencies [*Trone, 1991*]. The SIDA has also established a data bank and the management information system of the ODA contains key statistics on projects that might be expanded by data from evaluations. For all agencies, therefore, the co-operative efforts in the DAC – through the good offices of the CIDA – seem to be the first step to a shared, computerised information system. Even if not intended when the idea was first conceived, it cannot be ruled out that evaluation units and evaluators from developing countries may, in the future, share the accumulated insights contained in this system. So many arguments, some of which will be offered in the following section, point in that direction.

IX. PARTICIPATION OF THIRD WORLD PARTNERS AND EVALUATORS

Evaluation of development assistance has been initiated by the aid-providing countries, both for control and management reasons. Since development assistance, as far as the end use is concerned, is to a large extent channelled through administrative systems outside the civil service of the donor country, evaluation stands out as a particularly useful mechanism to gain insights of indispensable value in the exercise of the *control* function. As noted, evaluation also serves the function of legitimating the proper use of aid *vis-à-vis* the political authorities at home – and in the last resort also *vis-à-vis* the public at large (the electorate). These concerns loomed high when aid agencies – in most cases, with the blessing of the politicians – engaged in the expansion of aid evaluation.

The demands for more evaluation, which appeared in the late 1970s and became increasingly manifest in the 1980s, also followed, with a time lag, a new trend in aid relations, in particular, with regard to bilateral aid. Donor countries withdrew gradually from the more or less direct implementation of small projects and left the responsibility for implementation to the recipient governments. The combination of new forms of aid and the support of larger, more complex projects facilitated this change. However, this trend was not so pronounced in sub-Saharan Africa as elsewhere. Where applicable, it underscored the need for evaluation, as perceived from the perspective of donor countries.

Although perceptions of their own needs were the driving force and primary justification of the donors for engaging in evaluation, it might be expected that the particular environment of development assistance would also influence the approaches and forms chosen. After all, the primary objective of development assistance is to assist Third World governments in improving their capacity to run their own affairs. The involvement of host country stakeholders is also important from the perspective of implementation. As argued by Lawrence [*1989*], it seems inconceivable that useful information on project effectiveness can be extracted without substantial assistance from within the recipient country, or that an evaluation would not benefit considerably from being presented explicitly as improving capabilities in the recipient country to perform whatever project activities are being evaluated. And, as noted by Ginsburg [*1989*], there is no substitute for participation in the process to generate a feeling of ownership that should, in the long run, increase the participants' commitment to support and, it may be added, make effective use of evaluation studies. What, then, could be more natural than to involve the partners on the recipient side – and evaluators from the relevant milieus in the recipient countries – in the evaluation of aid?

The record of DAC countries on this account is not impressive. As noted by the Expert Group [*OECD, 1986*], recipient country involvement in defining the purpose and scope of evaluations has been very limited in all but the most operations-focused evaluations and even there their involvement has often been confined to a *pro forma* review and approval of the terms of reference which have been drafted by donors. Recipients have not been encouraged to participate in formulating issues and questions on some of the most influential determinants of project and programme success. They are explicitly excluded from the planning of certain types of evaluation, particularly those which address the donor's programme, policy, management or procedures. Overall, the Expert Group found that evaluation planning and the selection of issues to be addressed overwhelmingly reflected either the interests and concerns of donors or the interests and concerns of recipients as seen by the donors. Furthermore, evaluation reports were rarely translated into the official language of the recipient country, where this differed from the language of the donor. As noted by Lawrence [*1989*], these characteristics have a general bearing. They apply to World Bank evaluations as well. Even in the beneficiary assessment, a management information system recently experimented with by the Bank, it relied mainly on external participant observers [*Salmen, 1989*]. Although the UN Secretary-General, as early as 1966, had emphasised that every encouragement should be given to recipient governments to strengthen their own coordination and evaluation procedures, the UN Joint Inspection Unit observed, more than 15 years later, that the UN system had done little to support the development of national evaluation capacities [*JIU, 1982*].

A wide range of arguments has been offered to justify the exclusion of the recipient country authorities from an active part in the evaluation of aid. Their participation would affect the independence of the evaluation, one argument goes. This may be true; it may also apply to evaluations organised by the other party in the aid relationship, the aid-providing agency, with its own interests at stake and those of the public administration to which it belongs. Admittedly, if evaluation was organised as a joint venture, it might result in a reciprocal exclusion of the most critical themes, issues and questions from the evaluation assignments. However, it might also result in a reciprocality with regard to the focus through the inclusion of aspects for which the donor carries the main responsibility, which would be highly appropriate. If carried out as a genuinely joint enterprise, the timing would probably also be affected. Recipients are likely to prefer their own planning cycle (related to their development plan, usually with a four- or five-year-time horizon) to that of the project or programme of the donor agency. Adapting the planning cycle of the recipient would probably improve the follow-up of the evaluation findings where it matters most for the implementation of aid: on the recipient side.

A host of other reasons is also given – including lack of interest, competence and capacity on the part of the recipients. Recipient administrative authorities may quite naturally be reluctant to spend money and personnel on evaluations which are not adapted to their own needs but carried out in order to provide accountability to governing bodies abroad and to serve the management requirements of foreign aid agencies. As noted by the UN Joint Inspection Unit [*1982:7*], rather than assisting these governments to improve development administration and raise the overall effectiveness of their programmes, 'evaluation became merely a "necessary pill" for them to swallow along with the inflow of external assistance'.[21] Risks are involved, too; administrators tend to avoid being involved in activities that may result in a critical focus on their own activities or the government's policies and management and even lead to financial resources from abroad being cut off. The same applies to the individual evaluators and the institutions or firms with which they are associated; the sensitivity of some Third World governments and authorities is well developed and the fear of sanctions may be very real in some countries. Third World authorities and implementing agencies have also, to a large extent, regarded evaluation as a device for serving only donor needs for control and management, not for meeting their own needs and improving their development efforts [*Bamberger, 1989*]. Even so, both perceptions and attitudes seem to have gradually changed more recently [*Kjekshus, 1991*]. Given the particular field, the arguments referring to competence and capacity could easily be turned around into arguments for trying hard to find ways of including such participation. In addition, there is a persuasive cost argument for using in-country resources for evaluation.

The approach and performance of the countries included in this study vary somewhat on this account, too. Towards the end of the 1980s, there seemed to be a change to a less restrictive and more favourable attitude towards genuinely involving developing countries in evaluation efforts. By and large, however, their involvement so far has been rather marginal.

In some of the European countries, there has been a stated policy to involve the partner countries in the planning and evaluation of aid, and even in decision-making. However, commenting on the *Swedish* performance, Kim Forss concludes that no evaluation study has been initiated by a recipient country, although studies have been jointly agreed upon. The SIDA initiates, sets the terms of reference, recruits the consultants, finances the studies – and is the first to use the results. Consultants and researchers from the recipient country are rarely recruited as external evaluators. This is attributed to a combination of scarce relevant resources on the part of the recipient countries and the desire on the part of the SIDA's own staff for efficient implementation [*Forss, 1991*].[22] A similar situation prevails, to a large extent, in the case of *Norway*, although the evaluation manual of 1981 prescribed a joint venture approach, stating that evaluation should first of all serve recipients. In 1983, Parliament stated that evaluation should be organised in such a way as to ensure that the political authorities and the civil services of the recipients had a chance to benefit from the insights gained. The government agreed that evaluation should be a joint effort. In practice, however, the initiative has almost exclusively come from the donor, who, with a few exceptions, has also recruited the evaluators drawn from recipient countries. However, there have been a few joint ventures and about one-third of the evaluators who were recruited during the 1980s were drawn from the recipient countries. The evaluation (monitoring and reviews) carried out by the NORAD is organised more as a joint venture [*Stokke 1991*].

In the case of the *FRG*, nationals of the recipient country have increasingly been recruited. In many government agreements, joint evaluation studies have been provided for, and both parties have found the experiences positive [*Musto, 1991*]. In the case of *Denmark*, the recipient country is in most cases invited to select a member of the evaluation team; however, she or he tends to function more as a resource person than as a team member [*Schaumburg-Müller*, [*1991*]. In the *Netherlands*, the evaluations of the geographical and functional desks are supposed to be carried out jointly with the recipients [*Hommes, 1991*]. Basil Cracknell records an occasional success on the part of the *ODA* in encouraging Third World participation but adds that recipient countries, generally speaking, prefer to keep aloof [*Cracknell, 1991a*]. The *UNFPA* hires local consultants to provide a section on the population-related sectors of the country for evaluations on country programmes. Nationals of the recipient country are not included in teams. However, efforts have been made to recruit Third World consultants; in 1988, half of the team members were drawn from developing countries [*Trone, 1991*].

The Scandinavian countries have committed themselves to providing support for building up evaluation competence and capacity in the recipient countries. In 1982, the government-appointed commission to review Danish aid came up with recommendations to this end, but Henrik Schaumburg-Müller [*1991*] finds no evidence of any systematic efforts so far to implement them. This criticism also applies to some extent to Norway, although the share of Third World evaluators commissioned is relatively large. A strategy for improving the evaluation capability on the recipient side would include support for institution building in combination with an active involvement of Third World evaluators in the commissioned evaluation work.

The involvement of the public administration of the recipient countries – and their academics and consultancy firms – is therefore today, at best, only in its infancy. The bilateral aid agencies have made few efforts to meet the recommendations of the UN system to involve Third World governments in the process and to improve their evaluation capacity.[23] As Helge Kjekshus [*1991*] rightly observes, to improve this record is one of the greatest challenges to the DAC evaluation community. He suggests a DAC code of conduct which sets guidelines that would ensure an active and equal participation from recipients.

X. TRENDS AND CHALLENGES

The balance struck between evaluation as a management tool and as a control instrument, particularly related to the objectives set for aid, has been discussed in the above on the basis of several different indicators. The evaluation function, as institutionalised and performed, emerges as a predominantly managerial instrument, mainly oriented to serve the decision-makers at the civil service level. In some agencies, the trend is increasingly in this direction (the FRG, the UK, the UNFPA). However, this general picture is rich in nuances, and trends differ both for the individual agencies focused on and for the indicators chosen. Thus, for the Scandinavian countries and the Netherlands, a more even balance is struck between the two concerns and for some of these countries the general trend has clearly been towards accountability concerns. According to one of the indicators, the degree of openness, the general trend is towards accountability for all the countries included, except one (the FRG).

This overall assessment is based on the institutional setting and performance of the evaluation units. In several countries, however, a dual system has evolved. Monitoring has everywhere been vested in the operative units of the aid agencies. The ambition level of these 'monitoring' systems has increased, particularly where the evaluation unit has moved increasingly in the direction of the overall questions of aid (accountability), as evidenced in the case of Norway, where the aid agency has recently based its monitoring and evaluation on the 'logical framework' system adapted to its own needs. These 'monitoring' systems have been almost exclusively adapted to managerial concerns, with an emphasis on the requirements, as conceived by the operational level of the aid administration.

Evaluation is expected to serve many different functions and, as usual when limited resources are involved, different concerns will compete. The core conflict in this analysis, between management and accountability concerns, places the evaluation unit under pressure from stake-holders both *outside* (Parliament, the public) and *inside* the aid administration. In most cases, the evaluation unit has been included in the aid-implementing agency, although at some distance from the operational desks. It becomes, therefore, almost by definition a part of the aid-implementing organisation. No wonder that such an institutional setting has caused tension between evaluation units where leaders and staff have nurtured loyalty towards expectations set by external stakeholders (critical, independent and open scrutiny), and the aid agency, in particular, the operational units, wanting to keep a hand on the wheel and to have evaluations that can be immediately translated into improved aid. Such tensions led, in some agencies and particularly during the early phase, to a lack of co-operation by operational units in evaluation. The outcome has been either that the evaluation function has been increasingly integrated in the aid-implementing administration, with the primary function of serving managerial concerns (as in the case of the UNFPA) or that a dual system has evolved (as in the case of Norway).

These tensions – and outcomes – illustrate a more fundamental conflict between the implementation and evaluation functions, in particular, where the evaluation function is not appropriated by the implementing agency in order to serve managerial concerns only. Aaron Wildavsky [*1972*] goes further, arguing that evaluation and organisation may be contradictory terms as organisational structure implies stability, while the process of evaluation suggests change. The self-evaluating organisation, therefore, will have to convince its members to live with constant change.[24]

In our analysis and discussion, the focus has been almost exclusively on the main functions of evaluation, namely to control that aid works (accountability) and to improve the delivery system (management). Within these two broad categories, more particular functions may be discerned. One of these, twin of the accountability function, has already been integrated in our discussion, the *legitimating* function of evaluation *vis-à-vis* the funding authorities and ultimately the electorate. However, evaluation may also serve to legitimate changes that the management contemplates or even has decided upon.

Although, in some systems, the accountability function has been given emphasis, and increasingly so, the main emphasis has everywhere been on the management function. According to Basil Cracknell [*1991*], evaluation has increasingly become a tool in aid management. Another participant in the game, Annette Binnendijk [*1989*], observes a similar trend and argues for it, too. This is a very legitimate concern, particularly from the perspective of aid managers.

The more basic concern, however, is that evaluation should be useful and the results used. This has fundamental implications for the orientation of the evaluation; the core questions are what functions an evaluation should serve, what kind of information should be sought for what purpose and who the users of the information are. A good starting point is the needs of the users. The *users* have to be identified, their needs related to the particular evaluation to be clarified – and the evaluation has to meet these needs if the results can be expected to be put to effective use.[25]

The potential users of evaluation are, first of all, the policy-makers and aid agencies on the donor side, the political authorities and involved agencies on the recipient side – and the beneficiaries and other interested parties on both sides. The managers of aid are, therefore, among the most obvious potential users of evaluation. It is quite legitimate that priority is claimed for their particular needs and, given the present structure where the evaluation function is part of the donors' aid administration, understandable that they have succeeded. Imagination should, accordingly, be mobilised in improving present-day evaluation systems and methods to meet management needs. Within this perspective, some additional functions may crop up – not necessarily new functions of evaluation, but functions which have not been made explicit and for that reason may have been underplayed in actual evaluation work related to aid.

The major function of monitoring and evaluation within a management perspective is to assess the delivery system and report the results back to the decision-makers. In addition, the evaluators are almost always expected to come up with recommendations for improvements; for evaluation the scrutiny and recommendations may even include the objectives set for the aid intervention. These mainstream functions all deal with *inspection* and *judgment*, evaluation mainly from the outside, monitoring mainly from the inside. Evaluation is expected to come up with information which may be useful for improving ongoing activities and planning better for the future.

There are additional roles to be picked up by evaluation, too. The implementation of aid involves a complex social interaction between a wide variety of actors, including the beneficiaries (and victims!) and hierarchical social structures – with a duality that adds to the complexity, namely the recipient and donor administrative systems, rooted in different cultures – all with their vested interests in the subject matter, the ODA transfers. In this multi-faceted setting, conflicts are part of everyday life; some conflicts may seriously threaten the intended objectives set for aid – and the objectives set may cause conflict between different stakeholders. In such situations, the evaluator may take on the role of *mediator*.

To serve the broker function properly, however, additional qualities to those generally sought when inspectors and evaluators (judges) are picked would be in demand.[26] A combination of knowledge and power will be necessary. Knowledge is a prerequisite for making sound judgments. For the evaluator, a vital incentive is the prospect of seeing recommendations transferred into policy; his or her power position affects the access to information, too. As noted by Wildavsky [*1972*], the evaluation enterprise also depends on common recognition that the activity is being carried out in order to secure better policies and not in support of a predetermined position, otherwise people down the line will refuse to co-operate. These aspects apply to evaluation generally, but particularly when the evaluator takes on a broker function.

A related function is that of *catalyst*, which may also involve conflict resolution but is generally directed towards problem-solving.[27] Both functions presuppose a more direct involvement on the part of the evaluators than the traditional inspector and judge roles – the catalyst role may even involve direct participation.

Although these functions are not completely strange to many evaluators, they have not been identified as tasks for evaluators. The main challenge for evaluation, from a management perspective, is to explore the possibilities of using evaluators for these kinds of operation, which demand a greater involvement and additional qualities from the evaluator – and to identify the prerequisites, constraints and limitations involved.

Within the management perspective, there are also important institutional challenges. One relates to the *internal* structuring of the evaluation function. The ideal system would ensure that all aid channels (including the aid agency itself), forms and activities within all sectors became subject to scrutiny from time to time. Monitoring should be better coordinated with evaluation; whether evaluation and monitoring are organised in integrated or dual systems, reports emerging from monitoring and internal evaluation should be designed in such a way as to serve as building blocks for evaluation. Another challenge relates to *inter-donor co-operation*. Much would be gained – for the aid agencies, but even more for the often fragile, overburdened civil services on the recipient side, confronted with a trail of evaluation teams from abroad visiting in turn the same projects in distant areas and asking the same questions – if closer inter-agency co-operation in evaluation was sought, particularly between agencies with a similar aid orientation.

However, the main challenges, to my mind, are to be found in three different areas:

(1) Although there is still room for major improvements, management concerns have been increasingly attended to by most evaluation units. The main *neglect* has been the concerns of stakeholders *outside* the aid administration. The main, systemic, outside stakeholders belong to what we have termed the political level, namely first of all the policy-makers within the formal political institutions (government, Parliament and its committees), but even institutions on which these formal bodies are based – ultimately the electorate. What really matters, therefore, is a much greater concern for the political accountability of aid. After all, that concern was the one which triggered off the increased emphasis on evaluation in the late 1970s and early 1980s. At this level the most crucial question, which hitherto so much evaluation work has failed to address, is: does aid work? The overall objectives of development assistance would then be a point of departure for evaluation, and the main issues related to *development* and *aid*, including the aid relationship, would be given first priority. Evaluation would address policy issues head on, including values, strategies and the craft of aid administration.

These issues would probably be the most crucial ones from the perspective of the political decision-makers of a donor country. There are other neglected issues too. Hitherto, evaluation has mainly dealt with domestic concerns within the recipient country – most often within the confines of a single project and in a local context. Wider structural relations – in a regional or national context – have been left more or less untouched (and probably best so, when fast-travelling evaluation teams are involved!), although the relation between regional and national policies and the project or programme level may be of fundamental importance for the outcome. International structural relations of various kinds, so decisive in many regards, have been even more neglected in evaluation work so far.

Is it just wishful thinking to expect evaluation to address these more fundamental issues and concerns, given the present institutionalisation of the evaluation function? In most cases the answer is probably yes, although with some ambiguity. After all, the broader issues, even some of the overall objectives of aid, have been increasingly addressed in the late 1980s by some of the evaluation units focused on. But the present location of the evaluation function is not ideal for pursuing these tasks; ideally, it would be better situated outside the aid administration, with an independent institution or associated with the State Auditor.

However, to meet management concerns, including administrative decision-making, evaluation (and monitoring) would be best situated within the aid administration. The answer, at the institutional level, is probably a dual evaluation system; one within the aid administration adapted to serve management concerns and another outside the aid administration adapted to serve the accountability concerns. Needless to say, the need for coordination would arise.

Would the costs involved in addressing the political accountability of aid be prohibitive? Admittedly, they would, in most cases, be beyond the modest budgets of national evaluation units, if more immediate management concerns are also to be attended to. Additional resources would be one answer to this challenge, and pooling of resources an even more challenging answer. The Cassen Report emerged from international cooperation initiated by the World Bank and the International Monetary Fund (IMF); new efforts to evaluate the core issues related to aid and development in a systematic way, and other major efforts, such as country studies, may involve other international institutions and partners. Thus, the Development Assistance Committee of the OECD, for one, may take the initiative in coordinating this kind of evaluation. It is, however, representative only of the main, western aid providers; ideally, donors and recipients should be equally represented in a coordinating body of this kind, along with other major stakeholders outside the public sector. As indicated earlier, there should be no illusion that this kind of evaluation would be operating in a vacuum; values and political and economic concerns would affect the selection of issues to be evaluated, the orientation of the evaluation and the recommendations. The main stakeholders should, therefore, be part of both the decision-making bodies of such a consortium and be included in the reference group of the individual evaluation.

(2) Another major challenge, associated with the first, is to mobilise and

make use of the reservoir of resources available within the various disciplines, in particular, the social sciences, and to develop new evaluation methods in the interface between evaluation and research. The orientation towards various forms of non-project aid makes this even more urgent. Part of this challenge would be to involve the research milieus and higher education institutions much more than hitherto, as this task calls for both multi-disciplinary and inter-disciplinary research efforts.

(3) The Third World stakeholders – the authorities, the beneficiaries and the victims, the research institutions and the consultants – should be directly involved much more actively than hitherto. After all, these are the people who are most affected by foreign aid. This, therefore, is the most important challenge. Improving the recipient countries' competence and capacity in this field would also be in line with the ultimate purpose set for aid.

NOTES

1. This simple definition tries to be all-inclusive by avoiding the particularities of the more specific approaches. However, as argued by Palumbo [*1987*], just as it is impossible to define evaluation in a way that does not reflect a particular methodological or epistemological bias, there is no one correct definition, but many different ones.
    A mainstream definition is given by Rossi and Freeman [*1982: 20*]:

    Evaluation research is the systematic application of social research procedures in assessing the conceptualization and design, implementation, and utility of social intervention programs. In other words, evaluation research involves the use of social research methodologies to judge and to improve the planning, monitoring, effectiveness, and efficiency of health, education, welfare, and other human service programs.

    Lincoln and Guba [*1986*] cite four different definitions, each identified with a particular kind of evaluation, namely (1) determining the congruence between performance and objective (the conventional summative or impact evaluation), (2) obtaining information for judging decision alternatives (the approach of operations research), (3) comparing actual effects with demonstrated needs (Scriven's goal-free evaluation), and (4) critically describing and appraising an evaluation through connoisseurship (what art critics do). To these, Palumbo [*1987*] adds utilisation, focused, stakeholder, theory-driven, responsive, and political evaluations.
    Angela Browne and Aaron Wildavsky [*1987: 149–66*] offer a recommended *tour d'horizon* in the various approaches, addressing (and discussing) what evaluation *is*, related to the evaluator's answers to five basic questions about their craft: When? Where? For whom? What? and Why? They also offer some advice on separating implementation from evaluation.
2. Writing, in the mid 1980s, on the evolvement of evaluation in the US, Ross F. Conner *et al.* [*1984*] look back at the 'bubbling, exciting, fast-developing childhood years of the late 1960s and early 1970s'. According to the authors, evaluation research emerged in the mid 1960s, when a number of developments converged, such as the emphasis on the development of social programmes under Presidents Kennedy and Johnson and the appearance of two important books, by Campbell and Stanley [*1966*] and Suchman [*1967*].

Basil E. Cracknell [*1988: 76*] refers, with particular reference to evaluation of development assistance, to Albert Hirschman [*1967*] as the 'first evaluation report to catch the imagination of the public'. However, his study 'remains a fascinating but isolated oddity that has had very little effect on how the subject has evolved'. He finds that the 'logical framework' system, developed by Herb Turner during the early 1970s, had more direct impact. Cracknell argues that the 'massive volume of academic literature' on evaluation of social programmes in the US is little known outside that country and 'has had little impact on evaluation studies in Europe and elsewhere'. However, in the mid 1970s, the OECD invited two American professors to put their experience at the disposal of aid evaluation, resulting in a report in 1979 [*Freeman et al., 1979*].

3. Guba and Lincoln [*1987*] relate the first-generation evaluation to the early part of this century, stimulated by the availability of intelligence, aptitude, and achievement tests following World War I. This generation is characterised as technical and the evaluator as a technician. Evaluation meant little more than *measurement*. The second generation emerged from an eight-year study of the US school system coordinated by Ralph W. Tyler – later on recognised as the 'Father of Evaluation' – introducing programme evaluation. The second generation is characterised by description of patterns and strengths and weaknesses with respect to certain stated objectives and the evaluator's role came to be that of a describer. This *objectives-oriented descriptive approach* was followed, in the mid 1960s, by the third generation, adding *judgment* to description, championed in the first place by Michael Scriven [*1967*], implying that the objectives themselves should be subject to evaluation. Although evaluators only reluctantly agreed to enter into the new role, a range of different models (approaches) were developed during the following decade, of which most, explicitly or implicitly, placed the evaluator in the role of a judge. See also Guba and Lincoln [*1989: Ch. 1*].

4. Guba and Lincoln [*1987, 1989*] have given name and structure to the approach – and are its ardent champions. The class of models included take as their point of focus not objectives, decisions, effects or similar organisers but the *claims, concerns and issues* put forth by members of a variety of *stakeholding audiences* that are involved. It is based in *value-pluralism* and on this basis *negotiation* becomes the hallmark of fourth-generation evaluation. The evaluator retains the roles of earlier generations (technician, describer, judge) but in different forms, and takes on several others (collaborator, learner/teacher, reality-shaper, mediator and agent of change), of which those of a *negotiator* and *agent of change* are the most important.

Evaluation is conceived of as a *social-political process*, where the main stakeholders are given the right to provide inputs based on their own value positions; a *learning/ teaching process* involving the main stakeholders and the evaluator; a *continuous, recursive, and divergent process* (not as discrete, closed-ended, and convergent events); a process that creates 'reality' by bringing stakeholders face to face, it does not only 'discover' reality; an *emergent process*, as the 'design' can be completely described only retrospectively; a *process with unpredictable outcomes*; a *collaborative process* – judgments remain essential, but they should not be made solely by the evaluator or the client; and the agenda for negotiation is best displayed in a *case-study format*, with items requiring negotiation being spelled out in relation to the particulars of the case.

5. JIU [*1982*]. Whereas, up to the early 1980s, training in evaluation had been fairly limited in the Third World, the Indian government had established an extensive training programme. For a description and analysis of the role of bureaucratic and organisational factors in the utilisation of programme evaluations in Indian state government, see Eisendrath [*1988*], who concludes, *inter alia*, that evaluations are used intensively by civil service authorities in auditing the performance of executive agencies, but also that their findings and recommendations are often rejected (intentional non-use).

6. This definition may be compared with the definition generally endorsed by the UN system: 'a process which attempts to determine as systematically and objectively as possible the relevance, effectiveness and impact of activities in light of their objectives' [*JIU, 1982: 1*]. Evaluation 'is concerned with helping to achieve high *quality* in the way

they (the resources) are used to produce desired results. Evaluation is thus a learning and action-oriented tool, which should be an integral and continuous part of the basic management process along with planning and implementation. It provides managers and decision-makers with information and analysis of the extent to which stated objectives are being achieved and why, to help improve both current and future activities' (*idem*). See also JIU [*1979*] and the definition provided in Chapter 9 in this volume.
7. This definition of the term is adapted to the administrative control system involving public (state) expenditures in some donor countries (Government's Board of Auditors), less to the adopted control systems of the international aid agencies. The DAC glossary, however, distinguishes [*OECD, 1986: 62*] between *internal* and *external* auditing, defining the concept as 'determining whether, and to what extent, the measures, processes, directives, and organisational procedures of the donor, and its missions in the Third World, conform to norms and criteria set out in advance'.
8. In the DAC terminology [*OECD, 1986: 63*], monitoring is defined as 'a management function which uses a methodical collection of data to determine whether the material and financial resources are sufficient, whether the people in charge have the necessary technical and personal qualifications, whether activities conform to work plans, and whether the work plan has been achieved and has produced the original objectives'.

However, donor agencies may use different terms for the same basic concept and give slightly different definitions to the term. Thus, the United Nations (Glossary) refers to 'continuous oversight' to see that 'actions are proceeding according to plan', while the IBRD prefers the term 'supervision' for the monitoring function.
9. Annette L. Binnendijk [*1989*], drawing primarily on reports and experiences from the USAID, the DAC, the World Bank and other international aid agencies, maintains that a review of the many different concepts and definitions in current use to distinguish monitoring from evaluation suggests that monitoring and evaluation might be thought of as a continuum along several dimensions, of which she is offering the following [*1989: 207*]:

   (1) *the focus of the assessment* – with monitoring primarily concerned with tracking project inputs and outputs, and whether they are within design budgets and according to schedules, while evaluation focuses on measuring development results and impacts;
   (2) *the timing of the data collection and assessment efforts* – with monitoring typically involving a continuous, ongoing process of data-gathering and review, while evaluations are often considered as periodic, or even 'one-shot', efforts;
   (3) *the implementers of the assessment* – with monitoring viewed as a function implemented primarily by in-house project staff, while evaluation is frequently carried out by teams external to the project;
   (4) *the management uses of the assessment results* – with monitoring oriented primarily to serve the information needs of the project management to improve the project's implementation, while evaluation may serve the information needs of development managers above the project level; for example, to provide guidance for broader programme and sector-level decisions.

10. In this discussion, the focus is on these two categories of stakeholders, both belonging to the donor system. However, there are other important stakeholders, too, in particular, on the recipient side – both the assumed or actual beneficiaries of aid and the recipient authorities, centrally and locally. Beneficiaries and other stakeholders are also found on the donor side. There are other competing perspectives, too. As observed by Thomas D. Cook [*1978: 14*], discussing the utilisation of evaluation, the concept of Nathan Caplan of the two cultures may be illuminative even here: a knowledge-generating culture interested in truth, validity, and goal-oriented rationality; and a potential knowledge-utilisation culture interested in tough, pragmatic action, and a process-oriented rationality which stresses the feasible over the desirable, the timely over the accurate, and the self-protective over the true.

11. The organisation of Swedish bilateral aid has recently been subject to a major review [*SOU, 1990: 17*] which will most probably affect the future organisation of evaluation (see, in particular, Chapters 2 and 7). Since no action has been taken by the government yet, there will no reference to its various recommendations in this chapter.
12. Aid objectives, particularly at lower levels in the hierarchy, have been subject to assessment in aid evaluation involving several agencies, although attitudes differ somewhat, as will be seen in the following section. As values become involved, however, this stance has caused controversy in the debate on evaluation. In the tradition of logical positivism, science has nothing to say about values. Arguing that value-neutral research is neither possible nor desirable, Palumbo [*1987*] maintains that evaluations will take a political position about the desirability of various goals, whether *directly*, by judging that the goals are worthwhile, or *indirectly*, by concluding that the goals are being achieved efficiently. Evaluation, therefore, becomes a part of the goal-setting process.
13. This phenomenon is not limited to the confines of the aid policy. As observed by Martin Rein and Sheldon H. White [*1978: 27–28*] with reference to the US Congress, legislation does not generally, or even occasionally, arise out of a conception of a single objective or purpose.
14. Views may differ on this point. Thus Rein and White [*1978: 41*] – referring to the role of evaluators in a domestic US setting where the politicians, by failing to identify the values or value-derived goals to be pursued, passed on to the scientific community the problem of achieving consensus regarding social values and goals – answer in the negative, arguing that such a transfer of authority exceeds the professional competence of the researchers. They add that, in usurping some genuine political responsibility of the policy-maker, it is improper as well.
15. The function of evaluation to legitimate a policy – or to redefine priorities or policies – is discussed, in general terms, by Aant Elzinga [*1981*], who emphasises that an evaluation will most often reflect the standpoint and perspective of those commissioning it, and argues that it would be better then to speak of 're-evaluation', meant to cover up tacit shifts of policy and resource allocation.
16. Evaluation takes place in a political context with a wide variety of stakeholders, including politicians and administrators at different levels with different and competing interests and values, both on the donor and the recipient side – including the beneficiaries (and victims!) of an aid programme. Any outcome, therefore, may be used by stakeholders in a power game – within the administration or between this and outside actors. The main legitimation of evaluation, however, is to provide careful and unbiased data on the consequences of the programme to improving decision-making. As noted by Weiss [*1987*], failing to recognise the presence of political considerations in evaluation may confront the evaluator with shocks and frustrations. Thus, programmes and policies which evaluation deals with are creatures of political decisions – and remain, during their implementation, subject to pressures, both supportive and hostile. Evaluation reports enter the political arena, as an input in the decision-making process, where their conclusions compete with other factors that carry weight in the political process. By its very nature, an evaluation has a political stance in itself: it makes implicit statements on issues under political consideration, involving the performance of a programme, the legitimacy of goals and strategies, their utility and a wide range of other aspects.
17. The emphasis here is on 'more'. As rather convincingly conveyed by Henry M. Brickell [*1978*], external consultancy firms may also be under the influence of those who commission the evaluation; in fact, their present and future contracts may depend on their giving in to such pressures. Writing from long experience as the head of an (US) evaluation firm, Brickell concluded that external political factors were powerful in influencing the role and methodology of evaluation.

> Sometimes political forces control the populations we can sample. Sometimes they limit the data we can gather. Sometimes they shape our instruments. Sometimes they influence the designs we can use. Sometimes they shape our recommendations.

POLICIES, PERFORMANCE, TRENDS AND CHALLENGES

Sometimes they touch the wording of our report. And they always influence the impact of what we recommend. I think I have never written an evaluation report without being conscious of the fact that what I say will be used in the winning and the exercising of power, that my findings are to be lined up on one side or the other of a contest that somebody else has already set up, and that jobs are on the line – maybe my own job.

Although the settings may vary from one country to another and between policy areas, the independence of 'independent' consultancy firms should not be taken at face value – and even university institutes may look forward to new contracts. Professional ethics and norms in the environments of evaluation, in particular, if, as suggested by William J. Wright [1978], formalised in standard contracts, may be instrumental in reducing this kind of pressure.

The DAC Expert Group [OECD, 1986: 45–6] lists three reasons for the selection of external evaluators: the fact that most evaluation units have a very small staff, the need for specialists and experts in certain areas, and the assumption that outsiders are more objective or at least more neutral. The third assumption is not, according to the Group, justified by donor experience. They have found that 'a more meaningful way of avoiding bias is to distinguish between those closely associated with the project or its staff, and those having no direct association with the project, its staff, or even with the country programme in general. This second group can bring the same objectivity to an evaluation as outsiders can bring.'

18. Thus Wildavsky [1972: 91] argues that

> No matter how good its internal analysis, or how persuasively an organization justifies its programs to itself, there is something unsatisfying about allowing it to judge its own case. The ability of organizations to please themselves must ultimately (at least in a democratic society) give way to judgement by outsiders. Critics of organizations must, therefore, recognize that their role is an essential one. Opposition is part and parcel of the evaluative process.

A different view is argued by Donald T. Campbell [1984: 35], one of the early trendsetters in evaluation research. Looking back, he considers the recommendation (in the 1964–68 period) of external evaluation rather than evaluation of the delivery team itself as a mistake.

19. There is a conflict involved between the roles assumed by an administrator and (external) evaluator, too. As Palumbo [1987] observes, evaluators are trapped by several opposing imperatives: (1) to help administrators understand and improve their programmes, (2) to uncover facts about the programmes even if they are negative, and (3) to increase knowledge about evaluation research and programme evaluation. The more evaluators give emphasis to (2) and (3) (because of the prestige and recognition related to the creation or adding to knowledge, for example, reaching generalisations applicable to a wider number of circumstances), the less helpful they are to the administrators. Hence, it is essential to balance the dual roles of developing new knowledge and solving practical problems. If one or the other dominates, the results will not be good for evaluation research or for practitioners. Administrators, on the other hand, are trapped by two opposing imperatives: they are committed to the efficacy of the programme, yet they must also be its advocates and promoters. And the political structure in which they function will not allow even the slightest risk of failure.

20. Michael Quinn Patton [1987], discussing utilisation-focused evaluation, emphasises that various stakeholders look for different kinds of information for different purposes and uses and that no single evaluation is likely to be able to serve all constituencies equally well. He distinguishes between the immediate action impact of an evaluation and incremental impacts over a longer period of time. The question of where an evaluation is used is closely related to the question of who is the user. 'In a perfect world, the kind typically demanded by political rhetoric, a single evaluation would be useful at all levels, from the local agency up through the national government. In

reality, the information needs of these different units are dramatically disparate' (p. 111).
21. According to the JIU review [*1982: 7*], a number of Third World governments emphasised to the Inspectors that 'donor-imposed reviews and evaluations have often served to disrupt and distract national development management rather than to help it'. The report lists several factors which have contributed to the image of evaluation as an outside irritant instead of as a useful management tool.
22. The DAC Expert Group [*OECD, 1986: 48–50*], too, refers to the Swedish experience where the first of the three declared objectives is to support planning and evaluation activities in recipient countries. This is seen as a long-term goal to be kept in mind when designing and carrying out activities to achieve the other two: to assist in donor decision-making and to report on the effectiveness of Swedish aid. However, in the decentralised system pertaining, little has been done to satisfy this objective, mainly because of scant interest in the recipient countries in this kind of support. It is also reported that recipients have frequently acted as passive observers in joint teams and actually play a cosmetic rather than an active role.
23. See JIU [*1982*], especially p. 24 ff. See also comments by the UN Administrative Committee on Coordination (UN A/38/333/Add.1, 7 November 1983), supporting the report's recommendations.
24. See Wildavsky [*1972: 82–93*]. He starts with the following observations (p. 82):

Failing to understand that evaluation is sometimes incompatible with organization, we are tempted to believe in absurdities much in the manner of mindless bureaucrats who never wonder whether they are doing useful work. If we asked more intelligent questions instead, we would neither look so foolish nor be so surprised.

Who will evaluate and who will administer? How will power be divided between these functionaries? Which ones will bear the costs of change? Can evaluators create sufficient stability to carry on their own work in the midst of a turbulent environment? Can authority be allocated to evaluators and blame apportioned among administrators? How to convince administrators to collect information that might help others but can only harm them? How can support be obtained on behalf of recommendations that anger sponsors? Would the political problem be solved by creating a special organization – Evaluation Incorporated – devoted wholly to performing the analytic function? Could it obtain necessary support without abandoning its analytic mission? Can knowledge and power be joined?

Donald T. Campbell [*1984: 34–5*], discussing the application of post-positivist theory of science to applied social science, and looking at past experiences, points to the problems stemming from the one decision/one research ideal of his original programme evaluation model, which was conceptually tied to refunding. Such a policy violated both common sense and the sociology of knowledge. The recurrent conflict between evaluation staff and the programme delivery staff could be explained by this setting and programme evaluation became destructive of programme delivery morale.
25. This is an old truth in the operative sphere. Thus, among the major recommendations of the JIU [*1982: 21*] was the following: 'Evaluation is wasted if its findings are not used. It must be a decision-oriented management tool, responsive to the information needs of those who have the authority and capacity to act upon it. Evaluation does not end with reporting; it should lead to action by decision-makers.'

The concern for the use is also the point of departure for utilisation-focused evaluation. Michael Quinn Patton [*1987: 113–15*], discussing this approach and arguing for it, outlines six premises for its application, the most important ones being that concern for use should be the driving force for an evaluation at any point where a decision is made (focus, design, methods, measurement, analysis, reporting); that the evaluation should be oriented towards identified users; and that the users should be actively involved in making decisions about the evaluation (involving the stakeholders ('People who are *personally* interested and involved in an evaluation are more likely to use evaluation

POLICIES, PERFORMANCE, TRENDS AND CHALLENGES

findings. The best way to be sure that an evaluation is targeted at the personal concerns of stakeholders is to involve them actively at every stage of the evaluation')).
For a pointed warning of the risk of blurring the distinction between implementation and evaluation, see Browne and Wildavsky [1987].

26. These qualities will be similar to those outlined by Guba and Lincoln [1987: 223] in describing the characteristics that a fourth-generation evaluator must display to be effective:

> The new evaluator appreciates diversity, respects the rights of individuals to hold different values and to make different constructions, and welcomes the opportunity to air and to clarify these differences. The evaluator must possess the personal qualities of honesty, respect and courtesy and, like Caesar's wife, his or her integrity must be above suspicion . . . Nor can there be any question of the new evaluator's professional competence; training and experience that include not only technical skills but social, political, and interpersonal skills must be clearly demonstrable. The new evaluator must have a high tolerance for ambiguity and a high frustration threshold. The new evaluation is a lonely activity, for one must remain sufficiently aloof to avoid charges of undue influence by one stakeholder group or another. The new evaluator must be aware of the possibility that he or she is being used by clients or other powerful groups, as well as of the fact that stakeholders may, individually or in groups, engage in lies, deceptions, fronts, and cover-ups. Finally, the new evaluator must be ready to be personally changed by the evaluative process, to revise his or her own constructions as understanding and sophistication increase.

See also Guba and Lincoln [1989: 259 ff.].

27. Ross Conner et al. [1984: 20] emphasise the conflict resolution aspect, giving the example of disagreements between programme personnel over goals and objectives, where the evaluator can serve as the catalyst for goal and objective clarification.

REFERENCES

Addison, T. and L. Demery, 1987, 'Alleviating Poverty under Structural Adjustment', *Finance and Development*, Vol. 24.

Bamberger, Michael, 1989, 'The Monitoring and Evaluation of Public Sector Programs in Asia. Why are Development Programs Monitored but not Evaluated?', *Evaluation Review*, Vol. 13, No. 3 (June).

Binnendijk, Annette L., 1989, 'Donor Agency Experience with the Monitoring and Evaluation of Development Projects', *Evaluation Review*, Vol. 13, No. 3 (June).

Brickell, Henry M., 1978, 'The Influence of External Political Factors on the Role and Methodology of Evaluation', *Evaluation Studies Review Annual*, Vol. 3.

Browne, Angela and Aaron Wildavsky, 1987, 'What Should Evaluation Mean to Implementation?', in Palumbo (ed.) [1987].

Campbell, Donald T., 1984, 'Can We Be Scientific in Applied Social Science?', *Evaluation Studies Review Annual*, Vol. 9.

Campbell, D.T. and J.C. Stanley, 1966, *Experimental and Quasi-experimental Designs for Research*, Chicago, IL: Rand McNally.

Cassen, Robert and Associates 1986, *Does Aid Work?*, Oxford: Oxford University Press.

Conner, Ross F., Altman, David G. and Christine Jackson, 1984, '1984: A Brave New World for Evaluation?', *Evaluation Studies Review Annual*, Vol. 9.

Cook, Thomas D., 1978, 'Introduction', *Evaluation Studies Review Annual*, Vol. 3.

Cornia, G., Jolly, R. and F. Stewart, 1987, *Adjustment with a Human Face: Protecting the Vulnerable and Promoting Growth*, Oxford: Clarendon Press.

Cracknell, Basil E., 1988, 'Evaluating Development Assistance: A Review of the Litera-

ture', *Public Administration and Development*, Vol. 8.
Cracknell, Basil E., 1991a, 'The Evaluation Policy and Performance of Britain', in this volume.
Cracknell, Basil E., 1991b, 'The Role of an Evaluation Unit: Functions, Constraints and Feedback', in this volume.
Eisendrath, Allen, 1988, 'The Use of Development Project Evaluation Information: A Study of the State Agencies in India' (Ph.D. thesis, University of Wisconsin–Madison), Ann Arbor, WI: U.M.I.
Elzinga, Aant, 1981, *Evaluating the Evaluation Game: On the Methodology of Project Evaluation, with Special Reference to Development Cooperation*, SAREC Report R1: 1981, Stockholm: Swedish Agency for Research Cooperation with Developing Countries.
Forss, Kim, 1991, 'The Evaluation Policy and Performance of Sweden', in this volume.
Freeman, Howard E., Rossi, Peter H. and Sonia Wright, 1979, *Evaluating Social Projects in Developing Countries*, Paris: Development Centre, OECD.
Ginsburg, Alan L., 1989, 'Revitalizing Program Evaluation. The U.S. Department of Education Experience', *Evaluation Review* (Dec.).
Guba, Egon G. and Yvonna S. Lincoln, 1987, 'The Countenances of Fourth-Generation Evaluation: Description, Judgement, and Negotiation', in Palumbo (ed.) [*1987*].
Guba, Egon G. and Yvonna S. Lincoln, 1989, *Fourth Generation Evaluation*, Newbury Park: Sage Publications.
Hirschman, Albert, 1987, *Development Projects Observed*, Washington, DC: Brookings Institution.
Hommes, Enno, 1991, 'Aid Evaluation in the Netherlands', in this volume.
Joint Inspection Unit (JIU), 1979, *Glossary of Evaluation Terms*, New York: UN.
Joint Inspection Unit (JIU), 1982, United Nations System Co-operation in Developing Evaluation by Governments, Prepared by Alfred N. Forde and Earl D. Sohm, Geneva: JIU/REP/82/12.
Kamphuis, Elise and Catrinus J. Jepma, 1990, 'Tying of Aid', paper presented at the 6th General Conference of EADI, Oslo, June 1990.
Kjekshus, Helge, 1991, 'Evaluation Policy and Performance: The State of the Art', in this volume.
Lawrence, John E. S., 1989, 'Engaging Recipients in Development Evaluation', *Evaluation Review*, Vol. 13, No. 3 (June).
Lincoln, Yvonna S. and Egon Guba, 1986, 'Research, Evaluation, and Policy Analysis: Heuristics for Disciplined Inquiry', *Policy Studies Review* 5 (Feb.).
Musto, Stefan A., 1991, 'Evaluation Policy and Performance in the Federal Republic of Germany', in this volume.
OECD, 1986, *Methods and Procedures in Aid Evaluation*, Paris: DAC.
Palumbo, Dennis J., 1987, 'Politics and Evaluation', in Palumbo (ed.) [*1987*].
Palumbo, Dennis J. (ed.), 1987, *The Politics of Program Evaluation*, Vol. 15, Sage Yearbooks in Politics and Public Policy, Newbury Park, CA: Sage.
Patton, Michael Quinn, 1987, 'Evaluation's Political Inherency: Practical Implications for Design and Use', in Palumbo (ed.) [*1987*].
Raizen, Senta A. and Peter H. Rossi, 1982, 'Summary of Program Evaluation in Education: When? How? To What Ends?', *Evaluation Studies Review Annual*, Vol. 7.
Rein, Martin and Sheldon H. White, 1978, 'Can Policy Research Help Policy?', *Evaluation Studies Review Annual*, Vol. 3.
Riddell, Roger C., 1987, *Foreign Aid Reconsidered*, London: James Currey.
Rossi, Peter H. and Howard E. Freeman *et al.*, 1982, *Evaluation. A Systematic Approach* (Second Edition), Beverly Hills, CA: Sage Publications.
Salmen, Lawrence F., 1989, 'Beneficiary Assessment. Improving the Design and Implementation of Development Projects', *Evaluation Review*, Vol. 13, No. 3 (June).
Schaumburg-Müller, Henrik, 1991, 'The Evaluation Policy and Performance of Denmark', in this volume.
Scriven, Michael, 1967, *The Methodology of Evaluation*, AERA Monograph Series in

Curriculum Evaluation 1, Chicago, IL: Rand McNally.
Statens offentliga utredningar (SOU), 1990: 17, *Organisation och arbetsformer inom bilateralt utvecklingsbistånd*, Betänkande av biståndsorganisationsutredningen, Stockholm: Utrikesdepartementet.
Stokke, Olav, 1984a, 'European Aid Policies: Some Emerging Trends', in Stokke (ed.) [*1984*].
Stokke, Olav, 1984b, 'Norwegian Aid: Policy and Performance', in Stokke (ed.) [*1984*].
Stokke, Olav (ed), 1984, *European Development Assistance*, Volume 1, Tilburg: EADI.
Stokke, Olav, 1987, 'Norsk bistandspolitikk og bistandsadministrasjon', *Nordisk Administrativt Tidsskrift*, 1987: 4, Copenhagen.
Stokke, Olav, 1989a, 'The Determinants of Aid Policies: General Introduction', in Stokke (ed.) [*1989*].
Stokke, Olav, 1989b, 'The Determinants of Norwegian Aid Policy', in Stokke (ed.) [*1989*].
Stokke, Olav, 1989c, 'The Determinants of Aid Policies: Some Propositions Emerging from a Comparative Analysis', in Stokke (ed.) [*1989*].
Stokke, Olav (ed.), 1989, *Western Middle Powers and Global Poverty*, Uppsala: The Scandinavian Institute of African Studies.
Stokke, Olav, 1991, 'The Evaluation Policy and Performance of Norway', in this volume.
Suchman, E.A., 1967, *Evaluative Research*, New York: Russell Sage Foundation.
Svendsen, Knud Erik, 1989, 'Danish Aid: Old Bottles', in Stokke (ed.) [*1989*].
Trone, Kerstin, 1991, 'The Evaluation Policy and Performance of the United Nations Population Fund', in this volume.
Weiss, Carol H., 1987, 'Where Politics and Evaluation Research Meet', in Palumbo (ed.) [*1987*].
Wildavsky, Aaron, 1972, 'The Self-Evaluating Organization', XXXII (5) *Public Administration Review*. Reprinted in *Evaluation Studies Review Annual*, Vol.3.
Wright, William J., 1978, 'Comments on "The Influence of External Political Factors on the Role and Methodology of Evaluation"', *Evaluation Studies Review Annual*, Vol.3.

2

Evaluation Policy and Performance: The State of the Art

HELGE KJEKSHUS

Evaluation is a very recent discipline. In Europe, its development has – until recently – been connected almost exclusively with development aid management and administration and with the official aid community.[1]

In most European countries evaluation has been hooked on to public administration as a discipline, unlike in the United States, its country of origin, where it grew out of the many imaginative devices for public administration reform that spread from the universities in the 1950s. It then caught the interest of the legislators and came into full force in the mid-1950s and early 1960s with the 'Thou shall evaluate' exhortation of US federal legislation related to large-scale social and developmental programmes.

In the US the evaluation device seems to have quickly attracted funding as well as the support of politicians and scholars. Professional journals appeared quickly and a lively debate ensued within a broad-based and growing discipline. Today, the US evaluation community numbers several thousand professionals.

From a domestic focus the evaluation discipline spread into the US Agency for International Development (USAID) and through American influence into the United Nations (UN) organisations and the international financial institutions.

In Europe evaluation has for a long time remained an isolated foreign-aid phenomenon with little or no backing in the broader concerns of public administration teaching and practice. Moreover, the growth and coming of age of the evaluation discipline in European countries' aid organisations seem to have taken place largely in isolation from each other, and in response to unique national needs and circumstances, administrative traditions and political pressures. Homespun devices responding to these conditions have come to prevail, rather than standardised, international good practice.

I think this is a fairly accurate description of the historic record. It is true, of course, as Basil Cracknell has pointed out in his recent excellent

EVALUATION OF AID: THE STATE OF THE ART

study [*Cracknell, 1988*] that a series of important publications on aid evaluation emerged – partly under the auspices of the Organisation for Economic Cooperation and Development (OECD) – that were capable of giving some guidance and unity in this early formative period. I believe these had limited influence on national developments which were hesitant and exploratory. Quite widely differing aid evaluation practices came into being, fragmenting the oneness and commonality of the evaluation discipline. The way in which evaluation was organised and its place within the aid organisation in relation to policy-making, also differed widely from one country to another. In most instances the potential of the evaluation device was limited to the bare needs of aid managers and rarely put to use to explore the wider consequences of aid, its success or failure in achieving its goals and its impact in recipient settings.

A good illustration of the diversity in the evaluation field was given when aid managers and politicians in some of the OECD countries – under pressure of growing economic problems at home – became concerned with the question of popular support for the official aid effort. In response to this concern they turned in 1979 to the evaluation officers of the OECD countries for a collective view – based on evaluation work undertaken – on development aid as an effective instrument for furthering development and eliminating poverty.

This was a tough challenge to the evaluators of the aid agencies of the OECD. It led to the setting up of the so-called Correspondents Group on Aid Effectiveness in the OECD, which later became a permanent Expert Group on Aid Evaluation. The Group now consists of the 18 bilateral donors of the OECD area and the Commission of the European Communities. The international banks (the World Bank, the Asian Development Bank, the Inter-American Development Bank and the African Development Bank) and the UNDP are invited participants.

The question raised by aid managers and politicians was clearly about the impact of aid. They also wanted objective and independent answers. The challenge was: could the evaluators give a meaningful answer?[2]

What followed was a very interesting period of cooperation among the aid evaluators. This also provided a first opportunity to reflect on the state of the art in the evaluation community. I shall therefore dwell at some length on this early exercise. In the course of the exercise the differences in evaluation philosophy workstyle and goals, and the conceptual differences between the evaluation units of the OECD countries, were brought out into the open. These features revealed that diversity also set clear limits to fruitful co-operation. This was most clearly shown in the first collective report which the evaluators submitted to the Development Assistance Committee (DAC) in 1982 [*OECD, 1982*]. In it the evaluators stated frankly that – on the basis of nearly 200 reports subjected to joint analysis – they were unable to say one way or the other whether foreign aid had acted as a useful instrument for the elimination of poverty. The basic reason for this was that only a few of the evaluation units had been authorised to search for answers to questions of impact. The evaluators were not, therefore, in a position to answer the question 'does aid work?' suddenly put to the evaluation community. Summing up the exercise, the report stated:

> ... as regards the review's main task, ascertaining whether substantial evidence exists demonstrating the overall effectiveness of aid, the authors of the syntheses are unable to offer firm conclusions. There was a lack of quantifiable evidence in the component studies as regards impact and only a limited amount of information as to the factors determining effective and efficient project performance. These two points taken together meant that the information available was insufficient to allow higher level generalisations to be made on aid's effectiveness.

As to the reasons why the results were disappointing, the evaluators offered two explanations, one relating to methodological problems and the other to evaluation objectives and organisation.

With respect to methodology it was pointed out that the lack of common standards and indeed of evaluation methodology made synthesising work difficult, if not impossible. Further work in this field was accordingly called for.

The reasons related to evaluation objectives were even more revealing of the situation and indicated that until then aid organisations had never sought to utilise the full capacity for inquiry latent in the evaluation device. As the report puts it:

> If aid managers have indeed been seeking answers to questions about the lessons of experience to help them in this (goal achievement) task, it would seem, from the material made available in the course of this exercise, that their evaluators are not among those whom they have asked. Even the country studies examined are for the most part singularly imprecise on questions concerning the contribution aid has made to the realisation of the recipient's broad priorities and the attainment of the recipient's broad objectives, which donors always in principle respect and by which their allocations are in principle determined. At this level, as at the project level, evaluation has been aimed at identifying possible improve-

ments in programming and procedures, because that is what evaluators have been asked to do.

The evaluators thus recognised several shortcomings in their work in the early 1980s. First of all they pointed to a lack of clear goals for the aid effort as a basis for later evaluation. Secondly, evaluation work was in most agencies seen to be subjected to narrow managerial concerns with the technical/administrative problems of aid delivery. Limited interest has been shown by aid management in directing evaluation towards exploring the wider consequences of aid, its impact and effectiveness on poverty and developmental issues. Thirdly, the way in which evaluation work was organised tended to result in internal documents, not in independent assessments available for public scrutiny. Fourthly, the differences of concepts and practice put severe limits on the practical benefits of cross-agency efforts to synthesise and compare lessons from the aid experience.

The operational lessons of the 1982 report were subsequently re-examined by the Expert Group and emerged two years later as a separate document [*OECD, 1984*]. This report pointed to a number of practical lessons drawn from evaluation work. It indicated a series of typical reasons for qualitative deficiencies in development assistance. Most of these were found to originate at the project planning and appraisal stage. Notably, the report cited unclear goals and objectives, unrealistic time frames, technological bias, underestimation of recipient conditions of culture and politics and neglect of project beneficiary aspects as typical reasons for aid failures.

The publication of this report seems to have contributed to rethinking and reform, particularly in the planning methodology and practice of several major aid organisations in Europe. The so-called 'logical framework', or variations on this model, have lately been introduced as the central planning instrument in several aid agencies. This shows increasing concern among aid managers with the setting and achieving of goals for foreign aid, and also with the Expert Group's criticisms.

The experience has also contributed to greater clarity in the character and function of evaluations where care is now taken to distinguish between internal and external evaluations. In some aid agencies this has led to the emergence of a double system of evaluations. One is tied to the operative part of aid management whose review work is identified as self-evaluation, monitoring, or internal evaluation. On the other hand, there are evaluations carried out by external teams and organised by recognisable evaluation units separate from, and independent of, the operative units of the aid-delivery system. This tendency to greater precision in concepts and organisational matters regarding evaluation seems to be present in several of the DAC aid organisations at present.

Such changes have introduced a new and better foundation for subsequent evaluations and must be welcomed by the evaluation community as long-overdue improvements.

REGAINING THE COMMONALITY OF THE DISCIPLINE

The Expert Group on Aid Evaluation was established as a permanent group in late 1982 after the somewhat abortive attempt described above. It was then asked by the DAC High Level Committee to continue to document the impact of aid and to endeavour to strengthen future evaluation through joint undertakings relating to methodology and the exchange of information.

A number of initiatives has been taken by the group. Several contributions have been made on methodological issues, notably regarding the evaluation of non-project aid and of technical assistance. A useful inventory has been produced, comparing the evaluation units of the OECD countries, their organisations and activities. The initiatives are too numerous to allow substantial comments here and I shall, in the following pages, address myself to just three specific issues raised by the Expert Group, each of which is an important challenge for aid evaluation in the 1990s: first, the introduction of a cross-agency, information-retrieval system to benefit the Expert Group; second, initiatives to alter the relationship between the donor evaluators and evaluators in developing countries; and third, the Expert Group's concern with evaluation of development assistance channelled through multilateral organisations.

As a general observation on the achievements of the Expert Group, it is fair to say that the joint activities, studies and seminars conducted have significantly enhanced the commonality of practice and thinking in the donor agencies represented through the Expert Group. This has particularly resulted from a series of best-practice studies which seem to have acted as stimulants to self-interested reform in the aid agencies. An important contribution in this direction was the Expert Group's recommendations for a standardised evaluation vocabulary (glossary of evaluation terms) published in 1986 [*OECD, 1986*]. Thus a common basis for understanding and cooperation, that was certainly not present in the early 1980s, has now been established in the evaluation units of the OECD area.

EXCHANGE OF INFORMATION

Exchange of information has always been at the core of the Expert Group's interests. Each member has sought to learn from the evaluation experiences of the other, and to feed the lessons learnt into the knowledge bank of the home organisation. For such purposes the Expert Group experimented from its very beginning with the direct exchange of information among the members.

The idea of using the DAC secretariat as a clearing house for evaluation information was also discussed. At the same time some voices in the Expert Group expressed doubts about discriminate information-sharing and a concern about information overload. They called for information systems that could process and eliminate information as well as disseminating it; that is, systems capable of delivering manageable and relevant information packages to the greatest number of users.

What seemed to be needed in the Expert Group was a computerised information system with data banks and electronic networking which aid agencies such as USAID, the World Bank and the Canadian International Development Agency (CIDA) have for some time experimented with and brought into use – sometimes at a cost which appears prohibitive for smaller donors.

Through the good offices of the CIDA, the entire DAC group of evaluators were given the opportunity in 1987–88 to join CIDA's Evaluation Report Inventory System on an experimental basis. This promises to be a useful bibliography reference tool which will identify evaluation information available in all donor communities. The main purpose is to improve the dissemination of information between the donor agencies, facilitate evaluation research and reduce the time needed to acquire the necessary information.

The register will identify specific evaluation reports, subject matter, the responsible aid agency or NGO, geographical region, authors and dates. It will give short annotations on the content of the report, the lessons learnt and recommendations formulated on the basis of the report, and indicate tentative plans for future evaluations.

The system will operate through submission of simple standardised reporting sheets by individual donor agencies. The information will be processed, stored and disseminated by the CIDA, which has undertaken to answer all queries within 48 hours through the telex network. The network is expected to be operational in 1990.

THE PLACE OF THE RECIPIENT IN EVALUATION

The register is a system operated by and for the DAC evaluation community and will further enhance the possibilities of professional evaluators doing a better job. The system is not aimed at developing countries and their evaluators. The register may possibly widen the gap between donors and their colleagues in the Third World. This is an important concern, since the continued isolation from those taking on evaluation responsibilities in developing countries is perhaps the greatest challenge to the DAC evaluation community in the 1990s.

Until very recently it has been exceptional for evaluators from recipient countries to be accommodated in evaluation teams and given an equal say. Sweden may have been the first DAC country to make support for recipient countries' evaluation work part of the evaluation goals of its own aid organisation, the Swedish International Development Agency (SIDA). Equal participation in evaluation work came much later.

This neglect of recipient countries in the donor agencies' evaluation work must have been nagging the consciences of most members of the Expert Group from the very start. The recipient's role was a central subject in a number of informal talks in the first meetings of the group. Quite soon, the question of promoting the developing countries' own evaluation capabilities became an item on the agenda and several suggestions were made as to what to do and how to proceed. The general impression prevailing in the Expert Group was for a long time that the developing countries looked upon evaluation as a hostile donor invention – a form of aid conditionality which recipients wanted no part in.

The Expert Group's 1986 publication, *Methods and Procedures in Aid Evaluation* [*OECD, 1986*], recorded a series of experiences in donor–recipient cooperation in evaluation and discussed achievements and problems. On the whole there was marked reluctance to take a committed stand on this issue. It was therefore not until March 1987 that the DAC Expert Group was able to invite to a seminar evaluators and people responsible for evaluation from a number of developing countries [*OECD, 1988*]. This was an eye-opener to many, and an opportunity to correct a lot of misconceptions. To list only a few, it became evident that a number of developing countries are keenly interested in evaluation as a management tool and as a device for the betterment of public administration. It became equally clear that evaluation as a discipline already has some traditions in developing countries. In India these traditions go back to the early 1950s. This gives that particular country 20–25 years' lead on most of the DAC countries, which only geared up their evaluation activities in the 1960s and 1970s.

India may be a unique case, but, to judge from statements given at the DAC seminar, quite a few developing countries have established some form of evaluation unit and administration of their own. They are aware of and interested in evaluation as a public administration discipline and are committing funds and people to evaluation tasks. They are similarly eager to play a constructive and cooperative role in the donor community's efforts to evaluate effect, efficiency and impact of development aid. Finally, they express the view that they are part of the evaluation community and demand to be treated equally.

At the seminar, one could sense impatience with what recipients described as over-evaluation – burdensome demands of overlapping evaluation teams whose tasks are planned and initiated without consultation or input from the recipients' side and carried out by external 'experts'. The view was expressed that these exercises resulted in reports, the contents of which were deliberately concealed from recipients.

A new recognition was forced on the DAC evaluation community through the 1987 seminar. As a next step forward, I personally feel the need for some kind of DAC Code of Conduct, setting down guidelines for securing active and equal participation from recipients. Even if such a Code were not binding on all DAC members, it would mean a powerful push towards better practice that makes the recipients full partners in future evaluation work.

EVALUATION OF MULTILATERAL ASSISTANCE

A third initiative taken by the Expert Group pertains to the evaluation of multilateral assistance. A number of national evaluation units have from time to time ventured into this field. On an *ad hoc* basis they have produced the occasional report on international banks or UN agencies. On the whole, however, this has been a neglected field. The evaluation of multilateral assistance has been accorded low priority among DAC members, who have been much more concerned with their bilateral programmes and projects. This attitude has prevailed, in particular, among the greatest believers in the multilateral system; those countries that channel a large part – up to 50 per cent – of their aid budget through the multilateral agencies. For some reason it has been politically simpler to raise the evaluation issue *vis-à-vis* sovereign 'developing' states than *vis-à-vis* international organisations.

There are signs that this may be changing, in part, thanks to initiatives taken by the Expert Group, following up recent political signals from a number of donor countries. The issue has been on the agenda of the Expert Group for the last three to four years. Initially it led only to an increased exchange of information and experience relating to evaluation and multilateral assistance.

A report prepared by the Evaluation Department of Britain's Overseas Development Administration in 1987 [*ODA, 1987*] triggered the debate. The report analysed the evaluation systems of 24 multilateral agencies

(UN and international banks) and discussed their strengths and weaknesses from the point of view of a major donor and governing board member of numerous agencies.

The presentation of this report gave the Expert Group its first opportunity to assess its lack of engagement in the multilateral aid field and to ask for further work to be undertaken. It is expected that this issue will become a major concern in the Expert Group in the next few years.

So far this has resulted in a position paper prepared for the Expert Group by Norway. In it the DAC members are, among other things, asked to make more active use of the evaluation work produced by the multilateral agencies. At the same time they are asked to push for closer scrutiny of development funds channelled through the multilateral agencies. In particular, they are asked to press for improvements in the evaluation work undertaken by the multilaterals.

A third central suggestion in the position paper is to institutionalise joint evaluations of the multilaterals by all or some of the DAC members. In the past, such evaluations seem to have taken place as part of crisis management (FAO, UNESCO). In the future, joint evaluations should become a systematic undertaking, anticipating the need for independent advice on the multilaterals.

RESEARCH CHALLENGES

The majority of the official evaluation units of the OECD countries are small, understaffed units. They administer evaluation work, but very seldom practise their art in field situations. There is one notable exception to this, namely the Dutch Inspectorate, which inspects and evaluates.

For this reason, the research and consultancy communities in the OECD area offer vital resources of know-how and personnel to the evaluation units. This makes it possible for the units to carry out the independent, interdisciplinary work which most DAC evaluation units are aiming at today.

One should also recognise the importance of these communities as intellectual support groups for the evaluation discipline and its place in foreign aid. A pre-condition for such support is that there is openness about evaluation plans and procedures and access to the results of evaluation. Thus the right conditions must be created in order for useful interaction between aid agencies and the research/consultancy communities to take place. Where there is no access or openness, the conditions preclude scientific enquiry and constructive contributions.

DAC evaluation meetings generally confirm a tendency towards greater openness. Several aid agencies now regularly publish their evaluation reports as part of their concern for increased accountability and transparency for the foreign aid programmes. At the same time, much of the work of the Expert Group remains 'restricted to participants'.

But the usefulness of researchers and consultants is also found in more specific tasks. One of these is the type of review of the evaluation work of different aid organisations undertaken through the EADI project.

Within this project, several papers have traced the development of the function of evaluation in foreign aid and its institutionalisation in the different aid organisations. The papers have given explanations of organisational oddities. They have scrutinised the goals and purposes of evaluation and the performance of evaluators. Through this work the EADI project is performing a useful public function by 'evaluating the evaluation game', to borrow a phrase from a Swedish publication on aid evaluation [*SAREC, 1981*]. It is important for somebody to do this job, to act as a public conscience to remind the different evaluation units of their own stated intentions and to ask the awkward questions about their performance.

A final area where researchers may have much to contribute is in the development of new, better and more imaginative, evaluation methodology.

Evaluation within the aid community will over time become routine – and, it is to be hoped, good routine – representing time-tested solidity and predictability. But the evaluation field also needs experimentation and innovation. It needs the testing out of new ways of doing things. It needs new models and theories in its work.

I have indicated earlier that methodological deficiencies ten years ago partly explain the failure of DAC evaluators to provide answers to the question 'does aid work?' It is largely through the help of the research communities that the methodological issues of evaluation have in the meantime moved forward and placed the aid evaluators in a better position today to answer the mounting queries about aid in the 1990s.

NOTES

1. This study reviews a limited area of the evaluation discipline and is related to the author's experience as an evaluator of development aid and a member of the Expert Group on Aid Evaluation of the Development Assistance Committee (DAC).
2. A parallel investigation was later initiated by the Task Force on Concessional Flows set up by the Development Committee – the Joint Ministerial Committee of the Board of Governors of the World Bank and International Monetary Fund. It resulted in the publication *Does Aid Work*? [*Cassen et al., 1986*].

REFERENCES

Cassen, R. et al., 1986, *Does Aid Work? – Report to the Intergovernmental Task Force*, Oxford: Clarendon Press.

Cracknell, Basil E., 1988, 'Evaluating Development Assistance: A Review of the Literature', *Public Administration and Development*, Vol. 8.

Elzinga, A., 1981, *Evaluating the Evaluation Game*, Stockholm: Swedish Agency for Research Cooperation with Developing Countries.

ODA, 1987, *A Survey of Multilateral Agencies* (by A.G. Bovaird, D. Gregory and J.M. Stevens), London: Overseas Development Agency (3 vols.).

OECD, 1982, 'Evaluation Correspondents' Report on Aid Effectiveness', Paris: OECD.

OECD, 1984, 'Report of the Expert Group on Aid Evaluation on Lessons of Experience Emerging from Aid Evaluation', Paris: OECD.

OECD, 1986, 'Methods and Procedures in Aid Evaluation: A Compendium of Donor Practice and Experience', Paris: OECD.

OECD, 1990, 'Evaluation of Multilateral Assistance – An Approach Paper', Paris: OECD.

3

The Evaluation Policy and Performance of Britain

BASIL E. CRACKNELL

I. THE WIDER CONTEXT: THE ROLE OF EVALUATION IN IMPROVING EFFECTIVENESS AND EFFICIENCY – SEEN FROM WITHIN GOVERNMENT, AND FROM OUTSIDE IT

The purpose of this introductory section is not to discuss any particular aspect of evaluation philosophy or techniques in depth, that comes later, but rather to illustrate that evaluation is not something that evolves in an aid agency in isolation from other parts of government or from interested parties outside. Very much the reverse. Evaluation work in most aid agencies owes, if not its origins, then at least its present scale to the pressures emanating from potential critics of aid who seek reassurance that aid funds are being well spent. It is important to be aware of these pressures, and of their influence on the way evaluation work has grown. This first section describes how evaluation has evolved in the context of government generally, and then looks at the role of agencies outside the government, such as Parliament, the Development Assistance Committee (DAC) and the United Nations (UN) agencies, non-governmental organisations (NGOs) and the general public.

Evaluation as Part of the Machinery of Government
Since the word 'evaluation' can mean different things to different people, it is as well to define it. In this paper the word signifies an in-depth study of an ongoing or completed project or programme, by someone other than the project management, which covers not only implementation aspects but also basic objectives, and the purpose of which is to learn lessons for application in the agency as a whole. It is thus distinct from 'monitoring', which is carried out by the project staff and is aimed at ensuring that the project is implemented effectively according to the stated objectives.

Evaluation of aid began in the United Kingdom (UK) in the late 1960s and gathered pace during the following decade, and for most of that period the Overseas Development Administration (ODA) (originally known as the ODM – Ministry of Overseas Development) was almost the only government department that had a specific evaluation unit, although a few other departments, such as the Ministry of Agriculture, Fisheries and Food and the Department of Trade and Industry, were evaluating aspects of their activities in an *ad hoc* way. This was probably because the ODA was spending government funds outside the UK, and moreover in countries which often had severe economic and management problems, so that the need to carefully monitor and evaluate that expenditure was self-evident. In other government departments the need was less obvious, unless they were engaged in managing grant schemes, as were the two ministries mentioned above.

However, there was a growing interest throughout this period in improving the quality of management in the Civil Service, and many new techniques were introduced, such as Social Cost-benefit Analysis, Management by Objectives, Network Analysis, Systems Analysis, Critical Path Analysis, Operational Research, Time and Motion Study, Decision Trees, and Programme Analysis and Review (PAR). Thousands of civil servants were trained in the 'Coverdale' system of management, which was geared to the careful defining of objectives and the establishment of criteria of success, both of which are important components of the Project Framework (see below).

Undoubtedly there was some improvement in management efficiency as a result of all these efforts, but it was not very noticeable, and after a while a certain sense of disillusionment seemed to set in: all these ideas, although worthy in themselves, seemed to be unrelated to each other and uncoordinated. Above all, many of them were promoted as being vaguely 'desirable' techniques, but there was no generally accepted machinery whereby they could be applied in a consistent and focused manner.

A breakthrough came in the early 1980s with the introduction of the Financial Management Initiative (FMI) with all the authority of the Prime Minister (Mrs Thatcher) behind it. The FMI seemed to offer a way of encapsulating, and logically structuring, most of the management techniques that had been promoted previously. The FMI focused on two aspects in particular: (a) a clear statement of objectives, and (b) quantified and time-bound targets. Thus the FMI was presenting nothing new, but for the first time the known techniques were being promoted across the board with a new sense of vigour and determination.

A new joint Cabinet Office/Treasury Financial Management Unit (FMU) was set up in 1984, and one of its first tasks was to commission a few detailed case studies of ways in which a number of government departments had already been trying to apply the FMI principles: one of these was a study of the ODA's aid to Bangladesh, because it was recognised that the ODA had more experience of project monitoring and evaluation than many other government departments at that time.

The FMI was linked primarily to the performance of each civil servant individually, as it was considered that, if an individual has a clear vision of what is expected of him, and how his success or otherwise will be judged, then he is more likely to operate effectively, but it was applied also to the management of projects and programmes funded by government departments.

In June 1985 the UK government decided to launch a major new initiative, based on the FMI, to improve the quality of policy work, notably through evaluation procedures. A Joint Management Unit (JMU) was set up (eventually to be incorporated fully into the Treasury) with the following aims:

(a) To familiarise policy managers with the principles of evaluation, and, if possible, to persuade them to apply them.
(b) To find good evaluation methods and to develop better ones.
(c) To 'build in' evaluation as an integral component of policy work.

Since 1985 the JMU has been collecting case studies of evaluation activities being carried out by government departments [*Treasury, 1987a*], and it has prepared a 'Guide for Managers on Policy Evaluation' which was published during 1988 [*Treasury, 1988*]. The JMU has also organised a series of evaluation seminars for senior officials of Under Secretary rank and above, and it has studied the problems and potentialities of developing suitable 'indicators' of project success.

A great deal has already been achieved in getting evaluation widely accepted and applied within government, but there remain some problems. A 1987 House of Commons report on the FMI noted that 'scepticism and mistrust of the FMI seem to be widespread among the middle and lower management grades', and also quoted two Government White Papers (Cmnd 9058, September 1983, and Cmnd 9297, July 1984) as concluding that the FMI would be unlikely to succeed unless a more cost-conscious approach was adopted to government business [*House of Commons, 1987a*]. A FMU report in 1985 [*Treasury, 1985*] noted that: 'The pressures of day-to-day business are not conducive to adopting a systematic approach to performance measurement', and it went on to stress that top management would have to make it clear that they accorded such work high priority.

Summing up, there is no doubt that, in spite of the problems that still remain, evaluation is now firmly embedded in all government activity in the UK, and the ODA, the Department of Trade and Industry (DTI) and the Ministry of Agriculture, Fisheries and Food (MAFF) are no longer alone in taking evaluation work seriously. It is now mandatory that all new policies, and all policies deriving from formal reviews of policy, must have evaluation built in from the beginning, and departments are obliged to indicate what evaluation data will be required and how it will be collected. Policy proposals that have 'value for money' implications (especially those relating to large public expenditure decisions) must now state: what is to be achieved, by whom, at what cost, and how it will be measured. The only exceptions to this rule would be policies or projects which have broad political objectives, and which might not be amenable to measurement.

Whereas at one time the ODA was regarded as a front-runner on the evaluation scene, now that is no longer the case. The ODA is only one among many government departments which are developing evaluation systems to suit their requirements, and there is now a healthy interchange of ideas on evaluation between Treasury staff (who have regularly participated in the ODA's evaluation-training sessions, for instance) and their ODA colleagues. As part of their watch-dog role, the Treasury take a special interest in the ODA's evaluation results and have been supportive of the ODA's attempts to expand the coverage of its evaluation work, such as sector aid and programme aid, more effectively. They have also strongly supported the introduction of the 'project framework' system into the ODA and have themselves adopted many of its features in their own guidelines manual. Such co-operation can only be of benefit to all parties and should lead to a higher quality of evaluation activity all round.

The Interest of Parliament in Evaluation

Parliamentary pressure has been a significant factor leading to the strengthening of the ODA's evaluation activity. The most important of the parliamentary bodies in this context is the House of Commons Committee of Public Accounts. The Committee considered aid evaluation during its 1980–81 session, and the then Permanent Secretary of the ODA, Sir Peter Preston, was invited to explain why the expenditure on evaluation at that time (£55,000 in 1979–80) was so modest in relation to the total volume of aid (then around £800 million). He replied that, taken in conjunction with other kinds of continuous self-evaluation that were taking place in the ODA, it was thought to be adequate, and he added: 'You obviously cannot swamp people with the results of evaluations.'

The Committee, however, was not completely satisfied with this explanation and its spokesman said:

We are concerned at ODA's view that there is a limit to the rate at which the results of evaluation can be absorbed. In our view, if evaluation results are soundly based in the first place, and properly distilled and interpreted, they should be no more difficult to act upon than any other information which influences decisions, methods and procedures. We therefore recommend, first that ODA should examine the scope and balance of their evaluation programme in order to ensure that it covers a sufficiently comprehensive sample of bilateral aid projects and methods to provide all the assurance of effectiveness which is necessary, and second that they should review their priorities for drawing both broad and detailed conclusions from evaluation results and initiating appropriate action.

It was as a direct result of this pressure from the Public Accounts Committee (PAC) that the ODA's Evaluation Unit was increased in size from 2.5 person equivalents to 4.5 (now 9), and the annual budget was increased from £220,000 to £325,000 (now £500,000). It was also decided to introduce more rigorous methods of selecting the sample of projects for evaluation. However, the Committee's interests lay more in using evaluation to throw light on aid effectiveness in general (hence its interest in a comprehensive sample), whereas the ODA was more concerned to improve the effectiveness of its aid operations (which might imply an emphasis on, for example, problem sectors in the selection of projects for evaluation). This dichotomy of objectives has always been a major problem in evaluation work and will be discussed again later.

The Parliamentary Select Committee on Aid (more recently the House of Commons Foreign Affairs Committee) has also had a significant influence on the development of evaluation, especially, for example, in relation to their concern that aid should be focused on the poorest; their particular interest in the commercial spin-off from aid via the Aid Trade Provision (ATP) (a special pocket of aid used to fund development projects deemed to be of particular commercial benefit to Britain, while at the same time having developmental value), and their particular concern with the problems of food aid, especially with regard to famine in Africa. They have made effective use of the ODA's evaluation reports and have on occasion suggested that more evaluation resources should be devoted to specific issues [*House of Commons, 1981; 1986; 1987b; Comptroller and Auditor-General, 1985*].

The Interest of Independent Groups and the 'Aid Lobby'

In the UK there are a number of pressure groups that have had a significant impact on aid policy in general, and on the development of evaluation work in particular. One of the most important of these is the Independent Group on British Aid (IGBA), which has produced three reports [*IGBA, 1982; 1984; 1986*], the first of which focused particularly on evaluation and stressed the need for the ODA to evaluate the success or failure of its policy of more help for the poorest [*ODA, 1975*]. The Group's main protagonist of the need for more evaluation of the ODA's poverty-focus policy is Professor Paul Mosley, and in his evidence to the House of Commons Foreign Affairs Committee on 2 July 1986, he said:

> The main failing in ODA's evaluation procedures is that out of three hundred reports or so, which is what the Evaluation Unit has produced, there is not a single one which attempts to assess the impact of British aid projects on low income groups. We find this scandalous, and really surprising, because many of the evaluations were done during the period 1975–80 when the policy of more aid for the poorest was still technically in force, as well as in subsequent periods where it has been diluted by other objectives [*House of Commons, 1986*].

Professor Mosley again returned to this issue in a report commissioned by Action Aid and presented to a symposium on 5 October 1987 [*Mosley, 1987*].

This issue will be taken up again later, but the point has been made that outside pressure groups can, and do, exercise a considerable influence on the ODA's evaluation activity. Basically, of course, they are primarily users of the evaluation reports themselves, but they also have an interest in improving the quality of the ODA's evaluation work in general.

Another group that plays an important, if more academically oriented, role as a commentator on the ODA's aid and its evaluation activities is the Overseas Development Institute (ODI). In the mid-1980s one of its staff produced a monumental research publication [*Riddell, 1987*] which contains an authoritative and balanced critique of the ODA's evaluation work. This report will be extensively quoted later, but one of its main conclusions is that evaluation reports, for a variety of reasons, are a not wholly satisfactory basis for trying to answer the question 'Does aid work?'

This question was taken as the title of another monumental, independent report on aid which was edited by Professor Robert Cassen and commissioned by the World Bank Development Committee's Task Force on Concessional Flows [*Cassen, 1986*]. The various members of Professor Cassen's team examined a large sample of the ODA's evaluation reports and found many of them (often for good reasons) inadequate as evidence of overall aid effectiveness, mainly because many were more concerned with aid-delivery issues than with impact.

These two reports, representing a vast amount of human effort and having available to them a huge stock of evaluation reports, have highlighted the basic difficulty, referred to earlier, of trying to use evaluation reports that were carried out mainly to meet one objective (learning lessons on aid delivery and project implementation) to satisfy a different one (overall aid effectiveness).

Evaluation by Multilateral Agencies vis-à-vis *the ODA's Own Evaluation*

During the 1970s there was not a great deal of interaction between the ODA's evaluation work and that of the multilateral agencies, except in relation to such agencies as the World Bank (whose comprehensive and high-quality evaluation system has always served as something of a model for other agencies), the FAO and the World Food Programme, and the European Commission. The Joint Inspection Unit of the UN (JIU) also played an important part in developing evaluation terminology, while the ODA may itself have had some influence on the UN evaluation system through its participation in JIU evaluation seminars [*Cracknell, 1982*]. This writer strongly criticised the exclusive reliance in the UN system on internal 'built-in' evaluation and recommended that outside evaluators should also be used. The development banks (other than the World Bank) came on to the evaluation scene rather later, but the Asian Development Bank, in particular, soon established itself as a pioneer in some aspects of evaluation methodology, notably Project Benefit Monitoring (that is, the identification of beneficiaries at the appraisal stage and subsequent monitoring of benefit flows), and some of these ideas were in time incorporated into the ODA's evaluation thinking.

Among the bilateral donors, the USAID had a considerable influence through the training courses which it ran on the 'logical framework' idea during the early 1970s. The present writer attended one of these week-long training seminars in 1974. The 'logical framework' idea was a decade before its time, from the UK point of view, but in the 1980s it has been adopted by the ODA and by a number of other bilateral agencies.

During the 1980s, as a result of the pressure on aid funds being experienced by many agencies, many of them have taken a much greater interest in the effectiveness of UN organisations, and some (notably the ODA) have carried out major evaluations of the evaluation systems used by the main UN agencies [*Bovaird et al., 1987*]. The ODA study reveals a number of weaknesses in some of the multilateral agencies' evaluation systems, and there is no doubt that pressure will be put on those agencies to improve the quality of their evaluation work. This kind of interaction is surely much healthier than the former state of mutual ignorance and even disinterest, providing it is recognised that an evaluation system that may suit one agency may not suit another.

The Influence of the DAC

The DAC has played a significant role, since 1970, in helping to get evaluation work started in the ODA, among other bilateral donors, and giving it a multi-donor orientation. It was largely as a result of the two seminars on evaluation organised by the DAC in the early 1970s (at The Hague and Amsterdam), that evaluation work in the ODA began to develop along systematic lines and to acquire an impetus that it had previously lacked. Since 1980 the DAC, through its Expert Group on Aid Evaluation, has had a very important influence on the way the ODA's evaluation work has evolved, not only because the UK, along with other members of the DAC, undertook to participate in a series of joint evaluation activities, but also because there was important feedback, from the discussions of the Expert Group, into the pattern of thinking about evaluation in the UK and the direction in which it was heading. Very recently there has been important feedback from the DAC Expert Group in relation to the need for an evaluation data-bank and the use of computers for this purpose.

In the main body of the DAC, evaluation has been increasingly seen as an important operation, especially in view of the need to assure sceptics, at a time of financial stringency, that aid is worth while. Thus the same tension between the 'Does aid work?' approach and the 'Learning lessons or improving the quality of aid' approach expresses itself in the DAC and in turn is reflected back on the way the ODA plans and implements its evaluation programme, for example, leading to a major new interest in sector syntheses rather than in one-off project evaluations.

The Interest of Non-Governmental Organisations, and the General Public, in Aid Evaluation

Gradually, over the last 10–15 years, the non-governmental organisations (NGOs) have themselves developed a greater interest in evaluation, often setting up their own evaluation units, and they have also interested themselves in the quality of official aid. The recent Action Aid Symposium referred to earlier, which was addressed by the then Minister of Overseas Development, is one such example. The relationships between the ODA and the NGOs have become much closer as a result of the Joint Funding Scheme introduced by the ODA some years ago, and the ODA has already evaluated this scheme jointly with the agencies and has twice evaluated the Voluntary Service Organisation (VSO) Scheme and other voluntary agency schemes. There is a growing awareness in the ODA of the importance of the voluntary sector, and evaluations have suggested that the voluntary agencies can often get aid more effectively to the poorer people than can government-to-government aid.

As to the public at large, it would not be correct to say that there is widespread interest in the evaluation of aid, but there is certainly a small but articulate group of people, including teachers, research workers, journalists, politicians, religious leaders and writers, who interest themselves in aid issues and who often read evaluation reports. Some university researchers have pioneered experimental evaluation systems, such as scoring techniques [*Jennings, 1985*], while many others have participated as consultants in ODA-sponsored evaluation studies [*ODA, 1987a*]. It was in recognition of this important interrelationship between the ODA and the informed members of the public that the ODA organised a two-day international seminar on evaluation at the Institute of Development Studies, University of Sussex – a rather rare event in government circles [*ODA, 1984*].

Summing up, there is no doubt that evaluation, as an activity, is especially responsive to outside pressures, and this will always be the case so long as evaluation is required to meet not only the objective of improving the quality of aid administration and implementation, but also of satisfying the need for others (who may not require to be familiar with the details of aid operations) to be assured that 'aid works'.

II. THE ODA'S AID POLICY, AND HOW EVALUATION IS ORGANISED IN THAT CONTEXT

Aid Policy Objectives

Evaluation depends crucially upon a clear statement of objectives. That applies as much to the evaluation of broad aid policies and programmes as it does to specific projects. It is therefore important, when considering the performance of the UK evaluation system, to identify what are the objectives of UK aid policy.

The definitive statement of the UK's aid policy objectives for the 1980s was made by the then Minister, Mr Neil Marten, to the House of Commons on 20 February 1980. The key points of his statement were:

'We must seek to relieve poverty in the developing world.'

'Trade is of the greatest importance to the developing countries.'

'Private investment can and should play a greater part in development.'

'We believe it is right at the present time to give greater weight in the allocation of our aid to political, industrial, and commercial considerations, alongside our basic developmental objective.'

Subsequently ministers have reaffirmed that Mr Marten's statement remains broadly the policy of the ODA, although in recent years there has been special reference to the importance of:

- self-sustaining growth and the protection of the environment [*ODA, 1987c*];
- the need to give adequate weight to social factors [*Wilmshurst, 1986*];
- the need to enhance the participation of women [*ODA, 1986c*].

In 1987, the then Minister, Mr Chris Patten, summed up the ODA's aid policy in a speech [*Patten, 1987d*] as: 'To promote sustainable development, and to alleviate poverty in the Third World.'

Translating these broad aims into specific objectives for projects or programmes is, of course, very difficult, because they may well be mutually inconsistent. For example, the objective of serving the UK's commercial interest may well be better served by a policy focusing on western-type technologies and export-oriented commodities, whereas the objective of helping the poorest may suggest that priority should be given to traditional technologies and to subsistence crops. Again, the use of aid to encourage private investment may be difficult to reconcile with a poverty-focused policy. Often the way round this problem (for all but the Aid and Trade Provision (ATP) projects) is for the strictly 'developmental' objectives to be the ones formally identified in the appraisal, and at the monitoring and evaluation stages, leaving the commercial and political objectives to be left more or less as 'unwritten' and largely undocumented.

Perhaps the key issue is the same one that has already been identified, that is, to what extent is it the task of the evaluators to assess the effectiveness of ODA aid in general ('Does aid work?') or to adopt a much lower profile and to concentrate on the strictly developmental lessons to be learned regarding aid delivery and aid implementation and, so far as resources permit, aid impact?

Before considering this issue in depth, it would be useful first to consider how evaluation activity in the ODA is organised, and the role it plays in the ODA's aid policy.

Organisation of Evaluation in the ODA

In the ODA there is an Evaluation Department headed by a Senior Economic Adviser (equivalent to Assistant Secretary and reporting directly to the Principal Finance Officer), with a staff of eight, which comprises an Administrative Principal, two Economic Advisers, a Higher Executive Officer (D), an Executive Officer, a Clerical Officer and two support staff. It also has a budget of £500,000 per annum, which it can use to hire outside evaluators, who might be equivalent to say another ten person-years of effort per annum. The Evaluation Department has no other responsibilities and therefore is independent of any other department in the ODA.[1] It submits its reports directly to a committee of top management, called the Projects and Evaluation Committee (PEC), and in turn has to have its own annual work programme approved by the PEC. All evaluation reports of any significance have to be seen by the PEC, which is the same body as has to approve all medium to large aid projects. The PEC meets to receive and discuss evaluation reports roughly every six to eight weeks during the year. In all, about 18 reports go to the PEC annually, covering a wide range of projects and programmes. A previous chairman of the PEC has described the work of the committee in detail [*Browning, 1984*]. Because the committee's time is very limited, it requires the Evaluation Department to provide a 'Cover Note' to each evaluation that it submits. This summarises the key findings and describes the reactions of relevant ODA officials to the report, and especially to any recommendations that the evaluators may make. The Evaluation Department then makes its own action-oriented recommendations. It is the latter to which the committee devotes most attention. The chairman has to assume that the members of the Committee have studied the report and his main concern is to see that the ODA takes whatever action is called for as a consequence. The Cover Note is therefore a crucially important part of the Evaluation Department's work, and it helps to make it possible for such a hard-pressed committee of senior people (most of the under-secretaries are members of the committee, as well as the appropriate chief advisers) to devote the necessary time to evaluations.

It should be noted that evaluation in the ODA (as in most other aid agencies) is quite distinct from audit, although the Evaluation Department keeps in close touch with the Internal Audit Unit and in fact occasionally mounts an evaluation study on a joint basis with the latter.

It would be difficult to overestimate the importance of the role that the PEC plays in ensuring that evaluation reports are taken seriously in the ODA. The fact that such a top-level committee, one of the most influential in the ODA and representing all the senior management, is prepared to study every evaluation report and to take whatever action is called for conveys to the rest of the staff a sense of the importance of this activity, that is, it 'sets the tone' for evaluation work within the whole organisation. The burden on busy senior staff is at times rather frightening and more than once there has loomed the possibility that the committee might feel obliged to delegate the task to some more junior body, but happily that has not happened. Sir Peter Preston, in his remarks to the House of Commons Public Accounts Committee mentioned earlier, was making a very important point when he referred to the ODA's absorptive capacity for evaluation reports. No doubt there are ways of reducing the burden on the PEC (such as combining individual project evaluations into sectoral syntheses) and these should certainly be pursued, but fundamentally there is a limit to the number of evaluation reports that such a committee can effectively handle, and that limit is probably at about the present level.

The problem is that with only twenty or so evaluation reports per annum, how can the evaluation operation cover all the ODA's various objectives efficiently? There are bodies like the Independent Group on British Aid calling for more effective evaluation of the poverty-focus policy, while others, like the DAC, are calling for a more comprehensive sample so that aid effectiveness can be measured, while yet others, like the House of Commons Public Accounts Committee, are calling for a more representative coverage of different types of aid (including Aid/Trade Provision, Food Aid and Programme Aid) and aid to specific parts of the world, notably Africa. Reconciling all these objectives, with only 18 or so evaluations per annum, is a difficult task, and the result is that no single objective can be evaluated as systematically as one would wish – all one can do is to look basically at developmental effectiveness and then to include in the sample a few evaluations that are geared specifically at special issues, such as commercial objectives, role of women, sustainability, the environment and so on. This is basically what the ODA does, and, although it is an uneasy compromise, it is difficult to see what alternatives there are, given the limitations on the resources available.

The Independent Group on British Aid has criticised the fact that the Evaluation Department is not completely independent of other parts of the ODA, in that it reports to the PEC and not directly to the Minister.

The Group argues that it would avoid the risk of political influences being brought to bear on evaluation work if the Department were to report directly to the Minister (taking the World Bank's structure as its model) [*IGBA, 1982*]. However, this, in the writer's opinion, is ill-informed criticism: such a change would destroy the most successful and vital element of the ODA system – the reporting to the PEC, and in any case the incidence of political influence on the Evaluation Department is negligible.

In the House of Commons Public Accounts Committee one of the Members of Parliament asked if it might help to guarantee the impartiality of the selection process of evaluation studies if the Treasury were to make the selection [*House of Commons, 1981*]. However, the Treasury spokesman declared that the Treasury would not have the professional expertise, nor a specific view as to what should be evaluated, and added: 'It is not our business to second guess the Department.' Sir Peter Preston added: 'The safeguard for the Committee, I suggest, is the fact that the Comptroller and Auditor-General's staff have continuing access to our papers.'

Planning and Implementing Evaluations in the ODA – Problems and Solutions

Selection of projects and programmes for evaluation: The drawing up of the evaluation programme is the responsibility of the Evaluation Department, and it is free to include any project or programme it wishes. To quote Sir Peter Preston again, when he appeared before the House of Commons Public Accounts Committee: 'The Evaluation Unit now has the right to decide when an evaluation should be carried out quite independently of that part of the office which is running the project' [*House of Commons, 1981*]. In practice, of course, the selection of projects or programmes for evaluation is carried out as a joint operation with the geographical desks and the functional departments.

The PEC has to approve the programme each year, and it has laid down the main criteria for selection as follows [*Treasury, 1980–81*]:

- areas of increasing activity
- areas of uncertainty or particular difficulty
- areas which are innovative
- areas raising issues which are likely to recur elsewhere
- areas of particular commercial interest.

The Evaluation Department carries out a 'trawl' of geographical departments and functional departments once every eighteen months, in which they are requested to nominate topics for evaluation and to explain which of the criteria above they fulfil; why, in particular, the topic has been chosen and what they expect to get out of the evaluation. The Evaluation Department does not depend exclusively on this trawl, and increasingly it puts forward ideas of its own in line with what it knows to be currently relevant or likely to become so in the future. Also there is a growing emphasis on sectoral syntheses, and the Evaluation Department needs to plan a representative sample of projects within a sector to ensure that it will ultimately have a satisfactory synthesis (the ODA has recently completed, or is currently planning, syntheses for Fisheries, Technical Co-operation, Irrigation, Power, Minerals, Grain Storage, Forestry and Training). The Evaluation Department also finds out what topics the ODA's technical advisers would like to see evaluated and why. This mix of ways whereby projects are identified for evaluation diminishes the risk that geographical departments or functional divisions might try to draw a veil over failed projects, or ones which they think might be embarrassing if looked at too closely. The PEC takes very seriously its role of supervising the annual evaluation programme and may well delete proposals from the list and substitute ones it considers are more important. Evaluation, after all, is recognised by senior management to be one of the key means whereby they are enabled to test whether the decisions they took in the past, and those they are currently taking today, are likely to be the right ones.

In his evidence to the House of Commons Foreign Affairs Committee on 2 July 1986 [*House of Commons, 1986*], Professor Paul Mosley criticised the ODA for selecting only a sample (in fact around 20 per cent) of its medium- to large-scale projects, and contrasted this approach with the World Bank's (IBRD) complete coverage (through project completion reports) of all its projects. The report of the Independent Group on British Aid [*IGBA, 1982*] also recommended that *all* significant projects should be subjected to in-depth evaluation (as distinct from monitoring) by the ODA's Evaluation Department, and it went further, it suggested that a rate-of-return evaluation should be carried out immediately after the project's completion, with an impact study being made four or five years later. In this writer's opinion, to take the IBRD as a model in this way ignores the fact that the IBRD projects are typically many times larger than most of the ODA's and therefore would justify evaluation, and also that the IBRD does not evaluate all its projects at the same depth; many of its so-called 'evaluations' would be little more than expanded 'project completion reports', and the ODA is already carrying out a project completion report for every project. In fact the World Bank has recognised this fact by deciding recently that it will only evaluate half its projects and not try to cover all of them. In his evidence to the House of Commons Public Accounts Committee, Sir Peter Preston stated that the ODA's 20 per cent or so of significant projects being evaluated was typical of most aid agencies (see also the DAC Compendium [*OECD, 1986*]).

Implementing the evaluations: The Evaluation Department has produced detailed guidelines for evaluators [*ODA, 1986b*], which describe in considerable detail how the task should be approached and how the result should be presented. The guidelines make it clear that, in common with all the members of the DAC, the ODA requires every evaluation report to specifically cover these three issues: sustainability, impact on women, and impact on the environment. The guidelines state that: 'A main purpose of project evaluation is to assess what the project outcome and impact are; to consider how these compare with the objectives as originally set up for the project; and to draw lessons.' Comparison with the objectives is therefore a crucial component of any ODA evaluation. Other aspects covered in the guidelines are as follows:

(i) Lessons can be learned from successes as well as failures.
(ii) Where possible, beneficiaries should be identified.
(iii) Evaluations should not dwell at length on procedures that relate to a past period, and which have already been superseded.
(iv) The 'with and without' approach should be adopted where possible, although control samples may often not be feasible.
(v) Subjective data can be as valuable as objective data.
(vi) Evaluators should beware of hindsight in drafting reports. Comments on how effectively the project was planned and implemented should be kept separate from the discussion of the project's impact.
(vii) Recommendations relating to administrative procedures or operational practices should be produced separately and not incorporated into the main report.
(viii) If the team differ over points of substance, the respective points of view should be covered in the report and not obscured in an attempt to seek a compromise.
(ix) The reports are written for the ODA, and the ODA alone decides what will be done with them.

The general rule is for the ODA to choose mixed teams of evaluators, that is, usually one or two in-house staff members with one or two outside experts – this is to ensure an element of impartiality. The aim is that the reports will ultimately be made available to the public, and in fact that is the case with at least two-thirds of the reports [*ODA, 1986b*]. Recently almost all of its reports have been made openly available, which the ODA hopes to continue.

Although there is a brief reference in the Guidelines to the realised *ex-post* social rate of return on the project as one of the measures of success, it is given a low profile, compared, for instance, with the practice in the World Bank.

In only a minority of the ODA evaluations is any attempt made to measure the realised rate of return (Professor Mosely put it at 20 per cent [*House of Commons, 1986*]). Roger Riddell [*Riddell, 1987*] comments on the way inadequate and dubious data are often used to calculate realised rates of return, and in any case the rate of return may well be high or low as a result of good or bad luck rather than as a result of good or bad project management. He also points out that the rate of return cannot encapsulate many important social or administrative aspects (for example, beneficiary streams or institution-building), while the realised rate of return is in any case a relative concept (for example, two per cent may be creditable in Ghana but not in Singapore). He quotes Frances Stewart [*Stewart, 1978*] as saying: 'It is the nature of any exercise which is designed to put figures on, and add up, the result in costs and benefits, that results should appear to represent scientific and objective conclusions, although in reality they are largely based on hunch, estimate and judgement.'

The ODA's position is that where it is appropriate to calculate the realised rate of return (for example, in the case of projects with measurable outputs), this should be done, and in the process any shadow pricing used at the appraisal stage should be re-examined in the light of actual experience subsequently, but that in the majority of cases the circumstances are unlikely to lend themselves to this kind of quantification. Even in the latter cases, however, an attempt should be made to assess whether the realised rate of return would be likely to exceed, say, a minimum threshold level. An ODA press release in 1986 [*ODA, 1986b*] stated that in 1984–85 39 projects over £1.5 million were approved and of these 18 were susceptible to cost-benefit analysis: appraisals indicated likely rates of return for these projects to be estimated, however roughly, at the evaluation stage.

One of ODA's senior economists [*Wilmshurst, 1986*] has stressed the difficulty of reconciling the realised rate-of-return approach with the objective of helping the poorest. He concludes: 'The contribution of aid to the relief of poverty needs to be considered separately' because 'insofar as aid is a contribution to fighting poverty one would not expect to see aid linked to higher rates of economic growth'. This illustrates yet again the basic dilemma facing the evaluator when the same project has to try to satisfy a number of different criteria concurrently.

Effectiveness-vs.-efficiency and impact: The problems discussed in section I concerning the dichotomy between the 'Does aid work?' approach and the 'Learning lessons to improve aid effectiveness' approach are reflected in the implementation of any evaluation programme – they affect the selection of topics for evaluation, the choice of evaluators, the time allowed and the decision whether to include field surveys or not, the way the report is written, and the eventual feedback. The ODA has a mix of evaluations, some of which are clearly aimed at learning lessons about aid delivery and implementation (that is, effectiveness), while others are aimed more at trying to assess the efficiency of projects (that is whether projects were implemented cost-effectively) and their impact, for example, on the environment, on broad economic development, on women, on the poorest and so on. Impact evaluation tends to be very demanding in terms of the resources required (such as time, money, manpower, local involvement, etc.), and the ODA, like most aid agencies, cannot spare more than a proportion of its evaluation budget for in-depth impact evaluations. Perhaps one way of resolving this dilemma is for all the donors to share (and synthesise) the results of what impact evaluations they are able to do. Already a good start has been made with the decision to pool information gained in the three important areas mentioned earlier (sustainability, women, and environment), and this approach is now being developed further. Two new cross-cutting issues which have recently been added are institution-building and technical assistance methodology).

Projects-vs.-programmes, and capital aid-vs.-technical co-operation: While the evaluation of specific projects is more straightforward than the evaluation of programme aid, sector aid or Aid/Trade Provision, the latter types of aid have been tending to grow in importance and the need to evaluate them is therefore increasing. Balance of payments aid has also been growing in importance for countries like the Sudan and Tanzania. Despite the difficulties, the ODA has carried out some important evaluations of programme aid [ODA, 1984; Wilmshurst, 1986] and of ATP (jointly with the Department of Trade and Industry), while the various syntheses are providing valuable feedback on sector aid (such as the Power Sector synthesis). However, as donors and recipients evolve systems that leave greater scope for the private sector (for example, the foreign exchange auction system in Zambia), so the ability to evaluate the results may be reduced.

As to the evaluation of Technical Cooperation (TC), this has always been an important aspect of the evaluation work of the ODA and will remain so. The ODA has the special advantage that much of its TC aid in the education and training sector is handled on its behalf by the British Council, which has a substantial and experienced Evaluation Department of its own. The evaluation of training is well developed in the British Council, especially through interviews carried out in the developing countries a year or two after the trainees have returned. Thanks to the British Council's role, the ODA is probably further ahead in this area of evaluation than most other donors. The results generally confirm that education and training aid is very effective, and that the overwhelming proportion of beneficiaries return to their countries after their training and mostly rise fairly quickly to senior positions, although in the process some of them cease to use the specific skills in which they were trained.

Manpower aid, always an important element of the ODA's aid programme, has been a particularly important component in recent years, especially in Africa. The ODA has issued guidelines on institutional development and the role of manpower aid [*Wilmshurst, 1986*]. The ODA is now trying to 'projectise' its manpower aid, by linking it more definitely to specific sectors or institutions (such as Kenya Railways), and this should facilitate eventual evaluation. The 'project framework' is also increasingly being used as a tool for the planning and implementation of manpower aid and could eventually prove very useful for evaluation purposes.

Role of the developing countries: The ODA has had some success in encouraging the developing countries to participate in evaluation work (for example, in connection with a big sugar project in Pakistan), but generally speaking the recipient countries prefer to remain at arm's length. They tend to see donor-initiated evaluation as akin to audit, and they prefer to retain their manoeuvrability rather than being too committed through participation. They also have different criteria and objectives in evaluation, as the present writer has emphasised [*Cracknell, 1985a*]. Roger Riddell [*1987*] quotes the example of a project in South Korea aimed at providing village halls for public meetings. The halls were never in fact used for this purpose, so the donor decided that the project had been a failure, but the communities themselves found the halls very useful for other purposes and they regard the project as a success. In their evidence to the House of Commons Foreign Affairs Committee (on the ODA's bilateral country programme) in December 1986 [*House of Commons, 1987b*], the ODA recognised the importance of involving the beneficiaries when it comes to assessing the impact of projects on local communities. They stressed the sensitivity of any attempt to assess the impact on the poorest and also that it would be difficult to do this unless there were local bodies who could genuinely represent the poorest people, as such bodies are often dominated by local elites.

Perhaps the best hope for a more effective involvement of the recipient countries in evaluation work lies in the work of the DAC Expert Group on Aid Evaluation. They have already produced a Compendium of Donor Practices [*OECD, 1986*] with the intention of helping the developing countries when setting up their own evaluation units, and they have held the first international training seminar on evaluation methodology. They should be encouraged to develop still further along these lines.

Should success be judged according to whether the original objectives were achieved or not?: Some donors, including the ODA, were reluctant to adopt the 'project framework' approach, because they were afraid it would lead to evaluation being geared too precisely to the achievement of pre-set objectives. Experience shows (see especially the recent World Bank results published in the Tenth Annual Review of Project Performance Audit Results 1984) that most projects have to be substantially modified during implementation. The World Bank found that only 42 per cent of its projects had been implemented more or less as planned – the rest had been changed in some significant way. Reporting this, Roger Riddell [*1987*] comments: 'The question then arises whether success is to be judged by the degree to which original objectives were achieved, changed objectives were achieved, or objectives were not changed when they should have been.' The current emphasis on flexibility in the management of people-centred projects (the 'process approach') raises the fundamental question whether specific objectives should even be set in the first place. The ODA concentrated on the role of the 'learning process' approach in its recent evaluation of the Integrated Rural Development Project at Mpika in Zambia.

Can success or failure be objectively assessed? Role of scoring systems: The partial emphasis on public accountability that exists in the ODA's evaluation activity, as it must in that of every bilateral donor, has led to an increasing interest in the search for systematic and, if possible, objective ways of assessing success or failure. One approach is the use of quantified indicators, as in the 'project framework'. Another is to apply a simple scoring process according to a number of criteria of success. The ODA was among the first donors to experiment with this approach [*Jennings, 1985*] and the EC has also commissioned a major study along similar lines [*Wheatley et al., 1985*]. These are interesting experiments, but they suffer from the fundamental difficulty that at the end of the day it is a matter of someone making a personal judgement. Jennings realised this and arranged for several people independently to do the scoring to see if the results were reasonably close. Unfortunately they diverged quite significantly, and indeed it would be surprising if everyone were to form the same judgement about such aspects as sustainability, or the degree of help for the poorest.

The Robert Cassen Report [*Cassen, 1986*] and Roger Riddell's book [*Riddell, 1987*] represent another attempt to judge effectiveness, but they too had to admit that the task is a very difficult one: not only is most of the evaluation material deficient in terms of the aid impact, but it is often inherently impossible to decide, a year or two after the aid has ceased, whether a project is successful or not. It is often simply too early to form such a judgement.

This may partly explain why there is an understandable reluctance in the ODA, as in most bilateral aid evaluation departments, to get over-committed to the 'Does aid work?' type of evaluation activity. The effort could pre-empt a high proportion of the resources available for evaluation, and the results might still be very inconclusive, whereas in the meantime there are many useful lessons that can be learned of a more direct type which could improve the quality of aid-planning and implementation.

What is the right time to carry out an evaluation?: This is always a difficult problem. In the ODA the emphasis at first tended to be on learning lessons related to aid delivery rather than to aid impact, because until the early 1980s the monitoring system in the ODA was very rudimentary. However, monitoring was vastly improved during the early 1980s, and then Project Completion Reports (PCRs) were introduced. This meant that aid-delivery lessons could be adequately covered through the monitoring process, leaving evaluation to concentrate more on impact. The inference is that evaluations can now be timed to take place a little later than was the case previously.

However, there is an obvious limit to this, since, if the evaluation is delayed for too long, it becomes difficult to decide what can be attributed to the capital phase of the project and what is due to subsequent management, or to changes that may have taken place once a project begins to operate. One possibility, for certain large projects like the ODA-funded Songea–Makambako road in Tanzania, is to carry out a first in-depth evaluation a year or two after the road has been completed, and then to plan a second one to take place four or five years later, when the existence of the road will have had a chance to generate consequential economic changes. The proposal that evaluations should be carried out four or five years after the aid has ceased was put forward by Professor Mosley in his evidence to the House of Commons Foreign Affairs Committee in 1986 [*House of Commons, 1986*]. He saw it as essential as a test of the ultimate sustainability of 'projects. The inability of the ODA's evaluation reports to say much of value about sustainability was noted by the Independent Group on British Aid in 1986 [*IGBA, 1982*]. At present the ODA tends to carry out evaluations two or three years after 'projects have been completed, but, as PCRs become available, it may be possible to plan evaluations to take place a year or two later.

III. EVALUATION AND THE PROJECT CYCLE

Project Formulation and Appraisal

A very important new element in the ODA's 'project formulation and appraisal system is the 'project framework'. At the time when the revised ODA Guidelines to Evaluators were being issued (February 1987), the 'project framework' technique had only just been introduced into the ODA and it was as yet too early for it to be reflected in the evaluation procedures because it will take some years before new 'projects for which 'project frameworks' have been completed are ready for evaluation. It was no doubt the 'project framework' which the authors of the Guidelines had in mind when commenting: 'ODA is now paying increasing attention to more specific definition both of the objectives of aid 'projects and programmes, and of ways of measuring achievement against stated objectives' [*ODA, 1986b*].

The 'project framework' system (almost identical to the 'logical framework' mentioned earlier) was formally introduced into the ODA early in 1986 [*McCulloch, 1986*] following the recommendations of the present writer and his ODA colleague Mr. Rednall, in 1985 [*Cracknell and Rednall, 1985*]. The matrix comprises a hierarchy of objectives, and at each level of objective there are indicators of success, and key risks or assumptions. The system was introduced in response to the directive from the Prime Minister's Office that each government department should introduce some system of setting clear objectives and measures of achievement.

The ODA invited the present writer to evaluate the first year's experience of the ODA with the 'project framework' system early in 1987 [*Cracknell, 1987*], and the main conclusion was that, although the system had been successfully introduced, there was still considerable confusion as to the distinction between immediate objectives, and all too often the column 'Indicators of success' had been taken to mean simply listing the kind of indicators, and not the quantified figures themselves. The geographical-desk officers and technical advisers had tried to 'bolt on' the matrix at the end of the appraisal process, and therefore they hadn't found it particularly useful. The real value of the 'project framework' system is that it enables the 'project to be systematically formulated at an early stage in the project-selection process. However, senior management greatly valued the way the matrix encapsulated in a telescopic way the essential elements of the 'project. As a result, guidance was revised to indicate that the clear statement of objectives, and the introduction of indicators of success, should greatly help the monitoring and evaluation processes. Also training was provided for the formulators of 'project frameworks' on these specific points.

Already some ODA evaluators have made use of the 'project framework' approach, and undoubtedly it will play an increasingly important part in all future evaluation work.

One of the dangers of the 'project framework' approach, recognised by the present writer and his colleague, is that it may encourage 'project managers to take *too static* a view of projects, and it could be seen as a 'blueprint' rather than as a starting-off point for a project that may well have to change its shape in response to changing circumstances. One of the key lessons of evaluations of people-centred projects [*Rondinelli, 1987*] is that management has to be highly flexible and quickly responsive to the experience as the 'project is implemented. This implies that the 'project framework' has to be revised frequently if it is not to become a brake on flexible management.

The 'project framework' is now being taught at the Civil Service College as one of the techniques found particularly useful by at least one government department (ODA). As indicated earlier, the basic ideas of the 'project framework' have already been incorporated into the Treasury's Guide for Managers.

Evaluations have highlighted the crucial importance of social factors, and sometimes environmental factors, in the success or failure of projects, and this has focused attention on the issue of whether the existing project-appraisal techniques can accommodate such aspects. The ODA was among the first bilateral donors to develop a comprehensive social cost-benefit-analysis technique for project appraisal and a revised version was published in 1988 [*ODA, 1988*]; all projects submitted to the PEC carry a full, social, cost-benefit analysis as part of the appraisal. It is now mandatory for all 'project submissions to supply greater detail on the projects' intended beneficiaries, and on any groups likely to be disadvantaged [*ODA, 1986c*]. Environmental problems raise particularly difficult issues in terms of economic appraisal, because a high rate of discount can have the effect of discouraging project planners from taking into account any likely environmental impact which may not become significant until some years ahead. This issue is discussed in the new version of the ODA Manual of Project Appraisal. The then Minister for Overseas Development announced, in a speech on The Environment and Development in 1987, that his Department had commissioned a review by University College of the ODA's project-appraisal techniques, and this had concluded that they were robust enough to accommodate environmental aspects, but that some changes in emphasis in the existing techniques would be desirable [*Patten, 1987b*].

The Independent Group on British Aid, in 1986 [*IGBA, 1986*], urged that the ODA should put more resources into local consultation with intended beneficiaries, and into the project formulation and appraisal stages. However, the ODA in its evidence to the House of Commons Foreign Affairs Committee [*House of Commons, 1987b*] argued: 'It is not necessarily self-evident that identification and appraisal should be given more emphasis at the expense, for instance, of project supervision and monitoring.'

Monitoring and Review

As indicated earlier, monitoring has developed rapidly in the ODA in recent years, and this has relieved the pressure on the Evaluation Department to cover aid-delivery aspects. Now the Department is able to use monitoring reports, mid-term reviews and PCRs as the raw material for syntheses of lessons applicable to the ODA's work as a whole. The great advantage of monitoring reports, as a source of evaluation material, is that they are usually far more up-to-date in terms of the ODA's inputs than are evaluation reports.

It is now mandatory in the ODA for a monitoring plan to be an integral part of every project submission to the PEC. The ODA's Evaluation Department recently evaluated the Ministry's monitoring procedures [*Scott et al., 1987*], and concluded that: 'Effective reporting systems at the project level allow ODA's valuable advisory resource to spend less time on data collection, and the day to day problems of implementation, and to focus clearly on overall project effectiveness.' Thus monitoring can release skilled resources for the evaluation of project impact and effectiveness.

Project Completion Reports

In the ODA PCRs now have to be prepared for all projects and programmes of any significance, including technical cooperation and ATP. They are seen as the last step of monitoring, but they could equally be regarded as the first step in *ex-post* evaluation. The ODA's Evaluation

Department is still in the process of experimenting with ways of extracting the maximum evaluative value out of monitoring and review reports, especially as regards using them as an early warning system of projects that might need to be evaluated later. A technique now being explored is to grade each PCR according to the extent to which problems have been experienced. Not only will this provide a basis for selecting projects for evaluation, but a comparison over time might be a useful way of assessing trends in the incidence of problems, broken down by type of project, sector, region and so on.

Because the PCR is carried out when the donor's role has been completed, and the project starts its independent life, it cannot usually provide any evidence on impact or sustainability, except in the case of long-gestation, multi-component projects, where some components may already have been in operation for a number of years when the PCR is carried out. On the other hand the PCRs cover *all* projects and programmes (including TC and ATP) and so yield a full cross-section of all kinds of aid activities. For the 10 to 20 per cent of projects and programmes that are ultimately evaluated, it should be possible to make some judgement as to the extent that the PCR gave an accurate indication of the project's ultimate impact.

Feedback

The ODA is fortunate in that the procedure whereby all evaluation reports are submitted to the PEC provides feedback at a senior management level, and to the members of the organisation who most need it, those who have the responsibility for approving significant new projects, and who provide the technical advice to the administrators (the Chief Advisers). This is undoubtedly the most effective kind of feedback any donor evaluation department can have. However, it is supplemented in the ODA by several other systems as follows:

(a) *EVSUMs*. These are one-page summaries of the key findings from evaluation reports, which are distributed to all the middle-level and upper-level staff in the ODA, and more widely.
(b) *Sector Manuals*. These are technical manuals prepared mainly for use by the professional advisers, but available also to administrators and others. They cover the main technical, economic, and social aspects of each sector.
(c) *Policy Guidance Notes (PGNs)*. These are short pithy notes on selected topics which are circulated around the ODA from time to time as the need arises. Not infrequently evaluation reports provide the basis for the material used in PGNs.

(d) *Office procedure.* This is concerned mainly with internal ODA procedures, but it quite often happens that evaluation reports indicate that the ODA's existing procedures are not working adequately and revisions to office procedure have to be made.
(e) *Data-banks.* At present the ODA only has a very basic Management Information System (MIS), which comprises merely the key statistics for each project or programme. However, it could easily form the basis for a more comprehensive data-bank system, which might incorporate elements from evaluation reports. The ODA, along with other members of the DAC Expert Group on Aid Evaluation, is keenly interested in developing such a data-bank system along the lines being pioneered in the Canadian International Development Agency (CIDA) and building on experience gained over many years in the United States Agency for International Development (USAID), IBRD and other agencies.
(f) *Making evaluation reports available outside the ODA on request.* As indicated earlier, a high and increasing proportion of the ODA's evaluation reports are already made available to the public on request.
(g) *Use in training.* Evaluation reports are often used in ODA staff-training sessions, and occasionally special seminars are arranged at which the findings from evaluation reports covering selected sectors are discussed with the technical advisers. Seminars are also arranged from time to time with associated bodies like the British Council or with outside bodies, such as the British Consultants Bureau (BCB).
(h) *Feedback to the developing countries.* The ODA's Guidelines for the Preparation of Evaluation Studies [*ODA, 1987b*] state:
'Evaluators should not show copies (i.e., of evaluation reports they are preparing) to officials in the developing countries, or to anyone outside the ODA who does not have a direct involvement in the evaluation. If a developing country has supplied personnel to work closely with the evaluation team the content of an early draft may be agreed with them, but not the final draft or final report.'

Later, the Guidelines say: 'As far as possible, evaluation reports will be provided to the Governments of the developing countries concerned, and to others who have a direct interest in the subject' (that is, after they have been approved by the PEC). One possible way of ensuring a more effective feedback to the developing countries would be for the ODA to reserve a small proportion of the evaluation budget for each evaluation to enable the evaluators to return to the developing country to de-brief the officials there in detail on their findings.

IV. THE ODA'S PERFORMANCE AS JUDGED FROM EVALUATION

The most difficult task has been left to the last. What do all the 300-plus evaluation reports that the ODA has produced over the years [*ODA, 1987a*] say about the ODA's performance as an aid donor?

One of the ODA's Senior Economic Advisers, then Head of the Aid Policy and Research Group, reported in 1986 on the results of an informal review that the ODA had carried out in 1984 of 40 out of 217 evaluation reports [*Wilmshurst, 1986*] which 'suggested that in most cases the immediate objectives of the project and programme had been carried out.' Under the heading 'Does aid work?' he writes: 'The general conclusion from ODA experience is that most aid is reasonably effective in meeting its objectives.' He also points out that the team of consultants commissioned by the Task Force on Confessional Flows [*Cassen, 1986*]: 'reached a similar conclusion that the great majority of aid succeeds in its developmental objectives'.

Another independent assessment was the scoring system attempted by Jennings [*Jennings, 1985*]. He examined 40 evaluation reports in considerable depth, and his average scores out of 10 for three selected criteria were as follows:

	Score
Were project objectives achieved?	8.6
Were project objectives achieved efficiently?	6.3
Was the wider impact favourable?	8.1

In February 1986 the ODA issued a Background Information Leaflet with the title 'Making Aid Effective' [*ODA, 1986b*], in which it reported that during 1984–85 20 evaluation studies had been completed covering aspects of some £114 million of aid activities of varying duration carried out between 1972 and 1984. In two-thirds of the cases, where an overall verdict could be given or was appropriate, the studies found that the programmes or techniques examined had substantially achieved their purposes. They also identified changes in project planning and design and management methods, which would improve the cost-effectiveness, impact and durability of aid-funded schemes.

Such evidence as the above is hardly conclusive, and one observer who has done as much as any one person could reasonably do to weigh up the evidence of evaluation results [*Riddell, 1987*] came to the conclusion that 'The evidence remains unproved and in some instances simply does not exist in a reliable form.'

So much for the ability of evaluation, at its present stage of development, to answer the question 'Does aid work?' The fact is that it simply cannot be expected to provide the answer to such a question without much greater resources being poured into it, and that seems unlikely to happen. Yet the ODA's evaluations are all the time enabling the organisation to improve the quality of its aid operations, and thus its performance as an aid donor. Monitoring was developed by the ODA, or at any rate given a tremendous impetus, largely because of the evidence of the need for it from evaluations. The present emphasis on sociological factors was given a strong stimulus as a result of evaluation findings. There are many other examples of 'low profile' ways in which the findings from evaluation studies have been applied to improve the ODA's aid performance and these are referred to in several ODA publications [*Cracknell, 1984; ODA, 1983; 1984; 1986b; Wilmshurst, 1986*]. Whatever may be the answer to the overriding question 'Does aid work?', there can be absolutely no doubt that evaluation work has led to a definite improvement in the quality of aid administration, and aid-funded projects and programmes, and at a cost which is minuscule in relation to the sums involved.

NOTE

The author accepts sole responsibility for the contents of this paper, which does not necessarily reflect the opinions of the Overseas Development Administration.

1. A more detailed description of the ODA's evaluation system appears in Chapter 10, 'The Role of an Evaluation Unit: Functions, Constraints and Feedback.' See Figure 1 for an organogram.

REFERENCES

Bovaird, A.G. *et al.*, 1987, 'A Study of Multilateral Agencies' Evaluation Systems', EV 365 (3 vols.), ODA.
Browning, R., 1984, 'Evaluation in the ODA – A View from the Inside', in *Public Administration and Development*, Vol. 4, No. 2, April/June.
Cassen, R.H. and Associates, 1986, *Does Aid Work?*, New York and Oxford: Oxford University Press.
Comptroller and Auditor-General, 1985, 'National Audit Office: Report by the Comptroller and Auditor General – ODA Accountability for Overseas Aid'.
Cracknell, B.E., 1982, 'Evaluation in the UN System and Elsewhere, Viewed by the UK', Address to Informal Inter-Agency Evaluation Meeting Sponsored by the Joint Inspection Unit, Geneva, 29 March 1982.
Cracknell, B.E., 1984, 'Learning Lessons from Experience: the Role of Evaluation in the Administration of the UK Aid Programme', in *Public Administration and Development*, Vol. 4, No. 1.
Cracknell, B.E., 1985a, 'Learning Lessons from Past Experience: Evaluation Work in ODA', in *Crown Agents Review*, Oct.

Cracknell, B.E., 1985b, 'It Looks Different from the Other Side. Project Evaluation as Seen by the Developing Countries', Paper prepared for the Annual Conference of the ESRC Development Economics Study Group, Nov.
Cracknell, B.E., 1987, 'Evaluation of ODA's Experience with the Project Framework', EV 428, ODA.
Cracknell, B.E., 1988, 'Evaluating Development Assistance – A Review of the Literature', in *Public Administration and Development*, Vol. 8, No. 1.
Cracknell, B.E, and J. Rednall, 1985, 'Defining Objectives and Measuring Performance in Aid Projects and Programmes', ODA.
Freeman H.E. *et al.*, 1979, *Evaluating Social Projects in Developing Countries*, Paris: OECD.
House of Commons, 1981, Fourth Report from the Committee of Public Accounts, Session 1980-81 – ODA, HMSO.
House of Commons, 1986, Foreign Affairs Committee, Session 1985-86, ODA Bilateral Country Programmes, Minutes of Evidence, 2 July 1986.
House of Commons, 1987a, 'Thirteenth Report from the Committee of Public Accounts, Session 1986-87', The Financial Management Initiative.
House of Commons, 1987b, Foreign Affairs Committee, Session 1986-87, ODA Bilateral Country Programmes, Minutes of Evidence, Wednesday, 17 December 1986, and Tuesday, 27 January 1987, HMSO.
Independent Group on British Aid (IGBA), 1982, *Real Aid – A Strategy for Britain*, London.
Independent Group on British Aid, 1984, *Aid is not enough*, London.
Independent Group on British Aid, 1986, *Missed Opportunities: Britain and the Third World*, London.
Jennings, T., 1985, 'Measuring the Effectiveness of Aid: An Experiment in the Scoring Method for Aid Evaluation', University of Leicester.
Joint Inspection Unit, 1979, *Glossary of Evaluation Terms*, Geneva: UN.
Ludford, T., 1987, 'Report on the Questionnaire Survey of the Usefulness of Evaluation Summaries (EVSUMs)', EV Unnumbered Study, ODA.
McCulloch, M., 1986, 'Project Frameworks – A Logical Development for More Effective Aid', in *British Overseas Aid in 1985*, London: ODA.
Mosley, P., 1987, *Overseas Aid: Its Defence and Reform*, Brighton: Wheatsheaf Books.
Mosley, P., 1987, 'Poverty-focused Aid: The Lessons of Experience', an Action Aid Report.
Organisation for Economic Cooperation and Development (OECD), 1969, *The Evaluation of Technical Assistance*.
Organisation for Economic Cooperation and Development, 1972, *Evaluating Development Assistance: Problems or Methods and Organisation*.
Organisation for Economic Cooperation and Development, 1985, *Twenty-five Years of Development Cooperation*.
Organisation for Economic Cooperation and Development, 1986, *Evaluation Methods and Procedures: A Compendium of Donor Practice*.
Overseas Development Administration (ODA), 1975, 'The Changing Emphasis in British Aid Policies: More Help for the Poorest', Cmnd 6370, HMSO.
Overseas Development Administration, 1983, 'The Lessons of Experience: Evaluation Work in the ODA', HMSO.
Overseas Development Administration, 1984, *The Evaluation of Aid Projects and Programmes*. HMSO.
Overseas Development Administration, 1986a, 'Ensuring Value for Money: A Look at the Work of the ODA Evaluation Department', in *Overseas Development*, June 1986.
Overseas Development Administration, 1986b, 'Making Aid Effective', Background Information Press Release, Feb.
Overseas Development Administration, 1986c, *Women in Development and the British Aid Programme*.
Overseas Development Administration, 1987a, 'Evaluation Studies: A Summary

EVALUATION POLICY AND PERFORMANCE OF BRITAIN

Reference List of Reports of ODA Evaluation Studies, and of some other ODA Monitoring and Review Activities', EV 370.
Overseas Development Administration, 1987b, 'Guidelines for the Preparation of Evaluation Studies'.
Overseas Development Administration, 1987c, *The Environment and the British Aid Programme*.
Overseas Development Administration, 1988, *Appraisal of Projects in Developing Countries: A Guide for Economists*.
Patten, C., 1987a, 'Idealism and Self Interest: Britain's Aid Programme', Address to the Royal Institute of International Affairs, 18 March 1987.
Patten, C., 1987b, 'The Environment and Development', Address to IIED/IBRD, Seminar, 9 September 1987.
Patten, C., 1987c, 'Development and the Quality of Life', Address to the PACE-UK Meeting, House of Commons, 18 Nov.
Patten, C., 1987d, 'Poverty, Technology and Sustainable Development', Fifth O'Sullivan Lecture, 26 Nov.
Riddell, R., 1987, *Foreign Aid Reconsidered*, London: James Currey for Overseas Development Institute.
Rondinelli, A., 1987, *Development Administration and US Foreign Aid Policy*. Boulder, CO and London: Lynne Rienner Publishers.
Scott, M. *et al.*, 1987, 'An Evaluation of Bilateral Project Monitoring'. EV 408.
Stewart, F., 1978, 'Social Cost Benefit Analysis in Practice: Some Reflections in the Light of Case Studies using Little-Mirrless Techniques', *World Development*, Vol. 6, No. 2, Feb.
Treasury (UK), 1980–81, 'Treasury Minute on the First, Third to Sixth, and Eighth to Seventeenth Reports from the Committee of Public Accounts, session 190–191', Cmnd 8413.
Treasury (UK), 1983, 'Financial Management in Government Departments'.
Treasury (UK), 1984, 'Progress in Financial Management in Government Departments', Cmnd 9297.
Treasury (UK), 1985, 'Policy Work and the FMI', Report by the Cabinet Office (MPO)/Treasury, Financial Management Unit.
Treasury (UK), 1987a, 'Policy Evaluation – Departmental Case Studies', Note by the Joint Management Unit.
Treasury (UK), 1988, *Policy Evaluation: A Guide for Managers*.
Wheatley, C. *et al.*, 1985, 'Assessment and Interpretation of Development Aid Sources: A Proposed Scoring System for Application by the EEC and Other Development Agencies', *Integration*, Frankfurt.
Wilmshurst, J., 1986, 'The Effectiveness of British Aid', in *British Overseas Aid in 1985*, ODA.
World Bank, 1986, *Tenth Annual Review of Project Performance Audit Results*, Washington, DC.

4

The Evaluation Policy and Performance of Denmark

HENRIK SCHAUMBURG-MÜLLER

'Evaluation is an evolving work of art, a process in which accumulating experience is steadily allowing the boundaries of analysis to be pushed forward and the policy conclusions to become increasingly substantial.'

Cassen: *Does Aid Work?* [1986]

I. INTRODUCTION

As the above quotation indicates, the subject of aid evaluation is under constant change. The Danish aid programme is only a little more than 25 years old. In this period, evaluation policy has changed from something almost non-existent, being behind when the overall aid policy matured, and then to develop into the present solid evaluation programme. While there has been a very wide general support, both in the general public and from political parties, of the aid programme as such, the understanding of the need for evaluations has not had the same attention.

The support for the aid programme is no doubt best illustrated by the fact that the Danish aid budget has been increasing almost every year for the last 25 years, not only in nominal terms, but also as a percentage of the gross domestic product (GDP) from 0.08 per cent in 1962 to 0.86 per cent in 1988. Even in times of economic recession, and when almost all other public expenditures have been curtailed, there has been a broad political will to increase the aid budget.

Efforts have been made to make the Danish aid programme genuinely poverty-oriented. While the Danish tied aid has concentrated on industrial projects, the equally important untied grants have gone mainly to agricultural and social activities, where an important concern has been the inclusion in programmes of the poverty target groups. In other words, pressure to prove quantitative efficiency might not have been as strong as in the case of more direct productive activities where stipulated internal rates of return should be reached.

The Framework for Danish Aid

The framework for Danish aid policy is embodied in a law on 'International development co-operation' of 1971 which has been revised and amended a number of times. In its first paragraph, this law contains the objective of Danish official aid to developing countries: 'Through a co-operation with these countries' governments and authorities to support efforts, in order to achieve economic growth, thereby contributing to secure social progress and political independence.' In the interpretation of the objective it has, on a political level, been agreed that Danish aid should be 'poverty-oriented' in the sense that aid concentrates on the poorer developing countries, and the main aim should be to support lasting improvements of economic and social conditions for the poorer sections of the population within these countries [*DANIDA, 1987: 24*].

The Danish International Development Agency (DANIDA), responsible for the administration of the aid programme, is a department in the Ministry of Foreign Affairs. The administrative head of the DANIDA has direct access to the minister. The minister appoints to the Board of DANIDA nine members representing major interest groups and persons appointed in their personal capacity. The law gives the Board only an advisory function to the Minister of Foreign Affairs, and it has therefore no responsibilities as a true management board.

In 1987, the Danish aid budget increased to 5,688 million Danish Kroner (DKK)[1] or 0.85 per cent of the GDP. The Parliament has committed the government to increase aid allocations until they reach one per cent of the GDP by 1992 or some one billion US$. All parties in Parliament, except one, support the basic aid policy and principles, although there are occasional disagreements about the rate of increase. However, despite the prevailing slow economic growth, increasing unemployment and balance of payments deficits in Denmark, the broad political and popular support has been maintained.

The Danish law on aid co-operation does not contain details on which countries to co-operate with or in what form aid should be distributed. These issues are left to be settled by the government and the Parliament when the aid programme is discussed. For a very long period, there has been an understanding that approximately half of the aid budget should be distributed through the multilateral aid organisations and the other half should be given as bilateral aid. From 1989, bilateral aid has been given as grants (earlier about one-half was provided as loans) and at least half of the expenditures should be tied to purchases in Denmark. The number of recipients of bilateral aid is about to be limited to approximately 22 countries.

Compared to many other countries, a relatively large share of Danish aid is allocated through the multilateral institutions. For a certain share of these allocations, the financed projects are identifiable as so-called multi/bi projects.

Definitions and Outline of Study

In this study, the term 'evaluation' means the process of observing, analysing and assessing ongoing or completed development activities with the aim of determining the efficiency, effectiveness, impact sustainability and relevance of objectives of the aid.[2] In this sense, evaluation does not cover assessment of proposals and appraisal of aid activities. In relation to the DANIDA's activities, a review is part of the monitoring and supervising process of projects and programmes, initiated by the responsible implementing office, while evaluations are initiated and terms of reference formulated by the evaluation unit. This distinction has only become clear since the establishment of the evaluation unit in 1983.

Many donor agencies make country evaluations where recipient countries' development policy and performance are studied to identify aggregate development effects and are related to donor policies. So far the Agency has not made country analyses and programming on a routine basis, and there are no plans to engage in country evaluation studies.

Evaluation of aid could also mean a broader inquiry into the aid policy and performance in general, looking, for example, into the general efficiency of aid, in order to recommend future policies. The major inquiries of the Danish aid programme are mentioned in the following section on historical development, but they are not the object of study in this paper.

A large number of agents are involved in the formulation and implementation of aid policies in a donor country. In the following, the political level is used as a term which includes the Parliament and its subcommittees, the government, including the Minister of Foreign Affairs, and the DANIDA Board appointed by the Minister of Foreign Affairs. The term does not include the administrative management of the Agency in the Ministry of Foreign Affairs.

After the historical account of the development of aid evaluations in section II, the present objectives and policies for evaluations are discussed in section III. Section IV analyses the performance, while results and feedback are studied in section V. Conclusions are drawn in the final section.

EVALUATION POLICY AND PERFORMANCE OF DENMARK

II. HISTORICAL DEVELOPMENT OF AID EVALUATIONS IN DENMARK

The history of Danish aid evaluations goes back to a first major study made in 1968 of the Young Farmers Training Colleges managed by the Mysore State Adult Education Council in India and supported by the Danish Association for International Co-operation (Mellemfolkeligt Samvirke), a NGO which had provided technical assistance and funds to a couple of the agricultural training schools in the period 1960–66 [*Steen Folke et al., 1969*]. It was a thorough *ex-post* evaluation with collection of primary field data and a scientific approach to measure the impact on a traditional framework of comparing situations with and without the project (represented by trained farmers from schools which had not received Danish support).

The evaluation caused a considerable debate, mainly because the results showed that little impact from the Danish assistance could be traced to the farmers' level in the villages. Today this is easily understandable, taking into consideration the complexity of the rural Indian situation, the rather traditional Danish approach and the limited knowledge of Danish expatriates at that time of Indian agriculture and rural sociology. However, quite a lot of enthusiasm and honest efforts had been invested in the project, and the results of the evaluation therefore caused great disappointment.

Instead of discussing the project and its approach, the reaction turned against the evaluation. It was felt that this type of evaluation had given a bad reputation to sincere development work. As the evaluation method had a scientific approach supported by research with field interviews and investigations over several months, animosity was created against this type of evaluation in the aid administration.[3] For some time, there was an aversion on the policy level not only to *ex-post* evaluations, but also to some degree to social science development research in general.

On two occasions, when the law on 'International technical co-operation with developing countries' underwent major revisions, the government appointed a committee to make an investigation of the aid policy and to recommend future policies. The revisions were made in 1970 and 1982. Both reports discuss aid evaluation and comment on the role evaluation has played in the administration of the aid programme.

In the report of 1970, the aims of evaluations are stated closely in relation to the results of the projects. Aims are not seen from the standpoint of what should be the purpose and use of evaluations. On DANIDA practice, it is reported that ongoing evaluations or rather reviews of projects had been made for the DANIDA Board. A policy of doing this every second year for all major projects was abandoned for lack of resources, and the Board would instead have ten project reviews each year. Emphasis was put on ongoing evaluations, as few aid activities had terminated after the aid programme took off in the middle of the 1960s.

On future evaluation policy, the feeling of the committee can be learned from the following quotation: 'Because of the costs connected with comprehensive evaluations, including *ex-ante* 'mapping' of project effects, as well as *ex-post* evaluation by special missions, only a small share of the total aid programme can be included' [*Betænkning, 1970*].

With this background, it is no surprise that there was little reflection on the purpose of evaluations. However, it was said that those projects, selected for evaluation, should be able to illustrate project strengths or weaknesses of a more general nature. Basically, evaluations were looked upon more as a subject of development research than as a management tool.

In the following years, evaluation work continued to concentrate on project reviews undertaken by short-term missions of two to three weeks by two to three persons, of whom one would be an independent outsider and another employed in the Agency. No separate evaluation unit was established. The various country desks were responsible for arranging the project reviews.

The next major revision of the aid policy came in 1982. In the meantime, Danish aid had developed into a more mature programme. This is also reflected in the attitude to evaluation. The committee says that, with the increased recognition of the complexity of development assistance, the understanding of the necessity for evaluations has grown [*Betænkning, 1982*]. The committee considered a plan for establishing an evaluation unit in the DANIDA.[4] While such a unit was recommended, a majority of the committee would have liked to have had more resources allocated to the unit than were envisaged in the plan. The minority in the committee, whose advice afterwards seemed to have been followed, asked for a more gradual expansion of the new unit's activities. The minority included the members representing the DANIDA management and Board. It seems as if there was a reluctance among decision-makers to accept evaluations as a management tool in the formulation of aid policies.

The tendency to keep tight control of what should be evaluated and to have a selective approach rather than general rules is further supported by the Board's reaction to an evaluation of tied aid to Egypt in 1981. The evaluation was the first thorough evaluation of the tied aid made by people outside the DANIDA and rather controversial in its approach.

The Board appointed among its members a committee to review and comment on the report. The committee concluded with respect to evaluations 'that there is a need for future evaluations, and it is our opinion that this, for the present, is best solved by *ad hoc* evaluations, sanctioned by the Board in each case' [*Udenrigsministeriet, 1981b: 16*].

The two aid policy review committees of 1970 and 1982 were not allowed to look into the organisational structure of the DANIDA and its adequacy for the administration of the aid programme. A long-standing debate in Denmark has been the status of the Agency within the Ministry of Foreign Affairs, and whether DANIDA should be part of that ministry at all. In 1984, as a result of the questions posed by the 1982 inquiry, the Minister of Foreign Affairs asked the Minister of Finance to make a study of the administration of the aid programme and suggest suitable changes in the organisational structure of the Agency. Assisted by two management consulting firms and other outside consultants, the Ministry of Finance delivered a large five-volume report in 1986 [*Administrationsdepartementet, 1986*]. The report suggested a new structure and a more independent position for the Agency within the Ministry of Foreign Affairs. The report otherwise dealt in detail with how the DANIDA's structure could be changed to improve strategic planning and decision-making. In this connection it is interesting to note how little attention is given to evaluations, and what role evaluations could play in the formulation of strategic plans. The only comment is that the important function of evaluation should be located in a separate division together with administration of research funds and documentation. The location of the unit is given in Figure 1 below.

In the following years, the DANIDA worked on a strategic plan of action, published in 1988 [*DANIDA, 1988a*]. In a large section on strategic considerations on aid to specific countries and regions, recommendations for the future policy are – among other things – based on experience gained to which evaluations certainly have contributed.

In general, however, considerations given to evaluation as a tool of management are more or less absent, although the plan goes into details, dealing with institutional aspects of the aid programme. The notion of strategic planning for the DANIDA's activities is obviously taken from current thinking within business management, and it is therefore strange that the role of evaluation work is not considered. For a private company it would be essential to follow how its products perform on the markets and to make institutional arrangements to secure a systematic feedback of experiences gained in the field of customer relations – target groups – to product research and development and into policy formulation and decisions.

III. EVALUATION OBJECTIVES AND POLICIES

Evaluations of the aid programme, independent of government initiatives, are very rare, since the necessary access to government files and internal documents is difficult to obtain. Some larger Danish NGOs have recently started to make evaluations of their own projects, but, as most of the funding is coming from the DANIDA, it is in many cases the DANIDA which takes the initiatives.

Evaluations within the DANIDA

Evaluation policy: From the above historical narration it appears that evaluation policies have not played a very pronounced role in the aid debate and the formulation of aid policies. There are no guidelines from Parliament or its sub-committees on how the Agency's aid activities should be evaluated and what objectives the work should follow. No independent institution has been established within the administration to evaluate these aid activities. As all other government activities, DANIDA is subject to the general investigations by the Auditor of State Accounts as described in more detail below.

Evaluation policies have therefore mainly been developed within the DANIDA's own administration and of course in co-operation with the Board. In 1982, a separate evaluation unit was established in the Agency. Before that, the operational units were also responsible for evaluations. The main purpose of evaluations had been to make an assessment of the operation and the effects of single aid projects, in order to improve performance of the project concerned or projects of a similar nature. Most evaluations concerned ongoing bilateral projects. More thorough evaluations of project impact were only considered possible to perform some years after the end of projects, and provided necessary information on the situation of the project was available. Even then, the Agency had the impression from other aid organisations that expensive impact evaluations gave only limited results.

The Evaluation Unit in the Agency has now developed the definition and purposes for present evaluation practices, and updated the guidelines for evaluation work.[5] Evaluations are to examine the design, implementation of projects or programmes, with the aim of determining their efficiency, effectiveness, impact, sustainability and the relevance of their objectives. It is mentioned that the evaluation work comprises bilateral aid activities in general and is not confined to specific projects or programmes.

The purposes are now also spelled out in more detail to '. . . serve as *management tools* with a view to improve the projects evaluated and, being a systematic way of learning from experience, to provide lessons which can guide future decisions and thus improve Danish development assistance.' Furthermore, evaluation, together with monitoring activities, provides information to the Agency and host country managers about the performance of their projects and programmes.

Another important purpose of evaluation is to provide *accountability* about the aid process to the political community and to serve as a basis for informing the public about the results of Danish development assistance [*DANIDA, 1988b: 1*]. With this clarifying and almost all-embracing statement of purposes, the policy has moved a long way from the earlier situation. The question today is therefore rather whether the evaluation unit will have the capacity to accomplish these tasks, and to what extent the evaluation policies can penetrate the rest of the DANIDA bureaucracy and make an impact on the general aid policy process. The scope and objective of evaluation used now by the Agency seem to be in agreement with the intentions given by the government committee in 1982, when the evaluation unit was established, although the definition of evaluation objective was more general: 'The main objective of the evaluation system is to increase the quality of Danish aid, thereby using the given resources with greater efficiency to achieve stated detailed aims within the overall objective for Danish aid co-operation' [*Betænkning, 1982*].

However, it was also mentioned in operational terms how this general objective should be reached:

- establishing more systematic evaluations of the preparation, implementation and results of aid activities to draw conclusions to be used in the implementation of ongoing activities and in the identification, preparation and implementation of future activities;
- improving the receiving country's monitoring and evaluation capacity;
- establishing an information-storing and retrieving system to ensure that lessons learned from evaluations are made available for and used by those entities which participate in the preparation and implementation of aid activities, and the decision-makers of the aid policy;
- including relevant evaluation results from other donors.

While the first point is quite similar to the definition used today by the Agency, the other purposes of the evaluation effort will be further discussed in the section below on performance.

In the annual report of 1986, the Chairman of the Board dealt at some length with the DANIDA's evaluation activities and stated in relation to future work that it would evaluate more terminated aid projects. Evaluation should concentrate on fewer but more comprehensive evaluations of aid within certain sectors. The Board also recommended evaluations to include analysis of relations between costs and achieved results. This recommendation should be seen in relation to a very weak tradition within the Agency, as well as the Board, to emphasise quantitative analysis like cost-benefit or cost-effectiveness analysis in project appraisals and in evaluation studies. Finally, the Board also wanted evaluations – as far as possible – to look into the long-term impact of aid projects on the poorer sections of the population, even when they are not the direct target groups of the project [*DANIDA, 1986: 11*].

The above objectives and guidelines for evaluations relate to the bilateral share of the aid programme. For the approximately 45 per cent of the total aid budget allocated through the international organisations, the DANIDA policy has been to follow the work of the respective organisations' evaluation units closely. The condition, operation and reporting of these units are supposed to indicate the organisations' quality consciousness and results. The Agency has now commissioned a study of the multilateral aid, and the field effectiveness of the organisations through which it is distributed, seen in relation to Danish aid objectives and policies [*DANIDA, 1988b: 108*].

The DANIDA Evaluation Unit: Before 1982, the operational divisions drafted terms of reference for the evaluations and selected evaluation teams including members independent of the evaluated activity, either from inside or outside the Agency.

The evaluation unit, established in 1982, is separated from the operational divisions, but its independence is limited by its location within the administrative hierarchy, as indicated in Figure 1. It is placed within the normal command structure of the DANIDA and has no separate reference to either the Board, the Minister or other political bodies. On the other hand, the unit is strategically well placed within the DANIDA structure in the Secretariat, responsible for general policy formulation and development.

The unit prepares a rolling three-year programme for the evaluation work which is presented to the Board. The important policy features of this programme are now mentioned in the DANIDA annual report, together with major results of evaluation activities for the reporting year.

Besides preparing the general guidelines for the evaluation work, it approves the terms of reference and the composition of teams for all evaluation missions. In these tasks, the unit works together with the operational divisions and the DANIDA representations abroad when evaluations concern projects. For sectoral and thematic evaluations, the

FIGURE 1
ORGANISATION STRUCTURE OF EVALUATIONS

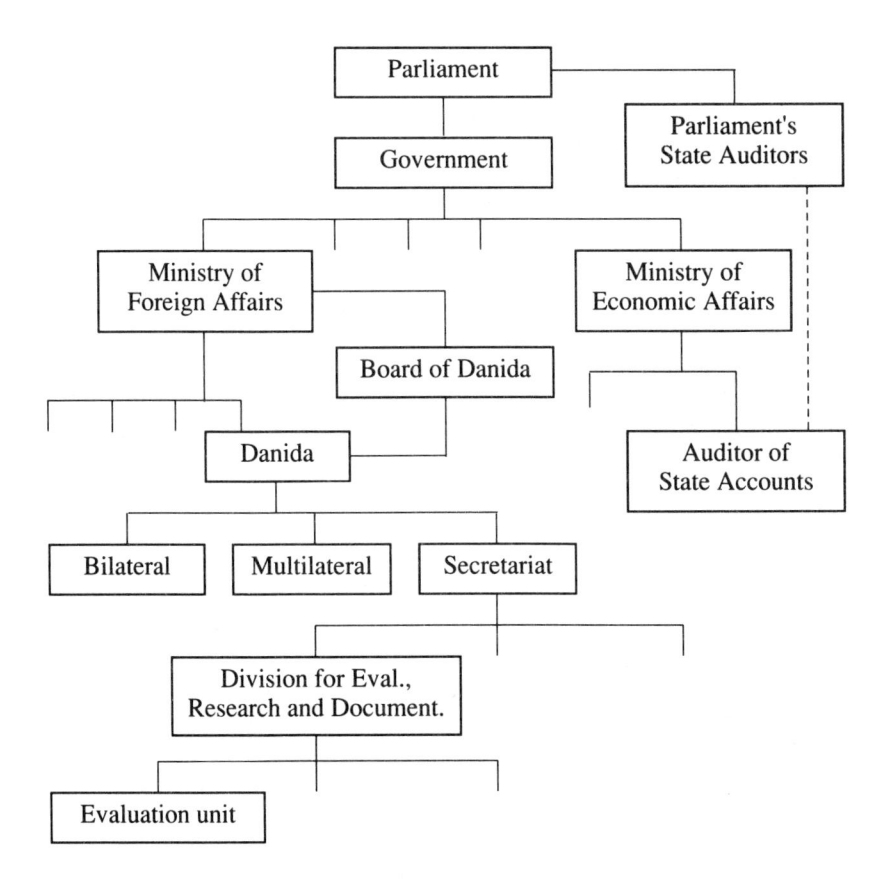

```
                    ┌─────────────┐
                    │ Parliament  │──────────────┐
                    └─────────────┘              │
                           │              ┌──────────────┐
                    ┌─────────────┐       │ Parliament's │
                    │ Government  │       │ State Auditors│
                    └─────────────┘       └──────────────┘
              ┌────────┼────────┐                │
    ┌──────────────┐      ┌──────────────┐       │
    │ Ministry of  │      │ Ministry of  │       │
    │Foreign Affairs│─────│Economic Affairs│     │
    └──────────────┘      └──────────────┘       │
              │  ┌──────────────────┐   │        │
              │  │ Board of Danida  │   │        │
              │  └──────────────────┘   │        │
              │          │         ┌──────────────┐
        ┌─────────┐      │         │  Auditor of  │
        │ Danida  │──────┘         │State Accounts│
        └─────────┘                └──────────────┘
         ┌────┼─────────┐
    ┌────────┐ ┌──────────┐ ┌───────────┐
    │Bilateral│ │Multilateral│ │Secretariat│
    └────────┘ └──────────┘ └───────────┘
                                 │
                  ┌──────────────────────────┐
                  │ Division for Eval.,      │
                  │ Research and Document.   │
                  └──────────────────────────┘
                                 │
                        ┌────────────────┐
                        │ Evaluation unit│
                        └────────────────┘
```

unit itself makes most of the preparations. Staffed with three professionals, the unit only occasionally participates directly in evaluation missions.

Aid-evaluation methods and forms: Although evaluation methods depend on the type of aid evaluated, the DANIDA's guidelines and standard Terms of Reference (TOR) for evaluations together describe how the performance of most evaluations is envisaged. The standard TOR lists the following aspects to be covered [*DANIDA, 1988b*]:

- The setting of the project
- Project preparation
- Project description
- Project implementation and performance
- Achievement of objectives, including effects and impact
- Project management
- Future operation and development of the project
- The need for further analysis
- Lessons learned.

The list indicates a very broad coverage and a descriptive way of narrating the history of a project. Central to this evaluation method is measuring achievement of stated objectives. The list includes both project effects and impact, but only a few pieces of practical advice are given on how to measure these. This is often left to the individual evaluation team and will depend on how well expected effects and impact are described in the project documents. The evaluation guideline realistically admits that measurement of impact (or effect) is 'a very expensive and difficult operation if it is to be done properly, and not all evaluations can reach this ultimate aim' [*DANIDA, 1988b: 10*]. Such impact evaluation requires information on the situation either before or without the project which needs resources and time beyond what is usually allocated. Beyond asking for cost-effectiveness, little is said about the requirement for quantitative analysis.

The above-mentioned guidelines and standard TOR focus on single project evaluations. When other types of evaluations are made, the scope and methods applied have been more or less individually designed.

For each evaluation, either a team is composed of individual external consultants or the task is given to a consulting firm or an independent institution. Professionals from the DANIDA participate in evaluations only as resource persons to the evaluation team. Normally, the evaluation teams consist of two to four persons, representing relevant technical and social science professions.

The recipient country is in most cases invited to select a representative to participate as a member of the evaluation team. Whether or not this is the case, the evaluation teams, when working abroad, are dependent on support from local authorities. For evaluations of projects or programmes in one recipient country, the team normally stays two to four weeks in the country.

In recent years, the evaluation effort has put more emphasis on sectoral evaluations, looking at activities spread out in many recipient countries and at thematic evaluations. For such evaluations, much larger resources are needed. Even evaluation of individual, but larger projects undertaken by outside institutions has been given resources and time beyond the old pattern of three or four men in three to four weeks.

For 20 bilateral aid evaluations in 1986–87, the number of man-weeks used was distributed as follows (Centre for Development Research 1987):

Man-weeks	No. of evaluations
4 or less	7
5–10	5
11–15	3
16 or more	5

In the case of evaluation teams composed of individuals, time should be added for preparation before work in the recipient country and possible finishing of a report written after return. When consulting firms are employed, the total number of weeks allocated might be included in the above figures. For more comprehensive evaluations of projects, like the Health Care and Family Welfare project in India, a large number of weeks (96) were allocated. However, in general, the average number of man-weeks per evaluation has increased fast since 1986–87.

For the terms composed of individuals, one reason for the short duration might be the practical one that the relevant and available persons cannot spend more time. This will not be the case for the consulting firms, which are prepared to spend as much time as the client is willing to pay for. However, as a man-week from a consulting firm easily costs two or three times the pay of an individual consultant, such a solution includes cost considerations.

When resources and time are limited and insufficient to measure the broader effects and impact of aid, the evaluation will either have to focus narrowly on project outputs or arrange complementary data collection and interviews to support the work of the evaluation team. These studies might often be made by local experts or consultants. This has often been the case when larger projects or more comprehensive aid programmes are evaluated. Taking such possibilities into consideration, resources for evaluations are flexible and not restrained, as the above figures might indicate.

The financial resources allocated to evaluation consist of cost of manpower allocated within the DANIDA plus a budget to cover other expenses of the evaluation work. The evaluation unit is staffed by three professionals, plus supporting office staff. To this should be added the support of other DANIDA professionals. The additional budget frame covers costs of using outside consultants and all travel expenses. There is no separate budget for these expenses. They are covered by a single budget, which also includes DANIDA's expenditures on feasibility studies and other aid-preparation activities. In 1988 the budget for all these activities was 1.9 per cent of the total aid budget or DKK 114 million. As there are only about 10–12 annual evaluations, the major share of this budget figure is used for aid-preparation activities. There is no specification of the evaluation expenditures, but it is safe to assume that they at present do not exceed DKK 20–25 million per year.

Today it is not so much financial funds for consultant fees, travel expenses, etc. which constitute a bottleneck for the evaluation work. It is more likely that the present staffing of the unit is a limitation. Taking into consideration that the three professionals are supposed to prepare, organise, digest, feedback, issue guidelines, etc., in addition to the general communication inside and outside the Agency on evaluation matters, they are at the moment only able to spend very little time on each evaluation project. In addition, the professionals in the evaluation unit are included in the general job rotation in the Agency which means that they will only spend three to four years in the unit.

Other Evaluations

A systematic evaluation outside the DANIDA of the effectiveness and efficiency of the aid programme is limited to the activities of the Auditor of State Accounts. Although there is an established tradition for development research in Denmark at the Centre for Development Research and at the universities, there are few examples of research directly focusing on an assessment of whether Danish aid works. Much of Danish development research is financed by DANIDA funds, and rather than undertaking their own evaluations of aid activities, Danish academics have tended to participate in the evaluations initiated by the Agency. There is not the same tradition as in the UK for an independent assessment of aid activities by the development research institutions.

The Auditor of State Accounts under the Ministry of Economic Affairs (see Figure 1), the official auditor of all government spending, also looks into how the aid funds are used. However, from being a rather simple auditing of the various aid projects' accounts and visits to the accountants of the project, the auditing has developed into a subject matter analysis.

EVALUATION POLICY AND PERFORMANCE OF DENMARK

Not only are the monetary flows included, but the Auditor of State Accounts now looks into whether the aims and objectives – which formed the basis for the financial allocations – are fulfilled. The material used includes review and evaluation reports, together with other documentation in the Agency. In addition, the staff of the Auditor of State Accounts make their own visits to the projects for collection of additional information. Today a separate section of the Auditor of State Accounts looks exclusively into the aid spending.

The provision for extending the scope of work into the non-accounting subjects and the qualitative aspects is found in the Law on State Auditing of 1975, where it is said that not only shall the accounts be audited, but also there shall be an evaluation of whether sufficient consideration has been given to the economic administration of the funds. In relation to the aid programme, the state auditors will look into whether the Agency has been sufficiently efficient in its administration and implementation of the aid activities. The auditors will, in particular, see if there have been deviations from objectives stated in the project documents forming the basis on which funds have been sanctioned.

As these evaluations are not discussed further in the sections below, some information is also given here on capacity and performance. The division in the State Auditor's Office dealing with DANIDA's fund is staffed with two or three social science graduates (economics or law) and three or four auditors. They are normally in the division for four to five years and their experiences with developing countries and development problems are in most cases obtained during this period through contacts with the DANIDA and on visits abroad [*Leif Grünfeld, 1988: 40*]. The staff is responsible for carrying out the investigations, since consultants are not used. The reports can deal with a single project or cover a broader area of the aid programme.

The strength of the investigations made by the State Auditor's Office, when it goes beyond auditing of accounts, is its total independence in forming opinions and its influence on public opinion, as all reports are freely available. Independent consultants, individuals as well as companies, used by the DANIDA for evaluations, may sometimes think of getting the next job and their terms of reference will, in any case, always be given by the Agency. The awareness of the press of the reports from the State Auditor's Office has made it possible in the public debate to raise a number of important issues in a very direct and concrete way. The fact that these issues are often critical of the Agency's work is no surprise, as this is more or less the nature of an auditing institution.

However, the independent auditing institution also has important limitations from an evaluation point of view. The State Auditor's Office has quantitative as well as qualitative limitations in making analyses of the aid activities. The staff have normally little experience of developing countries and are not professionally trained in development studies. While the auditors can look at efficiency in relation to output and possible effects, professional evaluations should also be able to give explanations of how and why the effects and impact of aid activities arise. Also the auditors have to work within the framework of stated objectives and resource allocations – to be 'immanent', as Kim Forss might term it, [*Forss, 1985*] – while there will often be a need for evaluations with a 'transcendent' approach, in which criteria are taken from the general theory and hypotheses of development.

With respect to the purpose and objective of the work of inquiry by the State Auditor's Office, on the one hand, and the DANIDA's evaluations, on the other, there are some confusions and misconceptions. From the law on auditing it is obvious that the State Auditor's Office is not only supposed to control public aid funds in a technical sense, but also to have the broader obligations of providing accountability and information on efficiency. But when the Auditor's Office finds that its inquiries have the objective – through demonstration of shortcomings in the Agency's administration of the programme – of improving future aid, while the Agency's own evaluations are looked upon as technical investigations mainly to suggest solutions for the project concerned, this is a fatal misconception.[6] Should that be the case, the aid programme would be in trouble as to how to make policy changes based on experiences well-founded in sound development practice and theory.

On the difference between 'evaluation' and 'auditing', the DANIDA guidelines of 1988 find it related to the aim of analyses where the Agency is primarily concerned to learn about the factors which led to either success or failure of a particular activity presented in a balanced manner. Here, audits differ, as they are 'concerned rather with identifying errors and shortcomings in the use of funds. Many evaluation reports have had the same bias, thus misrepresenting the aid effort and inviting negative mass media coverage' [*DANIDA, 1988b: 7*].

IV. EVALUATION PERFORMANCE

The DANIDA's evaluation unit prepares annually a three-year current plan for evaluations for presentation to the Board. One target has been to undertake about 30 evaluations and major project reviews each year. Before, the distinction between major project reviews and evaluation of ongoing projects was not clear in the DANIDA terminology. Now, reviews are initiated by the country offices concerned, while the evaluation unit is only responsible for evaluations. Since the single evaluation became more comprehensive, the target for evaluations has been limited to around 10–14 per year. The evaluation unit now operates with the following types of evaluations [*DANIDA, 1988b*]:

- Evaluations of ongoing projects (which is different from project reviews)
- Completion and *ex-post* evaluations
- Sector evaluations
- Thematic evaluations and special studies.

For the period after the DANIDA evaluation unit was established in 1982 to the end of 1987, a total of 170 evaluations has been made. Table 1 gives the distribution of these evaluations with regard to type of evaluations and forms of aid divided, into the periods before and after 1986, when the evaluation unit under the Agency's new structure was included in a separate division. The period as a whole, that is, after 1982, is characterised by significant developments in aid policies and changes in the DANIDA's structure after the inquiries mentioned above.

The number of bilateral grant project evaluations should be seen in relation to a total of about 250 ongoing projects in 1983. The number of active loan agreements was 35 also in 1983, comprising roughly 150 projects financed under these loan agreements. As the two forms of bilateral aid – untied grant (technical assistance) projects and tied loan/grant (investment) projects – have traditionally consumed almost equal amounts of funds, it is clear that the untied aid projects have been much more intensively evaluated than the tied aid projects. One reason is that the DANIDA has been more closely involved in the formulation, implementation and administration of these projects, compared to the tied aid, where these aspects have been left more to the recipient government and the Danish suppliers.

Evaluation of tied aid, where Danish suppliers have had major responsibilities for project performance, must also be regarded as a much more sensitive issue. A critical evaluation can easily be regarded as harmful to commercial interests by the supplier. As tied aid, until some years ago, was managed by an office separate from the country offices for untied grant aid in the DANIDA, there was little common interest and tradition in dealing with the two types of aid in the same way. While interest in aid effectiveness was more the concern of offices working on untied aid projects, the relation to Danish suppliers was more pronounced for the tied aid. This has been made painfully clear in a recent sector evaluation of land-based, fishery-support facilities. A main recommendation is to discontinue the procedure of starting project preparation with given

TABLE 1
DANIDA EVALUATION 1982–87

	1982–85	1986–87
1. Bilateral grant project[1]		
(a) Stipulated mid-term evaluations and major project reviews	48	7
(b) Evaluations related to extension of the project	17	4
(c) *Ex post* evaluations/project extension not verified	17	8
2. Bilateral tied aid	11	5
3. Multi/bi projects and programmes[2]	25	18
4. Programmes[3]	3	6
5. Thematic and cross-cutting issues	0	4
6. NGO aid activities[4]	12	1
Total	122	53

Source: DANIDA list of evaluations (without categories)

Notes:
1. The distinction between (a), (b) and (c) has been made mainly on the basis of project lists in DANIDA's annual reports. The category also includes bilateral-grant, non-project aid and Nordic aid activities.
2. Multi/bi is here defined as aid to which the DANIDA contributes funds, but where a multilateral organisation is responsible for implementation.
3. Includes global or general (e.g. technical assistance experts) aid activities, both under bilateral and multi/bilateral programmes.
4. Aid activities to which the DANIDA contributes funds, but a Danish NGO is responsible for implementation.

input (Danish supplies) rather than with objectives and identified constraints [*DANIDA, 1989*]. As mentioned above, the Agency does not provide tied loans any longer. Instead, it has a target whereby 50 per cent of the bilateral grant aid shall be used on Danish supplies of goods and services. Tying is therefore not fixed to specific projects, but to the total bilateral aid budget.

A significant change is the decline in mid-term evaluations in 1986–87. One explanation is that major project reviews are no longer regarded as evaluations. Instead, evaluation of cross-cutting issues has been introduced in recent years. It is also worth noticing the rather large number of multi/bi aid evaluations – much larger than the number of bilateral tied aid evaluations. In most cases the initiative to evaluate the multi/bi projects is taken by the respective international organisation, but a DANIDA representative will often participate. Sometimes the Agency itself will ask for evaluations and there is no doubt that the increased number of multi/bi project evaluations is a sign of greater concern in the Agency, particularly about the UN organisation's effectiveness. The Agency has now decided to make a more general assessment of the field effectiveness of multilateral organisations and to find indicators for current monitoring. A recent report from the Auditor of State Accounts has been very critical of surveyed multi/bi projects and recommends the Agency to be more active when projects are prepared [*Rigsrevisionen, 1989*].

The figures in the table above, however, do not sufficiently reveal the strong tendency in recent years to use more resources on evaluations, covering broader aspects and general themes, sometimes covering several activities in different countries. Examples here are not only a cross-cutting exercise based on evaluation reports on aspects related to women, environment and sustainability, but also larger evaluations of technical assistance experts and the role of women in aid projects. Sectoral evaluations are also taken up in, for example, an *ex-post* evaluation of support to the dairy sector in India over a long period, and a global evaluation of support to onshore fishery activities. The recently announced interest in evaluation, dealing with general development issues, has therefore already been founded in practice.

V. EVALUATION RESULTS AND FEEDBACK

Results

A discussion of the results of the evaluations and how they are used has to be related to the particulars of the aid programme. Two points stand out as particularly relevant in this regard.

The first relates to *the procedures* for project implementation that are applied by the DANIDA. As noted, a very large proportion of the project evaluations have not been *ex-post* evaluations but rather evaluations made when projects are extended or entering a new phase not covered by the original agreement. In these cases, the performed evaluations are either an element in the implementation of the project of interest to project management rather than to a wider target group within the aid community, or they are a phase in the formal procedures which is necessary in order to bring a continuation of the project forward in the new project cycle. Unless a project has been evaluated, it is difficult to bring a proposal for its continuation to the Board.

Also in this case, the results of the evaluations are mostly an instrument for decisions to be made by the Agency and its Board concerning the evaluated project. Of course, such evaluations can also provide experience for other projects and can be used in relation to policy issues, but this is rarely the main purpose. It can be seen that the results of these evaluations focus on aid delivery issues and project output rather than on impact. The evaluations can, of course, look into whether planned project activities and stated indicators have been achieved, but they will hardly be able to measure whether the project has been a success in relation to its overall and often long-term objectives.

The second point relates to *the orientation and composition* of the bilateral aid programme. Very few bilateral DANIDA projects financed by untied grants have been investments only in productive activities where efficiency of production has been the main concern. Many projects have been either in social services, training or provision or extension of other indirect services to production. In addition, aims and objectives have been broadly defined. These features may explain why the Agency has only made little use of quantitative economic analysis of projects, both in appraisals and evaluations. Only in some instances for the tied loans (now grants), where Danish companies have supplied turn-key project solutions, has an effort been made to calculate the projects' internal rate of return. The evaluations can therefore not tell by a single quantitative indicator whether a project has been a success or a failure in relation to either *ex-ante* expectations or an acceptable rate of return. Evaluations normally conclude in arguments 'pro and con' for a project's success.

On the basis of such often vague indicators, the DANIDA's own account of evaluations (of 30 projects) shows that 47 per cent of the projects have more than fulfilled the objectives, while 23 per cent have just reached them, and 30 per cent have not achieved stated objectives [*Administrationsdepartementet, 1986*]. This result is surprisingly close to what Cassen [*1986*] quotes as the result from other agencies.

However, in the enquiry into the DANIDA's structure, the consulting firm analysed a number of reports from the State Auditor on DANIDA bilateral aid projects, and calculated that only 29 per cent had fully achieved the objectives [*Administrationsdepartementet, 1986*]. About 59 per cent of the projects had only partly fulfilled the objectives. The main shortcomings were significant delays, less impact than expected, and lack of poverty orientation. The remaining 12 per cent of the projects had very low objective fulfilment, the main reasons being that they were either not initiated or their general development impact was lacking.

There might be some truth in the above, rather vague indications, but the State Auditor tends to judge projects harder than the DANIDA's own initiated evaluations. Also, the projects surveyed by the auditors do not represent a random sample. However, interpretation of project performance varies. The State Auditor, for instance, emphasises project-implementation delays as failures, while the DANIDA evaluation might tend to say that the original project-implementation schedules were too optimistic. Earlier short project periods might have been suggested with the intention of getting the project easily approved. The purpose of evaluations should then be to convince decision-makers to sanction projects with a longer and more realistic time horizon.

When comparing the results of the Danish aid evaluations with those of other agencies, not only the sectoral composition should be taken into account, but also the general poverty orientation of Danish aid. Particularly the bilateral, untied aid is concentrated on the poor countries and poor people within those countries.

Whether evaluations give material to indicate a relationship between efficiency and poverty focus has not been investigated, but the DANIDA investigation assumes a negative relationship [*Administrationsdepartementet, 1986, Vol. 2: 11*]. The impression is that the individual project evaluation rarely goes beyond an effort to document whether the aid reaches the intended target groups. That Danish aid has a particular poverty focus is not reflected in the general evaluation guidelines. The extent to which terms of reference for an evaluation include poverty aspects will therefore normally depend on how the poverty focus is integrated in the project formulation and design, particularly in the objectives and the definition of target groups.

While general or cross-project experience with respect to aid reaching the target groups, defined as poorer sections of the population, has been given little attention, the interest in gender aspects has been more articulated also in relation to evaluations. As part of the DANIDA's strategy of dealing with women as active participants in development, an evaluation of the women's aspects of six projects has been made [*Whyte, 1987*]. Although the evaluation showed an increasing awareness of gender issues in the project cycle, the impact part showed very little achievement of what was regarded as women's main interests in development.

Feedback

From a rather loose practice in which the evaluation reports and their distribution were main feedback elements, a more comprehensive routine has developed since the establishment of an evaluation unit. Earlier, an important part of informal feedback was the DANIDA staff participation in evaluations. It was hoped that this would spread evaluation experiences to other aid activities.

For the individual evaluations, the following feedback procedures are now normally followed:

- By the end of the stay in the recipient country, the evaluation team reports the main findings and conclusions or recommendations to the local DANIDA office and to recipient country authorities.
- The draft of the evaluation report, after comments have been received from the recipient country and the DANIDA office, is discussed in the Agency with representatives from the evaluation unit, the responsible operational unit and professionals from the technical division.
- The final report is distributed. Earlier, the reports were not freely available, but only distributed within the Agency, and sent to the recipient government. Now, with the consent of the recipient government, the evaluation report is freely available on request. The reports are not published for wide distribution. The regular recipients of the evaluation reports include the Chairman of the Board, the State Auditor and sometimes other donor agencies.
- A summary of evaluation reports (three or four pages) is drafted for all evaluations by the evaluation team and distributed widely, for example, to the press.

The responsibility of following up the individual evaluations will normally be with the operational units.

Feedback of more general experiences of the evaluation work includes:

- Annual reporting from the evaluation unit to the Board. A chapter on evaluation experiences and plans is now included in the DANIDA's annual report.
- Revision of the DANIDA's guidelines for appraisal, monitoring and evaluation.
- Internal staff-training courses.

To these more regular and formal ways of communicating findings and recommendations from the evaluation work, should be added the more informal ways which primarily arise when people meet and talk, and afterwards formulate new activities and policies. Some may find such informal communications more significant than the formal procedures and the reports on the shelves. Having the evaluation unit located within the Agency and the staff participating in evaluation teams increases the possibilities of informal feedback. An example – on the edge of informal and formal – of feedback for policy formulation has been seen when the head of division for the evaluation unit was a member of the consulting board for the working groups, formulating the strategic plan for the DANIDA, although the document, as mentioned does not say anything on the evaluation work.

From the general feedback systems it is difficult to get an idea of the impact of the evaluations on the policy-making. But the following observations point to some limitations:

- First, it is a question of how well-suited the formulation of the findings of the individual evaluation report is to make an impact on the general policy-formulation level. If mainly concerned with problems of on-going projects, the value might be limited.
- Second, in the organisational and hierarchical structure, the evaluation unit does not have direct access to the top decision-makers, represented by the head of the DANIDA, the Board, the Minister of Foreign Affairs and the Parliament's Finance Committee. In some other countries it is seen that the evaluation unit has this direct access. On the other hand, the unit is well placed within the secretariat to make an impact on the DANIDA's management. However, these possibilities should still be seen in relation to the meagre manpower resources of the unit.
- Third, the proposed information data-bank on evaluation experiences and results, mentioned by the last government committee, has not been established.[7] The need for such a data-bank should be seen in relation to the relatively quick staff rotation in the Agency. Guidelines do, to a certain extent, work as a substitute for an information bank, but in its absence concrete formulation of aid goals and activities might tend to follow the group of people which at a certain time is associated with the specific aid initiative, be it a project or another activity.[8] With the large number of reports arising in aid agencies, there will be a need for more systematic information retrieval if the mass of collected information and experiences is to be used in a systematic manner.

The recipient country's authorities receive a draft of the evaluation report and can make comments for the final version of the report. It seems to be the experience that very often no or very few comments are received. The evaluation team will have had discussions with the concerned officers at various levels of the administration before leaving the recipient country. However, only little information is available on how the final report is distributed in the recipient country and how it is used. Of course, when the report is made in relation to an ongoing or to an extended project, the report is included in discussions and negotiations on the project. Experience shows, however, that sometimes the circulation of evaluation reports has been limited, and the results of the evaluation have not even reached the local project authorities or the field staff project officers.

There is little information on how the evaluations initiated by the Agency penetrate into the recipient governments' own evaluation units, and how the results are used in their feedback systems. Seen from the recipient country's point of view, an inquiry into the issues of the value of aid evaluations might be wanted. As demonstrated in two separate evaluations, one made by the Agency and the other by the local authorities of the same DANIDA-assisted project, as early as 1971 and 1969, there were substantial differences in the issues and problems discussed [*Schaumburg–Müller, 1972*].

Apart from what happens within the management of the single project, there is no evidence of a systematic effort to improve monitoring and evaluation capacity in recipient countries, as recommended in 1982 by the government committee. The need might vary from country to country, but certainly there is one in some of the weaker administrations.

VI. CONCLUSIONS

Inspired by Cassen, we should ask: 'Does evaluation pay?' Unfortunately, the answer is not given by the analysis made here. However, it would in any case be very difficult to answer a question like that, particularly in a period when so many crucial parameters in aid policy and practice have changed significantly, as has been the case with Danish aid over the last decade. In a way, these changes can be seen as a result of evaluations of the aid programme in a broad sense. The expansion of the evaluation activities – particularly into all areas of the aid programme – can at least also be interpreted as a realisation of the fact that evaluation pays.

Assuming that evaluation does pay, the question would then be: 'How much evaluation?' When is there an increasing return and when a decreasing one? If a system has been established to make good qualitative evaluation reports, but the resources are lacking to make appropriate use of experience and results, there is an opportunity for obtaining an increasing return, provided that steps are taken to fill in the gaps. This is likely to be the case with the Danish evaluation programme at present. The scope and ambition for the single evaluation has expanded much more than the manpower in the unit, and it might be difficult to make proper use of the results. In any case, with the rather limited resources allocated to evaluations in DANIDA, the point of decreasing returns is unlikely to be close. But the question remains, where is it best to use additional resources?

Beside these benefit-cost considerations, our analysis leads to the following conclusions, characterising the present evaluation of aid in Denmark:

1. The scope and ambition of evaluation work within the DANIDA has changed significantly in the last four or five years since the establishment of an evaluation unit. The background for these changes has been the recommendations given by the latest aid inquiry committee for strengthening the Agency's evaluation work. Also within the administration, the need has been felt to have more thorough evaluations, in order to maintain the quality of aid when the budget increases. At the political level, that is, from Parliament there has been little interest in or demand for the formulation of evaluation policies and procedures, although the politicians have sanctioned increasing funds for aid. Political debates on aid policies and aid effectiveness have therefore not been based very much on actual information and experience drawn up for aid evaluations.

2. With the establishment of the evaluation unit, evaluations have been separated from the operational divisions. Located within the Secretariat Division, the evaluation unit is close to policy-planning and strategic formulation of the aid programme at an administrative level.

    The location of evaluation work is a result of weighing various interests. The present location does not give the unit an independent status outside the DANIDA's administration, with a greater possibility of influencing the political level. Being within the DANIDA structure, it has, however, close access to the top management level, and evaluation work can benefit from the daily formal and informal communication with the operational units. The evaluation work is less in danger of being separated from practical, aid-implementation problems. As interest at the political level in the formulation of aid policies and evaluation of the programme is not pronounced, but to a large extent left to the Agency's own management, the present location is suitable. Guarding the necessary independent status of the evaluation work is then primarily left to the Board, which reviews the evaluation programme and results. In addition, the Auditor of State Accounts acts independently.

3. The benefits of evaluations are closely linked to the feedback system. Such feedback messages have various forms and receivers. At the top level, feedback can go to those who formulate aid policies. It can also be expressed through the general procedures and guidelines which are formulated for implementation of the aid programme. At the bottom level, results of evaluations can be fed into formulation and appraisal of new aid projects and aid programmes.

With the evaluation unit located within the DANIDA, it is not easy for outsiders to evaluate the internal feedback procedures, and the impact they have on planning and policy-making. However, in respect of improvement of formal procedures and guidelines, the evaluation unit has significantly strengthened the Agency's performance. This is marked by improvement of guidelines for both evaluations and appraisals, by procedures for how evaluation results are disseminated inside and outside the Agency, and by formulation of development issues which need consideration in relation to the aid programme.

While dissemination of results from evaluation work has improved, the handling of the huge amount of experience and information, which is the collective result of many evaluation reports, is still weak. Information technology is available for that purpose, but the DANIDA has until now not made sufficient use of the technology to systematise its bank of knowledge and information. This requires careful design of how information is organised and fed into a databank, and considerations of how useful tools can be designed for policy and programme managers to make use of the information. In addition, those responsible for formulation, planning, appraisal, implementation and evaluation of aid ac tivities should also be able to make use of the information bank.

If proper information technology for evaluation experiences is established, this would also make it possible to exploit the international linkages which have been established for evaluations. The DANIDA's evaluation unit has been an active partner in the DAC Expert Group on Aid Evaluation in the OECD. For the DANIDA, this has been a very strong professional background and inspiration for improving the work of the evaluation unit. Strengthening of procedures and guidelines has its background in the work of the Expert Group. If, however, experience and information from other agencies' evaluation work is to be used directly by aid managers and professionals, the use of modern information technology will be necessary. With the very limited staff resources, which are set aside for evaluation at present, there is not enough capacity to design and implement a proper evaluation infor mation system.

4. Today, Danish aid activities are on a systematic basis evaluated both by the DANIDA's evaluation unit and by the Auditor of State Accounts and Parliament's State Auditors. Politically, it is unlikely that the auditors' evaluation will not continue, and from a professional point of view, it would be unfortunate if the DANIDA suspended its evaluations. Both forms are likely to continue. The auditors' evalua-

tions have succeeded in catching the headlines in the press and getting the ear of the politicians, and they constitute a healthy competition to the DANIDA's own efforts. But they are no substitute. The office of the Auditor of State Accounts does not have sufficient continuity and professionalism to bring about the necessary insight as to how aid works, and to raise development issues for the management of aid programming and implementation. What auditors bring are often well-known procedural problems. Their main functions will be control of budget allocation in a broad interpretation. The DANIDA's evaluation must therefore continue to go deeper into the substance of how aid works, and translate that knowledge into management tools for improving aid performance.

5. Involvement and integration of recipient countries was set as an objective for the DANIDA's evaluation work by the latest aid inquiry committee. This had not previously been the case, and the question is whether it matters.

Recipient countries need evaluation of development efforts as much as donor agencies do. But objectives and agenda for evaluations differ. The recipient countries have an interest in seeing whether their general policies and programmes work and need not be so interested in single donor-supported activities. Recipient country representatives function more as resource persons than evaluators with their own agenda when they participate in the DANIDA evaluations.

As long as its evaluations are project-dominated, participation by recipient countries will mostly benefit the DANIDA. As the Danish aid programme is small in relation to most countries' development programmes, general sectoral and programming issues of interest to recipient-country evaluators may be few. Should the Agency assist in strengthening recipient countries' evaluation capacity, a more direct institutional approach will be needed than the basic participation in the Agency's evaluation teams. As most evaluations are made by independent consultants or consulting firms, there could be an increasing recruitment of consultants from recipient countries, or establishment of true joint-venture evaluation teams.

NOTES

1. About 6.85 Danish Kroner (DKK) were equal to 1 US$ in December 1988.
2. This definition is close to the DANIDA definition of evaluation [*DANIDA, 1988b*: 1] and in line with OECD's terminology [*OECD, 1986: 15*].

EVALUATING DEVELOPMENT ASSISTANCE

3. One of the researchers in the evaluation team has since described the events following the publication of the evaluation [Jørgensen, 1972].
4. A consultant had made a report for the DANIDA on how the evaluation work could be organised and strengthened.
5. Latest revised issue: DANIDA [1988b], Project Guidelines, Evaluation, Copenhagen.
6. See Leif Grünfeld [1988: 40]. The author is head of the division in the State Auditor's Office dealing with the DANIDA.
7. A general project data-bank, intended also to include information on evaluation, is now under establishment in the DANIDA.
8. This impression is found in the study by J.-C. Wandel [1988: 72–3] which is based on interviews.

REFERENCES

Administrationsdepartementet, 1986, *DANIDA undersøgelsen*, Copenhagen.
Betænkning nr. 565, 1970, *Betænkning om Danmarks samarbejde med udviklingslandene*, Copenhagen.
Betænkning nr. 958, 1982, *Betænkning om principperne for den danske bistand til udviklingslandene*, Copenhagen.
Cassen, Robert and Associates, 1986, *Does Aid Work?* Oxford: Clarendon Press.
Centre for Development Research, 1987, 'Crosscutting Dimensions in Danida Evaluation Reports: Sustainability, Women and Environment', Copenhagen (for official use only).
DANIDA, 1986, *Danmarks deltagelse i det internationale udviklingssamarbejde*, Copenhagen.
DANIDA, 1987, *Danmarks deltagelse i det internationale udviklingssamarbejde*, Copenhagen.
DANIDA, 1988a, *Strategisk Planlægning, DANIDAs handlingsplan*, Copenhagen.
DANIDA, 1988b, *Project Guidelines; Evaluation*, Copenhagen.
DANIDA, 1989, 'Evaluation Report, Cooling, Cold Storage and Distribution of Fish, Sector Evaluation', Synthesis report, Copenhagen.
Folke, Steen, Jørgensen, Ib and Jakob Kjær, 1969, *An Evaluation of the Danish Mysore Project*, Copenhagen: Mellemfolkeligt Samvirke.
Forss, Kim, 1985, *Planning and Evaluation in Aid Organizations*, Stockholm.
Grünfeld, Leif, 1988, 'Statens kontrol', nr. 1., *Udvikling* 3.1988.
Jørgensen, Ib, 1972, 'Mysore-evalueringen i retrospekt', *Den ny Verden*, no. 4, 7 årgang.
OECD, 1986, *Methods and Procedures in Aid-Evaluation*, Paris.
Rigsrevisionen, 1989, 'Beretning til statsrevisorerne om 11 dansk finansierede multi-bi projekter i en række udviklingslande', Copenhagen.
Schaumburg-Müller, Henrik, 1972, 'Problemer ved evaluering af faglig bistand', *Den ny Verden*, no. 7, 7 årgang.
Udenrigsministeriet, 1981a, 'An Evaluation of the Danish Government Loans to Egypt and Proposals for Future Evaluation Procedures for the Danish Loan Programme'. Report submitted to the Board of International Development Co-operation by an independent commission, Copenhagen.
Udenrigsministeriet, 1981b, 'Beretning fra det af styrelsen den 15. april 1981 nedsatte underudvalg til gennemgang af evalueringsrapport vedrørende statslånsbistanden til Egypten', Copenhagen.
Wandel, Jens-Christian, 1988, 'Evaluering set ud fra to organisationsteoretiske perspektiver – et case-studie af DANIDA'.
Whyte, Susan Reynolds, Østergaard, Lise, Jespersen, Claus Branner, and Ann-Belinda Steen, 1987, 'Women in DANIDA – Supported Development Projects: An Evaluation', Copenhagen.

5

Evaluation Policy and Performance in the Federal Republic of Germany

STEFAN A. MUSTO

I. INTRODUCTION

Evaluation is procedure at the interface between fact-finding and value judgements, scientific inquiry and administrative decision-making, a learning process and a justification exercise. Some of the definitions offered by the relevant literature accentuate the cognitive function of evaluation. Jahoda and Barnitz write: 'Evaluation is an effort to learn what changes take place during and after an action programme, and what part of these changes can be attributed to the programme.'[1] In the *Handbook of Development Policy* edited by Besters and Boesch, evaluation is defined as 'a set of scientific measures taken to find out the effects of development projects and programmes.'[2] Other authors emphasise the role of evaluation in the administrative process relating to the allocation of resources. According to Klineberg, ' . . . evaluation is a process which enables the administrator to describe the effects of his programme and thereby to make progressive adjustments in order to reach his goals more effectively.'[3] In the framework of the development policy of the Federal Republic of Germany (FRG), evaluation is considered as a systematic inquiry into the efficiency of action programmes in order to provide the information necessary to guide administrative decisions with regard to these action programmes.[4]

Accordingly, evaluation implies an uneasy relationship between cognitive and normative statements, scientific capabilities and administrative requirements, objective knowledge and subjective convictions or interests. Contradictions and conflicts can never be ruled out when the criteria of scientific research into the effects of controlled social change are to be reconciled with the criteria for making transparent and justifying administrative decisions to legislative bodies, courts of audit, taxpayers and public opinion. Therefore, evaluation is a highly sensitive procedure subject to the forces exerted by divergent, conflicting interests located at the interface between science and politics, sincerity and consideration, factual validity and normative responsibility. For this reason a portrayal of the role of evaluation in development policy must take account of both aspects: the function discharged by evaluation as an integral part of the administrative process of decision-making and the function which evaluation has acquired in the advance of scientific knowledge.

The scope of the following article cannot allow for account to be taken of all aspects of evaluation research, least of all of those relating to its underlying scientific theory and a critical assessment of its methodologies. It is therefore confined to presenting and analysing the evaluation system as it is applied in the practical work of development co-operation in the FRG. The two final sections, however, shed light on a number of fundamental problems and raise a number of critical points as to methodology identified from the author's experience.

II. STRUCTURE AND ORGANISATION OF GERMAN DEVELOPMENT POLICY

The responsibility for federal German aid policy rests with the Federal Ministry of Economic Cooperation. Established in the early 1950s, this Ministry was largely concerned with coordination work until 1972 but has since been fully responsible for all considerations regarding planning, principles, programmes, and the implementation and coordination of development co-operation. It administers approximately 90 per cent of West German official development assistance (ODA).

The scope for the Ministry's autonomous political decision-making is limited by the general power of imposing guidelines held by the Federal Chancellor and the specific involvement of some other ministries – particularly foreign affairs, economics and finance – in overall decision-making in the field of foreign relations and development operation. Accordingly, the Federal Ministry of Economic Cooperation must coordinate its skeleton planning for each financial year with the other ministries and the Budget Committee of the *Bundestag*.[5]

Decisions relating to development co-operation are prepared and implemented under the supervision of the Ministry of Economic Cooperation (BMZ) by a variety of legal entities in the form of parastatal institutions and by the so-called independent agencies which carry out projects in developing countries with their own and government funds. The powers held by these institutions vary and are laid down in their respective statutes and in contracts with the Federal Ministry of

EVALUATION POLICY AND PERFORMANCE OF GERMANY

TABLE 1
INSTITUTIONAL STRUCTURE OF GERMAN DEVELOPMENT POLICY

LEVELS OF DECI-SION-MAKING	INSTITUTIONS	TASKS AND COMPETENCE
Government	Federal Government: – Ministry of Economic Cooperation – Ministry of Foreign Affairs – Ministry of Economy – Ministry of Finance	Basic policy decisions
Administration	Federal Ministry of Economic Cooperation (BMZ)	Planning Basic guidelines Coordination Supervision Evaluation
Executing agencies	– Bank for Reconstruction – Agency of Technical Cooperation (GTZ) – Other specialized agencies, such as * German Volunteers' Service (DED) * German Foundation for International Development (DSE) * Society Carl Duisberg (CDG)	Implementation Consultant activities Planning and evaluation on behalf and on request of the Ministry(BMZ) Autonomy in implementing own specialised activities
Non-Governmental Organisations	– Churches – Political Foundations – Other private NGOs	Autonomous cooperation measures; partly financed or co-financed by the Ministry (BMZ)

Economic Cooperation. A simplified account of the institutional structure of federal German development co-operation is given in Table 1.

Financial co-operation measures are largely handled by the Kreditanstalt für Wiederaufbau (KfW – Bank for Reconstruction). Endowed with equity capital amounting to about 2.3 billion DM, this institution is not subject to the provisions of the credit and loan legislation but is directly accountable to the Federal Ministry of Finance. It awards grants or loans to developing countries for investment projects, provides refinancing loans for local and regional development banks and makes available non-project-tied loans in the form of commodity aid. In addition, it supports technology-transfer measures, joint ventures and also subsidiaries of German companies operating in developing countries.

Technical co-operation falls within the competence of the German Agency for Technical Cooperation (GTZ), an institution operating under private law and fully responsible for the technical planning, implementation and supervision of technical cooperation measures, for providing consultancy services for their development assistance institutions, for selecting, preparing, assigning and supporting experts, and for technical project equipment. Its activities also include the carrying out of evaluation work with its own and specially commissioned external experts.

The private-law yet fully government-funded executive or consultative agencies also include the German Foundation for International Development (DSE), which organises international seminars, the German Volunteer Service (DED), which assigns experts to developing countries, the Carl Duisberg Society (CDG), which is responsible for training professional and managerial personnel from developing countries, and a number of other organisations operating in similar fields.

Finally, mention must be made of the large number of non-governmental organisations (NGOs), whose importance in the German development co-operation effort has increased significantly in recent years. The most important among these institutions include the development agencies of the Protestant Church and the Roman Catholic Church and the sociopolitical foundations of the political parties (FES, KAS, FNS, HSS). A further two dozen private organisations operate within an associative framework known as the 'Bensheimer Kreis', thereby introducing a large measure of social pluralism in German development cooperation. Government funds are awarded to NGOs in the form of grants on the basis of individual and clearly specified project applications. Except in the case of the political foundations, each NGO is itself generally responsible for contributing at least 25 per cent of the required project funds from its own resources.

III. MOTIVES AND OBJECTIVES OF EVALUATION

Within the framework of their respective field of competence, each of the above-mentioned development co-operation organisations has a set of mechanisms and instruments for monitoring and evaluating its own activities. As the superordinate authority, however, the Federal Ministry of Economic Cooperation bears ultimate responsibility for controlling government-funded, German development co-operation activities. The Ministry has a central unit for evaluation and supervision which is located outside the regular administrative hierarchy and has a right of direct audience with the policy-making authority within the Ministry.

Although the evaluation of aid has played a significant role even from the outset, the period from the mid-1970s on has brought an increasing awareness of the need to report the success and failure of development aid to the parliament and the public at large in a generally transparent manner. The role of the central evaluation unit has therefore been constantly strengthened and expanded. Three reasons are advanced by way of explanation: (1) the Federal Government attaches increasing importance to upgrading the efficiency of development aid; (2) by presenting a differentiated view of project realities, evaluation should contribute towards promoting the learning process on development policy and raise interest in co-operation practices; (3) evaluations should create the transparency required for counteracting the currently increasing 'development pessimism' among the general public.[6] Upgrading the role of evaluation can therefore be considered as a response to the challenges represented by the lessons and experiences of the past.

In recent years the general debate on development aid has indeed been characterised by ever more strongly voiced criticism and doubt. The development optimism of the early years has given way to a more sober view, this, of course, not only in the Federal Republic of Germany.[7] The public noted with ever greater amazement that, despite an increase in aid transfers, the prosperity gap between the industrial countries and the developing countries has tended to widen rather than narrow in recent years. The increasingly urgent question was therefore: Is development aid justifiable at all? The economic crisis and the employment problems of the late 1970s and early 1980s, from which even the Federal Republic was not spared, undoubtedly did nothing to raise public interest in the concerns of the Third World. And the experts who have long been professionally involved with development projects noted with increasing concern with how much meticulousness and precision the inputs are planned, allocated and managed and with how much obscurity the outputs, the actual impacts of the measures taken, are surrounded. That which was channelled into a project passes through numerous decision-making bodies and suffices to fill innumerable document files; that which comes out of the same project is the subject of brain-racking and quibbling on the part of researchers, experts and evaluators.

The competent Ministry increased its efforts to counteract the doubts about the success and efficiency of the measures taken, remedy the information deficits on their course, identify the reasons for repeated project extensions and find out which conditions are required to produce a 'model' project.[8] It being clear that it is not enough to carry out single studies on isolated projects or programmes, the Ministry endeavoured to draw on cross-sectional analyses covering a large number of different projects in order to home in on the planning, sectoral, regional, administrative and financial conditions which determine the success or failure of certain measures. Evaluation is, therefore, supposed to be a learning process; it should at least produce well-founded indicators for generalisable statements on the conditions for development project efficiency. The evaluation guidelines of the Ministry emphasise: 'Evaluation findings lead to a learning process which helps to improve the planning, implementation and control of development aid projects. They also serve as the basis for technical guidelines to govern specific types of project or entire sectors.'[9]

IV. THE ROLE OF EVALUATION IN DECISION-MAKING

How can evaluation contribute towards increasing the efficiency of aid? The life cycle of a project consists of several phases; each of these phases calls for decisions which directly affect the project performance. Project ideas and proposals must be examined for feasibility, relevance, and financial implications; projects in the implementation phase require permanent control in order to repeatedly monitor the individual measures and adjust them to changing conditions required for success; at the end of the phase envisaged for implementation, it is time for the decision whether the project should be extended, stopped, modified, linked with other programmes or handed over to national agencies. Such decisions presuppose the existence of such information and reliable assessments.

The various types of evaluation work can therefore be assigned to specific phases in a project life cycle, and one can distinguish between (1) *ex ante* evaluation ('appraisal'), the purpose of which is to review and, if necessary, correct the original project concept and provide the information required for the allocation decision; (2) *ex inter* evaluation ('monitoring') to exert a corrective influence on decisions by the project managers during the implementation phase; and (3) *ex post* evaluation ('assessment', 'measurement of impact') to identify and assess the impacts of the project, draw the appropriate conclusions for the execution of similar or future projects and justify the results achieved *vis-à-vis* the national control bodies. A simplified schematic overview of these

TABLE 2
SIMPLIFIED SCHEME OF THE FUNCTION OF EVALUATION IN THE
DECISION-MAKING PROCESS DURING THE PROJECT LIFE CYCLE

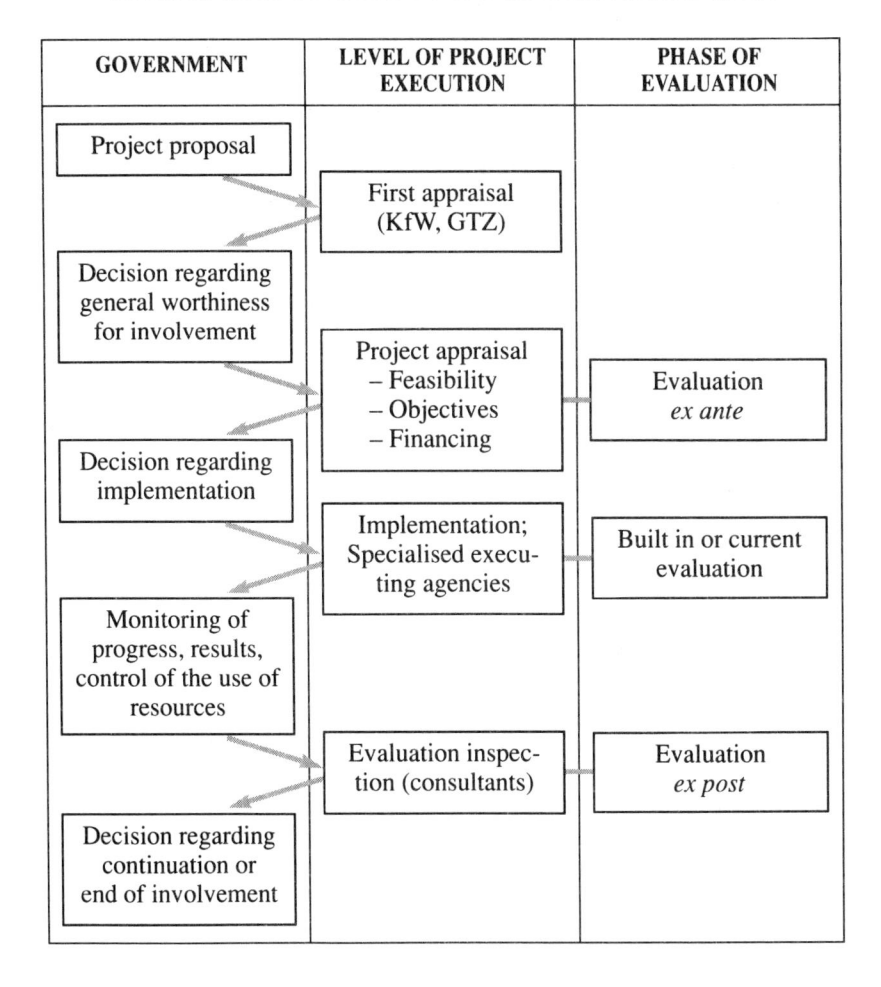

GOVERNMENT	LEVEL OF PROJECT EXECUTION	PHASE OF EVALUATION
Project proposal		
	First appraisal (KfW, GTZ)	
Decision regarding general worthiness for involvement		
	Project appraisal – Feasibility – Objectives – Financing	Evaluation *ex ante*
Decision regarding implementation		
	Implementation; Specialised executing agencies	Built in or current evaluation
Monitoring of progress, results, control of the use of resources		
	Evaluation inspection (consultants)	Evaluation *ex post*
Decision regarding continuation or end of involvement		

decision-related evaluation functions during the project life cycle is given in Table 2.[10]

Evaluation, thus, is intended to rationalise and clarify decisions on development aid. Presented in the form of analytical statements and value judgements, evaluation should provide information on whether the contextual conditions are suitable for a certain aid measure, whether the objectives set are realistic and achievable, whether the planning is adequate, the implementation and control are effective and the benefits of the project relevant to the development effort. In addition, the evaluator is required to draw up recommendations as to which decisions should be taken on certain aspects in order to increase overall efficiency.[11]

Whether or not evaluation has actually increased the efficiency of German development aid is a difficult question to answer. The staff of the competent Ministry are convinced that the evaluations carried out in recent years have indeed induced a learning process and thereby made it possible to learn from past mistakes and increase efficiency. But there are also independent experts whose own experience causes them to believe that a large number of projects have failed because of repeated corrections and improvements and unnecessary interventions in self-regulating processes.[12] No systematic research beyond the above-mentioned cross-sectional analyses has been conducted into the adjustments suggested in evaluation reports; the issue could only be resolved with the aid of an 'evaluation of evaluation'.

V. QUANTITATIVE AND QUALITATIVE DIMENSIONS OF EVALUATION

During the nine years between 1976 and 1984 the central evaluation unit of the Federal Ministry of Economic Cooperation commissioned a total of 262 evaluation studies. The main sectors concerned and the number of evaluations carried out in each are presented in Table 3.[13]

Most of these evaluations are concerned with individual projects. Since 1976, however, there has been an additional and constant increase in the number of comparative evaluations of the project series, country-specific and cross-sectional types. This shift has been justified with the claim that sampling individual projects without any basis for comparison is not sufficient for producing sound and generalisable statements on the prerequisites for the success of a development aid measure.

'Series evaluations' relate to projects in one and the same sector (for example, infrastructure, training) or projects of same type (for example short-term assignment of experts), and are intended to produce basic promotion criteria which are applicable to several projects and several countries. Such evaluations are required for drawing conclusions on the

TABLE 3
SECTORAL DISTRIBUTION OF EVALUATION STUDIES (1976-84)

SECTORS	NO. OF EVALUATION STUDIES	
	ABSOLUTE	PERCENTAGE
Agriculture, forestry, food aid, fishery	47	18
Industry, banking, mining, construction	50	19
Public services, mass media, transport and information	42	16
Education, science	58	22
Health projects	10	4
Planning, public administration	18	7
Self-help organisations	10	4
Multi-purpose projects	16	6
Other	11	4
Total	262	100

relative significance of individually country-specific, sector-specific or instrument-specific factors in generating a developmental impact.

'Country evaluations' have been carried out in numerous cases; these involve examining the efficiency of the overall aid contributed by the Federal Republic of Germany to a specific developing country. One example here is the global evaluation carried out with regard to German aid to Senegal (1980) since the commencement of cooperation here. The overall context of this African country was examined with a view to identifying the role played by the various aid instruments.

The 'cross-sectional evaluations' already referred to above are generally carried out annually. They involve examining and comparing all the evaluation reports prepared over the review year, this on the basis of a predetermined set of criteria. The purpose is to draw some general conclusions which are relevant for designing future development cooperation measures.

It is more and more frequently the case that nationals of the developing country concerned are involved in these evaluations. As the component bodies in some countries are increasingly interested in a dialogue to take place during the course of the project life cycle, joint evaluation studies have been explicitly provided for in a number of government agreements. However, involving a developing country in such evaluations presupposes that the country concerned can make available a sufficiently large manpower team for the evaluation and also communicates its interest in participation in good time to the German partner. The experience gained to date with such mixed evaluation teams has been largely positively assessed by both sides.

The central evaluation unit of the Ministry has also been keen to conduct evaluation studies jointly with international organisations in order to become familiar with the latter's operating modes and measures with a view to drawing suitable conclusions for its own evaluation work. Germany has been involved in the following cases in which the projects and programmes of international donors have been evaluated: EC (country evaluation in Africa), ILO (employment programmes), ESCAP (trade promotion projects), UNIDO (small-scale industry promotion), WHO (health projects), UNDP (country evaluation), the World Bank (agricultural projects in Africa), and the African Development Bank (dam project).[14] Such joint measures have also been valuable in comparing and contrasting the evaluation criteria and methods used by the various donor institutions and subsequently reviewing and, where necessary, improving the methodology used by the Ministry for carrying out its own evaluations.

VI. EVALUATION CRITERIA AND METHODS

Although virtually every donor country and every multilateral organisation (UN system, OECD, EC, World Bank, etc.) have their own criteria and methodology for evaluating their respective instruments of cooperation, comparison shows that they have much in common here and that the differences are relatively slight. In the case of German development policy the criteria and methods used display a marked similarity with the evaluation instruments customarily used internationally. Evaluations are carried out on the basis of a very largely standardised evaluation checklist drawn up in 1976. The method used owes much to the 'logical framework method' used by the USAID.[15] The evaluation check-list, to which the evaluation team must adhere strictly, contains three fundamentally distinct elements: (1) the general questions on the project and its environment; (2) the criteria for assessing the results of the analysis; (3) the method to be used for investigation.

(1) The general questions relate to the structural and functional con-

ditions prevailing within and around the project and the changes induced thereby. As a project can never be seen in isolation from its environment, the contextual conditions within which the project operates must be identified and their functions with regard to the project interpreted. This includes taking account of the general political and economic climate, societal power structures, legislation, and the objectives and intentions of the national public administration. Special attention should be given to analysing socio-cultural factors, as these may be of decisive importance for the success or failure of a project. A further question relates to the objectives of the project. Have the objectives been clearly defined and formulated for operational purposes? Are the objectives in any way conflicting? Have the target groups been clearly defined and are they within the reach of the project? Still other questions relate to the quality and adequacy of the project-planning. Did the planning take due account of all relevant influencing factors? Have the existing bottlenecks, teething troubles and other relevant difficulties been realistically assessed? Finally, the investigation addresses the subject of project implementation, calling for assessments of the efficiency of the project management, the counterpart inputs, the qualification level of the project personnel, the technical equipment for the project, the choice of technologies, the ongoing monitoring process, and the performance potential of the national project sponsor.

(2) The results of the investigations then have to be set in relation to the evaluation criteria proper. The evaluator is required to observe three main criteria: (a) effectiveness, that is, the extent to which the objectives of the project have been achieved; (b) cost-efficiency, that is, the relation between costs and benefits measured in operational (not necessarily monetary) terms; and (c) significance, that is, the extent to which the project has exerted an enduring relevant impact on its environment in terms of a contribution to overall socio-economic development. It is, of course, not always easy, especially in the case of the last-mentioned criterion, to find suitable indicators for measuring project impact. According to the guidelines of the central evaluation unit, a large measure of significance is deemed to be given if the project is instrumental in overcoming bottlenecks in terms of basic needs satisfaction, if it involves the target groups in the planning and implementation of the measures, if it can be integrated within a wider regional or sectoral context, and if the national project sponsor is sufficiently competent to continue operation alone after the termination of the external involvement.[16]

(3) The evaluation method originally used was the classical cost-benefit analysis. Two considerations have since induced the Ministry to restrict the use of this method; on the one hand, the considerable inputs required and, on the other, the practical difficulties involved in comparing monetary, quantitative-but-non-monetary and non-quantifiable factors and rendering these amenable to measurement and weighting in relation to each other. Drawing on the 'logical framework' method, the procedure used today is one which has the following predetermined elements: (a) definition of project inputs and outputs, goals and objectives on the basis of operationalised and reproducible indicators; (b) formulation of assumptions about causal relationships between inputs and outputs, means and ends, project goals and development strategies; (c) identification and analysis of external factors which might exert an influence on the context and configuration of these causal relationships; (d) measurement of goal achievement in terms of the indicators previously established.

This methodological procedure has proved to be fairly satisfactory in the planning phase and also in the phase for assessing the project results. A quite similar method referred to as 'target-group-oriented project-planning' (ZOPP) has been elaborated and is being used by the German Agency for Technical Cooperation (GTZ) for evaluating technical assistance projects.[17]

The limitations of this methodology are well known to the Ministry and also to experienced evaluators. There can be no doubt that measuring efficiency or establishing success is only conceivable from the viewpoint of an isolated intervention and with a view to isolated objectives. 'Overall efficiency', 'global success' and 'overall development impact' can never be definitively measurable in a causally interactive, dynamic and open socio-economic system. This implies that fundamental constraints, that is, constraints conditioned by the imperfections of the available methods and instruments, apply to every planning operation and every evaluation.[18] At the practical level, therefore, evaluation research operates with criteria and methods which cannot be considered to be complete and perfect but merely to represent satisfactory solutions.

VII. THE EVALUATOR AND HIS REPORT

Evaluations are generally carried out by independent evaluators commissioned by the Federal Ministry of Economic Cooperation. In some cases staff members from the Ministry, the authorities reporting to it or implementing agencies are also involved in the investigations. Basically, however, the Ministry is keen to ensure that ultimate responsibility for the findings of the evaluations rests with the external evaluators. The prevailing view is that an independent, neutral and interdisciplinary team is most likely to be able to present an objective, well-balanced judgement which takes due account of all relevant aspects and to formulate the corresponding recommendations.[19] The evaluators commissioned are generally commercial consultants, experts from universities and other scientific establishments or specialists from other private-sector and public-sector institutions. The central evaluation unit has an annual budget of about 3 million DM for funding evaluation activities.

The evaluation commissions to be awarded are listed annually by the Ministry in a so-called 'central evaluation programme'. Under normal circumstances they are awarded less frequently via a public invitation to tender than by direct contact with institutions and individual evaluators regarded as potentially suitable for carrying out a given study. Contracts specifying the terms of reference are concluded with the evaluators.

All the necessary formal precautions are taken to ensure that the evaluator can operate independently and freely when carrying out his work. Of course, this neutrality is subject to certain informal limitations. On the one hand, there is no absolute way of preventing evaluators, in particular, commercial consultants who rely on such commissions by profession, from emphasising in their conclusions and recommendations the need for follow-up evaluations with a view to obtaining follow-up commissions. On the other hand, in some cases it is difficult to steer a sound course *vis-à-vis* the national project sponsor and not cross the boundary between arrogance and complaisance. The evaluator is required to serve simultaneously as a scientist, an auditor, an administrative expert, a manager and a diplomat, demands which cannot always be met in full.

Even very sophisticated evaluation checklists cannot prevent the subjective premises and experiences of the evaluator from influencing the results of his investigations. Myrdal's well-known call to the effect that the expert should critically review and articulate his own premises, should stand back from his own cultural values and norms, is not easy to satisfy in practice: no researcher can 'levitate' himself out of his own activity. These are the practical limits to objectivity and neutrality, limits, though, which are set not by the administrative system governing evaluation but instead, so to speak, by anthropological constants.

At the end of the investigation in the field, the findings of the evaluation are communicated for discussion to the competent authorities in the developing country concerned. The final version of the evaluation report is also made available to the partner country. As developing countries are generally keen to ensure that the evaluation findings remain confidential, evaluation reports are not published, at least not in the case of individual project reports. In the view of the Ministry, publication might have the undesired effect of eroding the evaluator's courage to speak out openly lest he become implicated in the interplay of conflicting interests.[20] The report is, of course, made available to the competent bodies for inspection (Parliament, budget committee, cabinet, court of audit, etc.). The conclusions and recommendations are discussed in detail with the implementing agencies concerned. The Ministry undertakes an annual review to determine, on the basis of the information available, the extent to which the recommendations of each individual report have been followed and implemented.

VIII. SOME FINDINGS ON EVALUATION AND AID PERFORMANCE

It would be extremely difficult to generate exact but nevertheless generalisable conclusions regarding the performance of German development aid from the hundreds of evaluation reports in existence. The investigations carried out between 1976 and 1984 (cf. section V above) were assessed from the angle of their indications as to the future of the project under review. Accordingly, the recommendations were regarded as indicative of the quality of the project performance. It transpired that in 75 per cent of the cases investigated the recommendations called for continuation of the measure with modifications. 'Modifications', depending on the case concerned, may mean reductions, expansion, prolongation, or the introduction of conditionalities. In 15 per cent of the projects evaluated the recommendations called for continuation without modification. In ten per cent of the cases the evaluators called for the prompt termination of the project activities.[21] From this result one has the impression that the overwhelming majority of German projects in developing countries fall within the broad mid-field confines of efficiency measurement and that in principle there are possibilities of further increasing this efficiency.

A cross-section analysis of the 42 evaluation studies carried out in 1985 has been taken as the basis for a detailed assessment from the viewpoint of content.[22] Although the studies selected for this analysis were not strictly representative of all the evaluations, they do provide insight into the weaknesses, strengths, problems and accentuation to be found on the practical side of German development co-operation. Michael Bohnet summarises the findings of this cross-section analysis as follows:[23]

(1) Negative project results are most frequently found in cases where the contextual conditions, the external, political, economic and cultural

factors, were not sufficiently taken into account in the project-planning and implementation. Particularly grave problems arose in connection with projects in which the financial and manpower capacity of the national project management were not sufficiently analysed or wrongly assessed.

(2) Some weaknesses are ascribable to shortcomings in identifying the objectives and the target groups. In 40 per cent of the projects investigated the overall system of objectives was given a negative rating; in most of these cases the objectives were formulated without a previous field analysis of the problems.

(3) With regard to project-planning, clear shortcomings were identified in 50 per cent of all cases, the most important being: an inadequate data-base, absence of a thorough feasibility study, lack of concrete operational plans, no or unduly delayed adjustment to changes in the project environment.

(4) A positive judgement was forthcoming in the majority of cases with regard to implementation. The reasons given for this were mainly the adequacy of the technical equipment for the project, the qualifications of the German project personnel, and the fulfilment of the project specifications.

(5) Several weaknesses were identified and corresponding improvements suggested with regard to monitoring and control. The most important problems here concerned shortcomings in reporting and difficulties related to frequent personnel fluctuation and ill-defined areas of authority.

(6) With regard to the effectiveness criterion (goal achievement), 31 of the 42 projects were regarded as being satisfactory to good. As far as cost-efficiency is concerned (effectiveness with regard to costs), such a positive assessment could only be made in 19 cases. Examples of the problems encountered in this field include follow-up costs, over-dimensioned project endowment and in some cases the lack of quantifiable benefits. With regard to the significance criterion (development impact), 28 of the 42 projects were given a positive rating. The studies emphasised, in particular, the role of these projects in upgrading the living conditions of the target groups, utilising local resources and generating additional income and employment effects.

(7) Assessment of the projects by sector shows that the most positive effects were to be found in the fields of economic planning, public administration, education and scientific cooperation. Clear problems and shortcomings were to be found in projects related to agriculture, forestry and fishing. Assessment by region showed that the problem projects are largely concentrated in Africa, whereas those implemented in Asia were largely given a positive rating.

The Ministry and the various executing agencies are striving to learn from these and similar findings with a view to improving their future project policy. This task is made all the more difficult by the complexity, dynamic nature and singularity (that is, non-generalisability) of socio-economic and socio-cultural change processes. In the optimal case evaluations provide a 'freeze' photograph of existing circumstances; unlike a film they are hardly able to reproduce actual processes and the internal driving forces which precipitate events. Evaluations offer statements on present, momentaneous efficiency, but the conditions governing efficiency are not identical in the short and the long term. Something which is purposeful at the micro level of the project itself may be deleterious at the macro level of the national economy and vice versa; micro benefits cannot automatically be aggregated to form a macro benefit. Complex causal networks and dynamic self-reinforcing (or self-destroying) processes can hardly be planned, forecast and regulated; they are subject to mechanisms of self-regulation. This is, of course, not an argument against evaluation. Even freeze photographs are more informative than mere speculation. Seen from this viewpoint, evaluation is indeed a protracted and often frustrating operation but it is always a challenging learning process.

IX. THREE UNSOLVED PROBLEMS OF AID

As the author has had numerous opportunities over the past 20 years to carry out evaluations commissioned by the German Federal Government and other donors, it would be opportune at this juncture to outline three problem areas which his own experience indicates play a decisive role with regard to the performance of aid but which are either ignored or merely alluded to in many of the evaluation reports submitted to the Ministry. These, in his view, are the three main reasons for failure: recurrent costs, social polarisation and disincentives produced by aid.[24]

(1) Experience has shown that developing countries are only seldom able to cope with investment-induced recurrent costs. In cases where they

manage to meet their obligations, this is done at the expense of additional burdens elsewhere: the public budget, the balance of payments, or the foreign-exchange reserves. Accordingly, it is not surprising that of the projects evaluated by the author no more than some 20 per cent were found to be viable, that is, able to cover the investment-induced costs on a long-term basis. This problem is indeed a fundamental one. Projects are planned for allocating external aid; aid is used to initiate investments; the investments themselves incur recurrent costs. Since investments benefit certain sectors or subsectors, they initially create an imbalance between supported and non-supported fields. A discrepancy emerges between development in the capitalised and non-capitalised sectors; a growing disequilibrium develops between the requirement for funds to cover recurrent costs and the funds available. Aid is instrumental in generating a relative oversupply of resources without taking explicit account of the level of overall resource availability; it thus creates structural imbalances and at the same time places obstacles in the way of redressing them. Redressing these imbalances requires additional aid. The donors, in competition with each other and concerned with their 'pipeline problems', therefore approve new projects and thereby induce new costs for the future. The greater the number of projects implemented in this manner, the greater becomes the need for additional aid to cope with the additional project-induced costs. It is not easy to find a solution to this problem. One of the proposals is to calculate and take account not only of the project-specific costs but also of the macroeconomic and social recurrent costs. But even if, despite the improbability of such calculations, it were possible to forecast accurately and reliably the manifold, interacting, recurrent costs of a project over a given period of time, this would provide no compelling answer to the question whether or not the project is worth while. For the nature and quality of benefits and recurrent costs are open to various interpretations and value judgements; such judgements are ultimately political acts. If, for instance, a government wants to ensure its political survival, it will view even the highest recurrent costs for a project which serves its immediate interests as justified. This applies to governments and institutions in developing and developed countries alike; the difference is that the latter justify their action with the argument that they can afford such luxury.

(2) Our experience is that development aid fosters economic, social and regional polarisation. It has so far not been possible to fully synchronise growth and redistribution within a uniform and consistent process. Evidently, concentration effects need not be perceived as negative *per se*; egalitarianism is not necessarily the best of all ideologies and redistri-

bution not necessarily the most effective of all development strategies. No project can be of equal benefit to all citizens, but, where aid significantly contributes to the emergence of new disparities, it helps to create the very gap which it claims to close. Economic theory alone is not able to provide a satisfactory explanation for such polarisation and concentration effects. More illuminating is the assumption that the distribution of the additional resources induced by development aid depends on the internal power structures prevailing in the developing country concerned. Power structures exist, and their existence implies conflicts of interest. Regularly, the benefits of aid accrue to those who have the power to appropriate them. The motive to act thus is all the greater, the more relevant the tangible benefit. Accordingly, the polarisation effect of large-scale projects is significantly greater than that of micro-projects with only peanuts to distribute. In a social system where there is insufficient inherent dynamism, externally induced changes bring about positive (cumulative) but usually no negative (compensatory) feedback effects. Positive feedback without compensatory mechanisms triggers off cumulative processes without providing for a sufficient measure of self-regulation in the system. And where there is not a sufficient measure of self-regulation, there can be no autonomous dynamism.

(3) Finally, in many cases development aid stifles initiatives for finding one's own solutions, creates disincentives, fosters unjustified expectations and thereby has a negative effect on both the strength and the motivation of its recipients to rise to the challenge which their problems represent. Awareness of being responsible for solving a given problem breeds motivation and often creativity. Awareness that others can be called to account for one's own problems allows motivation and initiative to perish. In the latter case internal responsibility is transposed elsewhere. This strengthens governments and peoples in the Third World in their increasingly profound belief that responsibility for their future fate lies beyond their own national frontiers. The externalisation of problem-solving competence creates a strange situation: an increasing number of developing country governments have allowed or are allowing themselves to be manoeuvred into a position where they do not have to defend national interests *vis-à-vis* the donors but instead donor policies and interests *vis-à-vis* their own peoples. The international subsidy mechanisms then help to guarantee the survival of the beneficiaries but at the same time they tend to stifle both ability and willingness to undertake efforts to change the existing structural conditions. To the extent to which development aid contributes, as a side effect, to reinforce this attitude, it brings about precisely that which it is intended to prevent.

These problems imply new and difficult tasks for evaluation in the future. It is not merely a matter of the measurable effectiveness of aid, but also one of the negative effects which the aid itself induces. It is not easy to postulate whether and in what form solutions could be found for eliminating or minimising such negative effects. One could even raise the question of whether, given their essential point of departure, evaluations are even capable of solving such problems.

X. MEASUREMENTS AND SELF-REGULATION

The reasoning pattern of planners and evaluators is based on a striving to eliminate randomness; it perceives the state, the economy, and society as a functioning apparatus. According to this paradigm, the state, the economy and society are susceptible to disturbance but are repairable; they are not target-oriented *per se* but are steerable with a view to fixed objectives. This reasoning pattern is therefore used to reduce extremely complex, open and dynamic systems to relatively simple, quasi-deterministic systems. In other words, socio-cultural systems are reproduced by planners and evaluators as technical systems.

The problem here, however, is that socio-economic systems are not technical systems. Their changeableness, their dynamism does not automatically respond to deliberate technical interventions but instead to extremely complicated, non-linear mechanisms of self-regulation. This also means that the problems created by aid cannot necessarily be solved by even more aid and even better aid. The response given by aid administrations usually consists of perfecting the intervention techniques: increasing budgets, more projects, more differentiated criteria for allocation, better planning, more efficient implementation, more attentive monitoring, more accurate information systems, more sophisticated forecasting techniques, better-trained personnel, more reliable counterparts, more effective integration, improved progress control, better reporting, more efficient coordination, greater commitment. A bit more of everything and everything to be made a bit better. But such an incrementalism fails to take account of both the historical dimension of structural change processes and the interlinkage between individual actions and their implications at a higher aggregated level of system performance.

It is difficult to proceed from the view that it might be possible to pre-programme a certain desirable state in open and dynamic systems. Fredric Vester points out that even in a relatively simple game such as football, even the most detailed information on all players, the rules of the game, the conditions of the pitch, the wind situation and all other intervening factors would not suffice to allow one to predict whether or not a goal will be scored within the next six minutes.[25] Events and situations are not amenable to programming in an open system. It is the systems themselves which can expand their own ability for regulating themselves in a manner which allows for flexible and adequate reaction to unpredictable changes. Development, thus, is only to a limited extent amenable to planning; it is the upshot of a general improvement of mechanisms for self-regulation.

It is probably nonsensical to believe that certain desired characteristics of socio-economic systems can be synthesised in development laboratories. Development, whatever it may be, is not a technical operation and not a world repair workshop; instead, it is a historical process of accumulating faculties for coping with the imponderables of the future. Aid is effective to the extent to which it succeeds in improving these faculties. Undoubtedly, aid cannot initiate a development process; it can support such a process provided the latter is already in motion. But in this case, aid can only be effective if it minimises rather than maximises its own allocation costs, if it creates incentives rather than disincentives, indeed if it itself becomes an incentive for generating mechanisms for better self-regulation. If evaluation, beyond the measurement of standardised input and output categories, proves to be able to discover, describe and duly assess such self-regulating mechanisms, then it can indeed make a significant contribution towards increasing the efficiency of international development co-operation.

NOTES

1. Jahoda and Barnitz [*1955: 353*].
2. Besters and Boesch (eds.) [*1966: 1109*].
3. Klineberg [*1955: 347*].
4. Detailed analysis by Musto [*1972*].
5. A comprehensive analysis of German development administration can be found in Bendix *et al.* [*1985*].
6. See the official documentation prepared by the Federal Ministry of Economic Cooperation, Bundesministerium für wirtschaftliche Zusammenarbeit [*1986: 3*].
7. Multiple references in the same document.
8. *Idem*, p. 4.
9. *Idem*, pp. 7–8.
10. Comprehensive analyses and detailed presentation by Lembke [*1984*], Musto [*1972*], Bodemer [*1979*], Kantowsky [*1977*] and Lotz [*1984*].
11. See Bundesministerium für wirtschaftliche Zusammenarbeit [*1986: 7*].
12. Critical comments by Musto [*1987*].
13. Bundesministerium für wirtschaftliche Zusammenarbeit [*1986*], Annex. The number and types of evaluation studies prepared in earlier years could not be computed owing to the lack of systematic data.
14. *Idem*, p. 7.

EVALUATION POLICY AND PERFORMANCE OF GERMANY

15. Lotz [*1984: 296*]. See also Hedrich [*1986*].
16. Bundesministerium für wirtschaftliche Zusammenarbeit [*1986: 54–5*].
17. Analysis of evaluation methods by Lotz [*1984*].
18. See Musto [*1987*].
19. Bundesministerium für wirtschaftliche Zusammenarbeit [*1986: 7*].
20. *Idem*, p.5.
21. *Idem*, p.55.
22. The following analysis is based on Bohnet [*1987*] and the documentation in Bundesministerium für wirtschaftliche Zusammenarbeit [*1987*].
23. See Bohnet [*1987*].
24. The following comments are based on the author's own experience and subjective views; they do not represent the opinion of the German development aid administration. A more detailed presentation of these arguments was published by Musto [*1987*].
25. See Vester [*1983*].

REFERENCES

Bendix, P. *et al.*, 1985, 'Die Entwicklungspolitik der Bundesrepublik Deutschland' (working paper), Deutsches Institut für Entwicklungspolitik, Berlin.
Besters, H. and E.E. Boesch, 1966, *Entwicklungspolitik – Handbuch und Lexikon*, Berlin–Stuttgart–Mainz.
Bodemer, K., 1979, *Erfolgskontrolle der deutschen Entwicklungshilfe – improvisiert oder systematisch?*, Meisenheim/Glau.
Bohnet, M., 1987, 'Wie wirksam sind Entwicklungsprojekte?', *Entwicklung und Zusammenarbeit*, Nr.10.
Bundesministerium für wirtschaftliche Zusammenarbeit, 1976, *Zielausrichtung und Erfolgskontrolle der Entwicklungshilfemaßnahmen*, Bonn.
Bundesministerium für wirtschaftliche Zusammenarbeit, 1985, *Sechster Bericht zur Entwicklungspolitik der Bundesregierung*, Bonn.
Bundesministerium für wirtschaftliche Zusammenarbeit, 1986, *Aus Fehlern lernen – Neun Jahre Erfolgskontrolle der Projektwirklichkeit: Ergebnisse und Schlußfolgerungen*, Bonn.
Bundesministerium für wirtschaftliche Zusammenarbeit, 1987, *Wie wirksam sind Entwicklungsprojekte?*, Bonn, October.
Hedrich, M., 1986, 'Evaluation in German Development Policy', *The Courier*, No. 80, July/Aug.
Jahoda, M. and E. Barnitz, 1955, 'The Nature of Evaluation', *International Social Science Bulletin*, Vol.7.
Kantowsky, D., 1977, *Evaluierungsforschung und -praxis in der Entwicklungshilfe*, Zürich.
Klineberg, O., 1955, 'The Problem of Evaluation', *International Social Science Bulletin*, Vol.7.
Köhler, V., 1985, 'Evaluierungen wirken keine Wunder, aber . . .', *Entwicklung und Zusammenarbeit*, Nr. 6.
Lembke, H.H., 1984, *Evaluating Development Assistance Projects: Changing Approaches and the Conflict between Scientific and Administrative Requirements*, Deutsches Institut für Entwicklungspolitik, Berlin.
Lembke, H.H., 1986, 'Ökonomische Beurteilung von Projekten der Technischen Zusammenarbeit' (working paper), Deutsches Institut für Entwicklungspolitik, Berlin.
Lotz, R.E., 1984, 'Das Inspektionsreferat des Bundesministeriums für wirtschaftliche Zusammenarbeit', Hellstern und Wollmann (eds.), *Handbuch zur Evaluierungsforschung*, Berlin.
Musto, S.A., 1972, *Evaluierung sozialer Entwicklungsprojekte*, Berlin.

Musto, S.A., 1983, 'Die hilflose Hilfe: Ansätze zu einer Kritik der manipulativen Vernunft', D. Schwefel (ed.), *Soziale Wirkungen von Projekten in der Dritten Welt*, Baden-Baden.

Schwefel, D. (ed.), 1981, *Soziale Wirkungen von Projekten in der Dritten Welt*, Baden-Baden.

Vester, F., 1983, *Unsere Welt – ein vernetztes System*, Munich.

6

Aid Evaluation in the Netherlands

ENNO W. HOMMES

I. HISTORY

Aid evaluation in the Netherlands is possibly as old as aid involvement itself. In colonial times development projects were studied and on the basis of these studies new policies were formulated. But at that time the projects were not called aid projects and the studies were not called evaluation studies. Nevertheless it is important to mention them because the involvement of Dutch anthropologists, economists and orientalists in these studies in the colonies created the scientific basis on which later academic generations could build. When development assistance started in the Netherlands, a lot of knowledge about developing countries was available. The concept of development assistance started to play a role from the mid-1950s and we therefore start our story about evaluation in that period. The first decade from the mid-1950s to the mid-1960s shows a scattered interest in evaluation. In that period evaluation was much more developed in some developing countries, like India, than in the Netherlands. The evaluation of the community development programme in India started straight from the beginning in 1954. The evaluation was well organised in the Programme Evaluation Organisation.

In that period also international organisations became involved. In 1959 UNESCO published Samuel Hayes' book on 'Measuring the results of development projects'. After that, all international organisations became active and published their own handbooks. One of the latest publications is 'Methods and procedures in aid evaluation' [*OECD, 1986*].

The academic, theoretical interest in evaluation went hand in hand with the practical experiences. In the Netherlands, Dr G.J. Kruijer published his first article on evaluation in 1955 (together with Dr A. Nuis) and after that he was involved in the development of the theory on evaluation, culminating in his book on evaluation in 1969 [*Kruijer, 1969*]. His own experiences in evaluation work also started from the mid-1950s, especially in the Caribbean. My personal involvement in the develop-

149

ment of the theory on evaluation started when I was one of Kruijer's students in Amsterdam at the beginning of the 1960s.

I mentioned the institutional activities on evaluation in India and by international agencies like UNESCO because, compared to them, institutionalisation in the Netherlands was rather late. It was only in the mid-1960s that evaluation of foreign aid projects became an accepted practice and even then it took another ten years or more before, within the Ministry of Foreign Affairs, Directorate-General for Development Co-operation, evaluation was really institutionalised. (In the Netherlands the Minister of Development Cooperation functions within the Ministry of Foreign Affairs. His own ministry is called the Directorate-General for Development Cooperation (DGIS).) In 1969 we had one of the biggest evaluation operations in which the total bilateral aid programme was evaluated by an external, academic research institute. Since then we have never dared to start such an ambitious evaluation again.

From 1970 onwards there was an acceleration in the implementation of evaluation in foreign aid. There were three major reasons for this. In the first place there was a considerable increase in interest in development problems as such. This resulted in a fast growth in budgets and in an increasing complexity and number of programmes and activities, not only directly by the Ministry but also by the government-sponsored, non-governmental organisations (NGOs). The public interest in development cooperation included an interest in the objectives of aid and naturally in the results, especially of aid in the framework of bilateral aid. The second reason for the increased use of evaluation as a management tool was probably related to the fact that Jan Pronk, the Minister of Development Cooperation during this period (1973–77), had a professional background in planning and development economics and this affected the quality of the policy as well as the management of the Ministry. A third reason may have been that the more precisely the objectives of development projects were formulated, the more we were interested in knowing whether these objectives were reached. At that time especially poverty alleviation and emancipation were the topics of discussion amongst developmentalists and Mr Pronk himself was one of them. He brought clear objectives and policies to the Ministry, and he and we wanted to know whether these objectives were reached. Evaluation was supposed to be the proper tool.

But even before Mr Pronk's arrival in the Ministry, evaluation was already well accepted. Methodologies were improved and, partly under the influence of USAID experiences, staff were trained in the use of the 'logical framework' system (1972) and other techniques. Later on, we called this institutionalisation of evaluation of bilateral aid 'internal evaluation'. The concept 'internal' is a bit confusing because outsiders were also involved. 'Internal' means that these evaluations are carried out under the responsibility of the (country) desks, which are also responsible for the projects which are evaluated.

II. THE BIRTH OF THE INSPECTION UNIT

The rather leftist policy of Mr Pronk activated a critical attitude to foreign aid by some of the right-wing newspapers in the Netherlands. From time to time they published highly critical articles about the 'waste of taxpayers' money' in some Dutch-financed projects. To be prepared, Mr Pronk wanted a fast and reliable organisation within his Ministry that could inform him faster about the well-being of Dutch projects. So he established an 'inspection unit' (in Dutch: *Inspectie Ontwikkelingssamenwerking te Velde*, IOV) that was supposed to inform him more quickly and independently than the internal evaluations that were carried out by the country desks of the Ministry. Of course, the initiative to start the Inspection Unit was justified by more reasons than just the critical attitude of some right-wing papers. Also the Office of the Auditor General had published some critical observations which forced Mr Pronk to take action. But there were internal reasons too. The IOV was supposed to give much quicker answers to the question whether Dutch projects were in line with the policy Pronk had drawn up. Internal evaluations by the desks could not adequately fulfil that function, probably because their staffs were recruited in a more conservative period. Mr Pronk wanted to bypass them. At that time the main interest of the IOV was in the Dutch input, both in money and manpower. The reports were in Dutch, confidential and meant for the top of the Ministry. So in this way the Inspectorate was an inspectorate in real terms. But right from the beginning it was criticised just because of this inspection function. Inspection was a too limited concept to cover the objectives of the unit. One could also say that the name was most unfortunate because no evaluator wants to be called an 'inspector'. Inspection and evaluation cannot go hand in hand. J.H. Kramer, the former head of the IOV, in an article in 1983 [*Kramer, 1983*] avoided the name 'inspectorate' and used the term 'external review unit'. The Inspectorate (IOV) started in mid-1978 and from the beginning its functions were broader than just 'inspection'. The IOV was also supposed to make recommendations both at project and policy level. It was even supposed to provide an input in the general policy generation. But although these more general-evaluation types of functions were added, the strength of the IOV was, and is, that the seven inspectors can at very short notice visit any Dutch project in the world and inform the Ministry about its work.

III. INTERNAL AND EXTERNAL EVALUATION

Since 1978 we therefore have had within the Ministry two types of evaluation institutions. The already existing one we called 'internal', which means that the evaluations of projects in developing countries are executed under the direct responsibility of the country or programme desks involved. These evaluations are considered to be a management tool for the desk officers and for the project officers in the field. The terms of reference for this kind of evaluation are defined by the desk staff, who select the evaluation teams and receive the reports. As evaluation is today also one of the responsibilities of the staff of the Dutch embassies in the recipient country concerned, they are also consulted. These reports generally do not play a role in the higher echelons of the Ministry or in policy-generating. This can be considered as a waste, since many of the reports are very relevant for this purpose. The different methodologies in the reports make it difficult to compare them and to synthesise them. In 1987, about 60 to 70 of these evaluations were carried out. There is a large variety of evaluation studies in this category. Some are one-man studies, others have been carried out jointly with the country involved (which is supposed to be the rule now) and with big teams in which different disciplines are brought together. Sometimes the desk officers themselves participate in this type of evaluation study as resource persons. There are missions of a few days up to some weeks. Outsiders from consultancy bureaus or academic institutions are always involved. The reports are in English (or French or Spanish) and generally accessible, but not widely distributed. The institutional learning is rather limited. The high turnover of personnel at the desks and at the embassies would require a better institutional memory in the form of building up cumulative knowledge, but in the present structure this cannot be done. So the main function remains to serve day-to-day management at both the project and the desk level. Many of these evaluations are a kind of mid-term evaluation on the basis of which decisions have to be taken about the next stage of the project. Therefore it is understandable that there is opposition to making these evaluations more independent by bringing them under a separate unit. The desk staff is afraid that the studies will become more policy-oriented and less management-oriented.

The second evaluation institution is the new IOV, the Inspectorate. The IOV considers itself to be 'external' because it has a rather independent position in the Ministry. Its work cannot be influenced by the people who are responsible for the projects. But it functions completely within the Ministry. Since 1978, several changes have taken place in the IOV. The inspection function has been diminished and today it concentrates much more on policy development. For some years, the IOV has produced special reports on specific sector-related topics like drinking-water and health. These reports are based on existing evaluation studies. The latest development is its attention to specific policy matters like the commercialisation of foreign aid. 'Commercialisation' means that development projects are farmed out and carried out by commercial institutes like consultancy bureaux, while formerly projects were carried out by experts on the payroll of the Ministry. The evolution in the IOV during the last ten years has not only affected the objectives of the unit and the way it functions but also the methodology. In particular, the methods and techniques applied in evaluations of projects have been highly developed and standardised. The result is that the reports are of a uniform nature and comparable. The IOV has probably reached the highest professional level in the Netherlands, being the only purely professional group doing nothing else but evaluation work. There are about seven inspectors. Each inspector will form a team with outsiders from the academic community or from consultancy firms and this team will do the actual field visits.

At present there are at least three different types of evaluation studies which are carried out by the IOV. The first is the traditional ones, based on projects and programmes. The second category focuses on special sectors like drinking-water. These studies are summaries of Dutch evaluation studies of the first category. The third category covers special policy items like the commercialisation of Dutch aid projects. In the first category there will be a yearly production of 25 studies, in the second category two or three and in the third category probably one.

What is the relation between the 'internal' and 'external' evaluations within the Ministry? This question is not easy to answer. In principle the tasks are complementary. Duplications are avoided, if possible, but it may happen that a project is evaluated by both evaluation institutions. Being a professional evaluation organisation, the IOV is in principle supposed to play an advisory role for the terms of reference produced by the country desks for their own evaluation studies. The country desks do not have professional evaluators on their staffs and have to hire evaluators from outside. In fact, however, the IOV does not regularly see the terms of reference of the evaluation studies which are to be carried out by the country or sector desks of the Ministry. Although there may be exceptions, this is a weakness in the set-up.

EVALUATING DEVELOPMENT ASSISTANCE

The result is that the evaluation studies organised by the desks do have a different structure and their results cannot easily be compared with the IOV studies. As the IOV has moved from inspection in the direction of evaluations the whole situation today looks a bit artificial and outdated. Maybe the time has come to reconsider the set-up and to give the IOV a new name and extended responsibilities for the quality of the internal evaluations as well.

The standardised methodology of the IOV reflects the state of the art in evaluation methodologies which is found in many handbooks. They are related to the project-cycle approach, the 'logical framework', and include criteria like policy conformity, efficiency, effectiveness and impact.

IV. EVALUATION OUTSIDE THE MINISTRY

There are many Dutch organisations outside the Ministry involved in foreign aid. Non-governmental organisations may together spend more than 200 million dollars yearly. Most of their money, however, comes from the Ministry, although there are considerable private contributions. The major NGOs are not only involved in financing aid projects but also in raising consciousness about Third World development problems in the Netherlands. They run all kinds of information programmes and try to mobilise the Dutch public at large.

In these NGOs evaluation plays an important role. Together they produce hundreds of reports of an evaluative nature based on fieldwork, mainly by local evaluators from inside or outside the projects. Generally their own staff are not involved in the implementation of development projects. This is done by local counterpart organisations. There is even a tendency to be less involved in projects and more in programmes. Nevertheless the desk officers from the Netherlands regularly visit projects in the field and sometimes they organise evaluation missions from the Netherlands in which also outsiders, like members of the academic community, take part. Some NGOs have a specialist on evaluation in their staff who is fully occupied with evaluation work. Quarles van Ufford has pointed out that the increased attention to evaluation in the NGOs is also related to the fact that their relationship with the Ministry has changed [*van Ufford, 1983*]. Formerly their programmes had to be accepted by the Ministry before implementation. Since the end of the 1970s their programmes have been accepted after implementation. Thus, their relationship with the Ministry depends on their performance. Evaluation is the tool to show what they have done and is therefore of strategic importance. The evaluation by the NGOs is an internal evaluation mainly by evaluators in Third World countries. The lack of independent evaluations has created criticism in the Netherlands. Partly due to this criticism, a large-scale impact evaluation jointly by all the major NGOs and some external specialists is under way in 1990. This study will try to cover the whole programme.

In addition to the more project-oriented evaluations, a group of NGOs jointly and in co-operation with the Ministry organises country programme evaluations in which the activities of all the NGOs involved in that particular country are evaluated.

The NGOs differ slightly as far as their ideologies are concerned. Some, like NOVIB (Dutch Organisation for International Cooperation), have an outspoken policy related to poverty alleviation, emancipation, participation and the improvement of the position of women. Others concentrate on projects in the medical or technical field. TOOL, for instance, is an organisation in the field of appropriate technology. During the last few years a number of evaluations have been made of the total policy and programmes of these organisations. I have been involved in some of them, for instance, the evaluation of the SNV, the Dutch Volunteers Programme, which is a foundation. In this programme more than 500 volunteers are working abroad in developing countries. This evaluation took place in 1984–85 at the request of the Council of the SNV. The exercise took more than a year and about seven teams were sent into the field to evaluate a variety of projects. Such a large-scale evaluation is, of course, exceptional. More than 22 evaluators were involved and the whole exercise was controlled by a steering group and a full-time coordinator. The objective of this evaluation exercise was to formulate a number of general policy recommendations for the SNV. To give an example: one of the recommendations was to reconsider in the light of the professionalisation process of volunteer work the pay-scale system. We recommended a pay level between a professional from a consultancy firm and a traditional volunteer.

Like the internal evaluation reports in the Ministry, the reports by the NGOs differ in kind and quality. They are not widely distributed and not easily accessible. And, as in the Ministry, the cumulation of knowledge is a problem.

V. EXPENDITURE ON EVALUATION

It is extremely difficult to make a reliable estimate of the expenditure on evaluation of Dutch foreign aid. Nevertheless it must be of interest to have at least an idea of the magnitude. The following table is a very rough estimate:

TABLE 1
EXPENDITURE ON EVALUATION
(IN US DOLLARS ESTIMATED)

Ministry of Foreign Aid	1,000,000
IOV external evaluation	5,000,000
Internal evaluation (Ministry)	2,000,000
NGOs and others	

Total expenditure may be estimated as between seven and nine million dollars, which is less than one per cent of the bilateral ODA but nevertheless a considerable amount of money.

VI. THE IMPACT OF EVALUATION ON POLICY DEVELOPMENT

Much has been written on the impact of evaluation on projects. Project evaluations may have made their impact mainly at the project level only but also a little at the level of the desk officers in the Ministry or in the NGOs concerned. By and large, this impact on both levels seems to be satisfactory. Desk officers read the reports and are familiar with the recommendations.

It is much more difficult to assess the impact on policy. Here we enter a rather complicated field, where evaluation as an input has to compete with many other inputs from within the Ministry and from outside. We also enter the field of politics. At the project level and at the desk level evaluation can be considered a management tool of a technical nature. When it comes to policy, evaluation can no longer be considered in such terms. As far as the policy level is concerned, I would like to draw attention to some relevant aspects.

The effectiveness of evaluation for policy development strongly depends on the ability of the evaluation unit (for instance, the IOV) to convey their messages to the proper persons. It could also be maintained that the value of evaluation depends on the absorption capacity (or should one also say the readiness?) of the policy-makers to take the messages. I would not say that evaluation is useless if the messages do not directly reach the policy-makers (government). Indirectly the reports may exert influence via other 'consumers', such as advisers, Members of Parliament and other specialists.

How is the feedback into the administrative and political set-up organised in the Netherlands? As already pointed out, the 'internal' evaluation reports do not reach the higher echelons of the Ministry. Their relevance for policy-making is therefore limited to the desks involved.

They may only directly exert some influence on policy making at the higher levels, but no mechanisms have been developed for this purpose. It is my strong impression that policy-making even at the (country) desk level is not very much influenced by evaluation studies. Other influences are much stronger. Recently, country policy papers have been produced for some of the main recipients of Dutch bilateral aid. These documents could establish an interesting starting point for country evaluations, but such a systematic approach has not yet been implemented. Informally, such assessments are established as a basis for the bilateral negotiations. The World Bank reports are used in this context. If, in the future, general policies, like structural adjustment, become more important than programmes and projects, the 'internal' evaluations will have to adjust to these new developments. This will also give more scope for international co-operation (with like-minded donors?), as I see no reason why every donor country should make its own country evaluation studies. This work should not be left solely to the World Bank. Being a bank, its perspective is too limited and ideologically biased.

The IOV is in a much better position than the 'internal' evaluations in making an impact on policy-makers. And it certainly has such an impact. The reports are used by the policy unit of the Ministry. They have been used for the formulation of guidelines for consultants. They play a role in some of the policy-making committees of the Ministry, too. Moreover there is an interest in obtaining and utilising the reports by Members of Parliament and others.

Although much has been accomplished, I feel that there is still a long way to go. Let me point out a few shortcomings in the Dutch system. Although the IOV has been set up to provide rapid and regular information to the Minister, it has no direct and regular access to the Minister. Information can reach the Minister, but there is no institutionalised system to keep him directly informed. Regular meetings between the Minister and the IOV staff are not taking place. Of course, the information provided by the unit may reach the Minister through the normal administrative channels but that is not what I mean by direct access.

The results of the IOV evaluations generally do not reach the advisory community. The 50 members of the National Advisory Council for Foreign Aid never receive any report from the IOV, nor from the 'internal' evaluations. Nor do the evaluation reports which are produced by NGOs reach this body of advisers. Very little contact exists between the IOV and those Members of Parliament who are the specialists on foreign aid. Although meetings have taken place, there is no direct, institutionalised, frequent contact.

The results of the IOV are, therefore, mainly relevant for the Civil

Service leadership of the Ministry. However, the question whether instituionalisation of communication with the relevant parties is necessary might be raised. The information is available and everybody who would like to read the reports can do so. If, for instance, the Minister or the IOV feel it necessary, they can discuss the reports in more detail. My own experience from a number of evaluation exercises is different. I learned that it is necessary to make institutional arrangements for oral communication and discussions on the results, because otherwise the effects will be limited. The danger that evaluation will be degraded to rituals will always be present.

How relevant is the information for the Minister? Here we have to realise that a minister takes decisions on the basis of many inputs. Evaluation results could be just one of them. It is my impression that the influence of evaluation reports at that level is very minor. In the past I have known of cases in which the Minister – for political reasons – has purposely neglected the results of evaluation studies because they went contrary to his political preferences. In simple words one could say that it depends on the political usefulness of a recommendation whether it will be used or not. It is also possible that a minister with a professional background in development work will take more interest in evaluation results than a minister with a purely political background. Apart from the IOV, a number of other staff bureaux are involved in policy formulation and so is the National Advisory Council too. The impact of the IOV could be improved by informing these other institutions which provide inputs in the policy-generation processes, or involving them in the work of the IOV, via discussions on the work plan and on the evaluation reports. Joint seminars could be a solution to be recommended. A step in this direction has already been taken by the creation of steering groups for those IOV studies which address specific topics of aid, like the commercialisation issue. In these steering groups different bureaux are represented and even some outsiders are participating.

The absorption of evaluation results is a problem not only for the Ministry, but also for the councils of NGOs. In the past, I have had some very bad experiences, but, when evaluating the big SNV (Dutch volunteers), we had a very regular and institutionalised contact with the Council. In this case the communication between the evaluators and the Council of the SNV was excellent.

VII. WHAT IS EVALUATED?

Almost all Dutch evaluation studies are related to bilateral aid and especially to project aid. The type of evaluation studies referred to above was mainly based on short field visits of one to three weeks. Their limitations, both in research and in reporting, are clear. The limited fieldwork period makes it impossible to cover adequately a number of topics in which we are actually very interested. Such topics include participation, the position of women, institutional development and sustainability. To make assessments as far as these topics are concerned requires a much longer involvement in the local communities. Long-term research by researchers from the academic community is here the proper solution. The Dutch Ministry of Foreign Affairs has financed some studies of this kind, for example, on participation. There is a need for many more studies of this type. The IOV uses about 50 academic researchers for their evaluation studies a year and one could hope that the experience of these researchers also compensates for the relatively short field trips.

Another option is to have within the projects, evaluation and monitoring units which are able to implement the kind of impact studies that are required to answer questions on employment effects, participation, the role of women, sustainability and related topics. Some projects have built in such evaluation and monitoring units, like the IRDP project in Noakhali (Bangladesh), which came across during an evaluation mission for the Danish aid agency. But even for such units, permanently present, real impact studies are an exception. Also students who have to do field work as part of their studies can provide important contributions if their work is integrated in the overall evaluation process. This is still an underutilised source.

The limitations in the scope have even more far-reaching consequences than the limitations as far as topics are concerned. Which part of the budget for development aid is covered by evaluation studies? There has been a strong orientation towards projects and programmes and related topics. In the future it will be necessary to take up new topics like the country policy and the related structural adjustment. More work should be done on financial aid and on the role of the international aid agencies. The starting point should be the total aid policy. The question of whether it is still the role of the IOV to do this kind of work will be discussed in the final section.

VIII. LOCAL REPORTING

Reporting to the local staff and to local authorities is a weak spot in many evaluation studies. Lack of proper reporting creates misunderstanding and tensions between donors and counterparts. When I take responsibility for an evaluation, I therefore insist on reporting to local staff and local authorities before leaving the country. The modern tendency is to have joint evaluation teams. In that case, from a logistic point of view it is almost conditional to do the reporting at the local level.

From the point of view of local reporting the IOV has an unimpressive record. In the beginning the reports were confidential and did not go to the project staff and certainly not to local authorities of counterparts. When only the Dutch involvement was evaluated, one could find excuses for this approach. This approach became very soon old-fashioned and, as I have described above, the IOV went through an evolution process. Today there is much more openness but still local reporting is either non-existent or weak, although a debriefing takes place before a team leaves the country.

IX. SCIENTIFIC SUPPORT FOR POLICY-MAKING

Evaluation is just one input in policy-making. Other inputs are emerging from research projects and reports by academic advisory committees. It would be useful to try to link these inputs in one way or the other. Let me give some examples. The IOV may come across topics which are too difficult to include in the terms of reference for an evaluation team because of time constraints. These topics could be delegated to the research programme of the Ministry. In the same way internal evaluations could provide the research programme of the Ministry with interesting research topics. The sector programmes, like rural development and industrial development, could more often suggest topics for consideration for the IOV and for the research programme. Nowadays this is done incidentally, seldom and certainly not systematically. The National Advisory Council could suggest topics for both evaluation and research. In some of their reports this has already been done but to my knowledge there exists little systematic contact between the two bodies.

This approach would lead to a more coordinated research and evaluation programme within the Ministry. From a management point of view it could even be considered to bring these functions closer together.

Academic researchers have very little knowledge of the results emerging from evaluation studies. Access is difficult or impossible and even the information about what is available is not known in academic circles. In the same way there is very little knowledge in the IOV and in the internal evaluation units about research that is going on in the academic world and which is highly relevant for policy-makers and evaluators. It seems that the whole problem requires information management that is not yet available. The OECD/DAC initiative to make information available at an international level would be a very useful initiative for the internal situation within the Netherlands as well (and I am afraid we are not an exception).

The commercialisation of foreign aid projects is a complicating factor. Today, internal evaluations are usually carried out by consultancy firms. We have seen a fast growth of small-scale consultancy firms involved in evaluating the work carried out by the larger consultancy firms which are implementing development projects which via tenders have been farmed out by the Ministry. Although some of the information emerging from these evaluations is available at the Ministry, we can nevertheless state that the accumulation of knowledge takes place within private consultancy firms and it is not in their interest to share this information with others, including the Ministry.

In this matter a specific role is given to steering committees, advisory committees or so-called 'monitors'. They are supposed to write the terms of reference for the evaluation studies and to digest the information that comes forward. The members of these various committees are generally from the universities or from specialised institutes. They bring a certain continuity in the development of knowledge and the establishment and maintenance of these structures can, therefore, be considered as a positive development.

X. CONCLUSION

During the last two decades the evaluation of development aid in the Netherlands has been highly institutionalised. There has been a considerable increase in terms of both quantity and quality. The development of the IOV has, in particular, been fascinating and may be quite unique in its contributions. Although the general impression is positive, I have pointed out a number of shortcomings too, and much has still to be improved. The next step should be the establishment of an information management in order to be able to make the utmost use of all the evaluation work that is going on, both inside and outside the Ministry. What should be the function of the IOV? There are two different options.

The first option is to give the IOV an extended responsibility which embraces all the evaluation work within the Ministry or on behalf of the Ministry. The differentiation between internal and external evaluation is outdated and would then disappear. The role of this reorganised evaluation unit would then be to improve the quality of the evaluation studies, to standardise terms of reference and to 'translate' the reports into more general policy observations. The unit could develop a monitoring system at the desk level (like the British system) and take on a coordinating function. The unit should also coordinate all information coming from the outside. Other functions could be to keep the contact with the research community and to transmit evaluation results to interested parties. The unit could maintain most of the existing functions of the IOV but it should be more management-oriented.

The second option is to move away from management problems and be more policy-oriented. More relevant policy matters should be the object of their evaluation studies. The objectives of foreign aid would then be the primary concern for the unit. The IOV would then move in the direction of the policy-making units in the Ministry and a relationship with the National Advisory Council would also be important. Close relationships with other donors and international agencies would become a high-priority task.

In either case, the changes which take place in development policies will have to be followed up through changes in the functions and organisational set-up of evaluation of foreign aid, adapting evaluation to the new needs.

Acknowledgement: The first draft of this study was considered by the IOV staff and the author would like to thank them for their comments. The full responsibility for the final version is, of course, exclusively his. He would also like to thank the participants in the Lysebu seminar for their comments, which were very stimulating.

REFERENCES

Kramer, J.H., 1983, 'Evaluating Dutch Development Cooperation', *The Courier*, No. 80, 1983.
Kruijer, G.J., 1969, *Organiseren en Evalueren*, Boom, Meppel.
Ufford, Philip Quarles van, 1983, 'De opkomst van het resultatenonderzoek', *Ontwikkelingshulpgetest*, Coutinho.

7

The Evaluation Policy and Performance of Norway

OLAV STOKKE

I. INTRODUCTION

Evaluation as a tool in public administration is a recent activity in Norway. It has, in the first place, been related to the administration of development assistance, although slowly entering also other fields of public activities, especially education and research. Even in relation to development assistance, evaluation was introduced in a modest way only in the early 1970s.[1]

Evaluation is defined more or less narrowly by different authors. This applies also to the political and administrative authorities within the field of development assistance on which this study will focus, although some efforts have been made by the major donor countries to agree on concepts and language.[2]

In the Norwegian setting, aid evaluation is defined as a systematic assessment of official development assistance (ODA) activities, whereby the state of affairs is assessed against a given standard, such as an objective or a plan. An evaluation is expected to explain the course of events and factors influencing the outcome. Its practical value is related to recommendations offered to direct activities or inputs towards the objective aimed at or even suggestions for changes in the objectives set. The insights emerging from an evaluation should stand the test of a re-examination by others, which presupposes the use of methods that might be controlled or even used anew.[3]

Aid may be assessed in different ways. Distinctions are made between appraisal (by the recipient authorities and the aid agency, before it is finally decided to start an activity), monitoring (by the project staff, the continuous assessment and reporting of inputs and their uses during the project cycle), and evaluation. The distinction between monitoring and evaluation is admittedly difficult to establish in precise terms. However, an important difference would be that an evaluation should provide a more neutral assessment of the aid activities and usually be more comprehensive and of a more overall character than the regular reporting (monitoring). There is also a distinction between evaluations carried out during the implementing phase and *ex post* evaluations, carried out after a project has been completed (by the aid agency).[4]

This definition has been worked out by the Norwegian aid agency (NORAD) and adapted to the established administrative system. The justification and purpose are implicit in the definition, namely to improve the effect and efficiency of ODA. It was formulated by the NORAD evaluation office (in 1981) and may, therefore, be expected to be designed to serve the needs of the aid-implementing agency. However, due consideration may be expected to be given also to the concerns of the domestic policy environment, in particular, Parliament, given the active aid debate.

The evaluation policy has, during the 1980s, been formed and formalised at different levels. The policy has been stated in government White Papers and other government reports to Parliament and discussed – with recommendations – by Parliament's Standing Committee on Foreign Affairs and in Parliament. At the administrative level, the policy is formalised in an evaluation manual and other documents by the NORAD evaluation unit, instructions for evaluation of aid and standardised terms of reference (TOR).

In this study, I shall describe the main patterns of the formalised (declared) Norwegian evaluation policy, that is, the justifications, objectives, strategies and guidelines set for the evaluation of aid. On this basis I shall discuss to what extent the declared policy has been followed up. This discussion will be based on only part of the evaluation performance, namely the organisational setting, the resources invested and the evaluations carried out by the evaluation unit of the aid administration. This implies that one leg, the monitoring carried out by the aid agency (NORAD), is more or less cut off.[5] The research side has been only marginally dealt with. The external control (monitoring) carried out by the State Auditor is not included.[6]

Since evaluation has to be related to the aid policy – the declared policy, involving objectives, strategies and guidelines as well as its implementation – it is necessary to start out with a brief presentation of the Norwegian aid policy and the administrative structure which is implementing the policy.

II. THE MAIN FEATURES OF THE NORWEGIAN AID POLICY

Since 1961, the Norwegian aid policy has been formed in an interaction between governments of different political colours and Parliament. Over the years, the policy has been formalised in a series of propositions and reports to Parliament by successive governments, including several major policy reviews, and in Parliament's responses to these, in particular the recommendations from its Standing Committee on Foreign Affairs; most recently in June 1987, when Parliament considered the last major policy review, the 1984 White Paper by the Willoch government (non-Socialist coalition) and the 1987 addendum by the Brundtland government (Labour).[7] The main features of this declared aid policy are characterised more by continuity than change [*Stokke, 1988, 1989*]. In the following pages, it is the declared policy which is sketched, not the policy as implemented.

The Aims of Norwegian Aid

The predominant *objective* of Norwegian aid, established in 1962, is to contribute to social, economic and cultural development in the Third World. In 1972, this objective was further refined to include income distribution. In the 1984 White Paper (p. 20), the government confirmed that

> the overriding objective for the development assistance activities shall also in the future be to assist in creating lasting improvements in the economic, social and political conditions of the people in developing countries. Development assistance shall be used in a way that maximises its development effects for the poor sections of the people. Aid shall in the first place be directed to the poorest developing countries and be provided in a form that creates as little dependence on continued aid as possible.

In 1987, the Labour government confirmed these aid objectives and gave particular emphasis to a responsible administration of natural resources and environments, economic growth, improvement in the conditions of the poorest, in particular, women, support of social, economic and political human rights and the promotion of peace between nations and regions [*Report No. 34*].

The Main Strategies

The main *strategies* chosen to pursue these objectives have been [*Stokke, 1989*]:

(1) A welfare strategy, emphasising the improvement of both social services and services that will directly improve the ability of local communities to meet their own basic needs. The poverty orientation of aid is the core element of this strategy.
(2) An industrialisation and trade strategy, geared towards increasing the productive capacity and export potential on the recipient side.

The Main Guidelines

Several *guidelines* have been established to facilitate the predominant objectives. The general objectives and the guidelines are conceived of as a totality, which together constitutes the declared aid policy. However, the main components may at times conflict with each other, a fact that also applies to the guidelines. The following main guidelines have been established for Norwegian aid:

(1) *ODA is to be divided equally between bilateral and multilateral aid channels.* This key was established during the late 1960s and has been maintained ever since. Aid for specific purposes being administered by international aid agencies ('multi-bi') has been defined as bilateral aid. Since the mid-1970s, the multilateral aid component has been 40–45 per cent of total ODA, in line with the political authorities' understanding of how the guideline was to be interpreted.

(2) *Bilateral aid should be concentrated geographically on a few main recipient countries.* However, several activities have been explicitly exempted from this principle and a few countries, in addition to the (nine) main recipients, have received substantial assistance for various reasons. In the 1980s, three regions were added. Since the mid-1970s, approximately 60 per cent of bilateral aid has been concentrated on the priority countries. The trend has been a shrinking share to the priority countries.

(3) *Norwegian aid should be poverty-oriented.* The poverty orientation has been given the following components:

(a) Norwegian aid should go to poor recipient countries, in terms of their GNP per capita (LLDCs or LICs). This was established as a criterion for the selection of new priority countries in 1972.

(b) Norwegian aid should go to poor target groups (stated in 1972),[8] in particular women (stated in 1976, with increased emphasis in the 1980s. In 1985, a strategy to this end was adopted)[9] and children (added in 1987 [*Report No. 34*]).

(c) Norwegian aid should be provided to recipient countries with authorities pursuing a development-oriented and socially just policy for the benefit of all and especially for the worst-off groups of the population. This was one of the criteria established for the selection of new priority countries (established in 1972). In 1976, Parliament added that recipients of Norwegian aid were also expected to respect human rights, with reference to the UN Declaration and Convention.

In 1976, Parliament made it clear that the criteria for the selection of new priority countries were cumulative: all criteria had to be considered when new recipients were to be chosen. Up to 1987, there was an ambiguity as to whether the criteria should be limited to the selection of *new* priority countries (as stated) or were also to be applied to those already included, governing the distribution of bilateral aid. This ambiguity will probably linger on, although, in 1987, Parliament insisted that the criteria should govern most aid relations, excepting only targeted aid [*Recommendation No. 186*].

(4) The main stumbling block for (3) – and in particular for (c) – has so far been yet another guideline: *aid relations should be established with a long-term perspective* to make aid more predictable and easier to plan for the recipient.

(5) *Aid should be recipient-oriented.* Norwegian aid should be based on the development plans and priorities of the recipient countries. This guideline, established in 1972, was repeatedly confirmed up to 1984, when a redefinition took place [*Report No. 36*]: confirming the principle, the government added that equal weight should be given to the predominant objectives established for Norwegian aid, with particular reference to the poverty orientation, the emphasis on women as a target group and the concern for the environment. The aid programme for a main recipient country should evolve from a dialogue between the two parties. In some cases the Norwegian government wished to provide aid, outside the country programmes, which was not given priority by the recipient government.

This guideline, as conceived during the 1970s and early 1980s, has implications for the relations between donor and recipient, placing the initiative and also the responsibility for the implementation of aid with the recipient government. It also has implications for the forms of aid, giving emphasis to aid forms where the recipients obtained flexibility (programme aid, budgetary support), as contrasted with aid forms where the donor held the upper hand (project aid).

(6) *Aid should be provided as grants.* This guideline was established in 1972 and has been repeatedly confirmed.

(7) *Aid should be untied.* When this guideline was established in 1967, the government added some exemptions which should be used with great caution. In 1972, the guideline was repeated in less reserved terms. After 1975, it came under strong pressure due to the recession. In 1981, Parliament made an effort to correct the practice, recommending the NORAD as a general rule to buy at world-market prices but, in a quite unique formulation, allowing for the inclusion of Norwegian commodities in the aid programme (grants), even if the

price should be up to ten per cent higher than what could be obtained elsewhere, if particular reasons should justify this. As amended, this guideline was confirmed by Parliament in 1987. However, some exceptions have been made explicit during the 1980s, including the commodity aid and mixed credits.[10]

(8) *Ten per cent of ODA should be used for family-planning.* This guideline, established in the late 1960s, is the only one which has been formulated in quantitative terms, in addition to the distribution between multilateral and bilateral aid.

(9) Although not included among the guidelines, targets have also been established for the *volume of ODA*, to be reached at a fixed date, in combination with a stepped-up budgetary plan for attaining the target. In 1972, the Labour government proposed one per cent of GDP in ODA as a target to be reached in 1978. In 1977, when the budget for 1978 was decided, all political parties then in Parliament voted for a budget based on this target or higher. Since then, governments – and political parties – have committed themselves to even higher volume targets.

Guidelines do not all to the same extent directly expose the main thrust of the predominant objective set for Norwegian aid, although they all in various ways add to the understanding of how it is conceived by the Norwegian political authorities. The main thrust is poverty alleviation. This objective has been given added emphasis and extended to embrace all Norwegian aid, not only the government-to-government aid, but also the aid through the other main aid channels, including aid via the NGOs, the private enterprises and even the multilateral aid agencies and development-finance institutions. A crucial question to be addressed would, therefore, be the following: to what extent has this concern been governing the orientation of the applied Norwegian evaluation policy and the actual evaluation work?

The Administrative System

The administration of development assistance has been reorganised several times – most recently in 1989.[11] In the mid-1970s, the overall responsibility for all aid became vested in the Ministry of Foreign Affairs (before that, responsibility for part of the multilateral aid, the development-finance institutions, had been vested in the Ministry of Trade and the Ministry of Finance). Bilateral aid was administered by an executive agency outside the Ministry with a separate board appointed by the government (NORAD), whereas multilateral aid was administered by the Ministry. In 1983, a separate Ministry for Development Cooperation was established, with a Minister and State Secretary (Deputy Minister). This included most units of the Ministry of Foreign Affairs which were dealing with aid issues (leaving aside those dealing with North–South political issues) and even the aid agency. The Ministry was organised in four departments – one for planning, another for multilateral aid, one for administration (secretariat) and with NORAD intact as the fourth department responsible for the administration of bilateral aid. However, in 1989, NORAD again became an external agency, this time without an executive board. Whereas NORAD had previously been organised according to functions, the reorganisation this time gave emphasis to geographical criteria. With the change in government in the autumn of 1989, the Ministry was merged with the Ministry of Foreign Affairs. The political responsibility for aid issues was vested in a Minister for Development Cooperation.

Overall, about 54–9 per cent of all Norwegian ODA is provided as bilateral aid. However, a fairly large share of this aid (six to eight per cent) is administered by international aid agencies for specific purposes ('multi-bi'). Most of the bilateral aid is provided as direct aid and, for the most part, channelled to nine main recipient countries (priority countries). About 40–45 per cent is multilateral aid, mainly provided as general contributions to multinational organisations. Humanitarian aid is provided both bilaterally and multilaterally and amounts to about ten per cent of total aid.

This means that about half of the total aid is administered by the Ministry (since 1990 again the Ministry of Foreign Affairs) – almost all indirectly as general contributions to international aid agencies, although some of it is earmarked for particular purposes. Also the bilateral aid, administered by NORAD, is in the end administered indirectly, but planned and implemented by the Norwegian authorities in a much more direct and active way. Since the early 1970s, administration of bilateral aid has become increasingly decentralised. Offices of Resident Representatives have been established in the nine priority countries and in a few other major recipient countries, and both the number of staff and authority for planning and follow-up have been increased over the years.

III. THE DECLARED EVALUATION POLICY

The Norwegian evaluation policy has been formed and formalised at the highest political level – by the government (in reports to Parliament) and Parliament (in recommendations by its Standing Committee on Foreign

Affairs). In this interaction, Parliament has not limited its role to that of responding to government proposals; during the formative period in the early 1980s, Parliament initiated the policy.

In 1975, the government (Labour) committed itself for the first time increasing the number of impact studies of aid [*Report No. 94*] and was met with enthusiasm by Parliament, emphasising that impact studies should be given prominence [*Recommendation No. 192, 1976*]. In 1982, Parlia-ment's Committee on Foreign Affairs urged the government to give priority to the preparation of a report which dealt with the criticisms levelled against aid for lack of effectiveness [*Recommendation No. 137*]. The next year, in its annual report on aid [*Report No. 14*], the government (Conservative) responded by, *inter alia*, introducing a practice whereby the main findings of some evaluation reports were reported as illustrations. Parliament took advantage of this and established objectives and guidelines for the evaluation of development assistance [*Recommendation No. 189, 1983*].

The active role played by the political authorities at the highest level in forming the evaluation policy is a unique phenomenon and lends both authority and legitimacy to the declared policy. In describing the policy, emphasis will therefore be given to the sources involving the political authorities rather than those involving the administration.

The Main Objectives

Within the setting of development assistance, evaluation financed through the aid budget becomes, almost by definition, not an end in itself but a tool in the public administration of aid. Hence, the main objective will be to improve the effectiveness and efficiency of aid by providing insights into how an aid activity proceeds and even recommendations for future activities.

The more precise focus, however, will differ with different perspectives. The needs as conceived by Parliament may, for instance, be different from those of a project management. However, the common denominator will be the established aims set for aid, although perspectives may deviate from each other here too – Parliament may give emphasis to the overall objectives for aid, while the executive branch (project management) may wish to focus on the project objectives which may or may not reflect overall objectives. Thus, Parliament's main concern would be expected to be insights that can answer the question: does aid work? The executive organisation's main concern would be expected to be insights that can be used to improve present and future aid activities. Both at the policy-making level and the implementing level, there will exist a need for legitimating the aid-spending by evaluating the aid activities. There are other main actors that may influence the emphasis as far as the objectives are concerned too, and the two being identified would certainly have additional concerns. To what extent does the declared policy reflect these various concerns?

The active role of Parliament has clearly had an impact on the emphasis as far as objectives and guidelines are concerned. In 1975, the government (Labour) discussed impact studies in the context of mechanisms to control the use of resources effectively in accordance with the objectives set for aid [*Report No. 94*]. This perspective was strongly emphasised by Parliament in 1983 [*Recommendation No. 189*], which set the priorities in a direct way which justifies a direct quotation. According to Parliament's Committee on Foreign Affairs [*ibid.*, 7–8], the most important objective of evaluation was to find out whether aid, as implemented, was having the effects aimed at:

> This makes, in the view of the *Committee*, the objectives set for aid the central point of departure. The predominant objective established for Norwegian aid is that the development assistance shall create development and contribute to the promotion of social and economic growth in the developing countries. Norwegian aid is to be provided with the purpose of creating income distribution and social justice. It should be oriented in such a way that it benefits all social strata – and in particular those social groups which were worst situated. The poor social strata and women, in particular in rural areas, have been identified as particular target groups for Norwegian aid. The *Committee* wishes to emphasise that this objective governs both bilateral and multilateral aid. It also governs that part of the bilateral aid that is excluded from the guideline of geographical concentration of aid and aid channelled to projects run by non-governmental organisations or private enterprises in the Third World. It is of great importance, in the view of the *Committee*, that the aid administration makes strong efforts to implement aid within the various activity areas and projects/ programmes on the basis of this predominant objective. An evaluation of aid effectiveness must take as the point of departure whether the aid contributes to the promotion of the predominant aim set for Norwegian aid and objectives at lower levels which are derived from this. It is here the main efforts of evaluation should be made.

The control function in a more restricted way – ensuring the efficiency of aid by comparing results with the resources invested within the confines of a project – was also emphasised by Parliament, but clearly given secondary priority to the above. The importance of the feedback function was underlined – insights should be plugged back into the implementing units of the aid agency, made available to the decision-making organs within the administration and to the political authorities, in order to improve the planning and implementation of future aid or the adjustment of ongoing activities [*ibid.*].

This double objective of aid evaluation has been confirmed by successive governments. In 1984, the Willoch government (non-Socialist coalition) reversed the priorities between the two main objectives set out by Parliament. The main emphasis was given to evaluation as a tool for the implementation of aid.[12]

Strategy

Parliament and government have established a strategy for evaluation, too. Although strategy and guidelines are described separately, some guidelines are part of the strategy. The prescription of ways and means underscores the importance attributed by the political authorities to the evaluation of aid. Some elements of the evaluation strategy have been given prominence.

All aid channels and forms should be evaluated: Successive governments and Parliament have stated that the general aims set for Norwegian development assistance have a bearing on all Norwegian aid, including both multilateral and bilateral aid and all aid forms. The political authorities have also stated that these aims should be considered the primary point of departure in evaluating aid.

A similar, all-embracing commitment has also been established for the evaluation of aid: all aid channels and forms of aid should be evaluated. In 1983, Parliament [*Recommendation No. 189*] recommended that the administration should establish procedures to ensure that various forms of evaluation are included as an integral part of the aid implementation. A selection of activities within all areas should regularly be the object of a special evaluation effort. The NORAD's aid implementation should be critically examined, too. In 1984, the government followed up by stating [*Report No. 36*] that, although all aid activities should be critically assessed by independent evaluations, only a few could be selected for evaluation each year. However, over the years, the various aid channels (NORAD, multilateral and private organisations), recipient countries, aid forms and areas (sectors) of Norwegian aid should be evaluated. Also the different links in the aid chain should, over time, be evaluated.

Particular focus on the systems through which aid is provided: In 1983, Parliament recognised the important role played by the system through which aid was channelled for the outcome. For the direct bilateral aid, the priority countries are of particular importance. Parliament stated that it should be continuously explored whether the policies of the main recipient countries were attuned to the main guidelines on which the Norwegian aid policy was based. In its White Paper (1984), the government agreed: since Norwegian aid in most cases made up only a small proportion of the total resource input, a more extensive evaluation theme would be an evaluation of the total system into which aid is channelled.

Noting that, so far, evaluation had almost exclusively been oriented towards projects, the government, in a statement of intent [*Report No. 36*], declared that a limited number of projects would also in the years ahead be evaluated each year. However, more *general and overriding questions would increasingly be addressed, and the total aid engagement to a recipient country would be evaluated.* With reference to the demand by Parliament for a regular exploration of how the development policies of the recipient countries corresponded with the main guidelines on which Norwegian aid was based, the government announced that *country studies* for each of the main recipient countries (at present nine) would be carried out by the Ministry of Development Cooperation at least every fifth year.

According to the government [*ibid.*], the multilateral aid and bilateral aid through the international aid agencies and development finance institutions would also be more systematically assessed than before, although this posed problems of a particular kind, since multilateral aid was motivated not only by Norwegian development objectives but also by the broader, Norwegian foreign policy objective of strengthening the United Nations system. The control function would, as previously, be pursued mainly through participation in the governing bodies of the multilateral organisations and, therefore, be based on evaluations provided by the agencies themselves. From the Norwegian side, efforts would be made to make their evaluations more critical and independent. The government added, however, that its own initiatives might also be taken for more comprehensive evaluations of some of the main recipients of Norwegian multilateral ODA, although this might involve cooperation with other main contributors, in particular, the other Nordic countries, as well as with the agencies themselves.

Feedback to the administration and to the decision-makers becomes a *sine qua non* in order to achieve the objectives set for aid. In 1983, Parliament emphasised that the insights emerging from evaluation should be communicated not only to the Norwegian side but also to the political authorities and administration on the recipient side [*Recommendation*

No. 189]. The government agreed [*Report No. 36*]: evaluation is not an aim in itself. The real benefit of evaluation stems from the feedback of conclusions to the planning and implementing units of the system, which for the government-to-government aid would be the Ministry of Development Cooperation and the planning and implementing units within the recipient country. However, feedback should not be restricted to the administrative and political governing bodies of the donor and recipient countries. Evaluation reports might in many cases constitute a good basis for further discussions in fora outside these organs, where researchers, experts and media people could participate. According to the established practice, evaluation reports were public documents. The government announced that this practice would be continued but added that in exceptional cases, where general commitments to foreign governments (main recipients) made it necessary, some parts might be excluded. Popularised summaries of the evaluation reports would be prepared for dissemination to the general public.

In 1983, Parliament recommended *liaison with Norwegian research milieux* in order to strengthen the evaluation efforts [*Recommendation No. 189*]. The NORAD was advised to make use of Norwegian research milieux, in particular, within the social sciences. Norwegian competence ought to be further developed in this area. The following year, the government agreed [*Report No. 36*]. Noting that inter-disciplinary evaluation teams that carried out fieldwork and reported on this basis would be the most common method also in the future, it envisaged that methods and forms would have to be adapted to new and more complex evaluation tasks. Some of the more in-depth probing evaluations could be carried out only by research with a longer time perspective. Evaluation activities should, therefore, be considered in relation to research competence at home and abroad. The government recognised a need for external expertise in the evaluation work and even a need for competence-building both at home and abroad. In this connection, the Ministry indicated its intention of establishing co-operation agreements with institutes and groups of consultants, and emphasised the importance of building milieux for evaluation in the main recipient countries with a large degree of independence from the authorities.

Also in 1983, Parliament recommended co-operation with the other Nordic countries [*Recommendation No. 189*] in order to extend the evaluation capacity. In 1984, the government agreed to *international co-operation* in this field – both with the evaluation units of other donor countries and those of the multilateral organisations [*Report No. 36*].

A demanding strategy like this would be merely declaratory if competent administrative capacity and financial resources were not made available. In 1983, Parliament stated [*Recommendation No. 189*] that the administrative set-up within the NORAD ought to be strengthened and given more resources in order to handle the evaluation tasks in a satisfactory way. In its White Paper the following year, the government agreed. I will return to the follow-up.

Main Guidelines

The political authorities have established guidelines to govern some critical aspects of the evaluation of aid. These guidelines also reflect on the objectives and priorities of aid evaluation. As noted, Parliament has played an active role even here.

(1) *Independence*: In 1983, Parliament stated [*Recommendation No.189*] that evaluation work should be organised in a way that ensured an independence which made it possible to scrutinise even the NORAD's own administration of aid. In 1984, the government agreed that evaluations should be carried out in an independent way [*Report No. 36*]. The government emphasised that evaluations should be ensured maximum independence *vis-à-vis* both the commissioner (Ministry of Development Cooperation) and those subject to evaluation (aid channels, recipients). This guideline should have a bearing on both the formulation of evaluation mandates (terms of reference) and the composition of the evaluation teams. It added, however, a note of warning that reflected insights into the delicate balance existing between units within the same organisation having different main objectives to pursue that might even turn out to be conflicting: the prescribed independence did not imply that evaluation work should be isolated from the aid administration, as the feedback of impulses with a view to improving aid would be the most important purpose of most evaluations.

(2) *Open and accessible evaluations*: In 1983, Parliament stated that openness in the evaluation work should be aimed at [*Recommendation No. 189*]. In 1984, the Government agreed [*Report No. 36*]. Evaluation reports should as a rule be open and available. Routines and procedures had been established to ensure the feedback of information resulting from evaluations to the administrative planning and aid-implementing set-up both on the donor and the recipient side, but also to the interested public. However, there is a distinction between the evaluation report, which is the responsibility of the evaluation team, and the conclusions which were drawn on this basis by the Ministry of Development Cooperation after having obtained comments on the report by the involved parties.

(3) *Participation and involvement of the recipient side*: In 1983, Parliament emphasised [*Recommendation No. 189*] that the political authorities and the civil service of the recipients of aid should have a chance to benefit from the insights gained by evaluations. These should be organised in a way that served this purpose, by contributing to the building-up of evaluation competence and capacity in the recipient country. The administrative set-up and research milieux of the recipient countries should, therefore, be actively involved in the evaluation work.

In 1984, the government agreed [*Report No. 36*] that evaluation of aid should be carried out as a joint effort by the authorities on the donor side and those in charge on the recipient side. This implied that, for the government-to-government aid, recipients should be actively engaged in the preparation and implementation of the evaluations. Members of an evaluation team recruited in the recipient countries should maintain the same independent status towards the authorities there as the Norwegian members had towards the Norwegian aid authorities.

Summing Up

At the political level, the main elements of the evaluation policy were formed and formalised in 1983–84. In 1987, the Labour government agreed to the evaluation policy established by its predecessor [*Report No. 34*]. And so did Parliament, insisting strongly that the policy should be followed up and underlining the increased demand for quality in the development co-operation which the two government White Papers represented. 'The practical possibility to meet these demands requires, in the first place, increased access to relevant knowledge based on scientific research. Secondly, it requires a further build-up of the evaluation activities and the capacity and determination of the aid administration to integrate experiences in the planning and implementation of aid.'[13]

The Norwegian political authorities, Parliament and successive governments, have agreed on a dynamic evaluation policy. Both parties have insisted that evaluation is an important, integral part of the aid policy which needs to be expanded and given increased resources. They have agreed on evaluation at an ambitious level: what matters is not so much efficiency studies, although these too are important, but the evaluation of the effects of Norwegian development assistance, as viewed from the perspective of the predominant objectives and guidelines established for Norwegian aid. They have been concerned that the evaluations should be external, independent and critical and that the reports should be open and available. These guidelines should also govern evaluators recruited from the recipient side. Parliament and successive governments have insisted that the insights resulting from evaluation work should be integrated in the aid-planning and implementation: the feedback to the political and administrative decision-makers should be ensured in order to improve future aid.

To what extent has this declared policy been followed up by the government and the aid administration? Which components have been given priority by the different authorities and which have been given a low priority or even neglected? These questions will be addressed next.

IV. THE EVALUATION PERFORMANCE

The more fundamental questions to be addressed relate to the follow-up of the stated objectives, the strategy and the guidelines set for evaluation. These, again, have been strongly related to the Norwegian development assistance with its set of objectives and guidelines. During the late 1970s and early 1980s, some new aid forms came increasingly into use also for Norwegian aid. Another question to be addressed, therefore, is to what extent the evaluation performance has caught up with these changes. However, since administrative capacity and financial resources constitute a necessary precondition for any follow-up, I shall start there.

The Administration of Evaluation: Location and Resources

In 1977, a small office for research and evaluation was established within the aid-implementing agency (NORAD).[14] In 1983, when the Ministry of Development Cooperation was established, the evaluation function was moved from NORAD to the Ministry and located in the department of planning. Its mandate was extended to include evaluation of the whole spectrum of Norwegian aid activities, including multilateral aid and the responsibility for the administration and follow-up of the Norwegian participation in evaluation efforts carried out by multilateral aid agencies (previously the responsibility of the Ministry of Foreign Affairs). It was emphasised that the task of the unit was to *administer* evaluations and only in exceptional cases to participate in the actual evaluation work.[15]

In the 1984 White Paper, too, the government emphasised the importance of having the evaluation unit placed as independently as possible in relation to units with a direct responsibility for the implementation of aid. In addition to the task of administering evaluation, the evaluation unit was expected to be the connecting link through the different phases of the evaluation work and between the external evaluation team and the aid administration. The established link between evaluation and research was confirmed. Although the office was split into one office for evaluation and another for research, the government found it important to combine the responsibility for these functions within a common department of the Ministry in order to facilitate the use of commissioned research as a supplement to evaluation.

The staff of the evaluation unit was increased from two and a half man-years in 1984 to three man-years permanent staff (with an additional, one-man-year, non-permanent staff) at the beginning of 1990. The budget increased, too – from NOK eight millions in 1985 to NOK 14 millions in 1990.[16] If the salaries of the administrative staff are added, the cost of evaluations amounts to about 0.2 per cent of the aid budget. It should be emphasised, however, that the costs involved in monitoring have not been included.

As far as the location is concerned, a certain degree of independence *vis-à-vis* the operative units of the aid administration has been secured, particularly since 1984, in view of the fact that the evaluation function is an integral part of the aid administration. However, even when the unit was located in NORAD, some independence was ensured through structural arrangements, as it reported directly to the top management (the Deputy Director-General). It has obtained additional resources, too, but the achievement is less convincing on this point, given the new and extended tasks and the strong emphasis on the importance of evaluation in the declared policy.

The Focus: Have the Objectives been Followed Up?

Evaluations should scrutinise whether aid contributes towards the attainment of the predominant objectives set for Norwegian aid, such as, first of all, the promotion of sustainable development, involving poverty alleviation, social justice, concern for women, children and the environment and the promotion of human rights. This is the main thrust of the declared policy. To what extent has the objective been followed up?

The evaluation reports for the period 1981–89 have been analysed in order to answer this question, taking the terms of reference (TOR) as the point of departure. Given the fact that evaluations, by and large, have been carried out by external teams, it is assumed that the TORs, more than the actual evaluations, reflect the considered intentions of the aid administration. The results are summarised, for each year and the period, in Table 1.[17] The stated objectives have to a large extent been followed up.

The main objective for Norwegian aid – *poverty alleviation* and to create lasting improvements for the poorest sections of the people in the recipient countries – is reflected in the TORs, but not very convincingly. In almost one fourth of the assignments, the evaluators are asked to

TABLE 1
THE FOCUS ON THE MAIN OBJECTIVES AND PRINCIPLES OF NORWEGIAN AID
AS PERCENTAGES OF TOTAL EVALUATIONS 1981-89

	1981	82	83	84	85	86	87	88	89	Total
Effects of aid on										
Poverty alleviation/ social justice		50	75		50	17			25	23
Target groups										
(a) the poor	25	50	25	20	33	50	20	33	38	33
(b) women	25	50	25		67	67	20	67	50	44
(c) children		50			17	30	20	17		10
Growth/development										
(a) Economic	25	75	100	20	67	50	60	33	63	54
(b) Social	25	50	50		67	17	60		50	35
(c) Cultural			25		33		20	17	13	13
(d) Political					17					2
Human rights			25		17					4
Sustainability/ dependence	100	75	50	20	50	50	40	50	75	56
Environments/ ecology	25	25	75		33	17	40	17	38	29
Integration in recipients' development plans/policy	25		75	40	67	67	20	33	75	48
Local participation in decision-making	25	50	25	40	33	50	20	33	25	33
Universe	4	4	4	5	6	6	5	6	8	48

assess the impact of aid for poverty alleviation or social justice. However, the references are general and the evaluators are not provided with an operational definition or criteria on which assessments should be based.

One aspect of poverty alleviation concerns the effects (and impact) of aid on target groups – the poor, women and children. The performance here is better: in 33 per cent of the assignments an assessment of the effects of aid for the poor is asked for; the score is even higher with regard to women, 44 per cent; and less for children, ten per cent, but this may be explained by the fact that children were included as a target group late in the 1980s.

It is a major objective for Norwegian aid to contribute to *economic, social and cultural growth*. In the standard TOR outlined in the manual, an assessment of the impact of aid in these fields is asked for.[18] Economic and social development is strongly reflected in the evaluation assignments, too; the evaluators are asked to assess the effects on economic growth in 54 per cent, and the effects on social development in 35 per cent, of the assignments. The concern for cultural development is definitely less (13 per cent). Improving *human rights* became a concern in its own right in the mid-1980s; previously it was so indirectly. This concern is almost absent (asked for in four per cent of the evaluation assignments). Another stated objective is that aid should contribute to *sustain-able development* and not create dependence on future aid. In the standard TOR manual, an assessment of the performance of aid to this end is asked for and the concern has also been reflected in more than half of the evaluation assignments (56 per cent). The *environmental concern* became increasingly part of the Norwegian aid policy during the 1980s. It is reflected in the standard TOR manual and in 29 per cent of the evaluation assignments.

During the 1970s, a guideline established for the mode of cooperation obtained a particularly prominent position in the stated Norwegian aid policy: aid should be *recipient-oriented*, that is, integrated in the development policy and plans of the recipient country. This concern is reflected in the standard TOR and in almost half of the evaluation assignments. The evaluators are asked to assess the local participation in decision-making in the standard TOR and in one-third of the assignments.

During the second half of the 1980s, all nine priority countries, the main recipients of bilateral state-to-state aid, and Zimbabwe were subject to a particular evaluation effort – separate country studies. These studies were comprehensive evaluation efforts, describing the prevailing social, economic and political situation in the country concerned, the development policy of its government and the international assistance it received. The Norwegian country programme was described and discussed against this background. The objectives and main guidelines set for Norwegian aid, as outlined in the above, were central points of departure for these country studies, which were intended to serve as a basis for designing future aid.

The conclusions emerging from the quantitative analysis above need to be supplemented, particularly regarding human rights and women in development. Although the concern for *human rights* has been neglected in the evaluation assignments, they have been explicitly asked for in the country studies. Within this field, a major effort has been carried out, financed through the ODA budget (though not through the evaluation item), namely a yearbook on the human rights situation within the priority countries for Norwegian aid.[19] The initiative, however, came from outside (two Norwegian research milieux); the initiative could seek strength from the 1984 White Paper and received support in Parliament.

Evaluation of the effects of *aid for women* in development has resulted in several evaluation reports and, as noted, has been asked for in almost half of the assignments.[20] In the mid-1980s, a research programme on women in development was initiated, too, financed by the Ministry of Development Cooperation (but through a research grant, not through the evaluation budget) and administered by the Norwegian Council for Applied Research in the Social Sciences.

The Strategy: Some Ambitious Prescriptions have been Followed Up, but not All
The political authorities have prescribed a rather ambitious evaluation strategy. All channels and forms of aid should be evaluated and the main questions in the aid debate should be increasingly addressed. Insights emerging from evaluations should be fed back to the policy-makers and the aid administration and even to the general public of the parties concerned (donor and recipient countries). The research milieux should be strengthened and drawn upon in order to increase the capacity and competence of evaluation. And international co-operation should be sought for the same purpose. To what extent has this strategy been followed up during the 1980s?

The aid channels: An almost exclusively bilateral focus: The main focus should, according to the declared evaluation policy, be directed towards the systems through which aid is channelled. Systemic characteristics that were considered conducive to the attainment of the aims set for Norwegian aid, in the first place the policies pursued towards development, social justice, human rights and other areas of interest from this perspective, should be given particular attention. All channels of aid should be evaluated. To what extent has this commitment been followed up?

As noted, more than half of the Norwegian aid is channelled bilaterally, the largest part directly to nine priority countries. The aid agency (NORAD) administers some aid forms directly, such as the commodity aid and a few other schemes to stimulate Norwegian exports to and investments in the Third World. The multilateral aid – about 40 per cent of the total Norwegian ODA – is channelled mainly through the development finance institutions (the World Bank/IDA and the regional development banks) and the UN system (in particular the UNDP, agencies for agriculture and food aid, UNICEF and UNFPA) in the form of general contributions. In addition, six to eight per cent of the bilateral aid has been channelled through the multilateral system earmarked for specific purposes ('multi-bilateral aid'). Almost ten per cent of Norwegian aid is channelled through NGOs.

TABLE 2
EVALUATION INVOLVING AID CHANNELS AS PERCENTAGE OF TOTAL
EVALUATIONS 1981–89

	1981	1982	1983	1984	1985	1986	1987	1988	1989	Total
Bilateral	100	100	100	100	100	100	80	83	100	96
1. Priority countries	50	75	75	20	43	29	20	50	13	38
2. Other main recipients					14				38	8
3. Multi-bilateral		25		20		14		17	13	10
4. NGOs	50		25	40	29	29				18
5. NORAD/DUH					14	14	40	17	38	16
6. Others				20		14	20			6
Multilateral*							20	17		4
Total	100	100	100	100	100	100	100	100	100	100
Universe	4	4	4	5	7	7	5	6	8	50

* Involving the United Nations system.

A review of the evaluation assignments resulting in evaluation reports during the period 1981–89 provides a well balanced picture as far as the *distribution* between aid channels is concerned, with one exception: the glaring neglect of the multilateral aid agencies, particularly the development finance institutions. An overview for each year and the whole period is provided in Table 2, which is based on 50 evaluation reports.[21]

With the exception of two reports, both focusing on the UN system, all evaluate bilateral aid. Aid to the priority countries amounts to 38 per cent of all evaluation assignments. In addition, the total aid programme to each of the nine priority countries has been evaluated during the second half of the 1980s in a series of quite extensive country studies.

Bilateral aid through international organisations (multi-bi) has been scrutinised throughout the period, somewhat in excess of its relative share (ten per cent). This applies also to the aid channelled through NGOs – 18 per cent of the evaluations, almost twice their share of total ODA. Several of the aid schemes which are directly administered by NORAD have been evaluated during the second part of the 1980s – altogether eight per cent of the total assignments for the full period, far beyond their share of total ODA.

In Table 3, the country focus is given.[22] Most attention (eight per cent) has been directed to Tanzania, the main recipient of Norwegian aid, but Zambia, among those receiving least, obtained the same attention. Aid activities in four other priority countries (Bangladesh, India, Kenya and

TABLE 3
THE GEOGRAPHICAL FOCUS: THE DISTIBUTION AS PERCENTAGES OF TOTAL EVALUATIONS 1981-89

	1981	1982	1983	1984	1985	1986	1987	1988	1989	Total
Priority countries:	75	75	50	0	42	28	17	17	13	32
Bangladesh					14	14				4
India	25	25						4		4
Kenya		25			14					4
Sri Lanka	25				14					4
Tanzania			25			14		17	13	8
Zambia	25	25	25				17			8
Non-priority: Zimbabwe					14			37		8
Others	25			20		14				6
More than one country/not country specific		25	25	40	14	43	50	67	50	37
Donor country			25	40	29	14	33	17		18
Total	100	100	100	100	100	100	100	100	100	100
Universe	4	4	4	5	7	7	6	6	8	51

Sri Lanka) have been evaluated only twice (aid to India not after 1982) and aid to the remaining three (Botswana, Mozambique and Pakistan) not at all. Some additional countries – and the regional cooperation in southern Africa (SADCC) – have received programmed bilateral aid over several years. Of these, only Zimbabwe has been focused on – and quite substantially (eight per cent, concentrated in the years after 1985). An interesting feature emerging from this review is the large and increasing focus on aid which is not country-specific or goes to more than one recipient country.

The most crucial question, however, relates to the qualitative aspects: to what extent were the various aid channels effective and efficient in achieving the aims set for Norwegian aid? This concerns all aid channels. For the state-to-state aid, the policies pursued by the main recipient countries become of particular interest. To what extent has this question been addressed?

The decentralisation of the aid administration by the establishment of resident representatives in the priority countries has been considered the main tool to control and follow up aid-supported activities and to facilitate the aid co-operation. These were established in the early 1970s and were given more staff and extended authority during the early 1980s. Given the declared aid policy, in particular, the emphasis given to the criteria set for the selection of priority countries, it might well be expected that an additional task for these offices would be a continuous surveillance of the development profile and performance of the government. However, the striking stability over the years in the distribution of aid between the priority countries does not indicate that such a task has been given high priority. If it has, the political will to act on this basis has not matched lofty policy declarations.

The most potent follow-up of the government's commitment (in the 1984 White Paper) to look into the main systems through which bilateral aid is channelled, the main recipient countries, is the programme of country studies. The first study appeared as early as 1985. By early 1990, every one of the nine main recipient countries had been covered by a quite substantial and comprehensive study that described and even analysed the economic, social and political situation prevailing in the country – and the aid scene – and analysed the Norwegian aid programme against this background. Zimbabwe has been covered by a similar study.[23]

However, the country studies are only indirectly scrutinising the fitness of the recipient system as a channel for Norwegian aid, given the predominant objectives and guidelines set for this aid, although this was what Parliament had asked for as a basis for the allocation of future aid. Still, some of the studies have been more explicit than others. The TORs have, to some extent, been opened up for this kind of analysis, although the emphasis has been directed towards how the Norwegian aid fits into the recipient system and how this aid works in relation to the objectives set for Norwegian aid, rather than how the recipient system itself functions *vis-à-vis* these objectives.[24] In the terms of reference for the most recent country studies, reference is explicitly made to one structure which is critical in this regard, namely the administrative system of the recipient country.[25]

These studies, carried out by Norwegian research institutes and consultancy firms, have constituted the basis for a separate analysis by the department of planning – along with comments on the country study from the aid administration, in particular the Resident Representative of the country concerned. These analyses focus on the aid situation prevailing in the country, how the Norwegian aid fits into this and adaptations in the country programme which should be considered in view of the study. This analysis constitutes a basis for the dialogue which takes place annually related to the revolving, four-year country, programme with the main recipient countries.

The reviews of the country programmes to the main recipient countries represent a major effort that is unique among donors. In summing up, three other features deserve, for different reasons, to be highlighted.

(1) Activities for which NORAD itself has carried a direct responsibility have been quite strongly focused on. This scrutinising applies, in particular, to the various schemes established in order to stimulate Norwegian firms to engage in trade with and investments in the Third World. These schemes were controversial in the domestic aid debate, too.[26] However, Parliament played a decisive role in this regard by establishing these schemes on a temporary basis with a clause stating that they should be evaluated after a trial period (three years). But also other programmes for which NORAD carried a direct responsibility – such as the Norwegian Volunteer Service ('Peace Corps') – have been evaluated. However, it is difficult to assess to what extent the separation of the evaluation function from the aid-implementing agency has facilitated the focus on aid types where the aid agency itself poses in a real sense as the aid channel.

(2) The focus on NGOs may appear difficult for different reasons. Aid through NGOs attracts strong support from all political parties. NGOs are the main champions of aid in Norwegian society and as such are natural allies for the aid agency. Add to this that the political leadership of the Ministry of Development Cooperation from the very start has been recruited from NGOs with an active aid involvement. In face of such obvious constraints, several NGOs, and among them some particularly sensitive ones (missionary organisations and the Norwegian Trade Union Federation), have been subject to critical evaluations (though initiated before the pertinent ministers were appointed).[27] No new evaluation involving NGOs has, however, been commissioned since early 1986.

(3) The most important feature, however, is that the multilateral system, through which more than 40 per cent of total Norwegian aid has continuously been channelled, has been almost totally neglected. The various UN agencies (no evaluations have been made of the development-finance institutions) have not been scrutinised from the perspective of their performance in relation to the objectives and major guidelines established for Norwegian aid.[28]

There may be several reasons for this, including the natural preoccupation with bilateral aid for which the Norwegian aid administration carries a more direct responsibility and which it will be more able to influence. The political authorities have, after all, committed themselves to distribute aid through channels that would be most effective and efficient in achieving the aims set for Norwegian aid, not excluding multilateral aid and the different aid agencies within the multilateral system. Why then this demonstrated passivity?

The main reason is given in the White Paper of 1984, where the government stated that the control of multilateral aid would also in the future be exerted mainly through the participation in the governing bodies of the multilateral aid agencies. In addition, a Nordic office was established in the IBRD (Washington), presumably to serve also such a surveillance function [*Svennevig, 1982*]. A review commissioned in order to map evaluation practices within the multilateral system,[29] where Dr Helge Kjekshus, for years head of the evaluation and research unit, was one of the two consultants, provides additional insights. In its conclusion, arguments related to the competence and capacity basis and the costs involved in taking on an independent role are combined with considerations involving strategy. The main recommendation was that, if Norway really wanted to take on an active role the most effective strategy would be to utilise, more than before, the work that had already been carried out or could be done by the UN system itself by an active involvement in the evaluation work of the agencies and that of the Joint Inspection Unit. Also it could improve its own aid administration by establishing firmer routines in the reception and utilisation of feedback from the international system.[30] However, there has recently been an initiative, within the DAC Expert Group on Aid Evaluation, to focus more strongly on the multilateral system.[31]

Increased focus on overall issues and non-project aid: The main issues in the aid debate and all forms of aid should be increasingly addressed, according to the stated strategy. To what extent has this commitment been followed up?

Part of the answer has already been given in the above discussion related to the most crucial question of them all: does aid work according to the objective set? The distribution of the evaluation assignments between projects, programmes, types of aid and issues over time, summarised in Table 4, points in the same general direction: the commitment has to a large extent been followed up.[32] Thus, whereas evaluation, before 1984 (1981–84), mainly focused on projects (70 per cent), their share after

EVALUATION POLICY AND PERFORMANCE OF NORWAY

TABLE 4
EVALUATIONS INVOLVING PROJECTS, PROGRAMMES, AID TYPES AND
ISSUES AS PERCENTAGES OF TOTAL EVALUATIONS 1981-89

	1981	1982	1983	1984	1985	1986	1987	1988	1989	Total
1. Projects	75	25	100	80	14	14		17	25	33
2. Programmes	25	75			71	43	17	50	38	37
3. Aid types					14	14	33	17	38	16
4. Issues						29	17	17		8
5. Others				20			33			6
Total	100	100	100	100	100	100	100	100	100	100
Universe	4	4	4	5	7	7	6	6	8	51

1984 (1985-89) was reduced to 15 per cent. Since 1985, the attention has been increasingly directed to programmes, the various types of aid (of which several were controversial in the domestic aid debate, as noted above) and other broad aid issues, including the socio-cultural aspects of aid.

It is traditional to distinguish between four major forms of aid – project aid, programme aid, commodity aid and technical assistance. However, the policy statement did not limit its scope to the major forms; it included the main sectors (agriculture, fisheries, communications, industrial development, family-planning, etc.) as well as cross-sectoral aid. During the late 1970s and early 1980s, the balance between the major forms changed and new forms of aid came increasingly to the fore; in particular, financial aid in different forms (commodity aid, budget support earmarked for sectors, balance-of-payments support, etc.). The distribution of evaluation reports for the period 1981-89 between the various sectors and types of aid is summarised in Table 5.[33] The objective set for evaluation has been fairly well met over time also on this account.

The stated strategy involves a commitment to cover the wide spectrum of aid forms, not the relative emphasis given to each of them. It may still make sense to assess this balance. The distribution of bilateral ODA between the various sectors and types of aid may serve as the reference point in this regard. The distribution in 1986 has been chosen for this purpose [*Report No. 66: 44*].

The evaluation assignments cover a wide spectrum of aid activities (Table 5). Twelve per cent of the evaluation assignments during the period 1981-89 have focused on agriculture and rural development; the focus was strongest in the first half of the 1980s (23 per cent of the bilateral ODA was channelled to agriculture and rural development during the same period). The same attention was given to fishery development (four

187

TABLE 5

EVALUATION OF AID WITHIN DIFFERENT SECTORS AND CATEGORIES OF AID IN PERCENTAGES OF ALL EVALUATIONS 1981–89

	1981	1982	1983	1984	1985	1986	1987	1988	1989	Total
Agriculture/ rural dev.	25	25	25	20	14			13	12	
Fisheries	25	50			14	14		13	12	
Industries/ crafts	25		25							4
Health/ family planning					14		17			4
Education					14	14	17	13		8
Water supply		25			14		20	13		10
Commodity aid						29		13		6
Norwegian business schemes				20	14	29	40	13		14
Women in dev.					14			33	13	8
Multi-sector			25			14	40	13		10
Other sectors	25		25	60				33		14
Total	100	100	100	100	100	100	100	100	100	100
Universe	4	4	4	5	7	7	5	6	8	50

times its share of bilateral ODA). Eight per cent of the assignments have focused on aid for education (equal to its share of bilateral aid) and water-supply programmes, respectively, and the same attention was given to women in development, which is assumed to be integrated in all aid activities (particular projects for women amounted to 1.3 per cent of bilateral aid). Health and family-planning, and industries and crafts were both covered by four per cent of the evaluation assignments, the first sector well below its share of bilateral ODA (ten per cent), the second about its share. The schemes intended to stimulate the Norwegian private sector in trade with and investments in Third World countries have, as noted earlier, been strongly focused on: 14 per cent of the total evaluation assignments, with a concentration during the period 1984–87, almost ten times their share of total aid.

Technical assistance (13 per cent of bilateral aid in 1986) and commodity aid have also been evaluated. The first major review of technical assistance took place as a joint effort with the other Nordic aid administrations and focused on the aid to three of their joint major recipients in eastern and southern Africa [*Evaluation Report 5.88*]. It was followed up with an evaluation of the Norwegian Volunteer Service [*Report 3.89*]. Evaluations of commodity aid (23 per cent of bilateral aid in 1986) amounted to six per cent of the total evaluation assignments during 1981–89; all took place after 1985.

EVALUATION POLICY AND PERFORMANCE OF NORWAY

However, some forms of aid have attracted little attention. This applies, first of all, to humanitarian aid, which has received a large and increasing share of the total Norwegian ODA.

A clear reorientation has taken place since 1984. The more basic questions of the aid policy have been addressed more systematically. Although aid efforts of a more limited scope (projects) have also been included during recent years, the main evaluation efforts have been oriented towards the broader aid forms (programmes and types of aid) and issues, as noted also in the sections above on objectives and aid channels. This change in orientation coincided with the move of the evaluation function from the aid-implementing agency (NORAD) to the Ministry of Development Cooperation in 1984.

Feedback: In the declared policy, the importance of effective feedback to the policy-makers and the administration responsible for the aid activity in the donor (NORAD) and recipient countries was underlined. The main purpose was to improve aid effectiveness and efficiency. Even 'the extended family' (experts, researchers, administrators, information and media people) should be included. To what extent has this prescription been followed up?

In a passive sense, the follow-up has been quite extensive, although mainly to Norwegian institutions: the evaluation reports have been published (almost all in both a Norwegian and an English version) and are open to all who are really interested. The evaluation reports contain a summary, in which the main findings are highlighted. The major findings of an evaluation have, in recent years, been presented at a press conference, in Oslo, where the team is represented. A press release is worked out by the information unit of the Ministry, in co-operation with the evaluation division, and distributed to the Norwegian mass media and a network of interested people.

In addition, more specific measures have been taken in relation to special target groups:

(a) *Parliament* is informed of the main findings resulting from evaluations in the annual report of the Ministry of Development Co-operation. This practice was initiated in 1982 [*Report No. 14*]. The main findings have been related to the major policy concerns as expressed by Parliament.[34] At times Parliament responds directly to what is reported, as in 1983 [*Recommendation No. 189*], when policy directives based on the reported findings were given.

(b) *The aid administration* is more systematically informed, both the decision-making bodies and the operative units. During the early 1980s, the report was summarised in a memorandum which was forwarded to the NORAD Board. From the evaluation unit, it was expected that the message, then, as a matter of routine, would then be distributed into the administrative system. In 1984, when the Ministry of Development Cooperation was established, a similar routine was established, but with an important difference. A summary memorandum, *in which also action is proposed*, based on the recommendations of the report and the comments by the involved parties (particularly other units of the Norwegian aid administration), was to be presented to the regular staff meeting, consisting of the heads of departments (including NORAD) of the Ministry. The political leadership of the Ministry should also be informed and given the opportunity to check the press release. The action proposed was to be prepared by the department of planning in cooperation with the operative units involved. This implied a gradual change: a planning function was added.

The reports have been distributed, as a matter of routine, to all sectoral units of the aid administration. Occasionally, when the theme attracts special attention, seminars for the staff have been run by the information unit. With regard to the country studies, the feedback has been more systematically organised. The report has been the basis for a two-day seminar involving the top leadership in the aid administration, the resident representative in the country concerned, the sectoral offices with programmes or projects involved and representatives of the evaluation team. In this way the country studies have been instrumental in opening up for a major review, within the aid administration, of the country programmes, which involves a learning process; and they have been effective to this end, too.

No learning system has so far been established.[35] However, the insights emerging from evaluation have been available for the planning process and the reports have constituted a basis for the country studies. Some initial efforts have also been made at synthesising the experiences from several evaluation reports.[36] However, a memory system has not, so far, been conceived of. Still, the evaluation reports are there to be consulted whenever a new hand enters an operative unit – for what this may be worth in a system where changes are frequent with reference both to staff and administrative system,[37] and where pressure of time is the most common experience of everyday life.

(c) *'The extended family'* has, noted, an open access to the evaluation reports. Several relevant university and independent research institutes receive, as a matter of routine, the evaluation reports, the country studies and the country analyses for their libraries.

(d) The feedback to *the recipient countries* is particularly passive. A number of copies are handed over (normally to the Ministry of Finance or Planning) by the resident representative, to be distributed to all who have been involved with the 'draft final report' for comments. There is no dissemination of the evaluation reports to the research milieux, the mass media or other interested parties within the recipient country. However, the country studies, and the country analyses, are discussed by Norwegian and recipient country authorities at a high level.

Co-operation with research milieux: The declared strategy envisaged a *liaison with Norwegian research milieux* in order to strengthen the evaluation efforts. Competence-building in evaluation, at home and on the recipient side, was one element in this strategy. To what extent has this been followed up?

Norwegian research milieux have been quite extensively drawn upon for evaluation tasks (Table 6). Such assignments have taxed their scientific capital but at the same time given them new insights, experiences and contacts with Third World realities and provided 'learning by doing'. The same applies to other specialised research institutes, specialists, administrators and, increasingly during the late 1980s, consultancy firms whose services have been drawn upon. For the research milieux, consultancy firms and administrators of the recipient countries, such effects have probably been less, although their involvement has not been negligible.

However, if the scope is broadened to include commissioned research and support (through the ODA budget) for development research of a kind that contributes to general competence-building in areas of relevance for development assistance, a lot more has been done. Indirectly or even directly, such support may contribute to competence-building of relevance even for evaluation. Since the mid-1980s, the Ministry has financed a few targeted research programmes with competence-building as one explicit objective. So far, Norwegian research milieux have obtained the lion's share, and only small funds have been channelled into Third World research milieux. A few agreements with Norwegian research institutes, most extensively and for the longest time with the Chr. Michelsen Institute in Bergen, also aim at competence-building.[38]

International co-operation in aid evaluation: International, particularly Nordic, co-operation in aid evaluation constituted part of the declared evaluation strategy in order to extend the capacity. To what extent has this been followed up?

A few efforts have been made, but it is difficult to detect an active strategy in this area. A joint Nordic evaluation has been carried out in the area of technical assistance, headed by Kim Forss [*Evaluation Report 5.88*]. Another effort (not related to the evaluation division) may also be mentioned: a project, jointly financed by the Nordic governments and based in the Swedish Ministry of Foreign Affairs, has been initiated with the purpose of looking into the development efforts by the UN system.

The Guidelines

According to the guidelines set, evaluations should be independent, open and available. And they should be joint undertakings between donor and recipient. How have these guidelines been interpreted and to what extent have they been followed up?

Independence: Independence in the context of evaluation is a multi-faceted concept, involving both formal and informal aspects. The focus here will be on the formal aspects related to the selection of evaluators. Some obvious structural characteristics should, however, be pointed out. The fact that evaluation is part of the administration of aid has a bearing on the degree of independence as well: it is the aid administration that decides what should be looked into (the terms of reference) and who should look. The terms of reference are drawn up by the evaluation division of the Ministry in co-operation with the unit of the executive agency with the direct administrative responsibility for the activity to be evaluated; in the case of a country study, the office of the resident representative is also involved. The key persons in the evaluation team usually have an opportunity to comment on the terms of reference. Even more important, a 'security clause' allowing the team to address questions not listed which it finds of relevance has at times been included.[39]

Basically, evaluation has been carried out by external teams commissioned for the task. However, during the 1970s and early 1980s, it was almost the rule that officials of the aid administration were included (mixed external and internal).[40] The prime justification was that this arrangement might forestall misunderstandings at an early stage. After 1984, this rule was reversed, but one of the officials of the evaluation division has been included in most teams involving the country studies, though not the recent ones.

The majority of the team members have all through been drawn from

EVALUATION POLICY AND PERFORMANCE OF NORWAY

TABLE 6
MEMBERS OF EVALUATION TEAMS 1981-89 AS DISTRIBUTED BY
NATIONALITY AND INSTITUTIONAL RELATION (PERCENTAGES)

	1981	82	83	84	85	86	87	88	89	Total
1. Norwegian	45	36	52	69	49	68	74	58	32	50
(a) Consultants/experts	25	14	24	46	11	23	16	53	29	25
(b) University/Research	15	18	10	8	24	32	47	5	3	17
(c) DUH/NORAD/UD	5	5	14	15	8	14	11			7
(d) Others			5		5					1
2. Other Nordic countries	15	5	14	8	5	14	5	26	15	12
(a) Consultants/experts	5	5	14		3	9		16	10	7
(b) University/Research	10			8	3	5	5	11	3	4
(c) Others									3	1
3. Other northern countries	5	9		8	8		11	11	7	7
(a) Consultants/experts					8	5		5	11	5	4
(b) University/Research	5	9			3			5		3	3
4. Recipient country	35	50	33	15	35	18	11	5	46	31
(a) Consultants/experts	15	23	5	8	5				15	8
(b) University/Research	10	9	10	8	19	5	5	5	32	14
(c) Gvt./Public administr.	10	18	14		11	14	5			8
(d) Others			5							1
5. Other Third World countries					5	5				1
(a) Consultants/experts					5	5				1
Total	100	100	100	100	100	100	100	100	100	100
Universe	20	22	21	13	37	23	19	19	41	215

universities, research institutes, public and private institutions with the relevant, specialised competence and from consultancy firms – as will be seen from Table 6, which provides an overview for the period 1981-89.[41] Consultancy firms have been increasingly relied upon. During the most recent years (1988-89) most assignments have been given to such firms, mostly Norwegian ones, and in a few cases even in cooperation with consultancy firms based in the recipient country. The team members have been recruited, in the first place, from the Norwegian market (50 per cent for the period 1981-89), but quite a few are recruited from the other Nordic (12 per cent) and northern (seven per cent) countries. It is significant, however, that almost one-third of the team members during this period were recruited from the recipient countries, almost half of them from universities or research institutes. Almost no recruitment has taken place from the Third World outside the recipients (Table 6). The country studies have been commissioned, at the beginning mainly from Norwegian development research institutes but increasingly from consultancy firms, after a bidding procedure. The recruitment of team members then became the responsibility of the winner.

193

Open and available: As already noted, evaluation studies have, as a general rule, been publicly available, in contrast to the reviews (monitoring).[42] All evaluation reports have been published and are accessible. However, the memorandum which is prepared by the administration to follow up the recommendations is not open. The justification given is that they include the opinions given by the various units of the administration. These may be conflicting and the administration does not want to bring such conflicts into the open.

A Joint Enterprise between Donor and Recipient?
The evaluation manual [*NORAD, 1981: 22*] corresponds well to the guideline set, emphasising that evaluations should first of all serve the recipients.[43] This lofty ambition has seldom come true. For the *government-to-government bilateral aid*, the general agreement between the two parties includes a clause allowing for evaluation. The initiative to undertake an evaluation – and the decision – has in almost every single case rested with the donor. The terms of reference for an evaluation and the composition of the team are first cleared on the Norwegian side. The authorities of the recipient country are, however, invited to comment on the proposal. In real terms, therefore, the recipient orientation has been fairly weak.

As already noted (Table 6), almost one-third of the evaluators during the period 1981–89 have been recruited from the recipient countries, in some exceptional cases even with an equal distribution. With a few exceptions, however, the participants from the recipient country have been directly recruited by the Norwegian party. In a few cases, however, evaluations have been organised as a joint venture with the recipient government.[44] Occasionally the authorities on the recipient side have been asked to propose members of a team and have suggested the civil servants who were dealing with the matter. Experiences of this kind have probably reinforced an inclination to keep a low profile in involving the authorities on the recipient side, in view of the established norm to use independent evaluators.

An outcome of the kind referred to would not necessarily materialise if the nature of an evaluation and the principles guiding it were made clear beforehand. In some of the priority countries, evaluation units are growing up which may act as intermediaries between the donor and the national research milieux (with scarce resources) and consultancy firms. In some of the recipient countries, the culture is far more ripe for evaluation to take place and the experience and skills more developed than in the donor country (India is a case in point). To include evaluators from the recipient country has not, so far, been established as a matter of routine, not even for the country studies. Much could obviously be gained by making use of the existing opportunities.

To pursue such a policy would not be without problems. The country studies, where the TORs request an assessment of the prevailing human rights situation, may illustrate the point: in some of the countries, nationals may find it difficult to sign a critical report. Nationals of the recipient country have, for such reasons, been assigned specialised tasks and separate background papers.

The *problématique* involved is much the same also for aid channelled through multilateral agencies and NGOs, although the policy pursued has followed a different course. This applies, in particular, to the multilateral agencies where a direct and active Norwegian intervention, characteristic of bilateral aid, has been reversed, leaving it to the agencies themselves to evaluate their performance.

V. SOME CONCLUSIONS

Although most conclusions have already been given, a few deserve to be highlighted. The first concerns the strong involvement by Parliament, which, during the early 1980s, took the initiative in drawing up objectives, norms and guidelines for evaluation. The declared evaluation policy is, therefore, tuned to the needs of Parliament to know whether aid works according to the aims set (the *control* function). Parliament and government share a concern for effective and efficient aid. The stated evaluation policy reflects this concern, too, by emphasising the *management function* of evaluation, although not equally strongly.

During the 1980s, this policy has been followed up by the aid administration to a very large extent. Evaluations have focused on the main aid channels (though with the almost total exception of the multilateral system), the different types and forms of aid and even the controversial aid schemes where the NORAD itself carries the direct responsibility for the implementation. The focus has increasingly been on the broader aid issues and away from projects. The country studies, involving the ten major recipients of bilateral aid, represent a particular and unique evaluation effort that underscores this conclusion. The profile adopted is well suited to meet the needs one might expect from the policy-makers and which have indeed been expressed at the highest levels, particularly by Parliament. However, this does not necessarily imply a corresponding impact at that level.

Meeting such needs at this level serves management needs as well, although not necessarily at the operational level. Besides, the evaluations have also, by and large, addressed problems of direct relevance to the management of aid at the operational level. Evaluation teams doing so-called fieldwork seldom escape the operational aspects, nor should they, the fundamental problem being rather that it seems so difficult to approach questions which relate to higher management levels, involving decisions on policy. In dealing with problems at various levels, evaluation teams have, as a matter of routine, *combined the control function with the management function* by offering recommendations aimed at improvements in present or future aid activities in order to increase the efficiency and even the effects of aid in accordance with the objectives set for the particular activity or even the broader societal aims set for aid.

Evaluation has clearly been used as a tool in aid administration, both in adjusting a course during the project cycle in order to obtain better results, and even more as an instrument in the decision-making process at crossroads where a decision whether to prolong an activity, possibly in a new form, or to pull out is pending.[45]

In such cases, the evaluators – with wide-open eyes, it is to be hoped – serve the role of *brokers* between various actors active on the scene, including the recipient and donor sides, the various levels of the aid administration at home and in the field, and vested interests outside the administration, professional, economic and even ideological, particularly within the donor country. Clearly, evaluations also serve *a legitimating function*. In several cases, the political authorities have used evaluations for this purpose – quite explicitly so when the various mechanisms intended to stimulate Norwegian firms to engage in increased trade with and investment in the Third World were decided during the late 1970s and early 1980s, as this commercialisation of aid was controversial even within the government proposing the mechanisms. Their continuation was made dependent on the outcome of evaluations after a certain period.

In some cases, even the objectives set for the particular activity (project or programme) have been explicitly exposed to scrutiny and the evaluators have been expected to come up with recommendations that involved even the objectives.[46]

During the 1980s, a dual evaluation system has emerged in the aid administration, the system outlined and discussed above (situated in the Ministry) and the monitoring carried out by NORAD. The monitoring system belongs, in some respects, to a different world. It is clearly designed to serve management purposes, including decision-making at the administrative level involving policy. It is mainly carried out as *internal* reviews, but external consultants have been used for such purposes. The reports are not open and the feedback is concentrated on the administrative (including the operative) levels, although a summary of the activities and main findings was once included in the yearly report of the Ministry to Parliament [*Report No. 34, 1985–86: 172–9*], revealing a quite extensive review activity involving (during 1985) 40–50 bilateral projects and several multi-bilateral projects. And the professional ambition level has gradually been increased, as indicated by the introduction, in 1987–88, of the 'logical framework' system. Yet the two evaluation systems are almost totally compartmentalised.

The orientation of the evaluation work administered by the evaluation unit during the 1980s and the institutional split of the evaluation function, as broadly defined (including monitoring), between NORAD and the Ministry can probably explain the emergence of the dual system. An explicit invitation to critical scrutiny in combination with openness, which has been associated with the evaluation set-up, is a strange feature in most administrative systems. It rebels strongly against the culture nurtured in the aid agency during its formative years. The institutional setting during the early 1980s, when the evaluation policy was formed, was conducive to institutional rivalry, as the aid agency had, despite strong and loud protests, lost much of its autonomy *vis-à-vis* the Ministry. In such a situation, evaluation might well be considered by the aid agency as an instrument in the hands of the Ministry to exert control and influence. Expanding the monitoring function and initiating reviews of projects in order to prevent an external and open evaluation offered itself as an effective strategy to fend off unwanted control.

To keep up such a dual, compartmentalised, evaluation system has its price. The critical question that needs to be asked is whether, in the 1990s, this compartmentalisation can be defended, if at all. An integrated evaluation system where monitoring is organised in such a way that the reports can serve as building blocks in more comprehensive evaluations would represent a long stride ahead and be cost-effective, too.

Another form of integration would also be cost-effective, namely to fully explore and take advantage of opportunities for further co-operation in aid evaluation with other aid agencies, in particular, agencies of donor countries which, by and large, share the predominant objectives set for Norwegian aid. This relates, first of all, to the country studies and evaluations of the multilateral system. Much could be gained, both in quality and costs, by pooling resources to this end.

Equally important would be to explore and take advantage of the opportunities to include Third World researchers and research milieux (and genuine Third World consultancy firms) in the evaluation effort, also in countries without a strong evaluation tradition. This would serve a core-developmental objective as well.

This leads to my concluding point: the link between evaluation and research should be developed further. Some questions addressed by evaluation teams need a more penetrating and time-consuming scrutiny than what the tight time schedule of an evaluation mission allows. It is important, in this context, to bridge the expectation gap which exists. This implies, *inter alia*, providing researchers with a greater understanding of the need for an aid agency to settle for quick answers which can be directly used. It implies, on the other hand, that the aid administration at large gets a better understanding of the requirement, if more demanding issues are to be tackled, of resources and time that are adapted to the magnitude of the task. And the universities should more strongly integrate evaluation in their teaching and research programmes to improve its quality.

NOTES

1. The first evaluation report was produced in 1972. For a presentation of the early days of Norwegian aid evaluation, see Jensen [*1974*], with an introduction by the present author.
2. See Chapter 1 of this volume, 'Policies, Performance, Trends and Challenges in Aid Evaluation', by the present writer and Chapter 2, 'Evaluation Policy and Performance: The State of the Art', by Helge Kjekshus.
3. See NORAD [*1981: 1–3*].
4. Ibid. In 1984, the government [*Report No.36, 1984: 42*] made a similar distinction between project reviews (monitoring) and evaluation of aid. *Project reviews* (monitoring) were defined as regular, internal reviews by the aid agency, alone or jointly with the recipient, of the individual aid activity. External experts might be relied on, and even the broader effects of the activity might be assessed in such internal reviews. *Evaluation* was defined as an independent and critical scrutinising of the aid activity, which should concentrate on the effects of aid as related to the aims set for the activity. The predominant objectives established for Norwegian aid should be considered the primary point of departure, and lower-ranking objectives for the single activity were to be derived from the predominant one. Thus, both objectives, guidelines and organisational aspects are part of the definitions.
5. The monitoring system has characteristics particular to monitoring but has increasingly acquired features associated with evaluation, too. What here are termed 'evaluation' and 'monitoring' may, therefore, to a large extent emerge as the result of an institutional split: 'evaluation' is associated with the Ministry, 'monitoring' with the implementing agency (NORAD).

According to the procedures set for monitoring, most projects are scrutinised every year in an *annual review*, often combined with the annual meeting on the project, where the working plan and budget for the following year are discussed. The annual review is an integral part of the project management, regulated by the agreement. The projects are not run by NORAD but by the recipients (for aid within the country programmes by the host country). Such reviews are carried out by mixed teams involving representatives of the host country, NORAD–Oslo (the functional division and sometimes

EVALUATION POLICY AND PERFORMANCE OF NORWAY

also the country division) and the Resident Representative and sometimes an external consultant (specialist).

In addition, major *reviews* are undertaken for a variety of reasons (a major programme in terms of financial costs; a decision to invest new monies or to terminate a project; etc.), involving the same categories of evaluators, but with a more pronounced *external* participation (*mixed* teams). The decision to undertake such reviews is not centralised; usually the initiative comes from the Resident Representative, although the Director-General of NORAD (along with the Heads of Departments – the *Directors*) has at times initiated such reviews. In principle, initiatives may come from any office involved in the project or a body in the host country. Major reviews may involve the same kind of evaluators (even the same persons) from outside as those engaged in evaluations organised by the evaluation office of the Ministry; the main difference being that the implementing agency is also represented in the team (though not always) and the host country is always represented. As a matter both of principle and recent practice, monitoring is considered as a joint enterprise.

The terms of reference (TOR) are usually signed by the Director of the regional department (NORAD has two regional departments – one for Africa and one for Asia and Latin America) with the responsibility for the project and the team reports to this department. In NORAD, the report is occasionally discussed in the *advisory forum*, meeting once a week and consisting of the two regional directors and their deputies, the chief of division for the country concerned and the officer responsible for the project at headquarters (sectoral division), and the sectoral division involved (the sectoral divisions have a two-track reporting system: to the heads of the regional departments and to the Assistant Director-General of NORAD) – and the Resident Representative in the recipient country concerned. Decisions on follow-up are by and large confined to the regional department concerned.

The 'logical framework' system was introduced in 1988 – gradually and by persuasion rather than obligation (see MDC/NORAD [*1988*] and NORAD [*1990*] (not dated)). It is expected to be used in documents involving planning and decisions on projects, in a flexible way even from the recipient, and as a basis for monitoring.

The monitoring has not been guided by formal guidelines. No manual has been established (the NORAD Handbook for evaluation [*NORAD, 1981*] has not been in common use). Experiences have not been systematised. There are no instructions for feedback or procedures for follow-up.

The monitoring reports are *internal*. (A problem of definition is involved, however, as the management responsibility of NORAD-financed projects is vested in the recipient, unlike what is the case for some other donor agencies.) They have not been reported in a systematic way; though with one exception, in 1986, in the annual report on aid for 1985 [*Report No.34, 1986: 172–9*], where the reviews carried out in 1985 are extensively summarised. However, the NORAD Information and Documentation Unit is planning to make the reports more available than hitherto. The reports are mostly written in English.

6. The State Auditor (Riksrevisjonen) is an external controlling institution which is appointed by and reports to Parliament, not to the government as is the case with the State Auditor in Sweden (Riksrevisionssverket) and the United Kingdom. The Auditor, therefore, is at the service of Parliament to see to it that the policy set by Parliament is followed up.

The basis for the control are the main policy documents on aid policy, that is, Reports No.36 [*1984*] and 34 [*1987*] and propositions and reports dealing with specific aid issues, the annual budget propositions and the annual report to Parliament. Basically, the State Auditor looks into the administrative procedures and accounting by the aid agency (NORAD) and the Ministry of Development Cooperation. It limits its scrutiny to this level, and the focus is on the agreements that NORAD or the Ministry has entered into. As regards bilateral aid, it stops where NORAD's involvement ends. The implication is that the end use of aid is not followed up to the extent that this is the responsibility of a Third World government (bilateral aid), an international aid agency (multilateral and multilateral–bilateral aid) or of non-governmental organisations. However, if funds are used contrary to the agreement without interference by NORAD, this may appear as a case. And it has happened, though very rarely, that even field visits in recipient countries have been undertaken and reported (see Dokument nr. 1 [*1987–88: 22–4*]).

The State Auditor interacts directly with the implementing agencies and only cases where agreement is not reached are reported in its two annual reports to Parliament – in St. Dokument 1, where irregularities are noted, along with the explanation given by the Ministry, to be decided by Parliament and St. Dokument 2, where cases are brought to the attention of Parliament. All communications from the Auditor are confidential, though the recipients are allowed to make them public. The State Auditor has an office situated on the premises of NORAD with a staff of four or five.

The brief description given above indicates that the function of the State Auditor is distinct from the evaluation function as defined, limited as it is to management control of procedures and accounting. Given these limitations, mainly self-imposed, it cannot provide Parliament with answers of the type: does aid work? This is the most important question Parliament wants to be addressed. The State Auditor does not, therefore, substitute evaluation.

7. See Report No. 36 [*1984*], Report No. 34 [*1987*] and Recommendation No. 186 [*1987*]. For a description and discussion of the main features of the Norwegian aid policy, see Stokke [*1984, 1989*].
8. In the 1975 White Paper on aid [*Report No. 94, 1975*], the government stated, *inter alia*:

> When evaluating any development project or programme, a decisive criterion will be whether it will contribute towards promoting the development and well-being of the broad mass of population and in particular those who suffer most from poverty and need. Recent experience and research seem to indicate that it is precisely such a policy on development aid which in the long run provides the best incentive for growth, placing as it does the major emphasis on broad social (including health, nutrition and education) and economic development for the benefit of the broad masses of the population, hereunder not least the development of rural areas.

In 1984, the poverty orientation was given an even stronger emphasis [*Report No. 36, 1984: 8*]. The economic crisis of the 1980s made it

> even more necessary than ever to direct our development assistance towards the poor countries and to follow a strategy that aims at making it possible for them to satisfy their basic needs. A major objective is to further expand the poverty orientation of the Norwegian development assistance. It is the opinion of the government that our assistance must be directed towards poor strata of the population in the developing countries, and to increase their abilities to satisfy their basic needs, such as food, health, employment. In the opinion of the government, increased efforts within agriculture, water supply, health and education, in which primary health services and basic education are considered especially important, are elements in such a strategy. Aid directed to programmes which are contributing to a self-generating economic development may be obvious elements in this regard.

9. *Norway's Strategy for Assistance to Women in Development*, Ministry of Development Cooperation, Oslo, 1985.
10. The main concern, on which the guideline is based, was clearly expressed by the government (non-Socialist coalition) in the White Paper of 1984 [*Report No. 36, 1984: 28*]:

> We have to see to it that as little as possible of the aid disappears as a result of bad planning, corruption and inefficient administration in the recipient country. In a similar way the aid administration must see to it that the aid does not disappear on the Norwegian side because of too high a price or a quality that is not adapted to the purpose.

11. For an overview and discussion, see Stokke [*1987*].

EVALUATION POLICY AND PERFORMANCE OF NORWAY

12. The evaluation of aid had two main objectives, according to the government [*Report No. 36, 1984: 42*]:

    (1) The most important function is to systematise experiences in order to improve the current and future aid activities. Insights should be brought back to the units, within the aid agency and in the recipient countries, which had the responsibility of planning and implementing aid. Experiences should be integrated in the planning of new and the implementation of current activities. Routines should be established to ensure that this takes place.

    (2) The other main function is to provide independent information to the political authorities responsible for the aid budget and to the public at large on how the aid funds have been utilised.

13. Recommendation No. 186 [*1987: 21*]. See also ibid. [1987: 55], where Parliament's Foreign Affairs Committee emphasised

    the importance of further extending the work with evaluations, or result evaluation, both in quantitative and qualitative terms. The *Committee* wished to underline the importance of independent and critical evaluations and to stress that the experiences should be integrated into the practical implementation as far as aid administration was concerned.

    The committee recognised the difficulties involved in measuring the real effects of development assistance. Even so, an extended and intensified evaluation activity might assist in establishing a more solid basis for decisions involving future engagements, according to the committee. It agreed to the strengthening of the evaluation activity and its extension to include sectors and countries, adding the need for ecological country analyses.

14. This office started out by taking stock of what had been achieved till then and by establishing norms and procedures for the evaluation work. A brief report (commissioned) summed up the evaluation of NORAD activities in the period 1976–79 ('Kortfattet vurdering av evalueringer av NORAD-tiltak 1976–79', undated mimeo, 10 pp.), and an evaluation manual was prepared [*NORAD 1981*].

15. St. prp. nr. 1, Tillegg nr. 1 [*1983–84: 9–10*].

16. According to budget proposals by the government. In the budget proposal for 1985, evaluation got a separate budget allocation for the first time – for 1984, the expenses used for this purpose were estimated at NOK six to seven millions, which represented 'a large increase as related to previous years'. However, as a share of the total aid budget, the increase (excluding the staff) from 1985 to 1990 has been more modest than the increase in NOK may indicate: 0.15 and 0.2 per cent respectively.

17. This analysis is based on 48 evaluation reports published during 1981–89. The following reports have not been included because no terms of reference (TOR) are reported (or given): 7.85, 6.86 and 3.87. Reports 4.88 and 6.89 have to date not been published. With these exceptions, all evaluation reports during the period have been reviewed.

    In the TOR of several evaluation assignments after 1982 (from *Evaluation Report* 3.87 onwards), a general reference to the Norwegian objectives and principles for development co-operation is included, at times also a reference to the policy of the recipient country has been added (but not in all). These general references have not been included in Table 1. It should be added that for a few evaluation assignments, reference to some (or even all!) categories included in the Table could not be expected, as illustrated by *Evaluation Report* 5.84, where the assignment was to review NORAD's support to Norwegian NGOs for carrying out information and education work related to Third World development in Norway.

18. NORAD [*1981: Appendix II*].

19. See Andreassen *et al.* [*1986*] and Skålnes and Egeland (eds.) [*1987*].

20. See *Evalueringsrapport* [*6.86*] and Lexow [*1987*].

21. The overview in Table 2 includes all evaluation reports published during the period given, with one exception [*Evaluation Report 2.87*] which could not be classified

(focuses on the social-cultural aspects of aid). Two reports have not been published to date (4.88 and 6.89).
22. The overview in Table 3 includes all evaluation reports published during the period (4.88 and 6.89 have not been published to date).
23. See country study and Norwegian aid review on Pakistan (1985), Bangladesh (1986), Zambia (1986), Sri Lanka (1987), Kenya (1987), India (1977), Botswana (1988), Tanzania (1988), Zimbabwe (1989) and Mozambique (1990).
24. According to the TOR for the country study on Kenya, the purpose is: '... to provide a basic document for the assessment of aid policies and issues by the Ministry in respect of the country in question for the forthcoming 5-year period.' And the principal objective: '... to provide a comprehensive assessment of all Norwegian development assistance over the past 10 years, its real effects, effectiveness and conformity to the country's own development policies as well as Norwegian aid objectives.' See Tostensen and Scott (eds.) *[1987: 365]*. These are standard formulations.
25. Ibid. *[1987: 368]*. The terms of reference ask for a 'description of the private and public sectors, including parastatals, structure and degree of centralisation/decentralisation, planning and implementation of measures in selected ministries/sectors and regions/districts which is relevant to Norwegian initiatives.' For a follow-up in this particular country study, see pp. 235-43.
26. See, *inter alia*, *Evaluation Report 3.85*, *Evaluation Report 5.86*, *Evaluation Report 7.86*, *Evaluation Report 4.87*, *Evaluation Report 6.87* and *Evaluation Report 1.89*.
27. This has been a consistent policy and includes a wide range of organisations. It started with the Ceynor Development Project in Sri Lanka, involving the Norges Godtemplar Ungdomsforbund (the youth wing of a Norwegian teetotaller organisation) *[Evaluation Report 1.81]*, and subsequent evaluations include the Norwegian Church Aid, Sudan Programme *[Evaluation Report 2.81]*, two projects run by two Norwegian missionary organisations in Latin America, the Norwegian Santal Mission in Ecuador and the Pentecostal Mission of Norway in Paraguay *[Evaluation Report 1.83]*, a course in manpower training run by the Norwegian Shipping Academy *[Evaluation Report 2.83]*, Redd Barna (Save the Children) development activities *[Evaluation Report 4.85]*, trade-union training financed under the LO (The Norwegian Trade Union Federation)– NORAD framework agreement 1980-85 *[Evaluation Report 1A.85]* and organisations and countries supported through the agreement between NORAD and the Norwegian Trade Union Federation *[Evaluation Report 1B.85]*. The evaluation of the support for information on development issues given to Norwegian NGOs may also be included in this survey *[Evaluation Report 5.84]*.
28. In the TOR for the evaluation assignment leading to *Evaluation Report 5.87*, there is no specific request of this kind – except for a general reference to what is stated in the 1984 White Paper on Aid (the consultants, however, offered general assessments of the kind). In the TOR for the assignments leading to *Evaluation Report 1.88, UNIFEM*, there is not even a reference to Norwegian aid policy, nor in the report.
29. *Evaluation Report 5.87*. The main purpose of the review was to explore the existing needs from a Norwegian and Nordic perspective for evaluations of multilateral aid and their options in undertaking such evaluations (TOR: 38) and to come up with proposals for action based on a review of existing evaluation systems of some multilateral organisations and the Joint Inspection Unit and material produced by these agencies, along with the experiences of some major bilateral donors in evaluating multilateral aid.
30. Ibid., 27-30. Evaluations of the multi-bilateral aid could give insights into how effective and efficient the various UN agencies were as operators of aid. However, Norway lacked both policy and capacity in this area. The review also concluded that very little of the documentation provided by the UN system seemed to have been used as input to help the aid administration to evaluate the efficiency of the UN system and the effects of its aid-supported activities.
31. See DAC/EV(90)2.
32. Table 4 is based on all evaluation reports during the stated period with the exception of

EVALUATION POLICY AND PERFORMANCE OF NORWAY

two which have not been published to date [*4.88* and *6.89*]. The classification in Table 4 is somewhat arbitrary, particularly the distinction between projects and programmes. *Project* has been defined as aid activities integrated to attain designated goals within a determined time span and following an established plan of action, whereas a *programme* is defined as aid activities of several kinds, within different sectors, which converge to attain the same development objective. A programme may, therefore, include several projects. If an aid activity is spread to several geographical areas (countries), the term 'programme' is chosen. Included in the programme category (Table 4) are also *sector evaluations*, that is, evaluations of a variety of actions which all are all located in the same sector (within one or several country programmes). *Type* of aid refers to programmes of a specific kind, such as the Volunteer Service, the Women grant, various schemes to stimulate the private sector to engage in trade with and investments in the Third World.

33. Table 5 is based on all evaluation reports which have been published during the stated period (4.88 and 6.89 have not appeared to date), with one exception (2.87) which could not be classified within the categories chosen.
34. See, in particular, the reports for 1985 and 1986. In Report No. 34, St. meld. nr. 34 [*1985–86: 165–85*], the experiences of some more specific problem areas were also discussed, including the difficulties involved in reaching through to the poor. The monitoring of projects was also reported. In Report No. 66, St. meld. nr. 66 [*1986–87: 111–14*], some additional problem areas were discussed, namely conflicts in objectives between donor and recipient, co-operation problems at the local level and the choice of technology.
35. This point has been strongly put by outside insiders. See, in particular, Isaksen [*1982*] and Jansen [*1982*].
36. See *Evaluation Report 3.87* and *Evalueringsrapport 6.86.*.
37. See Stokke [*1987*]. In 1989, NORAD again became an external agency under the Ministry of Development Cooperation, but this time without an executive Board of Directors and reorganised according to geographical criteria (the previous organisation followed functional criteria). And later in the year, the Ministry merged with the Ministry of Foreign Affairs, while the political leadership continued to be vested in a Minister for Development Cooperation within the enlarged Ministry of Foreign Affairs.
38. In the government's budget proposal for 1990 [*Proposition No. 1, 1983: 61–2*] for the ODA, the research support was for the first time split between support for development research in Norway and other industrialised countries (NOK 22.6 millions; in 1988, NOK 24.7 millions were spent) and support for research in developing countries, South–South co-operation and North (Norway)–South research co-operation (NOK 24.4 millions, almost 2.5 times the amount spent in 1988).

The support for Norwegian development research has for most programmes been channelled through the national research council system. In the mid-1980s, it started up with support for two programme areas, namely women and development and technology transfers. These aimed at competence-building as well, and so did the research support included in a major aid programme to the Sahel (which also contains a component designed for Third World researchers). A third programme, initiated in 1988 (population, health and development) has the form of institutional support. Even a recruitment (Ph.D.) programme in development studies obtained the support of the Ministry. The grant for 1990 envisaged also support for competence-building within the subject of the environment and development and research related to human rights. For a description and discussion, see *Forum for utviklingsstudier* [*1987: 6–10*]. For an evaluation, see *Evaluation Report 6.89*.
39. In the instruction for evaluation given by the Director-General of NORAD, 22 January 1981 [*NORAD, 1981: Appendix I*], a rolling two-year plan for evaluation should be forwarded by the office for research and evaluation, based on proposals from the offices of the resident representatives in the priority countries and the offices at the home base and in consultation with the various departments of NORAD. However, the pro-

EVALUATING DEVELOPMENT ASSISTANCE

gramme, when accepted by the Deputy Director-General, should be discussed with the recipient countries in the yearly negotiations on the country programmes, where these countries could come up with proposals of their own or suggest changes. It was also stated that the evaluation 'should be carried out as a joint venture between donor and recipient'. Although this has occasionally happened, joint ventures have been the exception.

In the standard TOR (Ibid.: Appendix II), the 'safety clause' was included: 'Evaluate any other matter which the team finds relevant.' It has appeared also in some of the assignments, such as in the TOR to the evaluation assignment resulting in *Evaluation Report 1.84*. In the TOR to the assignment resulting in *Evaluation Report 8.89* it was stated that 'the work shall include but not necessarily be limited to the following points:', listing the points and adding, with regard to the recommendations, that the team should discuss 'any other aspect arising from the evaluation', after having listed a few areas to which attention should be directed.

40. In the evaluation manual [*NORAD, 1981: 25–8*], the evaluation team was supposed to be guided by a working group established by NORAD and drawn from the offices involved in preparing the TOR and the team and then serving as a secretariat for the team and ensuring the follow-up. One member of this working group should 'normally also take part in the field work during the evaluation'.
41. Table 6 gives an overview of all members of the evaluation teams for each year during the period 1981–89. In some cases, consultants of the recipient countries have been relied on for particular tasks. These have, with a few exceptions (*Evaluation Report 3.89*) not been included. The overview does not include *Evaluation Reports 4.88* and *6.89* (not published so far) and *9.89*.

    Some evaluation reports cover themes where Norwegian (or Nordic) evaluators stand out as natural choices (*5.84*), and some reports synthesise results from a series of evaluations (*6.86* and *3.87*). For the independence variable, it is of some interest that, when the Norwegian Trade Union Federation/ILO activities were evaluated (*1.85*), representatives from the NTUF and ILO (also a Norwegian) were included in the team – an exceptional feature.
42. In the early 1980s, this was not taken for granted. In the Instruction by NORAD's Director-General [*NORAD, 1981: Appendix I*], it is stated that the Director-General decides 'if and how the evaluation report should be made accessible for the public after having received the view held by the recipient country'.
43. It is stated that the prime responsibility for the development of the recipient country is vested in its own authorities. 'It is therefore the recipient countries that in the first place need information and information routines ... The evaluations by aid agencies must therefore be subordinated to a recipient-oriented purpose and become a supportive instrument for the recipient administration.'
44. *Evaluation Reports 3.81* (with the government of Zambia), *4.81* (with the government of India) and *5.89* (with the government of Tanzania).
45. In the case of the schemes established, on a temporary basis, in order to stimulate Norwegian private enterprises to engage in trade with and investments in Third World countries, this involved decisions at *the political level* on the continuation of the various mechanisms. This was made clear when the schemes were established. Thus, in the TOR for the evaluation of two of these schemes, parallel financing (PF) and mixed credits (MC), the consultants were, *inter alia*, asked to 'Describe objectives and guidelines for FP and MC as laid down in Parliamentary and Ministerial documents .... Discuss whether the aims, strategies and regulations concerning PF and MC are adequately clear and coherent, or whether the further development of guidelines would be advantageous (sic).' [*Evaluation Report 1.89: 103*].

    In other cases, it involved decisions at *the administrative level* (aid agency, Ministry – thus involving the Minister), such as decisions involving the WID grant [*Evaluation Report 2.89: 105*], the fisheries research vessel [*Evaluation Report 4.89*] or the Commodity Import Programme (CIP) in Zimbabwe [*Evaluation Report 8.89*], just to refer to a few recent assignments.

EVALUATION POLICY AND PERFORMANCE OF NORWAY

The TOR of a recent evaluation [*Evaluation Report 5.89*] of the Tanzanian Institute of Development Management may indicate that *joint* evaluations, more than others, are designed to serve the needs of the administration for administrative decision-making involving adjustments to improve effects and efficiency.
46. For illustrations, see *idem*.

REFERENCES

Andreassen, Bård-Anders, Jan Egeland, Asbjørn Eide, Bernt Hagtvedt, Tor Skålnes, Hugo Stokke and Bjørn Stormorken, 1986, *Menneskerettighetene i Norges hovedsamarbeidsland 1985*, Bergen and Oslo: Chr. Michelsen Institute and the Norwegian Human Rights Project.

Chr. Michelsen Institute, 1986, *Zambia. Country Study and Norwegian Aid Review*, Bergen.

Chr. Michelsen Institute, 1986, *Bangladesh. Country Study and Norwegian Aid Review*, Bergen.

DAC/EV (90)2, 1990, 'Evaluation of Multilateral Assistance. An Approach Paper (Note by the Delegation of Norway)', Paris: OECD, Development Assistance Committee, Expert Group on Aid Evaluation, Jan.

Evaluation Report 1.81, 'The Ceynor Development Project', Sri Lanka, Oslo: NORAD.

Evaluation Report 2.81, 'Norwegian Church Aid. Sudan Programme'. Oslo: NORAD.

Evaluation Report 3.81, 'Soil Survey, Zambia', Oslo: NORAD.

Evaluation Report 4.81, 'Industrial Tribology – India', Oslo: NORAD.

Evaluation Report 1.83, 'Norwegian Mission in Latin America', Oslo: NORAD.

Evaluation Report 2.83, 'Manpower Training – The Professional Shipping Course', Oslo: NORAD.

Evaluation Report 1.84, 'Worldview International Foundation', Oslo: The Royal Norwegian Ministry of Development Cooperation.

Evaluation Report 5.84, 'U–landsinformasjon til organisasjons-Norge', Oslo: The Royal Norwegian Ministry of Development Cooperation.

Evaluation Report 1A.85, 'Trade Union Training', Oslo: The Royal Norwegian Ministry of Development Cooperation.

Evaluation Report 1B.85, 'Organisations and Countries Supported through the Agreement between NORAD and LO–Norway', Background report prepared by the Norwegian Trade Union Center for Social Science and Research, Oslo: The Royal Norwegian Ministry of Development Cooperation.

Evaluation Report 3.85, Opplæringsstøtteordningen', Oslo: The Royal Norwegian Ministry of Development Cooperation.

Evaluation Report 4.85, 'Redd Barna Development Activities', Oslo: The Royal Norwegian Ministry of Development Cooperation.

Evaluation Report 7.85, 'A Case Study on the Administrative and Planning Model of HIRDEP, Sri Lanka', Oslo: The Royal Norwegian Ministry of Development Cooperation.

Evaluation Report 5.86, 'The Evaluation of Four Norwegian Consultancy Funds', Oslo: The Royal Norwegian Ministry of Development Cooperation.

Evaluation Report 7.86, 'Norway's Commodity Assistance and Import Support to Bangladesh', Oslo: The Royal Norwegian Ministry of Development Assistance.

Evaluation Report 2.87, 'Socio-kulturelle forhold i bistanden', Oslo: The Royal Norwegian Ministry of Development Cooperation.

Evaluation Report 3.87, 'Erfaringer fra 23 norske evalueringsrapporter', Oslo: The Royal Norwegian Ministry of Development Cooperation.

Evaluation Report 4.87, 'NORAD's Provisions for Investment Support', Oslo: The Royal Norwegian Ministry of Development Cooperation.

EVALUATING DEVELOPMENT ASSISTANCE

Evaluation Report 5.87, 'Evaluering av multilateral bistand gjennom FN-systemet', Oslo: The Royal Norwegian Ministry of Development Cooperation.
Evaluation Report 6.87, 'Promoting Imports from Developing Countries', Oslo: The Royal Norwegian Ministry of Development Cooperation.
Evaluation Report 1.88, 'UNIFEM: The United Nations Development Fund', Oslo: The Royal Norwegian Ministry of Development Cooperation.
Evaluation Report 4.88, 'Nordic Commodity Import Support to Tanzania', Oslo: Ministry of Development Cooperation (not published).
Evaluation Report 5.88, 'Evaluation of the Effectiveness of Technical Assistance Personnel', (financed by the Nordic countries; by Kim Forss, John Carlsen, Egil Frøyland, Taimi Sitari and Knud Vilby). A study commissioned by the Danish International Development Agency, DANIDA, the Finnish International Development Agency, FINNIDA, the Royal Norwegian Ministry of Development Cooperation, MCD/-NORAD (*sic*) and the Swedish International Development Authority, SIDA.
Evaluation Report 2.89, 'The Women's Grant', Oslo: The Royal Norwegian Ministry of Development Cooperation.
Evaluation Report 4.89, 'Fisheries Research Vessel "Dr. Fridtjof Nansen"', Oslo: The Royal Norwegian Ministry of Development Cooperation.
Evaluation Report 5.89, 'Evaluation of the Tanzanian Institute of Development Management', Oslo: The Royal Norwegian Ministry of Development Cooperation.
Evaluation Report 6.89, 'En evaluering av tre DUH-finansierte forskningsprogrammer', Oslo: The Royal Norwegian Ministry of Development Cooperation (not published).
Evaluation Report 8.89, 'Evaluation of the Commodity Import Programme, Zimbabwe', Oslo: The Royal Norwegian Ministry of Development Cooperation.
Evalueringsrapport 6.86, 'Virkninger for kvinner av norske bistandstiltak', Oslo: The Royal Norwegian Ministry of Development Cooperation.
Evalueringsrapport 1.89, 'Parallellfinansiering og blandete kreditter', Oslo: Det Kongelige Departement for Utviklingshjelp.
Evalueringsrapport 3.89, 'Evaluering av det norske fredskorps', Oslo: Det Kongelige Departement for Utviklingshjelp.
Forum for utviklingsstudier, 1987; 'Norsk utviklingsforskning, forskningssamarbeid og bistand til kompetanseutvikling i den tredje verden', 6–10, Oslo: NUPI.
Granberg, Per and J.R. Parkinson (eds.), 1988, *Botswana. Country Study and Norwegian Aid Review*, Bergen: Chr. Michelsen Institute.
Hansen, Stein, Ofstad, Arve, Das, Arvind N., Kjekshus, Helge, Mukhopadhyay, Maitrayee and Pamela Gwynne Price, 1987, *India: Development and Aid. Norway's Contribution and Future Options*, Bekkestua: Stein Hansen Economic Research, Policy and Planning.
Havnevik, Kjell, Kjærby, Finn, Meena, Ruth, Skarstein, Rune and Ulla Vuorela, 1988, *Tanzania: Country Study and Norwegian Aid Review*, Bergen: Centre for Development Studies.
Human Rights in Developing Countries. A Yearbook on Human Rights in Countries Receiving Nordic Aid, 1988, Copenhagen: Akademisk Forlag.
Isaksen, Jan, 1982, 'Evaluering skal gi innsyn, som vi bør formidle videre', *Forum for utviklingsstudier*, 8–10, Oslo: NUPI.
Jansen, Eirik G., 1982, 'Generelle erfaringer fra evalueringsoppdrag', *Forum for utviklingsstudier*, 8–10, Oslo: NUPI.
Jensen, Eskild, 1974, 'Evaluering av norsk bistand', *Forum for utviklingsstudier*, 1.
Jerve, Alf Morten and Aart van de Laar (eds.), 1985, *Pakistan. Landstudie og vurdering av norsk utviklingshjelp*, Bergen: Chr. Michelsen Institute.
Lexow, Janne (1987), 'Norway' (Chapter 10), in Cecilia Andersen and S.A. Baud (eds.), *Women in Development Cooperation: Europe's Unfinished Business*, Tilburg: EADI.
MDC, 1985, *Norway's Strategy for Assistance to Women in Development*, Oslo: Ministry of Development Cooperation.
MDC/NORAD, 1988, 'Introduction to Logical Project Analysis. A Preliminary Handbook', Oslo.

EVALUATION POLICY AND PERFORMANCE OF NORWAY

NORAD, 'Kortfattet vurderinger av evalueringer av NORAD-tiltak 1976–79', Oslo (undated and unpublished document): NORAD.
NORAD, 1981, *Håndbok for evalueringsspørsmål*, Oslo.
NORAD, 1990 (?) (undated), *The Logical Framework Approach (LFA). Handbook for Objectives-oriented Project Planning*, Oslo.
Proposition No. 1, 1983, St. prp. nr. 1. Tillegg nr. 1 (1983–84).
Proposition No. 1, 1989, St. prp. nr. 1 (1989–90), Departementet for utviklingshjelp.
Recommendation No. 192, 1976, Innst. S. nr. 192 (1975–76).
Recommendation No. 137, 1982, Innst. S. nr. 137 (1981–82).
Recommendation No. 189, 1983, Innst. S. nr. 189 (1982–83).
Recommendation No. 186, 1987, Innst. S. nr. 186 (1986–87).
Riksrevisjonen, Dokument nr. 1 (1987–88), 'Ekstrakt av Norges statsregnskap og regnskap vedkommende administrasjonen av Svalbard for 1986. Saker for desisjon av Stortinget og andre regnskapssaker'.
Report No. 94, 1975, St. meld. nr. 94 (1974–75), 'Om Norges økonomiske samkvem med utviklingslandene' (1975 White Paper).
Report No. 14, 1982, St. meld. nr. 14 (1982–83), 'Om Norges samarbeid med utviklingslandene i 1981'.
Report No. 36, 1984, St. meld. nr. 36 (1984–85), 'Om enkelte hovedspørsmål i norsk utviklingshjelp' (1984 White Paper).
Report No. 34, 1986, St. meld. nr. 34 (1985–86), 'Om Norges samarbeid med utviklingslandene i 1985'.
Report No. 34, 1987, St. meld. nr. 34 (1986–87), 'Om hovedspørsmål i norsk utviklingshjelp'.
Report No. 66, 1987, St. meld. nr. 66 (1986–87), 'Om Norges samarbeid med utviklingslandene i 1986'.
Skålnes, Tor and Jan Egeland (eds.), 1987, *Menneskerettighetene i Norges hovedsamarbeidsland*, Oslo: Universitetsforlaget.
Stokke, Olav, 1984, 'Norwegian Aid: Policy and Performance', in Stokke (ed.) [*1984*].
Stokke, Olav (ed.), 1984, *European Development Assistance*, Vol. I: *Policies and Performance*, Tilburg: EADI.
Stokke, Olav, 1987, 'Norsk bistandspolitikk og bistandsadministrasjon', *Nordisk Administrativt Tidsskrift* 1987: 4, Copenhagen.
Stokke, Olav, 1988, 'Norsk bistandspolitikk: kontinuitet og endring', *Norsk Utenrikspolitisk Årbok 1987*, Oslo: NUPI.
Stokke, Olav, 1989, 'The Determinants of Norwegian Aid Policy', in Stokke (ed.) [*1989*].
Stokke, Olav (ed.), 1989, *Western Middle Powers and Global Poverty. The Determinants of the Aid Policies of Canada, Denmark, the Netherlands, Norway and Sweden*, Uppsala: Scandinavian Institute of African Studies.
Svennevig, P.T., 1982, 'Evaluering av flersidig bistand', *Forum for utviklingsstudier*, 8–10, Oslo: NUPI.
Sørbø, Gunnar M., Brochmann, Grete, Dale, Reidar, Moore, Mick, and Erik Whist, 1987, *Sri Lanka. Country Study and Norwegian Aid Review*, Bergen: Centre for Development Studies.
Tostensen, Arne and John G. Scott (eds.), 1987, *Kenya. Country Study and Norwegian Aid Review*, Bergen: Chr. Michelsen Institute.

8

The Evaluation Policy and Performance of Sweden

KIM FORSS

I. INTRODUCTION

Swedish development aid started in the late 1940s through bilateral co-operation with Ethiopia. Evaluations started at the same time; the initial experience started an intensive debate on the nature of development and the possible contributions of Sweden. The early evaluations had a big impact on the organisational development of the Swedish aid organisations. The first was a public/private agency; the Central Committee (CK). In retrospect, its main accomplishment was to established international co-operation on the domestic political scene. In 1961, CK was followed by a governmental organisation, the Agency for International Assistance. Four years later, this was reorganised and renamed when the Swedish International Development Authority (SIDA) was created.

The objectives of Swedish development co-operation as laid down by Parliament in 1978, are to promote:

- economic growth
- economic and social equality
- economic and political independence
- development of democracy in society.

In 1987 another objective was added to the list – to promote careful management of the natural resources and concern for the environment.

Since 1975 around one per cent of the GDP has been appropriated for international development co-operation. In 1988–89 this amounts to 10,300 million SEK (1,745 million US$). Of this total, roughly 30 per cent is channelled through international aid programmes and 50 per cent is in the form of bilateral development co-operation. Other forms of bilateral co-operation, such as concessionary credits, and research co-operation account for 15 per cent. The remaining five per cent are used for information, administration, etc. Development co-operation is part of foreign policy and a Minister for International Development Cooperation within the Ministry of Foreign Affairs carries the overall responsibility. Multilateral development co-operation is administered by the Ministry, but other programmes are administered by independent government agencies, namely:

SIDA (the Swedish International Development Authority) is responsible for the bilateral development co-operation, including emergency aid, humanitarian aid, co-operation through non-governmental organisations, information and training;

BITS (the Swedish Agency for International Technical and Economic Co-operation) is responsible for technical co-operation, international training programmes in Sweden and concessionary credits;

SAREC (the Swedish Agency for Research Co-operation with Developing Countries) is responsible for research co-operation, science and tech-nology;

SWEDFUND (the Swedish Fund for Industrial Cooperation with Developing Countries) is responsible for joint ventures and investment co-operation; and

IMPOD (the Import Promotion Office for Products from Developing Countries) is responsible for support to developing countries' export efforts.

Each of the above organisations has its own policies and procedures in respect of evaluation. But there is also a continuous evaluation of development co-operation at the governmental level. The last comprehensive review of Swedish aid was the Public Enquiry on Development Co-operation, which was published 11 years ago [*SOU, 1977: 13*]. SIDA was subjected to a review of effective aid organisation [*Ds UD, 1984: 1*], which led to a reorganisation in 1986. SAREC was evaluated after ten years of operation [*Ds UD, 1985: 2*] – the evaluators appreciated the importance and effectiveness of research co-operation and recommended continued support for that purpose. SWEDFUND was evaluated in 1987 [*Ds UD, 1988: 4*] and the conclusions of that evaluation are presently leading to a major review of the objectives and organisation of the agency.

Other parts of development co-operation that have been reviewed in a similar manner are disaster relief, assistance through non-governmental organisations (NGOs) and 'movement to movement' co-operation. The Ministry of Foreign Affairs has also initiated comprehensive evaluations of the co-operation with specific countries, for example, Tunisia and Cuba. These evaluations were made after the countries had ceased to be major recipients of Swedish aid; that is, when they were no longer programme countries of SIDA, or if there was to be a change in the level of co-operation.

The National Audit Board undertakes studies of the performance of all government agencies. A major study of SIDA was presented in 1976. During 1983 two major components of bilateral assistance were studied: the aid agencies' employment of consultants [Dnr 1983: 172] and import support as a form of assistance [Dnr 1983: 173]. During 1986 the National Audit Board initiated a study of SIDA as a learning organisation, the objectives being to document how organisational learning takes place and the extent to which the organisation can be said to learn. The final report of this study was presented in late 1988.

At the level of the individual aid agencies there is also an ongoing evaluation of the various programmes and projects. But the need for evaluations, as perceived by the agencies, varies sharply between them. SWEDFUND is more oriented towards financial data. SAREC has an interest in the direct impact in terms of research results, as well as a longer strategic view of the growth of research capacities. BITS relies on external competence for most evaluation studies, the better part of which are *ex ante* studies or studies to support management decisions.

SIDA is the largest of the organisations; half of Swedish aid passes through its channels and it employs 600 people (SIDA's budget proposal, 1988–89), compared to around 70 in all the other agencies. SIDA is still seen by many as the one and only Swedish aid agency. When I now turn to discuss evaluation policies and performance, it is SIDA's evaluation system that I focus on; first, because it is the major channel for bilateral assistance, second, because it is older and has developed an evaluation system more explicitly than the other agencies have, and third, because it is more readily comparable to other bilateral or multilateral agencies. But it is important to have the other agencies and their evaluations in mind, particularly the Ministry of Foreign Affairs and the National Audit Board, as their activities have a major impact on the evaluation policies of SIDA.

II. EVALUATION IN THE SIDA

Definitions

Evaluation is an activity concerned with finding out whether things are good or bad. This is a basic fact that must not be forgotten. But when researchers and practitioners meet, we often speak of 'systems', 'procedures', 'methodologies' and 'methods'. We focus our questions on these concepts and categories and discuss them in detail, but we could equally well ask ourselves if there are other arenas of action where opinions concerning the good and the bad are formed – arenas that could be more important than the 'evaluation systems'.

Evaluation stems from the root word 'value'. In economics, 'value' is used in two senses: a narrow one equivalent to 'price', and a broad one, equivalent to 'utility' [*Bannock et al., 1972*]. Price is measurable, but utility can only be measured ordinally, that is, as a preference for one thing rather than another. As such, it has non-economic roots; it is essentially a psychological phenomenon. The etymological background of the word 'evaluate' justifies a vague, holistic and qualitative use, as well as quantitative and analytical use. But the tension between the two approaches causes confusion and may lead to a dysfunctional emphasis on the one rather than on the other.

I have chosen a practical approach to the subject of evaluation. I am primarily interested in finding out how and what SIDA learns on the subject of development co-operation; that is, how it as an organisation evaluates its activities. The 'official' evaluation system (using the established vocabulary, see OECD [*1986*]) is part of that learning, but no more. Describing the official evaluation system does not tell us how the organisation as a whole forms its opinions on the effect of programmes and projects. On the basis of the traditions of general system sciences, I treat evaluation as synonymous with feedback [*Wiener, 1954; von Bertalanffy, 1962; Buckley, 1967*]. Against this background, evaluation is part and parcel of a controlled feedback system of the organisation. The 'evaluation system' explored here comprises the constituents of that system, its leading subsystems, and its integration with other systems, such as planning systems. The use of the words differs from common practice, but I hope the reader will be patient with this. The perspective on evaluation as a phenomenon shifts with the vocabulary and perhaps it is possible to provoke new thoughts by an unconventional look at the 'system' (recognising that the usage is commonplace in other scientific disciplines).

EVALUATING DEVELOPMENT ASSISTANCE

The Order of SIDA's Evaluation System
The present discussion of SIDA's evaluation system will focus on three major aspects; (1) evaluation staff, (2) evaluation reports, and (3) the financing of evaluations. In doing so we will discuss both *ex ante* and *ex post* evaluations.

Evaluation staff: Who in SIDA evaluates projects and pro-grammes and to what extent do they rely on external competence for evaluations? Let me first note that all programme officers in SIDA evaluate. The staff at headquarters in Stockholm have a major role in preparing new projects, appraising them and recommending action to the director and the board. *Ex ante* appraisal is part of the ordinary job of headquarters staff. The procedures for appraisal as well as the criteria for assessment are described in the Guidelines for Project Support [*SIDA, 1987*].

Programme officers in the field office are usually involved in the elaboration of an idea for support; that is, the very first stages of the project cycle. The headquarters staff are responsible for the development of an idea into a project. At this stage external expertise may become involved, particularly if complex technical or institutional issues are concerned. In fact, most new projects are elaborated by external consultants, but it is programme officers at headquarters who prepare the decisions and appraise the projects in terms of the objectives of development assistance. As far as *ex ante* evaluations are concerned, all of SIDA's programme officers are involved.

Ex post evaluations are primarily handled by the field offices. The project monitoring is done by the programme officers in the field. They receive quarterly reports, annual reports, etc. from the projects, assess them and communicate their views to headquarters. Headquarter staff normally take part in monitoring reports and other types of progress reports, but this is not their main responsibility.

Apart from the monitoring reports and other types of progress reports, there are also *special project and programme evaluations*. Such evaluations can be initiated by the project personnel, SIDA's field office or headquarters, and by the recipient country. As for headquarters, these evaluations could either be initiated by the programme officers directly in charge of the activities, or by the central evaluation unit. The point is that most units at SIDA are engaged in *ex post* evaluation. All sometimes have a role to play, and the budget resources for evaluation are distributed throughout the organisations.

Let us make a rough estimate of how much time is spent on evaluation activities. A programme officer at headquarters will probably on the average spend about 25 per cent of his time on *ex ante* appraisals, but a programme officer in a field office will probably not spend more than 10 per cent of his time on such appraisals. On the other hand, personnel in the field office will spend roughly 25 per cent of their time on different types of *ex post* evaluations, and headquarters personnel probably around 20 per cent of their time. The real extent of time spent on evaluation activities will, of course, depend on the size and nature of the activities and it will vary from one year to another – but let us take these figures as rough approximations.

SIDA has a total staff of 600. Some 300 are programme officers and the rest are administrative staff, or have other duties than project management. Out of these 300 just over 100 are placed in the field offices and 200 are based in Stockholm. The total number of man-years spent on evaluation is approximately as follows:

	Ex ante evaluation	*Ex post* evaluation
Field office	10	25
Headquarters	50	40
Total	60	65

This means that SIDA staff in total spend around 125 man-years on evaluation. This rough approximation is supported by observations of the daily workload of programme officers. It also reflects the job descriptions in the organisation, which always mention evaluation activities as one of the most important tasks (not necessarily conducting evaluations but initiating them and using the results).

SIDA has a special evaluation unit which is part of the Planning Secretariat attached to the Director-General. The evaluation unit consists of four programme officers and one assistant. The resources of the evaluation unit may seem small compared to the 125 man-years of evaluation in the organisation, but they have a very important role to play. The tasks of the evaluation unit are:

(1) To ascertain that SIDA's projects and programmes are evaluated when need arises; evaluations are partly centrally planned according to the evaluation unit's plan of operations.
(2) To ascertain that evaluations are conducted professionally, objectively, and with the appropriate methods.
(3) To ascertain that the experience and knowledge gained through evaluations are actively used on SIDA's present and future co-operation and generally have an influence on the organisation.
(4) To ascertain that evaluation results are presented clearly and publicly and that they are accessible to all who could utilise them.

(5) To ascertain that evaluation results are disseminated to the government, the Parliament, the media and the general public.

The role of the evaluation unit is primarily that of a catalyst; to initiate action, establish quality standards, and ensure follow-up activities. The staff of the evaluation unit act as consultants to the programme officers in the organisation. They review terms of reference for evaluations and advise other staff on methodological issues. They have a data bank on evaluation studies and use this to transfer knowledge within the organisation. The evaluation unit publishes summaries of all SIDA projects annually in its 'Project and Programme Follow-Up'. This publication contains a fact sheet on each project, indicating objectives, activities, major results, budget and status of evaluation. The staff of the evaluation unit usually take part in one or two evaluation teams every year, to influence the study but also to remain at the forefront of evaluation practice.

Ex post evaluations are usually undertaken by external consultants. One of the problems here is to find qualified evaluators. The Swedish resource base is very limited and it is difficult to build international contacts. The evaluation unit can help programme officers find evaluators by maintaining a wider network of professional contacts.

Evaluation reports: Evaluation reports are the evidence that evaluation takes place. In fact, evaluation is often confused with systematic reporting in a written format. In the following pages I will discuss three categories of written information that can be said to summarise SIDA's evaluation activities.

First, each project or programme has some type of reporting procedure whereby the financial statements are handed to the programme officer in charge and where there is some type of feedback concerning the plan of operation for the activity in hand. These reports are often referred to as 'monitoring systems'. On some projects there are quarterly reports, on some semi-annual, and on some information is only given annually. The quality of the reports varies, but by and large they give little information that has an impact on the management of projects. Either the subject is already known by the programme officer or it is too technical to be of interest. The information contained in such reports is seldom useful from a managerial point of view. Their major function is to document activities that have taken place and as such they serve to legitimate actions.

It is important to note that SIDA has no standardised reporting procedures for such follow-up reports. The 'system' is designed according to the needs of each project and as such it is more or less formalised, more or less comprehensive, and more or less integrated with other project activities. Even if I have noted that the information in such reports is often not useful from a decision-making point of view, the magnitude of the reporting effort is huge. An average-size project generates approximately 200 pages of progress reports a year – which yields more than 200, 000 pages from all the projects in the organisation.

The second type of reports consists of *ex ante* or *ex post* studies of the impact of projects and the process of co-operation. The terminology for such studies varies; some are called evaluations, impact studies, studies of effectiveness, or some other name. They have in common an ambition to find out how good a project is and they are aimed at the target 'value'. *Ex ante* evaluations (appraisals) were mentioned above and there is, of course, always a study before a project is started. Appraisals are seldom published, they are used as *aides-mémoire* for the decision to embark on a project. The number of project appraisals depends on the state of SIDA's programme in each country. In some years, there are several new activities and thus a large number of *ex ante* appraisals; in other years, there are not so many. On the average there are now 10 to 15 new appraisals discussed by SIDA's board every year.

Ex post evaluations are generally of greater interest, as they reflect the value of something that has passed, which means that people can be blamed or praised. The evaluation unit's plan of operation includes around 30 projects to be evaluated per year. Besides, evaluations of all kinds are also initiated by the field offices and the sector divisions, but they are not as many as those initiated by the evaluation unit. Finally, some large projects have their own evaluations and impact studies. The total number of *ex post* evaluations can thus be estimated at between 50 and 80.

All evaluations are public according to Swedish law. They cannot be treated confidentially or withheld. But if I am to point out a problem in relation to the evaluations, it is the contrary – that they are not widely read. The evaluation studies are usually only read by those closely involved: the programme officers, project staff and the authorities in the recipient country. The average report is perhaps read by five persons – the summary might be read by another ten.

One of the activities of the evaluation unit is to disseminate evaluation results, to increase the use of such intelligence and to stimulate learning in the organisation. This is done through two series of booklets; (1) SIDA Evaluation Reports, and (2) *Bistånd utvärderat*. The latter is published in Swedish and is aimed at a general public interested in development problems. Each pamphlet contains a summary of a major evaluation. They are written in plain language and they have a fairly wide readership. The SIDA Evaluation Reports are aimed at a more initiated group of people – researchers, students and part of the general public which is more deeply interested in development co-operation.

There are about eight publications in each series every year and the aim is to keep to that level. These studies should be read and thus there should not be too many, the fear being that otherwise potential readers will only put them on the shelves. One of the most important features of the report series is that they disseminate information across countries and projects. Those working on a water project in Vietnam can become acquainted with results from a project in Zambia and find out if the latter has any relevant experience for them. The series also give the readers a good view of the diversity of SIDA's activities and facilitate contacts within the organisation. They stimulate the debate on development issues and thus in general raise the interest in evaluation, by putting questions about what is good or bad.

The third category of evaluation information is the informal correspondence that abounds in the organisation. This includes weekly letters between programme officers, telexes, notes on the file, memoranda from field visits, etc. All these sources contain a wealth of information about why some things are done and not others, why some questions are raised and not others. They indicate why some activities are considered poor and why others are good. The informal exchange of opinions is usually the first arena for the formulation of value statements, and perhaps the most important. The written information is, of course, supplemented by verbal communication of the same informal nature. It is difficult, if not impossible, to quantify such information. Nevertheless, I would suggest that there are fewer pages but better information in the third category than in the other two categories.

The financing of evaluations: I have now discussed who evaluates projects and how the results of evaluations are presented; now comes the question of how much the whole evaluation exercise costs. Let us first focus on the evaluation reports. The average SIDA evaluation costs between 200,000 and 300,000 SEK. Larger evaluation studies that cut across sectors, countries or functions cost more, but there are only one or two of that kind every year at present. If we speak of 50 evaluation studies, we thus arrive at a total of some 10 million SEK (1.6 million US$).

Monitoring and progress reports (category 1), and informal

communication (category 3), cannot usually be separated from other administrative costs. The cost of such reports can on the other hand be said to be included if we look at the cost per man-year for the evaluation staff – 130 man-years at a cost of one million SEK in a field office and 300,000 SEK at headquarters. We arrive at a total of 72 million SEK.

Note that the magnitude of evaluation in the ordinary officers' work is much larger than the 10 million SEK spent on 50 evaluation studies. But note that the total amount spent on evaluation – somewhere around 80 million SEK – is small in comparison to the size of SIDA's budget. It represents less than one per cent of the budget for bilateral assistance.

Let us now turn to the use of funds available for evaluation; that is, funds that are available for initiating separate studies of impact and effectiveness of projects (not including the cost of staff). Such funds are spread round the organisation, at the field offices, at each sector bureau at headquarters, and at the evaluation unit. The fact that funds are dispersed means that an evaluation study can be initiated from several sources. It happens that some part of the organisation is more interested in evaluating a particular project than another section. Neither part is dependent on the other for funds and it is thus more likely that critical evaluations will be undertaken as part of the internal competition for resources.

It is impossible to calculate the total funds available for evaluation. Evaluations fall under the budget post called IRV ('*insats- och resultatvärdering*'), which includes *ex ante* appraisals, *ex post* evaluations, special studies and various consultancy services. The total IRV budget was 30.5 million SEK in 1987–88. Considering the other expenditure items under this heading, the above mentioned estimate of 10 million SEK spent on evaluation studies appears to be quite realistic. The distribution of the funds, however, means that they are quite flexible and can actually be used for evaluation to a higher degree than that. There is also a 'grey zone' of studies and consultancy services which are not quite evaluations.

The Chaotic Nature of SIDA's Evaluation System

The review above has pointed to an orderly system in terms of staff, funds and publications that together constitute the evaluation activities of the organisation and yield the visible results of evaluation. But I have also noted that the aim here is to find out how opinions on the good and the bad are formed and translated into action. That process is not captured by looking only at the orderly side of the evaluation system, even if that side is as generously defined as here. The following notes on phenomena closely related to evaluation will be grouped under two headings; (1) SIDA's interactions with external organisations, and (2) integrating planning, evaluation and decision-making.

SIDA's interactions with external organisations: SIDA's evaluation reports are always publicly available. As a result there is often a public debate on development assistance. Daily papers are interested in 'scandals'. The political opposition has an interest in raising issues in Parliament that have a public appeal. Students at universities and researchers frequently select development projects for further studies.

But the public debate not only starts from the knowledge generated by SIDA and its evaluation reports. The debate generates knowledge, as new ideas are put forth, as independent journalists investigate development co-operation, as researchers and students go about their tasks. If we look at the most significant sources of new ideas concerning SIDA's projects and programmes, we find that these often come from research at the universities.

Among other things, SIDA stimulates such activities by making funds available for students to write their exam papers on development problems. These funds serve the purpose of engaging young people in development co-operation. At the same time there is a possibility that their reports will be useful to the organisation.

Furthermore, SAREC supports Swedish research on development problems – research which is often closely connected with a problem area that bilateral assistance is occupied with. The research reports that are produced help to increase SIDA's knowledge of the problem in hand and help to form an opinion on the value of the activities.

SIDA encourages journalists to write on development problems and SIDA staff contribute to the debate by occasional articles in the daily papers. This process is, of course, something that can never be controlled and it has drawbacks for the 'management' of Swedish aid – opinions put forth are not always comfortable to live with. By and large SIDA has promoted and encouraged the debate and the results are primarily positive.

It is important to recognise the 'open systems' nature of the organisation and to facilitate the exchange of information rather than closing the borders. It is particularly important to recognise that the function of evaluation is very closely connected with inputs from the environment, from the press, researchers and politicians. At times the press is seen as hostile, but it is also a source of information and ideas and as such performs an important task in respect of evaluation.

Integrating planning, evaluation and decision-making: One of the major areas of concern in aid administration is how to link planning and evaluation into an integrated management process. Bachrach [*1980*] concluded that the principal constraint on evaluation was the initial design of a project. The evaluation cannot be better conceptualised than the project itself. However, this seems to contradict the experience of most aid organisations. There is widespread evidence of projects that are well conceived but the evaluations contribute little or nothing to their future development. On the other hand, we may witness successful evaluations that play a key role in improving projects with preparation deficiencies.

Imboden [*1978*] argued that projects should have an experimental design as the only means of achieving meaningful feedback. As that presupposes a rather sophisticated administrative system, which is value-laden and part of foreign social systems, they may have little application in a development context, perhaps even sharpening the divergent interests of aid organisations and recipient governments.

SIDA's assistance programme is evaluated by the monitoring system, informal communication and evaluation studies, and by the environment in a wider sense. All these sources of information are integrated through the annual sector reviews when SIDA meets with the recipient countries' governments to review the aid programmes. This is when evaluations are considered, discussed and evaluated. It is also the occasion when future activities are planned and when a number of management decisions are taken. The annual reviews are the most important planning, evaluation and decision-making events. They are the instruments whereby those three functions are integrated.

The development of overlapping projects, sector programmes and import support necessitates a holistic view of aid. Fuzzy boundaries between activities, overlapping goals and a large number of 'informal' considerations thus strengthen the integration between planning, evaluation and decision-making. The annual reviews are also rather lengthy processes and may take two to three weeks on the larger programmes. Sometimes they are also supplemented by minor reviews in between the annual reviews.

Design principles: The two features mentioned above – an open system and an uncertain internal environment – point to an example of system design that is interesting. Emery and Trist [*1973*] have described two opposite design principles that both serve to increase the system's adaptiveness in a turbulent environment. An adaptive, self-regulating system has to have built-in redundancy. If not, the system is confined to a limited set of responses that are adaptive only to a similarly finite, strictly identified set of environmental conditions. But there are different ways of introducing redundancy.

The first design principle can be called 'redundancy of parts'. Having redundant parts implies that the system must have specialised parts, that is, control mechanisms, that determine which parts are active or redundant for any particular adaptive response. The control mechanism must, of course, also have its own specialised part, and so on *ad infinitum*. In this type of system, the tendency is towards continual reduction of the functions of the individual part.

The second design principle is to increase the redundancy of functions of the individual parts. This entails effective mechanisms within the part for setting and resetting its functions and the system operates by means of overlapping assemblies based on a similar sharing of parts. The reality of organisational design is, of course, never similar to theoretical constructs, but, all things considered, SIDA's evaluation system has many of the characteristics of the design 'redundancy of functions'. Evaluation is part of the daily job of all programme officers. It is closely interlinked with other functions, it does not follow any standardised procedures, and it is chaotic, but a sense of order in the chaos can nevertheless be perceived.

Some Notes on the System's Properties

After this brief description of the evaluation system I will turn to three related questions, namely whether the evaluations are good, whether they are used and to what extent the recipient countries are taking part in them.

Quality: Let me first note that I think most of us recognise good evaluations when we see them, but it is often difficult to pinpoint why we think they are good. In the following pages I would like to introduce two criteria that can be used to assess the quality of an evaluation system.

First, what aspects of the environment do evaluations focus on? Following Emery and Trist [*1965*], Sachdeva [*1984*] introduced a model to analyse factors which affect organisational complexity. The project environment is a wide concept and not every event affects the project, nor do the project activities have an impact on all aspects of the environment. A useful distinction can thus be made between the contextual and the transactional environment. The transactional environment consists of the organisations and the people with whom the project is interlinked. The project affects their activities and is, in return, affected by them; they are in a situation of interdependence. The contextual environment has an impact on the project's behaviour but cannot be influenced in return by it. Finally there is the internal environment of the project: its technology, its people, the processes whereby it operates.

A first approach to an assessment of quality would be to examine which type of environment the system is focused on. In a review of SIDA's industrial development projects in Tanzania, the present author [*Forss, 1985*] found that all the SIDA projects covered the internal and transactional environments, and 50 per cent also assessed the contextual environment. It was also argued that, in order to perform well, an evaluation system has to make sure that all environmental levels are addressed and, in particular, that the contextual environment is not left out.

In general it seems as if SIDA's evaluation more often addresses questions related to the transactional and internal environments. However, the present trend is towards larger and more comprehensive evaluations and these are more likely to address issues of the contextual environment. But there has been no review of the overall quality of evaluations, so I am left with the indications from the above-mentioned study.

A second criterion regarding the quality of an evaluation system was proposed by Apthorpe and Gasper [*1982*]. Simplifying their argument, it becomes possible to distinguish evaluation as 'immanent' or 'transcendent'. An immanent evaluation uses as leading criteria for the evaluation those objectives stated within, and for, the project itself. Consequently, if the criteria are instead taken from a general theory of development, which may have been unknown to those designing the project or is even hostile to those starting and implementing the project, this is termed a transcendent evaluation.

In the same study [*Forss, 1985*] it was noted that transcendent approaches were present in a majority of the SIDA projects. I would also propose that it is extremely important that the evaluation system ascertains that transcendent approaches are made – perhaps not in every instance but at least once during the lifetime of any particular project.

There has never been an analysis of SIDA's evaluation outside the industry programme in Tanzania in these terms, but I think there are reasons to believe that transcendent approaches are less common in other parts of the programme. The trend appears to be towards more immanent approaches. SIDA is becoming more operational, but a transcendent approach thrives on freedom. When evaluators, particularly external evaluators, are closely controlled by the aid agency, they become more preoccupied with the stated objectives in their terms of reference. But transcendent questions are seldom specified in advance by those who order evaluations.

In sum, the quality of evaluations leaves much to be desired. It is encouraging that evaluations are becoming more concerned with the contextual environment. But it will be regrettable if the signs of increasingly immanent evaluations prove to develop into a trend.

The evaluation unit has a very important role to play in influencing these trends. It has taken initiatives to start more comprehensive evaluations that assess the contextual environment of development co-operation. The unit has also influenced the evaluations to the extent that more questions regarding the transactional environment are asked. In my opinion the evaluation unit will in the future have a very important role to play in ascertaining that evaluations also make a transcendent approach to their subjects.

Impact: Having looked at the extent of environmental analysis and the scope of assessment of a project – two indicators of the quality of evaluation systems – we are left with one disturbing question: do they have an impact on the project's performance? Does the combination of an assessment of all environmental layers and a transcendent approach lead to better projects? Do such evaluation systems help to (1) identify when project activities follow undesirable routes, (2) identify a need to change activities to achieve objectives, and (3) perceive shifts in national development priorities that require changes in project objectives?

In the review of industrial development projects in Tanzania, it was found that evaluation systems have been most useful in changing and adapting projects when the transcendent approach has predominated and when the entire environment has been assessed. Such projects were also found to have made the best contribution towards national development objectives. The question is how representative this sample is of SIDA activities, and that is a question that cannot be answered here. If it is true that the contextual environment is not assessed in half of the projects (as was the case in Tanzania), and if an immanent approach predominates, then it would not be likely that the evaluation system on the whole has any major impact on development co-operation.

But apart from the three functions mentioned above – warning, guidance and reconceptualisation – evaluations may serve yet another purpose, that of mobilising support. Programme officers can use evaluation results to help build a winning coalition. Evaluation becomes a means of persuasion [*Weiss, 1987*]. As such it can legitimate the activities by convincing the practitioners that they are doing the right thing. It can legitimate the organisation by showing the general public that the results are desirable. When activities are not successful, evaluations help to show that the organisation knows about it and, by implication, is doing something to change the situation.

Evaluations in SIDA are to a large extent used as a means of persuasion. As we have seen above, evaluations can be initiated by all sections and they are mostly initiated to mobilise support for some management decision. The evaluations initiated by the evaluation unit are less motivated by such reasons; on the other hand they often serve to legitimate the organisation in the eyes of the general public.

The role of recipient countries: When we discuss evaluation systems, we mostly do so in terms of a learning system where there is an actor who learns and takes action. That actor is the aid agency. The evaluation systems are by and large the processes whereby that actor learns and forms opinions on the value of his activities. But there are several actors in an aid project, the most important of whom is the recipient country. Obviously the organisations and the persons in the recipient country also form an opinion on the value of the aid projects, but they largely do so outside the evaluation system of the aid agencies.

I doubt whether a single *ex post* evaluation study (out of the 50–80 that SIDA conducts every year) has been initiated by a recipient country. Most of them have, of course, been decided upon jointly, but there should not be any doubt that it is SIDA which initiates such studies, sets the terms of reference, recruits consultants, finances the studies, and is the first to use the results.

The recipient countries also have a minor role to play in actually making evaluations. It is rare that consultants and researchers from recipient countries are recruited as external evaluators. Less than ten per cent of the IRV budgets are used in the recipient countries, and only a small share of that is used for evaluations. Using local consultants would, of course, have many advantages, such as better familiarity with the local scene, closer contacts with local decision makers, and perhaps lower costs to the aid organisation. Locally conducted evaluations could also stimulate the research capacity of the consultants. SIDA seems to favour the use of local consultants in principle, but it is a slow change from the present reliance on domestic resources.

The recipient country authorities are naturally partners in all decisions regarding the projects. It is, however, well documented that aid projects are often dominated by the foreign staff and the aid organisations (see, for example, Forss *et al.* [*1988*]). To the extent that evaluation results are used they are thus in fact primarily used by some of the representatives of the donor country. This is not a reflection on SIDA policies; on the contrary, SIDA's policies are to integrate the reccipient governments as much as possible in planning, evaluation and decision-making. The annual reviews are the primary instruments for doing this. But the implementation of the policies faces several constraints, not least the managerial capacity of the recipient country authorities and the ambitions of SIDA's own staff in efficient implementation.

III. SUMMARY

The task of an evaluation system is to provide feedback on the results of activities, which can be used for managerial purposes or as information. The approach in this paper has been to include all activities that are related to such learning and form opinions on whether the results of development co-operation are good, bad or in between. This is not an orderly system; it can better be described as fluid, overlapping and ambiguous processes.

Major policy issues concerning Swedish development co-operation are addressed by the Ministry of Foreign Affairs. The aid organisations themselves are subjected to evaluations from the Ministry and the National Audit Board. Each of the aid agencies has its own evaluation system. The nature of these systems differs as the tasks of the agencies differ. SIDA is the most important organisation and in this paper I have chosen to focus on how SIDA learns from its own experience and how that learning is translated into action.

SIDA's evaluation unit, which is part of the planning secretariat, is an important catalyst for evaluation activities. The unit is small in comparison to the overall evaluation effort in the organisation, but its role is primarily to initiate evaluations, to work for a high qualitative standard of evaluations, and to disperse the results of evaluations inside the organisation and outside. The unit is closely integrated with the rest of the organisation and works together with other sections in planning, implementing and using evaluation studies.

But it would be a fallacy to equate the evaluation unit's activities with evaluation in SIDA. Whether the organisation learns and improves depends on the dedication and interest of all staff members. The evaluation unit is the tip of the iceberg that is evaluation.

The division of labour between the evaluation unit and other units, as well as the other aspects of the evaluation system, do not emanate from policy decisions. The solutions to the problems of learning and improving development co-operation have grown out of the tension between budgetary constraints and the successive reorganisations of SIDA. The word 'policy' implies a rationality coupled to decisions that cannot be detected in the messy reality of development co-operation. The design of the system can nevertheless be interpreted as an illustration of the principle of 'redundancy of functions' and as such it is found to be effective in the turbulent environment that characterises aid. Quality and impact could be improved, but the weakest link in the evaluation chain is at present the lack of integration with the recipient country authorities.

NOTE

During 1989 and 1990, the organisation of Swedish development assistance in general, and the decision-making and evaluation systems in particular, was subject to detailed reviews. A public inquiry on the organisation of bilateral development co-operation [*SOU, 1990: 17*] suggested changes in the overall structure, working processes and division of tasks between the five Swedish aid agencies referred to above. A review by the Ministry of Foreign Affairs (*Ds UD, 1990: 63* – '*Bra Beslut: om effektivitet och utvärdering i biståndet*') recommended changes in the structure of the evaluation system, in particular, the establishment of a separate and independent unit for studies in development co-operation. The purpose of this unit would be to provide analytical support to strategic decisions, to develop methods and procedures for the evaluation work within the aid agencies, and to undertake specific studies of topics in development co-operation.

REFERENCES

Apthorpe, R. and D. Gasper, 1982, 'Policy Evaluation and Meta Evaluation: The Case of Rural Cooperatives', *World Development*, Vol. 10, No. 8.
Bachrach, P., 1980, 'Evaluating Development Programmes: A Synthesis of recent Experiences', D. Miller (ed.), *Studies on Project Design, Implementation and Evaluation*, Vol. 1, Paris: OECD.
Bannock, B., Baxter, R.E. and R. Rees, 1972, *A Dictionary of Economics*, Harmondsworth: Penguin.
Buckley, W., 1967, *Sociology and Modern Systems Theory*, Englewood Cliffs, NJ: Prentice Hall.
Ds UD, 1984, 'Effektivare Biståndsadministration, Betänkande av Biståndsorganisationsutredningen', 1.
Ds UD, 1985, 'Tio År med SAREC. En utvärdering av SAREC's verksamhet med särskild tonvikt på de bilaterala insatserna', 2.
Ds UD, 1988, 'Kunskapsöverföring genom företagsutveckling. Betänkande avgivet av Swedfund-översynen', 4.
Emery, F.E. and E.L. Trist, 1965, 'The Causal Texture of Organizational Environments', *Human Relations*, 18:1, pp. 21–3.
Emery, F.E. and E.L. Trist, 1973, *Towards a Social Ecology*, London and New York: Plenum Press.
Forss, K., 1985, *Planning and Evaluation in Aid Organizations*, Stockholm: IIB/EFI.
Forss, K., Carlsson, J., Frøyland, E., Sitari, T. and K. Vilby, 1988, 'Evaluation of the Effectiveness of Technical Assistance Personnel Financed by the Nordic Countries' (A study commissioned by DANIDA, FINNIDA, MCD/NORAD and SIDA).
Imboden, N., 1978, 'A Management Approach to Project Appraisal and Evaluation – with

special reference to Non-directly Productive Projects', Paris: Development Centre of OECD.
OECD, 1986, *Methods and Procedures in Aid Evaluation*, Paris: OECD.
Rossi, P.H., Freeman, H.E. and S.R. Wright, 1979, *Evaluation – A Systematic Approach*, London and Beverly Hills, CA: Sage.
Sachdeva, P.S., 1984, 'Development Planning – An Adaptive Approach'. *Long-Range Planning*, Vol.17, No.5.
SIDA, 1987, *Guidelines for Project Support*, Stockholm: SIDA.
SOU, 1977, 'Sveriges utvecklingssamarbete med u-länderna, Huvudbetänkande av Biståndspolitiska utredningen', Stockholm: Utrikesdepartementet, 13.
Weiss, C.H., 1987, 'Evaluation for Decisions: Is Anybody There? Does Anybody Care?' Plenary address for meeting of American Evaluation Association, Boston, Massachusetts, 16 Oct. 1987.
Wiener, N., 1954, *The Human Use of Human Beings: Cybernetics and Society*, Garden City, NY: Doubleday Anchor.

9

The Evaluation Policy and Performance of the United Nations Population Fund

KERSTIN TRONE

I. INTRODUCTION

The view of evaluation taken by the United Nations Population Fund (UNFPA) closely resembles that of the Joint Inspection Unit (JIU), the organisation in charge of the overall evaluation of the United Nations system. The JIU defines evaluation as follows [*Sohm, 1978*]:

> Evaluation is a learning and action-oriented management tool and process for determining as systematically and objectively as possible the relevance, effectiveness and impact of activities in the light of their objectives, in order to improve both current activities and future planning, programming and decision-making.
>
> Evaluation is *not* a decision-making process, but rather serves as an input to provide decision-makers with a full knowledge of problems, circumstances and opportunities. Therefore, it is decision-oriented.
>
> Evaluation is *not* basically concerned with the routine administrative or financial aspects or operational problems of an activity, but rather goes beyond these areas to a concern with critically assessing the objectives, design and results of the activity.
>
> Evaluation should *not* be concerned with justifying past activities or merely identifying their inadequacies, but rather with serving as a decision-oriented, participative, learning process to assist in the posi-tive improvement of present and future activities.
>
> Evaluation efforts should also *not* be excessively ambitious or elaborate, but rather be as rigorous, systematic and objective as is possible under existing constraints, in keeping with the basic evaluation purpose of providing useful analytical information to decision-makers.

EVALUATING DEVELOPMENT ASSISTANCE

In this study I attempt to describe and analyse UNFPA's efforts at developing evaluation policies and programmes in line with JIU's concepts. In order to facilitate the understanding of the role of evaluation in UNFPA, I first provide some background information on the organisation and on the programming system used by it. Next I discuss the evaluation policy and the system for monitoring and evaluation. The remainder of the study is mainly devoted to the experience with independent, in-depth evaluations, feedback and the use of evaluation results and the major results of the evaluations. Finally, I discuss some of the issues which have emerged.

II. THE UNITED NATIONS POPULATION FUND – SOME BACKGROUND

The Fund was set up in response to a General Assembly resolution in late 1966 [*General Assembly, 1966*], which for the first time authorised the United Nations to provide assistance in the population area. Since this area, and in particular family planning, at the time was a very sensitive issue, the regular channels for UN assistance could not be used. Therefore, a separate fund for voluntary contributions was established. This fund, named the UN Fund for Population Activities (renamed UN Population Fund in 1988), started functioning in 1969. Over the past almost twenty years the Fund has grown considerably. In 1987 it received contributions from 90 countries, both in the developed and in the developing world, and the annual budget increased from about $3 million the first year to $157 million in 1987.

The aims of the organisation are:

(a) To build up the knowledge and the capacity to respond to national, regional, interregional and global needs in the population field;
(b) To promote awareness, both in developed and in developing countries, of the social, economic and environmental implications of national and international population problems and of possible strategies to deal with them;
(c) To extend systematic and sustained assistance to developing countries at their request in dealing with their population problems; and
(d) To play a leading role in the United Nations system in promoting population programmes and to coordinate projects supported by the Fund [*ECOSOC, 1973*].

In the beginning, the awareness creation was extremely important, as was the building up of knowledge in the population area. These areas are still part of UNFPA's programme. However, the main emphasis of the programme has always been, and is increasingly so, the on provision of assistance for operational programmes in developing countries. In 1987 more than 2,000 country projects and 674 intercountry projects received support.

Certain principles guide the Fund's allocation of resources [*ECOSOC, 1976*]. UNFPA promotes population activities proposed in international strategies, particularly the World Population Plan of Action; assists developing countries which have the most urgent needs in the area of population (certain countries have been designated priority countries, using both economic and demographic selection criteria); respects the sovereign right of each nation to formulate, promote and implement its own population policies; promotes the recipient countries' self-reliance; and gives special attention to meeting the needs of disadvantaged groups.

The substantive areas receiving support are in order of priority: family-planning; population education, communication and information; basic data collection; population dynamics (mainly training and research); and formulation, implementation and evaluation of population policy [*UNDP, 1981*]. In recent years special emphasis has also been given to the integration of women's concerns in the programmes, as well as to the provision of assistance to sub-Saharan Africa.

UNFPA is mainly a funding organisation with close ties to UNDP (same governing body and field offices). Most of the programmes/ projects supported are carried out by other organisations, in particular, FAO, ILO, UNESCO, the United Nations Department of Technical Cooperation for Development and WHO. UNFPA was also one of the first organisations to encourage direct government execution and the use of international, non-governmental organisations for execution.

III. UNFPA'S PROGRAMMING SYSTEM

UNFPA's programming system has changed over the years from providing support to single projects to assistance to comprehensive programmes. The programming cycle includes population needs assessment, programme development, project formulation, monitoring and evaluation [*UNFPA, 1984b*].

The population needs assessment exercise assists the government in analysing the population situation within the context of national development goals, identifying the programme needs and the national capacity to fill the needs. As a result the needs assessment mission produces recommendations on programme areas requiring external assistance.

Next, the government and UNFPA agree on which of the assistance needs should be covered by UNFPA, and a country programme is developed outlining the sectors and subsectors to receive support. This programme is presented to the Governing Council for approval. However, no funds are allocated until specific project proposals are formulated, appraised and approved.

The individual projects are designed by the government, usually with the assistance of an adviser from the potential executing agency or from UNFPA. There are guidelines for the presentation of the project proposal to UNFPA. Since the early 1970s, these have been based on the 'logical framework' concept. They require, *inter alia*, a clear description of the objectives as well as a plan for monitoring and evaluation.

Once a project is approved by UNFPA, the daily implementation of it is left to the government and the executing agency. UNFPA's role is basically confined to monitoring and evaluation of the project and the overall programme. For these activities there are certain standard requirements. These requirements and the experience in applying them will be further discussed below.

IV. EVALUATION POLICIES AND ATTITUDES

The Executive Director very early felt the need to introduce a system by which the performance and effectiveness of UNFPA-assisted projects could be ensured. In 1972 an evaluation unit was set up, one of the very first in the UN system. The objectives of the evaluation activities have remained the same ever since, even though the interpretation and implementation of them has changed over the years. The objectives are:

(1) To help meet the requirements of accountability to the Governing Council, and
(2) To provide timely, analytical information for decision-making within UNFPA.

Initially the accountability objective took precedence. There were various reasons for this, but the main one concerned the attitude to evaluation among the staff of the organisation, as well as at the government level. Although the Executive Director saw the importance of evaluation, others merely recognised its usefulness for accountability purposes, and they did so only after the Governing Council had expressed a need for evaluation reporting. Evaluation was looked upon mainly as a controlling function and often seen as an unnecessary complication. Its usefulness for the project management was not adequately understood. Therefore, at the beginning it was not always easy to find candidates for project evaluation.

In line with the thinking of the evaluation community in the early days, only independent, in-depth evaluation was considered true evaluation and therefore was the kind to be undertaken in UNFPA. Consequently, the evaluation unit was set up separately from the programme unit. This arrangement, though clearly providing the required independence, may also have contributed to the difficulties in promoting the concept of evaluation internally.

Over time, the attitudes to evaluation have changed and both objectives are now actively pursued. The second one is in fact the most important today, and special efforts are made to ensure that the evaluations are useful not only for decision-making in UNFPA but also for governments and executive agencies. Three factors have contributed to this change, namely actions in the Governing Council, the work of the JIU, and the efforts made by the evaluation unit.

The Governing Council, by asking for periodical (biannual) reports on evaluation results, helped provide in-house arguments for undertaking more evaluations. Furthermore, by endorsing methodologies and procedures proposed by the evaluation unit (through the Executive Director), it also helped advance and expand the evaluation function of the organisation. The Council has several times praised the evaluations for their candour and frank discussion of both achievements and problems. The Council also endorsed proposals for expansion of the evaluation activities to include internal evaluations. It furthermore requested a report on the comparative results of the evaluations in 1986 , which was very well received, and asked the Fund to go one step further and report on the development and institutionalisation of procedures for feedback and use of evaluation results. This report was presented and endorsed in 1987. In the two latter cases, the Council played an active, rather than a reactive, role in promoting further development of the evaluation activities of the Fund. In addition, because of the special reports, the evaluation discussion in the Council was intensified, as it has lately taken place annually.

The JIU started making assessments of the evaluation activities of the UN system in the late 1970s, but UNFPA was not included in the first exercise. The second report, in 1981 [*Sohm, 1981*], concluded that

Evaluation appears to have become a well-established and useful process in UNFPA, which is understood by the staff, top management and the Governing Council. While the accountability function is felt to be adequately fulfilled, however, there is a demand from all these groups for more internal feedback through an increase in the number and speed of evaluation studies, improvement or development of new feedback mechanisms to provide intermediate analysis of specific problems to ensure timely corrective actions, or both. Given staff resource constraints and the desire to maintain the in-depth nature of the current independent evaluations, this will be a particular challenge.

The report recommended that 'UNFPA should further strengthen its project design processes and then consider the possibility of developing a built-in self-evaluation system. The additional feedback and coverage which such a system could provide could usefully supplement the present effective activities of its central Evaluation Branch.'

A follow-up to this report was made by the JIU in 1985. This time the JIU [Sohm, 1985] concluded that

> UNFPA has further improved the coverage, feedback, and usefulness of the independent, in-depth evaluation work done by its Evaluation Branch. However, despite a commitment to strengthen project design and monitoring and introduce built-in self-evaluation and related training in the overall UNFPA programming system, progress in these areas has been rather slow. The UNFPA internal task force needs now to follow through with specific steps and actions to develop, install and effectively use these new or revised processes.

This time no specific recommendation was made. This report, like the previous one, was presented to and endorsed by the UN General Assembly. This fact made the reports especially useful for discussions within the Fund.

In order to make the evaluation concept more acceptable, the evaluation unit made use of the strong support provided in the recommendations and resolutions from the two bodies mentioned above, but it also needed other arguments to convince the programme staff, and indirectly the governments, that the evaluation results could actually be useful to them. As mentioned above, it was at first very difficult to get agreement to undertake evaluation of any project. Those done were few in number and mostly dealt with intercountry projects, such as regional training activities. It took many years and careful efforts before the attitude was changed.

It was only after the introduction of a system of annual consultations with programme and technical staff to ascertain what projects needed evaluation, and when, that more interest in evaluating country projects emerged. Furthermore, by changing the reporting system to one where the report is prepared and immediate feedback provided in the field, the results were more timely and could more easily be used for management decisions and not just for accountability purposes. Furthermore, when the results of the independent evaluations became more useful, interest in undertaking internal evaluation (by now an accepted activity in the evaluation community) also emerged.

V. THE SYSTEM FOR MONITORING AND EVALUATION

UNFPA now has a fairly well-established system for evaluation. As mentioned above, evaluation is seen as an integral part of the programming cycle, in regard both to individual projects and overall programmes, country or intercountry. Also, during the last few years the close relationship between monitoring and evaluation has been recognised. Monitoring in UNFPA has always been the responsibility of programme staff, while evaluation in the past was the exclusive domain of the evaluation unit. However, as evaluation increasingly became viewed as useful for managerial purposes and the importance of internal evaluation was acknowledged, it became clear that a coordinated system for monitoring and evaluation was required.

Many independent evaluations had pointed to the need for better project design, both to improve the projects and to allow evaluation of the achievements. Therefore, UNFPA first revised its guidelines for project formulation [*UNFPA, 1986a*]. As mentioned, emphasis was put on providing guidance for formulation of objectives and on the need for a plan for monitoring and evaluation. Among other things, this plan should indicate if self-evaluation would be sufficient or if other types of evaluation would also be necessary. Indicators of progress and means of verifying them are required for each objective. These guidelines were issued for testing in early 1986. The experience of their use is now being analysed and they will be further revised on the basis of this analysis.

The next step was to develop guidelines for a complete system of monitoring and evaluation. Even though there were previous separate guidelines for monitoring and for independent evaluation, the new concept of internal evaluation had not been incorporated in any of them. An internal task force, with members from both headquarters (programme and evaluation) and the field, reviewed the experience with the existing guidelines, as well as the implementation of previous circulars in regard to internal evaluation. Furthermore, the task force was asked to harmonise the guidelines, as far as possible with those recently developed by UNDP. The new guidelines [*UNFPA, 1986c*] were issued at the end of 1986 for testing, with finalisation expected to take place late in 1989.

The components of the system, as far as projects are concerned, are outlined in Table 1. The requirements for programmes are described in Table 2. (Both tables are taken from the 1986 guidelines.) Although the tables provide a fair amount of information, a few additional comments are in order. As mentioned in the introduction, we shall discuss the independent, in-depth evaluations in a later chapter. The comments here, therefore, are limited to some of the other components of the system.

The project progress report was revised drastically for two reasons. First, the previous format, while indicating areas to be covered, left it to the writer to decide on the content. This led to many reports which focused on description of inputs and activities, while the outputs and problems were seldom identified. Furthermore, there was little analysis. The new format, therefore, requires a listing and a discussion of each output, activity and input. The second reason for the new format is that it follows closely that of UNDP, which should help reduce the potential confusion at the government level, where the same officials sometimes deal with both organisations. It is also in line with the present emphasis within the UN system on harmonisation of procedures for operational activities.

The Internal Evaluation Report form (IER) was also patterned on that of UNDP. This form should enable the project management to undertake a simple self-evaluation. Specific questions are asked about progress towards the achievement of the project's objectives, unexpected effects, effects on women (planned or unplanned), and needs for revision of the project design. Many projects, for example, those which are large-scale or innovative, require more elaborate evaluation exercises. Plans for such exercises, including the necessary budget, should be part of the original project design, but they can also be included in the course of project implementation. These evaluations are also called internal, even though they may be undertaken by outside consultants, for the simple reason that we wanted to keep the distinction between them and the independent evaluations organised by the evaluation unit. The terminology is not ideal, but so far no better alternative has been found. To assist project managers, who will organise this kind of internal evaluation exercises, the guidelines provide a set of standard terms of reference.

TABLE 1
MONITORING AND EVALUATION REQUIREMENTS FOR PROJECTS

TYPE OF M & E	TYPE OF PROJECTS	TIMING	RESPONSIBILITY
Project Progress Reports (PPR)	All projects over 1 year duration	Every six months	Project Management*
Field Monitoring Visits	Those requiring particular attention for technical or administrative reasons	As often as required	Proj. Mngt.*, Gov't., UNFPA, exec. agency
Internal Evaluation Reports (IER)	All projects over 1 year duration	Annually	Project Management*
Internal Evaluation Exercises	Those requiring particular attention for technical or administrative reasons	Periodically, depending on need	Proj. Mngt.*, Gov't., UNFPA, exec. agency
Tripartite Project Review (TPR)	Projects over $100,000 or those requiring special attention, e.g. innovative or complex projects	Annually	Gov't. including project management*, UNFPA, executing agency
Independent In-depth Evaluation	Special criteria**	Once during life of projects chosen	Evaluation Branch of UNFPA
Final Projects Report (FPR)	All projects	2 months before end of project	Project Management*
Final TPR	Same as TPR	Termination of project	Gov't. including project Mngt.*, UNFPA, exec. agency

* The leaders of the national staff and international staff of a project together constitute the project's management. See definition of project management (UNFPA 1986c, p. 7).
** See UNFPA 1984a, p. 8.

TABLE 2
MONITORING AND EVALUATION REQUIREMENTS FOR PROGRAMMES

TYPE OF M & E	TYPE OF PROGRAMME	TIMING	RESPONSIBILITY
Country Review (CR)	Countries with: country programmes, or significant number of projects over $100,000 UNFPA budget; or innovative, complex programme	Periodic – normally yearly or every other year	Government and UNFPA
Independent, In-depth Evaluation	Special criteria*	Once during life of programmes chosen	Evaluation Branch of UNFPA

*See UNFPA [1984a: 8].

The tripartite and the country reviews are important events for discussion of the findings of monitoring and evaluation reports and for initiation of corrective measures, if necessary. In the past, this opportunity was not always well utilised, partly because of the limited reporting presented to the meetings (scanty progress reports for the projects and seldom any evaluations of either projects or programmes). The new guidelines, therefore, put much emphasis on encouraging the active use of the review meeting as a management tool to ensure the best possible programme implementation.

VI. THE ROLE OF THE EVALUATION UNIT IN THE ORGANISATION

As mentioned above, the evaluation unit was deliberately established as independent of the programme unit of the Fund. This is still the case. Its placement within the organisation has varied over the years. For a period, it was an Office reporting directly to the Deputy Executive Director. In connection with a reorganisation in 1981 it was made part of the Policy and Evaluation Division, which reported to the Deputy Executive Director. In the next reorganisation, in 1987, it was made part of a new Technical and Evaluation Division, which reports directly to the Executive Director. The latest change reflects an increased emphasis on the part of the Executive Director on the quality aspects of the programme. Therefore, the technical units were considerably strengthened and put together with the evaluation unit to ensure that the lessons learned from evaluations could be fed directly back into the development of policies and strategies in the substantive areas.

These various locations of the evaluation unit in the organisation do not seem to have mattered very much in terms of the ability of the unit to perform its work. It could, perhaps, be argued that a closer association with the programme unit would have facilitated the change in attitudes to evaluation. However, it was and still is considered important to safeguard the independence of the unit.

The tasks of the evaluation unit include, *inter alia*, the undertaking of independent, in-depth evaluations, the development of evaluation methodology, providing advice on evaluation to other parts of the organisation (particularly in regard to more elaborate, internal evaluation exercises), collection, analysis and feedback of lessons learned from evaluations, and follow-up of the use of evaluation results. The unit is represented on the committees that make recommendations to the Executive Director for decisions regarding policies, programmes and projects. Therefore, evaluation concerns – in terms of using evaluation results as well as plans for evaluation – can be addressed before final decisions are made. It would, of course, be better if such concerns could be dealt with at an earlier stage. However, there is no formalised system for consultation with the evaluation unit during the development of, for example, new projects. Nevertheless, such consultation takes place on an *ad hoc* basis and, given the staff limitations (five professional posts) of the evaluation unit, more systematic and frequent consultations could probably not be accommodated. Instead, the aim is to train all programme staff in the field and at headquarters to be able to review evaluation plans as part of their regular tasks.

VII. INDEPENDENT, IN-DEPTH EVALUATION

A two-year work programme for independent, in-depth evaluation is developed each year (revising one year, adding on another) in consultation with programme, technical and field staff. The work programme is reviewed by the Policy and Planning Committee, chaired by the Executive Director. In view of the increasing amount of internal project evaluations and the need for information for policy decisions, the work programme today includes programme and comparative evaluations, but no evaluations of a single project. The programme evaluations cover either a country programme or an intercountry programme, for example, recent evaluations dealt with the UNFPA-supported programmes in Tanzania, WHO and FAO. The comparative evaluations cover issues of concern to the organisation, such as training of family-planning service staff and integration of population in development planning. These evaluations are based on assessments of individual projects, using available project monitoring and evaluation reports and, in some cases, field visits, but they provide conclusions and recommendations of a general nature rather than for the specific projects. The independent, in-depth evaluations are financed from a separate project administered by the Evaluation Branch. This project is used mainly for the hiring of external evaluators, staff travel on evaluation missions and the printing of evaluation reports. The budget for 1988 was US$562,000.

Preparatory Phase

The independent, in-depth evaluations have three components: preparation, field mission and follow-up. Thorough preparations are needed so that the mission members can concentrate on assessment rather than fact-finding. A background paper is prepared by the officer in charge of the evaluation, often with the assistance of graduate student interns or, if no qualified students are available, consultants. This document describes the objectives and the planned performance of the projects involved, as well as the actual performance as reported in progress reports. The background paper for the comparative evaluations also includes an analysis of the 'state of the art' regarding the issue to be studied and those for programme evaluations review the overall programme. The scope of the country programme evaluations has recently been expanded to include an aspects-of-needs-assessment update. The background papers, therefore, now also include descriptions of the various population-related sectors in the country. For this latter task, local consultants are hired.

The preparation of background papers is time-consuming and various attempts have been made to cut down on the amount of work required. However, we have always come to the conclusion (and so did a consultant we hired to look into this issue) that a thorough background paper is essential for the successful performance of the evaluation mission and, therefore, we continue giving it as much emphasis as before. The background paper preparation also serves the purposes of identifying issues to be addressed in the terms of reference (the methodology) for the evaluation and the type of consultants needed for the mission. In addition, the programme staff find the document useful in their daily work.

The terms of reference have a general part which is fairly standard, dealing with, *inter alia*, achievement of objectives and the adequacy of the design and strategy. All evaluations are also expected to look into the role of the executing agencies, women's concerns and the adequacy of the monitoring and evaluation components. In addition, for each evaluation specific terms of reference are prepared, dealing with those issues identified during the process of preparation. The terms of reference are discussed with the various parties concerned, such as the programme staff and the government, before they are finalised.

A third aspect of the preparation process is the identification of the consultants for the evaluation mission. Only after some of the background paper preparation has been done can we usually decide which technical capacity we need to have represented on the team. Then follows a very time-consuming process of identifying the persons. The individuals have to be experts in the technical area, have knowledge of developing countries, preferably the country or region to be visited, speak the UN language used in the country, be fluent in English, work well in a team, be analytical and understand evaluation, write well, concisely and quickly and be available for four to five weeks. In addition, in order to ensure independence, they should not have been previously involved with the projects evaluated, nor be nationals of the country studied. Furthermore, there has to be a mix of nationalities in the team. Special efforts are made to include nationals of developing countries and women in the team. (In 1988 almost half of the consultants came from developing countries and a quarter were women.) Very few people meet all these criteria and our roster of potential consultants, while useful, is frequently insufficient. Finally, all logistics and the paperwork for the hiring and travel have to be initiated and constant follow-up of the implementation is required, since problems in this area sometimes jeopardise entire evaluations.

The preparatory phase frequently requires several months, especially now that the evaluations include several projects and sometimes several countries, as well as a more complicated methodology. At least a month before the field mission, the background paper, including the draft terms of reference, is sent to the consultants and to UNFPA's field offices in the country or countries concerned and through them to the governments. They are also shared with the executing agencies and various departments at UNFPA headquarters.

Evaluation Mission

The evaluation mission, consisting of independent consultants and an evaluation officer, who is a full member of the team and acts as mission coordinator (since the reorganisation in 1987, technical officers also undertake some of the evaluations), starts with a briefing session at UNFPA in New York. In addition to discussions with staff members concerned, for example, programme and technical officers, a day or more is devoted to discussions of the evaluation methodology. This aspect has taken on an increased importance for the comparative evaluations, which frequently involve more than one team visiting various countries before assembling in one location to write a joint report. We have found that it is important for the success of the mission that the teams agree in advance on the methodology for the country studies, the outline for the country notes needed to inform the other team their findings, as well as the draft outline of the final report and the responsibilities for writing the various chapters.

The field mission includes interviews with the persons concerned in the country, visits to project sites, frequent (usually daily) discussions between team members and report writing in the field. If it is a country programme evaluation, the report is given to the government, UNFPA's field office and any executing agency represented and a session is held to discuss the results with them before the mission departs. At the same time the government's permission to give unrestricted distribution to the report is sought. Such permission is almost always granted. Comparative evaluations are usually organised by region. The whole mission, in most cases two teams, meets in one place to write the regional report.

We do not usually have either chairpersons or rapporteurs of the teams, since we have found that such assignments tend to make some of the other members feel less responsible for the final product, the report. Instead, every team member is expected to write a pre-agreed part of the report. An important vote is played, therefore, by the evaluation officer, who coordinates the writing. He or she reads the first draft of every chapter and guides the rewrites to ensure adequate analysis and uniformity of style. Generally, we request the consultants to write concise reports focusing on conclusions and recommendations and to avoid, as far as possible, descriptive parts. They are also asked to be frank and constructive, analysing both positive and negative aspects, and to use diplomatic language as far as possible. All parts of the report are read and agreed upon by all mission members to ensure that it is a true joint report.

Follow-up

The draft report is sent to the relevant persons at UNFPA and executing agency headquarters for comments. If any changes have been made as a result of the discussions of the report in the country, the revised version is transmitted to the government for comments. A different procedure is used, however, for comparative evaluations. Here the various regional reports are analysed and a report with general conclusions and recommendations is prepared by the evaluation unit or a consultant before official comments are requested. The draft regional reports are nevertheless shared with and used by the executing agency concerned, as well as by programme and technical people at UNFPA.

Since the evaluation missions present reports *to* not *by* UNFPA, the Fund has to take a stand on the recommendations made. The results of the evaluation, therefore, are presented to the Programme Committee (PC). The minutes of the Committee are shared with the UNFPA staff, as well as the government and executing agency involved. After the PC discussion the report is printed and distributed.

The implementation of the agreed recommendations addressed to UNFPA rests with the programme, technical and field staff of the Fund, but the evaluation unit makes a follow-up of the use of the evaluation results for the projects evaluated a year after the PC discussion. It also synthesises and disseminates the results of selected evaluations in the same area for use in the preparation of new projects or programmes or for the development of technical strategies and policies.

Guidelines

To assist the evaluation consultants as well as new evaluation officers, guidelines and procedures for independent, in-depth evaluations were drafted in 1982 [*UNFPA, 1984a*]. After a period of testing they were printed in three languages (English, French and Spanish) in 1984. They provide information about the evaluation system in UNFPA and step-by-step procedures for the various phases of the evaluation exercise. A supplement for internal use provides further details, regarding, for example, the practical arrangements for the missions, and gives examples of the required correspondence. The guidelines have been widely used and we have received positive feedback on them. Most of the content is still valid, but some minor modifications are required, in view of the recent organisational changes in UNFPA. A revision will be undertaken during the second half of 1989.

The terms of reference for the missions always include a requirement to look into the role of women in the various projects evaluated. We found that it was sometimes difficult for consultants not familiar with gender issues to undertake this task. Guidelines for evaluation of the women's dimension in UNFPA-assisted programmes were prepared to help with it [*UNFPA, 1986b*]. After a period of testing they were printed in 1986, also in three languages. Finally, draft guidelines for country programme evaluation have also been prepared and various versions have been tested during the last couple of years. The methodology for this kind of evaluation is still undergoing changes, and so the guidelines are kept in draft form for the time being.

VIII. FEEDBACK AND USE OF EVALUATION RESULTS

Evaluation activities do not make much sense unless the results are used as extensively as possible. They should serve to improve ongoing programmes and projects but they also have to be made part of the accumulated knowledge that should facilitate better programme and project design and assist the Fund as well as governments and the Governing Council in making more rational decisions regarding future policies. It has always been difficult to disseminate evaluation results to those not directly concerned with the projects evaluated, and even for those who were concerned this latter task was not always easy.

We are concerned about the need to expand the use of the results and in an effort to deal with this issue a computerised system for lessons learned from evaluation has been established. After careful consideration of the options, we decided to set up a data-base with quotes from evaluation reports (both independent and the more elaborate internal) which imply a potential lesson. These potential lessons are classified both by substantive area and by a list of other issues, identified after consultation with the main intended users of the system, namely UNFPA programme and technical staff. Furthermore, they are classified by region and country (if applicable). The user of the system gets a print-out with all the quotes under the classification requested. Information on the system and how to use it has been sent to all UNFPA headquarters and field staff as well as the various participating UN agencies. It is hoped that they in turn share the information with the governments. Some requests for information have already been received, although the system has only been operational for a short time. At present all requests have to be made to the evaluation unit, but once the plans for a Fund-wide management-information system are implemented, any staff member at headquarters or in the field should have direct access to the evaluation data-base. So far, the costs of the data-base have been low; the direct costs have been limited to a short-term consultant to help analyse the backlog of reports in the beginning. Indirect costs are part of the time (maximum 20 per cent) of one officer and one secretary.

In order to further increase the use of the system, the evaluation unit occasionally selects an issue, analyses and synthesises the lessons learned in regard to that issue and disseminates the results through Fund- and agency-wide circulars. The most recent one dealt with institution-building. These activities are obviously only a beginning of more systematic efforts to disseminate and use evaluation results. We are still looking for more and better methods of dissemination and we also have to find ways of finding out the extent of actual use of the lessons. One way of doing this is by requesting information on the use of evaluation results in the presentations of new programmes and projects for approval. Another way is to provide more and improved training in the design and evaluation of programmes and projects. Both of these methods are now being pursued.

IX. LESSONS FROM EVALUATIONS

When preparing the comparative study of evaluation results for the Governing Council in 1986, we found that it was very difficult to identify lessons applicable to all programmes and projects, particularly regarding substantive matters. One constraint was that projects were implemented under different political, social, economic, cultural and geographical circumstances. Another constraint was that the number of evaluations was too limited to allow generalisations about which strategies and elements were most effective. Furthermore, the evaluations had not been prepared with comparability in mind but were rather tailored to specific programmes and projects, and therefore may not have covered the same substantive issues. Nevertheless, it was possible to draw some conclusions, in particular, regarding obstacles to successful implementation. These conclusions relate mainly to managerial issues. They have been further substantiated by the additional information now provided in the evaluation data-base. Since they do not seem to be confined to the population sector – others have reported similar findings – it may be worthwhile to mention a few of the most important ones here.

1. Project formulation was often undertaken by consultants from executing agencies and UNFPA with insufficient involvement of national personnel. This led to inaccurate and inadequate assessment of local conditions and created confusion regarding responsibility for project implementation.
2. Although some improvement has taken place lately, many evaluations concluded that programme and project objectives were unclear, the strategy was not adequately defined, and the logical links between inputs, activities, and so on, were not made explicit. This problem of project design is partly a reflection of the inadequate assessment of needs and partly a reflection of the difficulties of identifying each step needed to achieve the objectives.
3. Many planners of institution-building projects aimed, unrealistically, at simultaneously securing the legal mandate, establishing the basic organisational unit and programme, and initiating actual

delivery of the product (for example, research studies or education services). This lesson shows the need for a detailed and realistic work plan, highlighting the importance of step-by-step consolidation of progress before proceeding.

4. Limited availability of local staff and of national technical specialists appeared as a major constraint on implementation, regardless of the type of project. Assessment of the need for and availability of local staff is essential, as are plans which are realistic in time and scope, for training needed during the course of project implementation. This lesson is closely related to the next.

5. Implementation was greatly facilitated in projects in which training needs had been accurately ascertained from the beginning, where provision had been made for meeting these needs locally or abroad, and where arrangements had been made for drawing upon the skills of returning trainees.

X. REMAINING ISSUES IN EVALUATION

On the basis of our experience in UNFPA, we can identify various issues in need of further discussion before a properly functioning evaluation system can be in place. Some of them may apply in other organisations as well and are therefore mentioned below.

(1) *Attitudes towards evaluation*, although considerably improved, need to be further changed before the desired participation in the planning and use of evaluation can be accomplished. Of major importance for such a change is top-level support for evaluation as a tool for both design *and* implementation. As long as many governments and organisations continue to place emphasis on project approval alone and not on implementation, there is limited incentive for the staff to make use of evaluation during the life of a project. In UNFPA there has been a recent positive change in the top-level attitude to the importance of the quality and effectiveness and therefore also the implementation of the programmes and projects. In this context evaluation is considered a necessary tool to achieve better quality. How this new emphasis is to be enforced at the working level is an issue that still needs discussion.

(2) *Type of evaluation*. There is now considerable agreement that a mix of types of evaluation, ranging from simple self-evaluation to indepen-dent, in-depth evaluation, is desirable. However, the optimum mix for an organisation, such as UNFPA, is still not apparent. The best mix in terms of who organises the evaluation, whether the

evaluation unit or the project management, is also not given. In our opinion, both have justifications, but the distribution of the tasks needs further review.

(3) *Focus of evaluation*. At present, UNFPA's evaluation system covers ongoing projects and programmes as well as selected technical issues. However, there is no systematic *ex post* or impact evaluation. The former has been neglected in view of the more urgent need for evaluation results to be used directly in the projects and programmes. However, now that a system for evaluation as a management tool for projects and programmes has been established, some thought has to be given to whether there is a need for *ex post* evaluations as well. They could certainly be useful as an input into the accumulation of lessons learned, in particular, with regard to the sustainability of the projects.

Impact evaluation has not been undertaken, partly for the same reason as the lack of *ex post* evaluation, but also because few programmes and projects so far have been designed well enough to allow measurement of impact. There is usually limited baseline information and clear and measurable objectives are lacking. Some efforts to study impact are now being made in a few countries, but, to accomplish this, special projects have had to be organised, since, for the reasons given above, this issue could not be handled through regular evaluation. It is encouraging, however, that some new projects are now designed to include baseline studies. A different, but related issue is, of course, the difficulty of finding appropriate indicators of impact. Here again, more study is needed.

(4) *Training*. Although there is now a recognition that training in programme and project design and evaluation for project personnel as well as for staff from UNFPA and executing agencies is important, little has so far been done in this area. Until very recently UNFPA did not have a staff-training programme. Now that such a programme has been established, some efforts have been made to include design and evaluation issues as part of the briefing and training sessions for, *inter alia*, national programme officers, but a concerted effort at professionally prepared training has yet to take place. We still have to find the most effective way to provide the design and evaluation training within the limitations of staff and financial resources.

(5) *Dissemination and use of evaluation results*. The first question in this connection is what type of reporting on evaluation is most likely to be useful. In regard to the independent evaluations we emphasise that the report should be as concise as possible and, preferably, not include any descriptive parts. Furthermore, it should be ready immediately, at least

in draft form. We introduced this kind of reporting to make the reports more accessible for the decision-makers. It has served this purpose, but there is still a demand for more details from those at the working level dealing with the projects. To a certain extent this is provided in background papers and in annexes. In any case, this illustrates the dilemma in preparing a report which is useful to a variety of audiences – in our case mainly project managers, programme staff and decision-makers at UNFPA and agencies, and the Governing Council. It is not possible to please all with one report, nor is there time to prepare various versions. For this reason, we have had to focus mainly on one group, the decision-makers, while hoping that others can also find some use for the report.

The next question concerns the best way of disseminating the evaluation report to ensure that it is read and used. We have found it useful to provide a draft report on programmes or projects to the parties concerned in the field and at UNFPA immediately following the mission. However, the issue becomes more difficult in relation to the comparative evaluations and syntheses of lessons learned, which do not have such an immediate and captive audience. At the moment we are experimenting with a mixture of circulars, reports, seminars and the data-base. We still do not know which of these or any other method is the best for reaching each group of potential users.

(6) *Coordination with other evaluation systems.* At the recipient government level the same person often has to deal with various aid providers, such as bilateral and multilateral agencies, and the profusion of different requirements for project formulation and evaluation is not only confusing but also time-consuming. Coordination and simplification of the various donor-imposed systems, therefore, is called for. Coordination is beneficial also from the donor-agency point of view, in that time and effort can be saved through application of lessons learned in systems development in other agencies. In spite of these good reasons for coordination, there is still not much to show. Granted, there have been coordination meetings for the agencies in the UN system and also within the OECD Development Assistance Committee, which have served to at least make us aware of some of each other's activities, even though there has been little interchange between the two groups.

However, coordination of the overall evaluation systems and, above all, harmonisation and simplification of procedures, still need much more effort. It seems that stronger political will, expressed in clear instructions from all the various governing bodies, is needed before we shall see any significant change in this situation, since everybody is for coordination, but nobody wants to be coordinated. Of course, this would require coordination between the different governing bodies, which it might be unrealistic to expect. Meanwhile, we all need to make an effort to learn about any existing simple systems and try to adjust to them. It will be difficult, as we are all part of bureaucracies, with elaborate rules and procedures and with a built-in resistance to change, but in the long run it will be to our own advantage.

In conclusion, we have come a long way in the development of evaluation in UNFPA and, although many issues, such as those discussed above, still remain to be resolved, the problems are not insurmountable. A major issue confronting the development community in the 1990s will be the improvement of the quality of the programmes and, therefore, evaluation will continue to play an increasingly important role. However, in spite of a fairly positive outlook, we must keep in mind that such evaluation, like any other development-related area, is constantly evolving. Before we have found the solutions to the issues identified today, many new ones will have emerged, and this will ensure that the area of evaluation will continue to be one of challenge, discovery and learning.

REFERENCES

ECOSOC, 1973, *Resolution 1763* (LIV), 18 May.
ECOSOC, 1976, *Resolution 2025* (LXI), 4 Aug.
General Assembly, 1966, *Resolution 2211* (XXI), 17 Dec.
Sohm, Earl D., 1978, *Glossary of Evaluation Terms*, JIU/REP/78/5, Geneva, Nov.
Sohm, Earl D., 1981, *Status of Internal Evaluation in United Nations System Organizations*, JIU/REP/81/5, Geneva, Feb.
Sohm, Earl D., 1985, *Third Report on Evaluation in the United Nations System: Integration and Use*, JIU/REP/85/11, Geneva, Oct.
UNDP, 1981, *Governing Council Decisions*, 81/7 I, 23 June.
UNFPA, 1984a, *Guidelines and Procedures for Independent, In-depth Evaluations*, New York, March.
UNFPA, 1984b, *Report of the Executive Director Reviewing UNFPA Programming Procedures*, DP/1984/35, New York, 11 April.
UNFPA, 1986a, *Third Revision of 'UNFPA Instructions for the Preparation of a Project Document'*, UNFPA/19/rev. No. 3, New York, 22 Jan.
UNFPA, 1986b, *Guidelines for Evaluation of the Women's Dimension in UNFPA-assisted Programmes*, New York, April.
UNFPA, 1986c, *UNFPA Guidelines on Monitoring and Evaluation of UNFPA-supported Projects and Programmes*, UNFPA/CM/86/63, New York, 3 Nov.

10

The Role of an Evaluation Unit: Functions, Constraints and Feedback

BASIL E. CRACKNELL

I. FUNCTIONS AND CONSTRAINTS

The Staffing, Structure and Status of an Evaluation Unit

There are a number of key decisions that have to be made when an evaluation unit is set up. First is the fundamental issue of what its main objectives are. There are basically two possible emphases and, although in practice most evaluation units have to try to incorporate both, their relative importance in the eyes of the agency's top management will have a critical influence on how the unit will evolve. The first possible emphasis is to use evaluations as a means of enhancing the *accountability* of the organisation towards its paymasters; its main purpose is to answer the question: 'Does our aid work?' The second possible emphasis is to *learn lessons* about what happened as a result of previous aid administration and implementation activities, so that improvements can be made in the future, either in relation to the project or programme being evaluated or in relation to future projects or programmes. The first objective is geared more to external needs, and the second to internal ones.

The first objective would call for a high degree of independence and impartiality on the part of the staff carrying out the evaluations, a wide cross-section of skills among the evaluation staff, and a fully representative selection of projects and programmes to be evaluated. On the other hand, the second objective would call for a much greater involvement of the agency staff, since they would know where the agency's main weaknesses are likely to be, and they would want to be highly selective in the choice of projects for evaluation. For instance, it may be that the technical advisers are not particularly concerned about, for example, road projects, because these are numerous and on the whole seldom present any severe technical problems, but an innovative project (such as a solar energy scheme) they would want to have evaluated in depth, even

248

though it may account for only a small proportion of the total aid being disbursed, because they are anxious to learn about what is an unfamiliar area.

It is clear that the relative emphasis on accountability versus learning lessons will have a major influence on the size of the evaluation unit (fully representative samples are likely to be much larger than highly selective ones and more resources will be required), on the choice of staff (in-house vs. out-house), and on the organisational set-up (independent vs. integrated). The latter issue, the status of the evaluation unit, has proved to be a contentious one, and different aid agencies have resolved it in different ways. In some agencies, such as the World Bank, the Operations Evaluation Department is given a special independent status, even to the extent that the Director-General is told that he can expect no other subsequent appointment in the Bank, so that he is free to be as critical as he wishes without having to worry about the possible impact on his future career. However, many other agencies, including the ODA, regard the evaluation unit as an integral part of the structure, administratively independent of the other main spending departments but equivalent to them in being responsible to senior management. Commenting on this distinction, the then Chairman of the Projects and Evaluation Committee in the ODA (Mr R. A. Browning), who had also served as the Alternate UK Executive Director on the Board of the World Bank, commented [*Browning, 1984*]:

> The evaluation system at the World Bank is designed to help the Board, but in the minds of some of the Directors when the system was introduced, the intention was that the evaluation system would act very much as a check on senior management, or even more than a check. There was a definite desire to separate the management of the programme from the overseeing of the evaluation process. We ourselves put the two together: we find that we are able to criticise ourselves, and in fact we criticise each other with considerably more relish when it happens, as it inevitably must from time to time, that one of the members of the PEC was actually, in an earlier incarnation, responsible for the project under review when it was identified and first worked up.

The organisation of the ODA's Evaluation Department is shown in an organogram in Figure 1. It is striking that in the ODA's structure administrative and professional people are working side by side. This is relatively unusual in the UK Civil Service, but it works very happily. Of the three Heads of the Evaluation Department, two have been Senior

EVALUATING DEVELOPMENT ASSISTANCE

FIGURE 1
ORGANOGRAM OF ODA'S EVALUATION DEPARTMENT

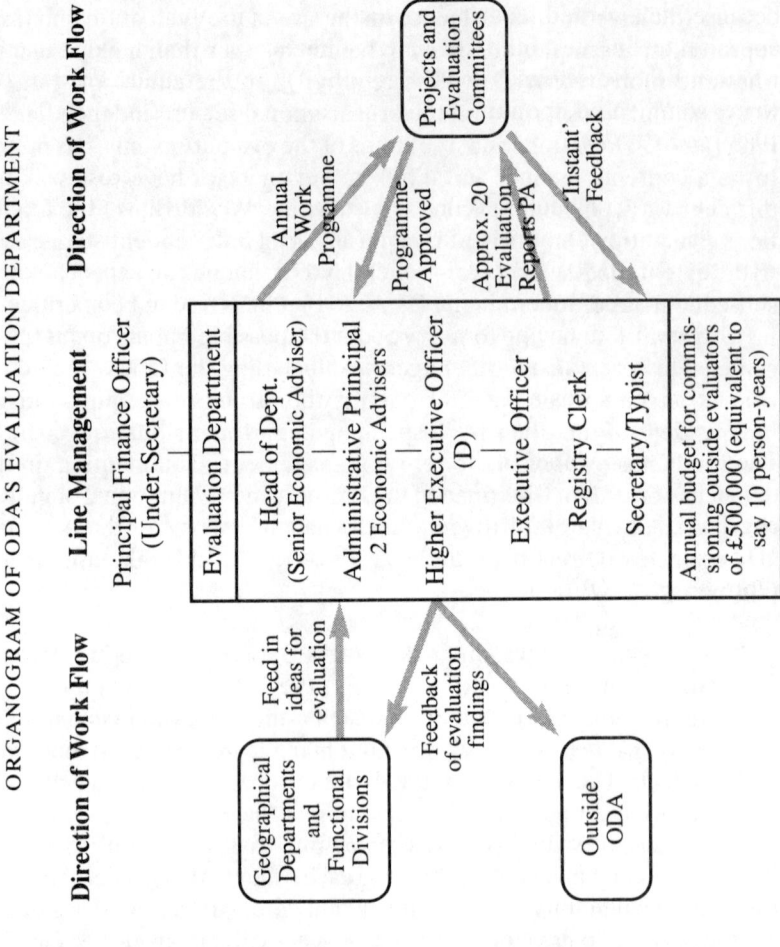

Economic Advisers, and one an Administrative Assistant Secretary. For many years, the Evaluation Department was staffed only by economists, but administrators were introduced in 1981. Economists had had the major role in getting the subject of evaluation started in the ODA because they wanted feedback on the success or failure of their project appraisal techniques, but from time to time the question had been raised whether other disciplines should not also be represented. The present writer commented upon this at the conference organised by the ODA in 1983 [*ODA, 1984*]:

> Doctor Cracknell said that although the economists had taken the lead in evaluation work, more and more the ODA was moving towards the concept of a wider mix of disciplines. The problem was that with only 20/25 new evaluations to be carried out per annum, it would hardly be possible to have an engineer, an agronomist, or a medical expert, attached permanently to the Department, whereas economics was a skill required for almost all evaluation work.

The ODA is now able to draw on a wider range of skills, thanks to the introduction of the administrators, who spend about half their time engaged on evaluation work. The Economic Department can also 'hire in' outside specialists, thanks to its annual budget of £500,000, and this represents an additional ten person-years of input which is available to the Department. The great advantage of this is that the ODA can select just the specialist skills it needs from outside for each evaluation. Generally speaking, the Evaluation Department uses mostly individuals from outside the ODA, such as academics or senior retired members of the ODA, but occasionally it uses commercial consultants. Interestingly, one problem with using consultants is that some of them in the past seem to have been most reluctant to be critical of the role played by the ODA for fear of prejudicing their chances of being engaged for projects in the future. Now that it is mandatory for each evaluation to cover the three topics of sustainability, the role of women and the environment, there is a growing need to have people on the evaluation teams who are capable of dealing with these issues.

The key role in the ODA's evaluation system is played by the Projects and Evaluation Committee (PEC). This comprises the Deputy Secretary, most of the Under-Secretaries, and the Chief Technical Advisers, as may be appropriate for the projects coming before the Committee. It meets every few weeks and approves all projects or programmes of £5 million or more. Every such project has to be submitted to the Committee for approval, in the form of a detailed, technical, economic and social, project appraisal. When possible, the economic appraisal will include a social cost-benefit analysis, and approval is usually only given if the project is shown to be capable of yielding a positive Net Present Value at a given rate of discount for the country concerned. It is now mandatory for the project submission to include a Project Framework. This is a matrix of the objectives of the project, indicators of success, and risks and assumptions (see the outline of the Project Framework in Annex 1). It is also mandatory for every project submission to contain an assurance that relevant evaluation studies have been considered, and that the findings have been taken into account in the preparation of the submission. More recently, it has also become mandatory for project submissions to cover a number of specific issues, notably the expected sociological impact [*Browning, 1984*]: 'Individual ODA departments seeking management approval for proposed projects must now supply far greater detail on the projects' intended beneficiaries – and in particular any group likely to be disadvantaged.' Writing in an ODA publication [*ODA, 1987*], Sir Crispin Tickell, the then Permanent Secretary of the ODA, stated: 'Our aim in the ODA has been to find ways by which environmental factors can enter by right into the complex of calculations, political, social and economic, which lie behind aid in whatever form.'

The PEC not only approves all significant new projects and programmes, but also receives all the evaluations of past ones. It allocates a number of meetings during the course of the year which are intended specifically for evaluation reports, usually about eight, and at each meeting two or three evaluation reports are taken one after the other. Since the meetings seldom last longer than about two and a half to three hours, the time allowed for the discussion on each evaluation report is usually about an hour. There is little time for any discussion in depth about the project or programme which is the subject of evaluation, and the Chairman also has to concentrate on the key lessons that have emerged and, in particular, on what the ODA should be doing about it. To assist the Committee in this, the Evaluation Department prepares a very important document called the 'Cover Note'. This gives a very brief introduction to the background of the evaluation, who did it, when, what it cost, and any problems that were encountered in carrying it out. Then it summarises the main reactions of ODA colleagues to the report's findings and recommendations and, on the basis of these, it presents the Evaluation Department's own recommendations of specific action that the ODA might take to improve the quality of its aid operations. The final section of the Cover Note contains the Evaluation Department's recommendations on feedback.

One of the slight snags with the Cover Note procedure is that the process of getting reactions from interested ODA colleagues can sometimes be a protracted business and can delay submission of the report for some months. On the other hand, it quite frequently happens that the recommendations put forward by the evaluators (even though they may include members of the staff of the ODA) are often either rather vague or tend to be off-target so far as specific action within the ODA is concerned. The Committee simply does not have the time to translate vague generali-sations into specific action proposals. To quote Browning again [*Browning, 1984*]: 'We must know how *we* as an aid agency can do things better, not how things can be done better in some general cosmic sense.' The Evaluation Department translates often vague recommendations into specific decisions-oriented proposals, even to the point occasionally of drafting terminology for 'Office Procedure' if some change in administrative procedures seems to be called for.

The fact that the same body which approves projects or programmes also receives the evaluations, ensures that there is vital feedback at a senior level. To quote the Chairman of the PEC once more [*Browning, 1984*]: 'We gain a lot from studying the evaluation reports, from judging them, and deciding what has to be done about them, and because we are the body which considers all new projects, the lessons are often very quickly applied.'

Relationships between the Evaluation Unit and other Parts of the Aid Agency
The evaluation unit needs to be very well informed about what is going on elsewhere in the agency, at all points of the project cycle.

Project formulation and appraisal: It is important for the evaluation unit to know what kinds of projects and programmes are entering the 'project pipeline', because this provides it with an early warning of what are likely to be the most significant sectors and sub-sectors which will be occupying the agency's attention during the years immediately ahead. Armed with this knowledge, the unit can then ensure, as far as possible, that it selects projects for evaluation that might help to throw light on these sectors. In the ODA it was largely due to the Evaluation Department's concern to obtain this kind of information that the 'Early Warning Project Pipeline System' was set up some years ago. This was simply a questionnaire sent to all the geographical departments and functional divisions, every six months at that time (now every four months), asking them to describe the new projects and programmes that were entering the agency's pipeline. The other objective of doing this was that it enabled the Evaluation Department to feed information, based on evaluation findings of previous projects, back to the geographical departments and functional divisions, so that it could be taken into account at a very early stage. As stated earlier, it is mandatory for project submissions to indicate to what extent evaluation findings of past projects in the same sector have been taken into account in the preparation of the project submission, and this often involves the Evaluation Department in sending evaluation reports and summaries at the request of those preparing submissions.

Another very important role for an evaluation unit at the project formulation and appraisal stage is to advise on whether a base-line survey should be carried out. Time is usually very short, so there is a great deal of urgency if the base-line survey is to be carried out before the first contractor's vehicles and machines arrive. In the ODA the Evaluation Department may assume the responsibility of carrying out the survey, or the Geographical Department may decide to do it as a basis for future monitoring and implementation.

At present the Evaluation Department tends not to be very closely involved in the drawing up of the monitoring plan, which is unfortunate, since the monitoring system will provide vital data for the Project Completion Report (PCR) and any evaluation that may ultimately be made. Therefore the Evaluation Department has a keen interest in ensuring that effective monitoring systems are set up. However, the Department does see the monitoring plan for each project at the approval stage and is able to bring its influence to bear at that stage if necessary.

Project implementation: The evaluation unit's role concerning implementation is mainly to collect and synthesise all the PCRs with a view to extracting wider lessons which might be appropriate to the agency as a whole. In the UK the Evaluation Department was for a long time specifically instructed not to get involved in ongoing projects, except Technical Cooperation or Manpower projects which are often by definition ongoing, because it was thought that this would lead to confusion with the monitoring process. However, at the conference at the Institute of Development Studies in 1983 [*ODA, 1984*], the ODA was severely criticised for this, particularly by R. J. Berg, who had until recently been head of the evaluation division in the USAID. He commented that:

> Rather than differentiate monitoring and evaluation on the basis of the timing of the exercise, it was surely more satisfactory to concentrate on the different purposes of the two operations. Thus monitoring was concerned with the progress in the implementation of an aid activity, whilst evaluation was concerned with the socio-economic results.

In his closing address at the conference, R. S. Porter, the ODA's Chief Economist, commented that the ODA would have to reconsider its compartmentalised approach, 'if only for no other reason than that one clearly had to rely to a considerable extent on the information generated during the monitoring process as a basis for evaluation.'

In practice, however, the ODA still tends to keep the two separate. The Evaluation Department only gets involved in the evaluation of ongoing projects, other than those in the Technical Cooperation or Manpower fields, when a mid-term evaluation or review can provide useful lessons both for the project and often for ODA activities. This is in marked contrast with the situation in some other aid agencies, where the interest has switched from *ex post* evaluation towards ongoing evaluation, mainly because the lessons derived from the former tended all too often to be out of date. This viewpoint is reflected in the OECD's 'Methods and Procedures of Aid Evaluation' [*OECD, 1986*] which comments:

> There is a tendency to increase mid-term studies as opposed to *ex post* evaluation. The reason is that the latter easily becomes dated, and the procedures they examine have often been changed by the time the final evaluation reports are completed. The dominant pragmatic approach to evaluation also favours early evaluation, in that it is easier to follow up such studies with concrete action. With *ex post* studies the donor's role is over before the reports are delivered.

The ODA's Evaluation Department has recently carried out a desk evaluation of the ODA's monitoring system [*Scott et al., 1987*]. This found that financial (audit-type) monitoring was the most effective, followed by monitoring of implementation, with monitoring against objectives the least effective. The evaluators suggested that the present use of the Project Framework should play a significant role in improving current monitoring effectiveness. One important conclusion was that the monitoring missions spent far more time than should have been necessary in data collection. If ongoing project-reporting could be improved, this would release the ODA's technical advisers to focus more definitely on overall project effectiveness; steps have been taken to focus monitoring in this way.

Project completion: When the ODA's principal involvement comes to an end, a Project Completion Report (PCR) is prepared which is intended to record the main achievements of the project, and any problems that may have been encountered. The PCRs provide another important, if relatively new, source of material for evaluation syntheses.

The Evaluation Department has recently designed an improved format for PCRs to enable them to be completed more effectively. The PCRs are likely to be most useful if the ODA staff who were closely involved in the project (especially the technical advisers) use them to record the key lessons they feel they have learned from the project. The Evaluation Department is naturally keen to improve the coverage and quality of PCRs and sees scope in introducing the new format together with some kind of a grading system, along the lines of that developed by the Swedish aid agency (SIDA) for its projects, geared to the degree of problems which have been associated with the project during implementation.

The main weakness of the PCR, for evaluation purposes, is that it takes place too soon for impact to be properly assessed. Often the end of the donor's involvement marks the beginning of the project's life.

Ex post evaluation: The evaluation process is not carried out in isolation from the rest of the office; very much the reverse. Not only do the geographical desks and functional divisions play an important part in the basic selection of projects to be evaluated, but they also play an integral role in carrying out the evaluations themselves. They advise on the terms of reference, on the suitability of the proposed evaluators, and on the approach to be made to the developing country. If there is a development division, it will take a keen interest in the process and may well participate in an 'associate' capacity. The ODA does not appoint to evaluation teams anyone who has been directly involved in the project or programmes to be evaluated, and most of the Development Division staff are likely to have been in some way associated with projects in their region. If it is a big evaluation, the geographical desk or functional division will participate in a Steering Committee and, when the evaluation report is submitted, their views will be immediately sought on the report, especially on any recommendations produced. In drawing up the Cover Note, the Evaluation Division is basically trying to draw lessons from particular projects or programmes which can be applied across the board. This is obviously a risky business, and therefore the Evaluation Department tries to find out whether what is being recommended fits in with the 'conventional wisdom' of the office and especially its technical advisers. If it doesn't, it is very unlikely that the recommendations will be included in the Cover Note. This process involves the Evaluation Department in very close liaison with colleagues throughout the organisation, which is good, because it makes everyone aware of the evaluation process and ensures that they feel involved in it. This improves feedback and subsequent action on the findings.

The Main Constraints on the Evaluation Unit

Relationship to policy-making: Two of the unresolved issues which continue to act as constraints on evaluation activity in most donor agencies are (1) the extent to which policy aspects should be evaluated directly, and (2) the extent to which evaluations concerned with projects or programmes should also comment on broad policy implications. These issues are not confined to the ODA; they apply to many other aid agencies and indeed were among the most sensitive and controversial issues tackled by the DAC Expert Group on Aid Evaluation. Some donors, notably USAID, regard evaluation of policy as a crucial aspect of their evaluation work. The ODA sees policy-making as the responsibility of senior management, and even if evaluations can make a major contribution to this, that is not their major purpose. The DAC Expert Group on Aid Evaluation's report [*OECD, 1986*] states that the objectives of evaluation are not only to improve the delivery of aid, and to provide accountability, but also 'to place development aid in a broader context', and it singles out the following examples:

- to examine the outside constraints on development aid
- to examine the institutions involved and their influence on aid delivery
- to examine alternative ways of accomplishing a goal, for example, private vs. public alternatives, project aid vs. non-project aid, etc.

These fall short of an outright adoption of the position that evaluators should directly address themselves to major policy issues. Probably most evaluation units are increasingly reluctant to get involved in directly evaluating highly sensitive aspects of aid policy, where systematic and quantified techniques of evaluation are not feasible, but rather prefer to evaluate selected individual instances of the results of such policies.

Relationships with developing countries: One of the anxieties of evaluators is that over-critical comments about the roles of the developing country institutions or personnel could so affect the relationships between the two parties that the developing countries might refuse to co-operate in evaluation work in the future. This has rarely happened in practice, which is a tribute to the flexibility and tolerance of the developing countries, as well as to the care that evaluators have taken to avoid it. More recently there has been a welcome change of emphasis away from the negative attitude of fearing adverse reactions to a more positive attitude of involving the developing countries more fully in the whole of the evaluation operation.

Fear of weakening the public support of aid: Another constant fear of all evaluation units is that, if absolute frankness is exercised, and details of aid disasters are made available to the public, this may result in a cut-back in the public support for aid. Others argue, however, that the public should be trusted, and that, if they are presented with the facts, and with a reasonable cross-section of projects, good and bad, they can be relied upon to form a fair judgement by themselves. In any case they ought to be made to realise that, just as any private company which is investing overseas must reckon that it will make mistakes, so mistakes are inevitable with the aid operation. The argument flows back and forth, but without any real conclusions being reached. Some donors, particularly the Dutch and the Scandinavians, seem more ready to be completely open (perhaps because they are well assured of strong public support for aid), whereas others take a more cautious line. There is general agreement, however, that a continuous diet of disaster stories will surely damage public support for aid, so evaluation programmes must be sure to include success stories as well as failures. One can in any case learn useful lessons from success just as one can from failures.

At the broad policy level, there are usually seriously conflicting objectives surrounding any aid project or programme. Thus the Foreign Office may favour a programme to a politically sensitive region, in the hope of winning political advantages for the donor country, whereas the aid agency will be more concerned about developmental criteria. The Department of Trade will tend to favour the newly industrialising countries, because they are likely to offer more opportunities for trade, whereas the aid agency may favour the poorest countries, because their needs for development assistance are greatest. The aid agency may offer Western-oriented resources, if only because with tied aid it is not free to offer anything else in many instances. But it may be that the desirable path of development would favour the upgrading of more traditional technologies.

At the project level, there are also nearly always a number of competing objectives. Aid for a rural development project may be intended to help the peasant, but its effect may be to widen still further the differential between rich and poor. If the poor are made a little better off, does it matter that the rich are made much richer still? It is extremely difficult for evaluators to cope with issues of this kind. They are not well equipped to make policy-type value judgements. The tendency, therefore, is for them to side-step such issues, and to concentrate mainly on technical and physical changes, so they will describe a new road but will shrink from passing a judgement on whether it helps or harms the poorest. However, one or two detailed studies are now being carried out to examine the distribution of benefits to the poorest. It may be that the growing use of the Project Framework system will help, in that the various objectives are spelled out in the matrix.

Relationships with colleagues: Evaluation is always a rather sensitive operation. If the evaluator comes from within the agency, he will seem to be setting himself up in judgement on his own colleagues. If he comes from outside, he may be reluctant to be too critical of the agency that is employing him, especially as his knowledge of how that agency operates is likely to be partial.

It is a basic rule in all evaluation units that individual names are never mentioned. The purpose is to focus on systems, procedures and policies rather than on individual performance. But even so, it is usually possible to identify at least the section which has been responsible. One way of diminishing the possible adverse impact of this is to constantly change round some of the staff of the Evaluation Department, so that over a period of years a fair number of the staff of the agency will themselves have spent a year or two doing evaluation work and therefore are likely to be sympathetic to the operation. This should mean that, when their turn comes to be evaluated, they should be co-operative. The administrative staff are likely to spend a shorter period doing evaluation work than the economist, although too rapid a turnover is not desirable. Another way of coping with sensitivities is to plan and implement evaluations in a totally co-operative way with the colleagues involved, that is, instead of deliberately keeping them at arm's length, it is preferable to carry out the study alongside and with them, although they should have no part in the writing up of the report. Use of outsiders does not in itself diminish the risk of harming relationships with colleagues. Sometimes outsiders, especially academics with their reputations to make, are severely critical of what they see as incompetence, when often it may be due to extreme pressure of work or to difficult inter-relationships that the evaluator has failed to understand.

The need to optimise scarce resources: All evaluation departments struggle with the problem of how to make the optimum use of scarce resources, when there are so many competing calls. As indicated above, there is a basic conflict between the aim of having a representative sample (for accountability reasons) and the need to look at specific projects and programmes at the request of colleagues, so that lessons can be learned. The same conflict of priorities expresses itself as between the desirability of cross-sectional representativeness in the selection of projects and programmes for evaluation and the need to concentrate resources by sectors in the hope of being able to carry out syntheses which will yield more useful general observations. Then there is the conflict of interests between trying to cover a reasonable number of projects, on the one hand, and the realisation that to get useful evidence on 'impact' it will usually be necessary to set up field surveys that could well spread over a considerable period of time and could quickly soak up a high proportion of the available resources. Again every evaluation unit is keen to establish base-line surveys, wherever possible, but these too usually involve field surveys and are relatively expensive, so that one often has to weigh up the relative merit of a base-line study as against an evaluation, since the available resources may not stretch to both. These are just some of the severe constraints which are related to scarcity of resources, and it is vital that the evaluation unit has a clear lead (as in fact the PEC gives to the ODA's Evaluation Department) concerning where the emphasis should lie and what the priorities are.

In-house evaluators vs. outsiders: There is always a certain tension associated with the decision as to the relative roles of outsiders and in-house staff in the building up of evaluation teams. Sometimes the choice is obvious (if, for example, the evaluation calls for specialist technical skills, which are either not available within the agency or the technical officer concerned has already been too committed to the project), but often there are no such factors steering the decision one way or the other. Sometimes there may have been some controversy associated with the project, and it may seem advisable to have an impartial opinion. At other times speed may be of the essence (as with base-line studies) and it may be more practical to use a commercial consultancy. The views of the geographical desks (and in the ODA's case also the Development Divisions) will have to be weighed up very carefully, as well as the sensitivities of the developing countries. Most aid agencies have found that mixed teams are the most satisfactory, and that the evaluation report is more likely to be geared to specific action appropriate to the agency's needs if one of its in-house staff members has had a major part in its formulation.

Absorptive capacity of the PEC: One of the constraints of the ODA's Evaluation Department is the absorptive capacity of the PEC. At present the Committee devotes about eight meetings a year to evaluations, but this is stretching its capacity to the limit, since its primary function is to decide on new projects, and this must have first claim on its resources.

Yet it is vital that the PEC should make time available for evaluation work. One of the ODA's under-secretaries at the 1983 Conference [*ODA, 1984*] commented:

The burden, in terms of the reports that have to be read, is considerable (ODA's evaluations are usually detailed studies and can sometimes run to 150–200 pages), but it is held to be justified in terms of the benefits from instant feedback. This consideration is one factor that explains why in ODA we have always tended to put a higher premium on quality than quantity. We feel that a few good 'impact' evaluations can give more useful and worthwhile results than a larger number of evaluations of the Project Completion Report (PCR) type can hope to do.

The Evaluation Department always has to plan its operations so as to optimise the limited amount of time that the PEC can spare for evaluation work. But this is not really a disadvantage, because it forces the Department to look for such ways of extracting the maximum benefit from evaluations as combining one-off project evaluations into syntheses or devoting a lot of care to making the Cover Note as useful and as action-focused as possible. There can be no doubt at all that this small degree of constraint is more than justified by the advantages of instant feedback at a senior policy level.

II. FEEDBACK

Need for Feedback

It is rather ironic that the most important phase of the evaluation process, feedback, has hitherto been given the least attention. It is obvious that any evaluation study, no matter how well it has been prepared, will have little effect unless there are specific arrangements for ensuring that action is taken in the light of the findings. Why then has feedback been so often ignored? Perhaps it is because the mere existence of evaluation reports may seem to be sufficient to meet the public-accountability objective. Or it may simply be that very different skills, even different people, are required to ensure effective feedback, compared with the requirements for carrying out the evaluations. The former operation is a matter of communication, the latter of investigation.

There is no doubt that most evaluators are far more interested in carrying out the evaluations than they are in ensuring feedback. They stand to gain personal prestige from their role in doing the evaluations, but trying to persuade colleagues or institutions to act on the basis of their findings can lead to confrontations and conflict, which people tend to shrink from. Or it may simply be that the best machinery for ensuring feedback is not self-evident – indeed it has to compete with many other seemingly more pressing claims on people's time. Inevitably evaluations of past projects have a slightly *passé* air about them, compared, for instance, with a decision that has to be taken immediately on a project which may cost millions of dollars. The pressure in most aid agencies to disburse aid funds is usually far more urgent than the pressure to improve the quality of aid: success or failure, so far as the former is concerned, is immediate, transparent, and irreversible, since aid funds not spent during a given financial year can seldom be transferred to a succeeding one, while the latter only becomes evident years later, by which time probably someone else will be sitting at that particular desk.

However, in spite of these factors, the need for effective feedback is so self-evident that most agencies in recent years have accorded it high priority, and some very interesting and effective feedback mechanisms have been introduced, some intended to improve the internal feedback within the aid agency, and some to improve the external feedback of results to the general public and to others. The purpose of the second part of this paper is to describe and review these mechanisms and to assess how effective the existing feedback systems are.

Feedback at the Policy Level

The most important kind of feedback must surely be feedback at the policy-making level. It is vital that those who have the responsibility for settling the policy of the aid agency should receive a constant flow of findings from evaluations which throw light on the effectiveness of their past decisions. Without this, they could simply be repeating past mistakes. Yet the DAC Expert Group on Aid Evaluation found that in many aid agencies there is no effective feedback at the senior policy level comparable with the PEC in the ODA. The EC's Basic Principles procedure, excellent as it is in some respects, cannot be compared with the ODA's PEC system for getting evaluation results into the 'bloodstream' of the aid agency at a senior level. The USAID also lacks a comparable system and there the tendency is to call together *ad hoc* groups of people to discuss specific evaluation reports, but these tend to lack the executive authority of a body like the PEC. The present writer once heard a senior USAID official complain that all too often the evaluation reports produced by his agency finish up unread, on his colleagues' window sills. Time is at a premium for senior policy-makers in any aid agency, and unless there is a specific mechanism, such as the PEC, which obliges them to read and act upon evaluation reports, they are unlikely to do so. It should, of course, be emphasised that even a discussion forum is not enough: it needs to be a decision-taking committee. The PEC's procedure of focusing on action-oriented recommendations ensures that reports are followed by action.

One of the Evaluation Department's tasks is to keep a watchful eye on the key findings emerging from the evaluation activities of other donors (the Department keeps a library of evaluation reports issued by IBRD and other donors, particularly any synthesis studies), so that it can brief the Chief Economist and other Chief Technical Advisers on important findings relevant to new projects that may be coming before the Committee. This source of information supplements the ODA's own growing stock of evaluation reports and can occasionally fill a gap in the ODA's coverage.

Feedback at the Operational Level

Most evaluations contain lessons of an operational, as well as a policy nature, and these need to be taken on board by aid administrators and technical advisers within the agency. The evaluation reports themselves are the obvious vehicle for this, and there is no doubt that professional advisers read them and note the contents carefully. After all, there are not many reports annually that fall within their special area, and they will probably have been involved in the planning and implementation of the evaluations, so they naturally have a keen interest in seeing the results. But with the geographical desk officers it tends to be different. They handle all kinds of projects, and they cannot be expected to read all the evaluation reports in full. Yet they too need to be aware of the main gist of the evaluation findings. The ODA has resolved this problem by introducing the EVSUM (short for 'Evaluation Summary'). An example of an EVSUM is given in Annex 2. The EVSUM is a one-page synopsis of the main findings of each evaluation. The sector reference is shown at the top and, as the staff receive the EVSUMs, they place them in ring-binders sector by sector. As they insert the fresh sheets, the idea is that they will glance again at the other EVSUMs in that particular sector, and this should remind them of the key findings. As they have to deal with new projects, so they look up the EVSUMs at an early stage. To reinforce this system, the Evaluation Department operates the Early Warning System mentioned earlier, whereby it sends EVSUMs to geographical desks which are relevant to new projects.

The ODA has recently carried out its own evaluation of the EVSUM system [*Ludford, 1987*]. The purpose was to assess how useful the system was, and the extent to which it has actually been used in practice. About 200 questionnaires were sent out, covering a representative cross-section of recipients, and there was a very high response. Only 19 said that they had not seen any EVSUMs during the last six months and this was mainly due to staff movements. Their results show that the EVSUMs were widely used by ODA staff and that three-quarters of the staff on geographical desks who had worked on preparing project submissions had made use of EVSUMs in the course of their preparation. Where they had not been used, it was because there were no EVSUMs relevant to the particular projects or programmes being processed. The main findings were:

- EVSUMs (that is, the evaluations upon which the EVSUMs are based) need to be as relevant as possible to the kinds of project currently being handed by the ODA.
- Timeliness is vital. EVSUMs need to be used as soon as a new project enters the project pipeline.
- All new staff need to be introduced to the EVSUM system in initial training sessions.

There are three other vehicles that can be used for carrying evaluation findings into operational use. The first of these is the *Policy Guidance Note*. The PGNs are internal policy notes that are circulated around the ODA from time to time as the need arises. Each year there may be one or two new PGNs. A recent one, for instance, relates to the Project Framework System and sets out guidelines on how the matrix should be used, based on the results of an evaluation carried out for the ODA by the present writer [*Cracknell, 1986*]. This is a typical illustration of how the results of an evaluation study can be disseminated in a more detailed and authoritative way than is possible with the EVSUM. The second vehicle is the *Sector Planning Manual*. This is a technically oriented manual aimed primarily at meeting the needs of the professional advisers, but available also to others. Manuals now exist for such subjects as power, railways, water, telecommunications, roads, and others. Evaluation findings are incorporated into the text of these manuals when they are revised from time to time. Thirdly there is *Office Procedure*. This relates specifically to administrative and procedural aspects. It is a codification of current practice in the ODA. Occasionally it will happen that an evaluation finding calls for an amendment to be made to Office Procedure.

The Evaluation Department will usually prepare a suitable text, and this will be included in the Cover Note when the evaluation is submitted to the PEC. A recent example related to a change in the procedure over the manning of monitoring missions.

The emphasis on synthesis by sectors in recent years has opened out the possibility of feedback through internal staff seminars devoted to such evaluations covering whole sectors. One such seminar was held on the power synthesis in 1985, and others are planned. Evaluations are also used for training purposes, in conjunction with the ODA's Training Division. It is noteworthy that the Evaluation Department ran two training workshops on the Project Framework, before this task was transferred to the Training Division. The Department also participates in evaluation training sessions run by the Civil Service College from time to time.

Lastly, so far as internal feedback is concerned, there is need to incorporate evaluation findings into data-bank systems. These have developed far more in some agencies (notably CIDA, USAID and IBRD) than in others (such as the ODA or the EC). In the former, elaborate data-banks have been set up which absorb a substantial proportion of total evaluation resources, but hitherto other agencies have not been altogether convinced that the results justify the costs. The ODA has preferred to develop its EVSUM system as a simple but cost-effective way of disseminating evaluation findings. However, as evaluation as a subject becomes more mature, there is a growing desire among the different aid agencies to ensure that the growing stock of evaluation findings is shared more effectively, and that probably points towards some kind of computerised data-bank service. There is already a mountain of evaluation reports (around 9,000 in 1986 [*OECD, 1986*]), and no one can possibly have time to read all the reports that other agencies have produced. This probably explains the renewed interest, among evaluation experts, in computerised data-bank systems, of the sort developed by CIDA. These enable the key findings of evaluations to be recorded alongside the appraisal data and monitoring results for each project, giving a comprehensive story of project success or failure. The data can also be analysed in a number of ways to meet agencies' data needs.

The ODA's Management Information System (MIS) provides a skeleton round which such a system might be built, and no doubt some experiments will be made in the years ahead to see how to optimise the potential for a synthesised computer system among the main aid agencies. One problem is likely to be that too much information can be as much an obstacle as too little. If a geographical desk officer, or technical adviser, faced with a roads project, for instance, seeks help from a computerised data-bank, only to find that it throws back at him a thousand bits of information covering all aspects of roads, he will quickly lose interest, because he cannot cope with so much information. However, if he can obtain information, say, on a gravel-top road, in a wet tropical climate, built and maintained by local labour, and all that corresponds roughly with the problem he is currently facing, then he may well make use of the information . . . if he can still find time, that is! The experience of other agencies that have developed data-banks is that all too often they are used more by research workers (who, of course, tend to have the time) than by hard-pressed, operational-agency staff. Maybe the evaluation units in aid agencies will have to act as intermediaries, using the computerised data-bank to produce their own synthesis data that can be fed into sector manuals and similar documents. The DAC Expert Group on Aid Evaluation is looking closely into these issues and deserves full encouragement.

Availability of Evaluation

The first and obvious form of feedback is to make evaluation reports available on request to anyone who wishes to read them. Hitherto there has been a marked reluctance on the part of many agencies to do this, because they fear that the reports may be used to attack the aid programme. However, there has been strong pressure from bodies like the Independent Group on British Aid in the UK [*IGBA, 1982, 1986*] for evaluation reports to be made freely available, and there is a growing acceptance that this is desirable, provided there are adequate safeguards. As mentioned earlier, the ODA now hopes that it will be possible to make all reports available to the public. It is a remarkable fact that, although about two-thirds of the ODA's evaluation reports have been made available to the public over the last 15 or 20 years, there have been very few instances indeed where the results have been used as a stick with which to beat the ODA.

Because evaluation reports can be expensive to produce, the ODA has tended in recent years to substitute the EVSUMs for the full reports in its circulation to outside recipients. Some development research institutions still prefer to receive the full reports, usually for their libraries, but others seem to be satisfied with the summaries, so long as they know that they can always ask for the full report if they wish. EVSUMs, and sometimes full reports, also go to consultants, and this is an important element of feedback. Consultants frequently have to submit proposals to the ODA for new assignments, and it is important that they should be aware of the results of past aid activities. It was for this reason that the British Consultants Bureau, some years ago, suggested that the ODA's Evaluation Department should join it in mounting a series of training seminars based on the ODA's evaluations. The BCB is also, of course, concerned to ensure that its members have an opportunity to participate in the carrying out of evaluation assignments, and the ODA bears this in mind when selecting evaluators.

Feedback to Institutions in the Donor Country

Development research institutes in the UK play an important part in the UK's evaluation system. All of them have participated fully in the ODA's evaluation teams, and the staff concerned find that this helps them a great deal with their own teaching, research and consultancy work. Some of them, notably the Overseas Development Group at the University of East Anglia, are also engaged in the training of evaluation techniques to people from the Third World, and it is obviously important that there is close liaison with the ODA in that field. The Overseas Development Group, which had been teaching the 'logical framework' approach long before the ODA adopted it, was invited by the ODA to participate in the training workshops on the new Project Framework System. Another institute that has made particular use of the ODA's evaluation reports is the Overseas Development Institute, where Roger Riddell carried out a major review of the ODA's stock of evaluation reports as a basis for his book *Foreign Aid Reconsidered* [*Riddell, 1987*].

The ODA is aware of the need to inform the public, especially those informed members who constitute the 'aid lobby', of the results of its evaluation work, which is why it took the unusual step of calling a two-day international conference on the subject at the Institute of Development Studies at the University of Sussex in 1983 [*ODA, 1984*].

Parliament, through its various bodies such as the Foreign Affairs Committee, takes a keen interest in the ODA's evaluation activities, as also does the UK Treasury. The meetings of the Foreign Affairs Committee are reported openly and, in the Minutes of Evidence, evaluation reports are frequently quoted, especially when academics and others come before the Committee. Evaluations provide, in encapsulated form, very useful evidence on the success or failure of different kinds of aid activity and thus help to ensure that debates are firmly based on real evidence rather than merely on people's opinions.

The role of the DAC Expert Group on Aid Evaluation has already been mentioned. It has been a very important avenue of feedback, especially through the syntheses that it has organised in the past, not only for use by the full DAC but also by others. Feedback has been one of the important issues that the Group has considered, and there are current proposals for joint action to ensure more effective feedback through computerised bibliography as a consequence of this concern.

Feedback to the Developing Countries

The usual practice is for evaluation teams to discuss their evaluation reports and findings in draft with their developing country colleagues before they leave the country, and then for the final report to be sent to the developing country once the PEC has given its approval. The ODA does not go so far down the road of cooperation with the developing countries as does the World Bank, which seeks the developing countries' written comments on each evaluation report. Because the ODA, through its technical advisers and its Development Divisions on the spot, works so closely with the countries it is assisting, there is a lot of interchange on evaluation reports, even if this is not always formalised. In recent years many developing countries have set up their own evaluation units, and there has been more interchange over methodology and technique. The present writer was able to assist such new evaluation units in Indonesia and Malawi when he was in the ODA, and the DAC Expert Group on Aid Evaluation has organised its first international training seminar mainly intended for the developing countries.

Undoubtedly this kind of feedback needs to be taken much further, along the lines pursued by the Director-General of the Operations Evaluation Department of the World Bank some years ago, when he made a tour of developing countries to see how the Bank could help them with their own evaluation problems. However, it has to be recognised that evaluation models that may suit the requirements of the developed countries may not be appropriate for the aid recipients [*Cracknell, 1985*]. The EC's system, whereby evaluation findings are used to prepare 'Basic Principles' for each sector, which are then discussed and agreed jointly with the developing countries (ACP), has a lot to recommend it, since it transforms evaluation from being exclusively a donor preoccupation towards becoming an operation of equal interest to all parties in the development process.

REFERENCES

Browning, R., 1984, 'Evaluation in the ODA: A View from the Inside', *Public Administration and Development*, Vol. 4, 133–9.

Cracknell, B.E., 1985, 'It Looks Different from the Other Side: Project Evaluation from the Perspective of the Developing Countries', A paper presented to the Annual Conference of the ESRC/Development Study Group, November 1985.

Cracknell, B.E., 1986, 'Evaluation of ODA's Experience with the Project Framework', EV 428, ODA.

Independent Group on British Aid (IGBA), 1982, *Real Aid – A Strategy for Britain*, London.

Independent Group on British Aid, 1984, *Aid is not enough*, London.

Independent Group on British Aid, 1986, *Missed Opportunities: Britain and the Third World*, London.

Ludford, R.A., 1987, 'Report of the Questionnaire Survey of the Usefulness of Evaluation Summaries (EVSUMs), EV (Unnumbered Desk Study), ODA.

Overseas Development Administration (ODA), 1984, *The Evaluation of Aid Projects and Programmes*, London: HMSO.

Overseas Development Administration, 1986, *Women in Development and the British Bilateral Aid Programme*.

Overseas Development Administration, 1987, *The Environment and the British Aid Programme*.

THE ROLE OF AN EVALUATION UNIT

Organisation for Economic Cooperation and Development (OECD), 1986, *Methods and Procedures of Aid Evaluation*, Paris.

Riddell, R., 1987, *Foreign Aid Reconsidered*, London: James Currey for Overseas Development Institute.

Scott, M. et al., 1987, *An Evaluation of Bilateral Project Monitoring*, EV 408, ODA.

ANNEX 1
ODA'S PROJECT FRAMEWORK MATRIX

PROJECT TITLE:
BRIEF DESCRIPTION OF PROJECTS:
MIS CODE NO:
FILE REFERENCE:

PERIOD OF ODA FUNDING:
FROM F/Y   TO F/Y
TOTAL ODA FUNDING: £
DATE FRAMEWORK PREPARED/REVISED:

PROJECT STRUCTURE	INDICATORS OF ACHIEVEMENT	HOW INDICATORS CAN BE QUANTIFIED OR ASSESSED	IMPORTANT ASSUMPTIONS (ASSESSMENT OF RISK)
WIDER (i.e. SECTOR OR NATIONAL) OBJECTIVES What are the wider objectives or problems which the project will help to resolve?	What are the quantitative ways of measuring, or qualitative ways of judging, whether these wider objectives have been achieved?	What sources of information exist or can be provided cost-effectively?	What conditions external to the project are necessary if the project's Immediate Objectives are to contribute to the Wider Objectives? What risks have been considered? Are any conditions attached to ODA's aid to improve the prospects of success?
IMMEDIATE OBJECTIVES: PROJECT PURPOSE What are the intended immediate effects on the project area or target group? What are the expected benefits (or disbenefits) and to whom will they go? What improvements or changes will the project bring about?	What are the quantitative measures (including the realised internal rate of return), or qualitative evidence, by which achievement and distribution of effects and benefits can be judged?	What sources of information exist or can be provided cost-effectively? Does provision for collection need to be made under Inputs-Outputs?	What are the factors outside the control of the project authorities which, if not present, are liable to restrict progress from Outputs to achievement of Immediate Objectives? What risks have been considered? Are any conditions attached to ODA's aid to improve the prospects of success?
OUTPUTS What outputs (kind, quantity and by whom) are to be produced by the project in order to achieve the Immediate Objectives? E.g. teaching institution, miles of road built or rehabilitated, irrigation system and associated management installed, persons trained.		What are the sources of information?	What external factors must be realised to obtain planned Outputs on schedule? What risks have been considered? Are any conditions attached to ODA's aid to improve the prospects of success?
INPUTS What materials/equipment or services (personnel trained, etc.) are to be provided by – ODA – other donors – recipient?		What are the sources of information?	What decisions or actions outside control of ODA are necessary for inception of project? What risks have been considered? Are any conditions attached to ODA's aid to improve the prospects of success?

THE ROLE OF AN EVALUATION UNIT

ANNEX 2
TYPICAL EXAMPLE OF ODA 'EVSUM'

EVSUM	**ENERGY EV 326**
SUMMARY OF EVALUATION HIGHLIGHTS	
AN EVALUATION OF DIESEL GENERATORS IN NEPAL: 1984	

The Project

A 10 Mw diesel generating station with 4 x 2.5 Mw generating units was provided at Hetauda, Nepal at a cost of £2.54 m. The project was expected to make a cost effective contribution to reducing power cuts pending the completion of further hydro electricity capacity. It was intended originally to move the diesel capacity to other localities after 1981.

The Evaluation

The evaluation was undertaken by J. N. Stevens, Economic Adviser, ODA and P. W. Beard, Consulting Engineer, who visited Nepal and had access to documents.

The main findings were:

a. project planning and the contribution of the recipient government were inadequate to meet the implementation schedule and the project was delayed by over one year;
b. the difficulties of transporting heavy equipment in Nepal were not fully appreciated;
c. design weaknesses were identified in the project, the most important of which was the lack of easy mobility of the generators;
d. the Units have been virtually unutilised for lack of funds to purchase fuel;
e. electricity tariffs are such that they do not cover even diesel fuel costs;
f. neither staff nor procedures for maintenance were adequate;
g. the Units will not be relocated but could still have a useful life if properly maintained and if a budget for fuel supply is created.

Lessons

Lessons learned in this evaluation were brought together with those from other projects reviewed in a synthesis study (EV 374 – see separate EV-SUM).

Evaluation Department, Overseas Development Administration
Eland House, Stag Place, London SW1E 5DH
Telephone: 071-213 5413

Index

Indexer's note. The headings and sub-headings in this index are arranged in alphabetical order, not letter by letter but word by word. When a word appears within parentheses, for example, (total), this means that this word also occurs occasionally in a few of the references. An extra indentation in the run-on sub-headings, followed by a sub-heading in **bold type**, indicates the beginning of a particularly important set of sub-headings. A subsequent extra indentation denotes the resumption of the ordinary sub-headings. Singular headings include the plural and *vice versa*.

access, 157, 160, 176, 190; accessible evaluations, 175
accountability, 25–7, 43, 45–6, 69, 107, 114, 230, 233, 248–9, 257, 259; concerns, 45–6, 50; function, 47, 232; political accountability of aid, 49–50; public accountability, 89; public-accountability objective, 261
achievement, 89, 91, 110, 231, 270; evaluation of the, 233; goal achievement, 138, 141; measures of, 91; of the project's objectives, 234, 238
actors, 1–3, 9, 22, 48, 54, 171, 196, 223; political actors (political parties), 16
administration (*see also* administrative system *and* aid administration), 129, 169–70, 172–3, 177, 205, 208; administrative staff, 259; German development administration, 146–7; national public, 137; of development assistance, 163; of projects, 115; of the Danish aid programme, 101; on the recipient side, 173; public, 60, 66, 135, 142, 163, 170; public-administration reform, 60
administrative systems (*see also* administration), 139, 164, 168, 190, 197, 219; administrative capacity, 174, 177; decisions, 127; level, 164, 197, 204; donor, 48; recipient, 48
(aid) administrators, 94, 127, 189, 191, 251, 263
Africa, 82, 88, 136, 142, 199; eastern, 188; famine in, 75; southern, 188; sub-Saharan, 41; provision of assistance to, 229
agency (*see also* aid agency), 245–6, 259, 263, 265–6; Agency for International Assistance, 208; (operational) agency staff, 248;

265; executive/executing, 142, 230, 235, 238–40, 243, 245; government, 210; independent, government, 209; public/private, Central Committee (CK), 208
aid (*see also* development assistance *and the specific forms of aid*), vii, 1, 9, 12–13, 16, 19, 21, 24, 26–7, 29, 31, 34–5, 37, 46, 49–50, 63, 69, 75, 76, 78–80, 82, 86–7, 90–1, 96–7, 100–1, 112, 119, 123, 125, 142–6, 150, 163, 165–73, 175–8, 180–1, 183–4, 186–9, 195, 198, 200–2, 209, 219, 225, 248–9, 252, 258; aid channels, 21, 24, 26, 48, 172, 175, 181–6, 189, 195; distribution between, 182; community, 69; forms (types), 24, 26, 172, 181, 186–7, 189, 195, 203; funds, pressure on, 77; aid-providing countries, 41; relationship (relations), 19, 21, 36, 41–2, 49; allocations of aid monies, 20; balance-of-payment aid, 87; bilateral, state-to-state, 2, 19, 27, 34, 36, 180, 183; capital aid, 87; channelled through multilateral agencies, 195; channelled through NGOs, 26, 171, 182, 195; commercialisation of, 26; compartmentalisation of, 17, 19; cross-sectoral, 187; developmental objectives of, 20; ecological dimension of, 4; economic dimensions of, 3; education and training aid, 88; effectiveness and efficiency of, 21–2, 35, 62, 87; end use of, 199; external, 143; financial, 159, 187; foreign, 15, 36, 51, 69; future, 180, 184; general aims for, 16–18; geographical concentration of, 171; government-to-government, 168, 174; humanitarian, 169, 189; impact of,

272

INDEX

on poverty alleviation, 27; (overall) impact of, 23–4, 179; effects and impact of, 111; planning and implementation of, 88; role of, 88; multi-bi aid evaluations, 117; multilateral, 34; multilateral-aid component, 26, 166; new forms of, 41, 187; official, quality of, 78; non-project aid, 18, 27, 51, 186, 257; evaluation of, 64; bilateral-grant, non-project aid, 116; overall, 135; overall objectives for, 14–16, 22, 24, 50; planning and evaluation of, 44; planning and implementing of, 35; poverty-oriented, 34; project aid, 18, 27, 257; public administration of, 170, 176; public support of, 258; quality of, 123, 262; socio-cultural aspects of, 187, 201; socio-economic dimension of, 4; targeted, 167; tied, 20; use of, for import support, 26

aid activity, 4, 7, 15, 34, 94, 96, 102, 104, 106, 116, 120, 163, 170, 172, 182, 188–9, 196, 198, 201, 203, 227, 234, 243, 266–7; administration and implementation of the, 113; aid-financed/supported activities, 33, 284; analysis of the, 114; appraisal of, 124; (independent) assessment of the, 112, 164; concrete formulation of aid goals and activities, 121, 124; effectiveness and efficiency of an, 7; effects and impact of, 114; evaluations of (multi-bi), 27, 112, 124; NGO, 116; Nordic, 116; planning of ongoing and future, 34, 124; positive improvement of present and future, 227; preparation, implementation and results of, 107; single, donor-supported, 125; socio-economic results of an, 254

aid administration, 8–9, 12, 14, 16, 19, 23, 28, 32, 34, 37, 40, 46, 50, 60, 97, 103, 145, 164, 171–2, 175–8, 181, 184, 186, 189–90, 193, 195–6, 198, 200–2, 219, 248; (closed) administrative system, 35; aid-implementing units of the, 23; civil-service, decision-making level of the, 25; compartmentalised, 12; craft of, 49; Danish, 25; decentralisation of the, 183; decision-making bodies of the, 40; donor's, 47; Dutch, 13; improving the quality of, 79; managerial level of the, 11–12; Nordic, 188; Norwegian, 190; officials of the, 193; operational departments of the, 11; operational level of the, 46; operative units of the, 11, 13; sectoral units of the, 190; systems, 10; centralised, 10; dual, 10, 12–13, 46, 49–50; integrated, 10, 49; top leadership of the, 190

aid(-implementing) agency (*see also* agency *and under the names of countries*), vii, 1–3, 7, 9–13, 17–20, 23–4, 26–34, 37, 41–2, 45–9, 63–5, 68, 71, 81, 85, 87, 121, 163–4, 169, 173, 185–6, 195, 197–8, 201, 210, 221, 223–5, 249, 253, 255, 257–8, 260–2, 265–6; aid agencies' employment of consultants, 210; aid-implementing agency/ organisation/administration, 32, 46; decision-making level of the, 12; donor agencies, 64; European development-assistance, 8; evaluations by, 204; evaluation system of the, 223; executing agencies, 142, 230, 235; external, 169; five Swedish, 225; implementing units of the, 172; independent, 128; international, 8, 14, 27, 53, 159, 162, 166, 169, 173, 199; management requirements of foreign, 43; multilateral-aid agencies, 26, 67–8, 168, 182; of the OECD, 61; operational/operative units of the, 1, 29, 46; policy of the, 262; specialised administrative units of the, 17; voluntary, 79

(aid) aims (*see also under the names of the respective countries*), 14, 18–19, 22, 26, 113, 118, 170, 198; broader societal aims set for aid, 196

aid budget (*see also* budget), 170, 178, 201

aid, commodity (*see also* commodities)

aid, community (*see also* community), 117

aid co-operation (*see* co-operation)

aid delivery, 9, 25, 77, 81, 87, 90, 257; delivery team, evaluation of the, 55; issues, 24, 77, 118; system, 12–14, 24, 26–7, 46–7; operative units of the, 63; technical/administrative problems of, 63

aid forms, 28, 115, 167, 177

aid funds, 112, 201, 262; economic administration of the, 113

aid implementation (*see also*

273

implementation), vii, 2, 32, 34, 81, 172, 177; aid-implementing authorities, 13; function, 10; level, 33; problems, 123
aid intervention, 4, 7, 21; evaluation of the effectiveness of an, 7; of the efficiency of an, 7; of the impact of an, 7; formulation of objectives for, 17; objectives set for the, 47
aid management (*see* management)
aid managers (*see also* managers), 6, 24, 32, 47, 53, 61–3, 124
aid, multi–bi, 25–6, 116, 181, 202
aid objectives (*see* objectives)
aid operations, 79, 252, 258
aid organisations (*see* organisations)
aid performance, 1, 25, 36, 102, 125, 140, 142, 154, 179–80, 195, 230; performance measurement, 73; performance of all (Swedish) government agencies, 210
aid-planning, 34, 90, 177
(overall) aid policy (*see also* policy), vi, 10, 14, 19–20, 22, 27, 31, 54, 76, 100, 102, 123, 164, 184, 202, 257; aid policy and practice, 122; aid-policy review committees, 105; Danish, 101, 108; decision-makers of the, 107; declared, 165–6; developments in, 115; formulation and implementation of, 102, 104, 106, 123; objectives, 79; strategies, guidelines and instruments of, 21
aid programmes (*see also* programmes), vii, 1, 10, 17, 19–20, 27, 54, 100, 104, 111, 113, 117, 122–4, 167, 203, 219, 266; compartmentalised, 15; bilateral share of the, 108; effects of, 127; evaluations of the, 106, 122–3; formulation and appraisal of, 123; management of, 23; strategic formulation of the, 123
aid projects (*see also* projects), 149–50, 154, 233; long-term impact of, 108; management of, 23; medium-to-large, 81; new aid-project proposal, 38; preparatory stage of a, 38; terminated, 108; value of the 223
aid(-providing) systems, 172, 211, 214; evaluation of the total, 173; main, through which bilateral aid is channelled, 184
analysis, 110, 122, 184, 233–4, 237–8, 240; cost-effectiveness analysis, 108; country, 191; cross-sectional, 132, 134, 140; ecological country, 201;

intermediate, 232; of external factors, 138; previous field, 141; quantitative, 110; results of the, 136
appraisal, 6, 80, 91–3, 118, 120, 124, 132–3, 163, 215; appraisal data, 265; economic appraisal, 92, 252; *ex-ante*, 212–13, 215, 217; new, 215; of aid activities, 102; procedures for, 212; process, 92; project, 133; project-appraisal techniques, 92; stage, 63, 77, 86
assessments, 4, 7, 20, 25, 31, 39, 53–4, 106, 112, 132, 137, 140–1, 157, 159, 164, 179–80, 202, 221, 238, 243; by region, 142; continuous, 163; criteria for, 212; inaccurate and inadequate, of local conditions, 243; inadequate, of needs, 243; independent, for public scrutiny, 31, 63; methods of, 4; needs-assessment mission, 230; update, 238; of aid policies and issues, 202; of all environmental layers, 222; of individual projects, 238; of poverty alleviation, 25; of proposals, 102; of project impacts, 23; of risks, 270; of the evaluation activities of the UN system, 231; of the projects by sector, 142; overall, 45; population-needs, 229; processes, 8; scope of, of a project, 222
assignments, 20, 28, 179–81, 191, 193, 202, 204, 240, 266; evaluation assignments, 23, 43, 180, 182, 186–8, 201–2, 204, 266; planning system for, 23; research and evaluation, 6; short-term, of experts, 134; total 182
auditing (*see also* State Auditor), 6, 113–14; audit, 81, 88, 114; courts of audit, 127, 140; external auditing, 53; internal, 53; auditors, 13, 113–14, 119, 125; auditors' evaluation, 124; Auditor of State Accounts, 109, 112–13, 117, 123–5

background papers, 238–9, 245; background-paper preparation, 239
Bangladesh, 159, 182–3, 202; aid to, 73
baseline, 254; study, 260; survey, 254, 260
beneficiaries, 2, 47–8, 51, 53–4, 85, 88, 92, 144, 252; beneficiary assessment, 42; streams, 86; identification of, 77; local consultation with intended, 93; project-beneficiary aspects, 63

INDEX

benefits, 134, 137, 143, 270; lack of identifiable, 141; macro, 142; micro, 142; of aid, 144
bilateral aid/assistance (*see also* aid), 17, 34, 41, 101, 105, 150, 157, 159, 166, 168–9, 171, 181–4, 186, 188, 195, 199, 210, 217–18; administration of, 169; agencies, 40, 45, 77, 210, 246; bilateral grant aid, 116; bilateral projects, 67, 75, 118, 197; bilateral financial aid, 34; bilateral, state-to-state aid, 180; budget, 116; channels, 166; evaluations, 111, 150; evaluation departments, 90; government-to-government, bilateral aid, 194; multilateral and bilateral aid, distribution between, 168; programme, 34, 67, 150; orientation and competition of the, 188; Swedish, 54, 210; major channel for, 210
bilateral (aid) donors, 40, 77–8, 89, 92, 202; of the OECD area, 61
British Council, 88, 95; Evaluation Department of the, 88
budget, 23, 145, 150, 178, 234; aid budget, 170, 201; budgetary constraints, 224; plan, 168; processes, 19; support, 167; control of, allocation, 125; for development aid, 159; for evaluation, 23, 181; frame, 112; project budget, 214; public, 143

Canadian International Development Agency (CIDA), 40–1, 65, 95, 265; Evaluation Report Inventory System, 65
capacity, 43, 51, 113, 186, 228; evaluation capacity, 45, 122; national, to fill the (programme) needs, 230; technical, 239
Cassen, Robert, 24, 76, 118, 122; Cassen Report, vii, 50, 90
children, 4, 166, 178–9; child care, 18
commercialisation: issue, 158; of Dutch aid projects, 153; of foreign aid, 153, 196; of foreign-aid projects, 161
commodities: commodity aid, 130, 168, 181, 187–8; evaluations of, 188; export-oriented, 80; Norwegian, included in the aid programme, 167
communications, 187, 229, 261; informal, 216, 219; institutional arrangements for oral, 158; institutionalisation of, 158;
systems, 32
community: academic community, 153–4, 159; advisory, 157; development, 246; evaluation, 61–2, 64, 67, 233; local, 159, 165; official aid, 60, 69, 117; research, 162; US evaluation, 60, 231
compartmentalisation (*see also* aid, aid programmes *and* objectives), 18, 197
competence, 43, 51, 186, 193; competence-building, 174, 191, 203; in evaluation, 191; evaluation competence, 45; external, 210, 212; externalisation of problem-solving, 144; Norwegian (in the social sciences), 174; research, 174
completion, 27; completion evaluations, 115; project-completion report, 12; report on, 7
conflicts, 48, 261; basic, 259; conflict resolution, 48; conflict-resolution aspects, 57; of interests, 260
consultancy firms/services/bureaux, 6, 29, 110–11, 118, 125, 130, 152–3, 155, 161, 191, 193–4, 219; commercial, 260; consultancy work, 267; external, 54; independent, 55; Norwegian, 184; Third World, 45, 197
consultants, 26, 44, 69, 96, 111, 113, 126, 133, 186, 192, 199, 202, 204, 210, 214, 223, 238, 240–1, 243, 251, 266; activities, 129; commercial, 30, 139, 251; evaluation consultants, 241; (outside) external, 29–30, 110, 112, 197, 212, 214, 234; fees, 112; formulation of guidelines for, 157; from the recipient countries, 44; groups of, 174; identification of the, 239; independent, 113, 125, 239; local, 44, 223, 238; Third World, 45, 51
control (functions), 2, 11–14, 27, 34, 41, 43, 45, 132, 134, 141, 171, 173, 195–7, 199–200, 231; control mechanisms, 220; samples, 85; external, 164; national control bodies, 132; of evaluation, 35, 231; of multilateral aid, 186; progress, 145; unwanted, 197
co-operation (*see also* development co-operation), 61, 64, 135, 173, 203, 210, 213; aid co-operation, 184; autonomous, measures, 129; between donor and recipient

275

authorities, 39; bilateral, 208; closer, inter-agency, in evaluation, 49; co-operation agreements, 174; Danish law on aid, 101; on international technical, with development countries, 103, 267; development, 176, 216; donor-recipient, in evaluation, 66; evaluation of, 88; financial, measures, 129; instruments of, 136; inter-donor, 49; international, 157, 174, 181, 208; in aid evaluation, 192, 197; investment, 209; mode of, 180; 'movement to movement', 210; Nordic, in aid evaluation, 192; overall objectives for Danish aid co-operation, 107; practices, 131; problems, 203; process of, 215; research, 203, 208–9; scientific, 142; technical, 87, 93–4, 130, 209, 254–5; through NGOs, 209; with research milieux, 191
co-ordination, 50, 128–9, 145, 246; co-ordination and simplification of the various donor-imposed systems, 246; meetings, 246; of the writing of the report, 240; procedures, 42; UN Administrative Committee on, 56
costs, 137, 186; additional, project-induced, 143; macro-economic, 143; new, 143; of using outside consultants, 112; recurrent, 142–3; investment-induced, 142–3; social, 143; relations between, and achieved results, 108
cost-benefit analysis, 86, 92, 108, 138; cost-benefit considerations, 122; social, technique, 92
country (*see also* recipents/recipient countries), 134, 201–2, 216, 239; country evaluations, 136, 157; country-evaluation studies, 157; country level, 157; policy, 159; policy papers, 157; country pogramme, 237; programme evaluations, 155, 238, 240–1; country projects, 229, 233; inter-country programme, 237; inter-country projects, 229, 232–3; Nordic, 174; poor countries, 119, 200; poorest developing countries, 165; priority countries, 166–7, 169, 173, 229; criteria for the selection of new, 166, 229; programme countries of the SIDA, 210

country programmes (*see also* programmes), 26, 39, 55, 167, 184, 190, 198, 203–4, 230, 236; Norwegian, 180; ODA's bilateral, 88; revolving, four-year, 185
country studies, 8, 25–7, 29, 36–7, 40, 50, 62, 173, 180, 182, 184, 190–1, 193, 195, 197, 202, 239; country-evaluation studies, 102; programme of, 184
cover note, 38, 81, 252, 256, 261, 264
coverage, 232, 256, 263
Cracknell, Basil E., ix, 3, 5, 26, 30, 37, 44, 52, 60, 71, 248, 251
credits: concessionary, 208–9; mixed, 168, 204
Cuba, 210; programme country of the SIDA, 210; recipient of Swedish aid, 210

data: agencies' data needs, 265; financial, 210; objective, 85; subjective, 75; synthesis, 266; data-bank, 39–40, 65, 95, 124, 214, 265; computerised, 265–6; evaluation databank/base, 78, 243; information, 121; project, 126; (computerised) data-bank service/ system, 95, 265; data-base, 141, 242, 246; (complementary) (basic) data collection, 93, 111, 229, 255; data-collection techniques, 8
decisions, 133–4, 196, 212, 215, 224, 248, 260, 262, 270; decision-oriented evaluation, 227; on development aid, 133; strategic, 225
decision-makers, 6, 9, 34, 47, 53, 104, 107, 119, 121, 173, 227, 245; at the civil-service level, 45; local, 223; political, 32; political and administrative, 177; political, of a donor country, 49
decision-making, 12, 32, 34, 37–8, 40, 44, 54, 105, 127–9, 132, 179–80, 215, 218–19, 224–5, 227, 230–1; administrative, 50, 196, 205; bodies/organs, 50, 131, 172, 190; (civil service), body of the ODA (PEC), 23; (administrative), process, 54, 128, 133, 196, 227; unit of the aid administration (ODA), 12; decision-taking committee, 262
delivery (*see* aid delivery)
Denmark (*see also* aid policy, aid programmes, co-operation *and* tied aid), 3, 11, 13, 20, 23, 25, 29, 31,

276

INDEX

37, 44, 101, 103, 105, 112, 125; Auditor of State Accounts, 106; Centre for Development Research, 111–12; Danish aid evaluations, 119; Danish aid policy, 103–4; Danish aid programme, 102, 104, 113–14, 125; administration of the, 103, 105; budget, 100–1; effectiveness and efficiency of the, 112; general poverty orientation of Danish aid, 119; Danish Association for International Co-operation (Mellemfolkeligt Samvirke) 103; Danish development aid/assistance, 45, 101–2, 104, 107, 112, 119, 122; (major) objectives of (*see also* objectives), 25, 101–2, 107–8; Danish development research, 112; evaluation of aid in Denmark, 123; evaluation programme, 122
Danish International Development Agency (DANIDA), 11, 23, 29, 31, 37, 101–2, 104–110, 112–18, 120, 122–6, 159; administration/administrative hierarchy/management of the, 102, 104, 106, 108, 123; annual report, 116, 120; bilateral (aid) projects, 118; Board of the, 102, 104–6, 108–9, 114, 118, 120–1, 123; command structure of the, 108; definition of evaluation, 125; (own) account of evaluations, 118; (own) evaluations, 114–16, 119, 124–5; evaluation activities/work, 108, 123, 125; evaluation expenditures, 112; evaluation of the, aid activities, 106; evaluation teams, 125; Evaluation Unit in the, 106, 122; expenditures on feasibility studies, 112; guidelines, 110, 114, 120; management, 121, 123; manpower resources of the, 121; organisation structure for evaluations, 109; organisational and hierarchical structure of the, 105, 121; performance, 124; relatively quick staff rotation in the, 121; representations abroad, 109; staff participation in evaluations, 119; structure, 118, 123; changes in, 115; shortcomings in, administration of the programme, 114; strategic plan for, 121; technical division, 120
Law on State Auditing, 113; main objective of the Danish evaluation system, 107; Ministry of Foreign Affairs, 11, 101, 105, 109; Danish NGO, 116; suppliers, 115; supplies, 116 design, 227, 242, 244–5; adequacy of the, 238; better programme and project design, 241; design 'redundancy of functions', 220; first design principle, 220; principles, 219; project design, 243; reality of organisational, 220; second design principle, 220; system design, 219, 224
desks, 30, 37, 151–2, 154, 157, 262; country desks, 104, 1513; desk level (in an aid agency), vii, 152, 156–7, 162; desk officers, 29, 92, 152, 154, 156; desk staff, 152; functional, 11, 23, 44, 83; geographical, 12, 23, 44, 83, 91; operational, 29, 46; programme desks, 152; sector desks, 153
developed countries, 143, 228, 268; least-developed countries (LLDCs), 166
developed countries/states (*see also* recipient countries), 32, 41, 44–5, 65–7, 80, 88–9, 95, 101, 113–14, 128, 130–1, 135–6, 139, 142–4, 149, 152, 155, 165, 200, 203, 228–9, 239, 256–7, 260, 267–8, African, Caribbean and Pacific countries (ACP), 268; authorities of the, 39; developing countries' own evaluation capabilities, 66; evaluation in, 64; evaluation responsibilities in, 66; evaluators of, 66; German projects in, 140; governments, 144; institutions, 257; internal power structures prevailing in the, 144; nationals of the, 135; operational programmes in, 229; personnel, 257; poorer, 101; poorest, 165; role in the, 88; subsidiaries of German companies operating in, 130; support for developing countries' export efforts, 209
development, 35, 49–50, 61, 80, 93, 143, 146, 171, 179–81, 200, 203, 258; administration, 43, 146; approach to, 15; (development) criteria for development, 17, 258; cultural, 180; development division, 256; issues, 117, 124–5, 216; management, 56; practice and theory, 114; problems, 150, 154, 218; process, 146; programmes,

277

125; studies, 114; theory, 17; work, 103; economic, 87, 200; fishery, 187–8; general theory and hypotheses of, 114, 221; industrial, 160, 187; institutional, 159; national-development goals, 229; nature of, 208; objectives, 16, 20–1, 203; of strategies, 237; rural, 160, 187–8, 200; rural-development project, 258; social, economic and cultural, 179; social, economic and cultural, in the Third World, 165; socio-economic, 137, 179; sustainable, 15, 80, 178, 180
development activities, 102, 202; ODA financing of, 11
development aid (*see* development assistance)
(official) development assistance/aid (ODA), vii, 1, 3, 5–6, 8–9, 14–16, 18, 21–2, 27, 31, 41, 61, 104, 131, 134, 143–4, 149, 159, 163, 165–6, 168, 170–1, 191, 200–1, 218, 257–8; activities, 165; administration of, 163, 168; bilateral ODA, 156, 187–8; efficiency of, 131, 164; efficiency of German, 134; European, agencies, 8; evaluation of, vi, 5, 41, 64, 161, 170; institutions, 130; Norwegian ODA, 169, 172, 176–7, 181; multilateral, 173; total, 182, 189; objectives of, 212; overall objectives of, 49; primary objectives of, 41; ODA activities, systematic assessment of, 163; outside constraints on, 257; particular environment of, 41; performance of German, 140; planning, implementation and control of, projects, 132; qualitative deficiencies in, 63; Swedish, 208; through NGOs, 209; volume of ODA, 168
Development Assistance Committee (DAC) (*see also* Organisation for Economic Co-operation and Development), 3, 6, 24, 31, 40–1, 50, 53, 62, 64–5, 67–9, 71, 78, 82, 85, 246, 267; Compendium, 85, 89; countries, 42, 66; DAC evaluation community, 45, 65–7; evaluation meetings, 68; evaluation units, 68; Expert Group on Aid Evaluation, 3, 10, 24, 28, 40, 42, 55–6, 63–9, 78, 89, 95, 124, 186, 257, 262, 266–8; glossary, 53; group of evaluators, 65, 69; High-Level Committee, 64; suggested, code of conduct, 45, 67; terminology, 53
development banks, 77; local, 130; regional, 130, 181
development co-operation (*see also* co-operation), 34, 128, 135, 150, 176, 208–9, 211, 216, 218, 222, 224–5; a separate and independent unit for studies in, 225; bilateral, 208–9; evaluation of, at the governmental level, 209; German, 130, 140; German, activities, 131; German, effort, 130; implementation and co-ordination of, 128; institutional structure of federal German, 129; international, 50, 101, 208; efficiency of, 146; messy reality of, 224; multilateral, 209; Norwegian objectives and principles for, 201; organisation of, 225; organisations, 130; Swedish, 208, 224
development policy (*see also* policy), 128, 162, 180; German, 136; institutional structure of German, 129; learning process on, 131; Norway's own, 202
development projects (*see also* projects), 131, 149, 153, 161, 218; implementation of, 154; industrial, 221–2; objectives of, 150
development research (*see also* research), 104, 112, 191, 203; institutions, 112, 299; social-science development research, 103
disincentives, 144, 146; produced by aid, 142
documentation, 11, 105, 112
donors/donor countries, vii, 14–23, 27–8, 32–3, 36, 41–3, 49–50, 53–4, 62, 65–7, 87–9, 96, 102, 136, 142–4, 157, 160, 162–3, 167, 176, 181, 183, 185, 192, 194, 196, 203–4, 246, 257–8, 263, 266, 270; administrative and political governing bodies of the, 174; administrative planning and aid-implementing set-up of the, 175; agencies of donor countries, 197; bilateral aid of a donor, 17; bilateral donors of the OECD area, 61; civil service of the, 41; donor administrative system, 48, 53; donor agencies' evaluation work, 66; donor agency, 24, 36, 53, 65, 102, 120, 125, 199, 257; donor communities, 65, 67; donor

INDEX

evaluation department, 94; evaluators, 64; experiences, 55; donor-inspired systems, 246; donor's involvement, end of the, 256; donor needs for control and management, 43; policies, 144; role, 94, 255; donor's selection of projects, 23; evaluation a donor pre-occupation, 268; evaluation units of other, 174; foreign policy of the, 19; formal policy-making structures of the, 35; like-minded, 157; policy objectives of the, 21, 102; political authorities of the, 19; political, industrial and commercial concerns of the, 20; projects and programmes of international, 136; representatives of the, 223; west European, 2

drinking water (see also water supply), 19, 153, 188; rural, 18

dual evaluation system (see aid administration)

early warning system, 24, 94, 263; early-warning, project-pipeline system, 253

education, 200–1; aid for, 188; basic, 200; services, 243

effect (of aid) (see also aid *and* aid activity), 67, 110, 196, 198, 202, 205, 270; additional income and employment effects, 141; assessments of, 28; concentration effects, 143–4; development effects, 102, 165; of aid programme, 127; of development projects, 127; of ODA, 164; on poverty alleviation, 27; on social development, 180; on the environment, 4; possible effects, 114

effectiveness (of aid) (see also aid *and* activity), 7, 25, 33, 71, 75, 82, 87, 90, 102, 115, 123, 137, 145, 154, 170, 189, 227, 230, 244; cost-effectiveness, 7, 96; effectiveness criterion, 141; evaluation of the, of an aid intervention, 7, 171; field, 108; information on project effectiveness, 41; lack of, 170; measurement of, 110; monitoring effectiveness, 255; of evaluation for policy development, 156; of past decisions, 262; of the ODA's aid operations, 75; on women, 234; overall, of (aid) programmes, 43, 75, 77; (overall) project effectiveness, 93; studies of, 215; studies of the, of projects, 216; unexpected, 234

efficiency (of aid) (see also aid *and* activity), 7, 25, 67, 71, 87, 102, 106–7, 114, 119, 132, 138, 140, 142, 154, 170–1, 189, 196, 205; cost-efficiency, 137; evaluation of the, of an aid intervention, 7; of development aid, 131–2; of German development aid, 134; of international development co-operation, 146; overall, 134, 138; quantitative, 101; studies, 176

environment, 4, 15, 24–5, 82, 87, 93, 117, 136–7, 167, 178–9, 203, 208, 218–20, 222, 251; aspects of the, 220; contextual, 220–2; cultural, 3; distinction between the contextual and the transactional, 220, 222; environmental analysis, extent of, 222; aspects, 93; concerns, 15, 167, 180; conditions, identified set of, 220; factors, 4, 92, 252; impact, 85, 93; levels, 221; external (international), 14, 19; internal and transactional, 221; internal (domestic), 14, 19–20; policy environment, 164; political, 3; protection of the, 80; responsible administration of natural resources and, 165; transactional, 220, turbulent, 225; type of, 221

European Association of Development Research and Training Institutes (EADI), vi; EADI project, 69

European Community (EC), 61, 89, 136, 265; Basic Principles, procedure of the, 262, 268; Commission of the, 40, 61, 77; the EC's system, 268

evaluation (of (development) aid/ assistance) (see also assignment, institutions, monitoring *and* work programme), vi, vii, 1–17, 19–33, 35–44, 46–57, 60–7, 69, 71, 73–6, 78–9, 81–2, 84–5, 87–92, 95–7, 100, 102–29, 131–6, 138–40, 142, 145–6, 149–52, 154–8, 160–4, 170–9, 181–2, 185–99, 201–4, 208–24, 227, 230–4, 236–9, 241–8, 250–7, 259–65, 267–8, 271; administration of, 177; aims of, 103–4; as a control instrument, 45; as a management tool, 45; attitude towards, 230–1, 244; availability of, 266; built-in or current, 133; by multilateral agencies, 77; by the NGOs, 155; capability/capacity, 45, 66, 174; 'central evaluation programme', central systems for monitoring and, 24; closed, 30; comparative, 237–40, 246; evaluation competence, 45; cost of, 178; 'country evaluations', 135; criteria and objectives in, 88; 'cross-sectional evaluations', 134–5; decentralised, 26; (general) definition of, 3, 53, 164; (OECD) definition of, 6; (UN) definition of, 52; desk, 255; (historical) development of, in Denmark, 102–3; differentiation between internal and external, 161; directions for, 23; donor-imposed, 56; donor-initiated, 88; double objective of aid, 172; effectiveness of, for policy development, 156; evaluation of a donor pre-occupation, 268; evaluation activities, 56, 66, 73–4, 90, 108, 122, 139, 174, 201, 212–13, 217, 230–1, 241, 263; joint evaluation activities, 78; proposals for expansion of the; 231; chain, 225; check-list, 136, 139; data-bank, 78; experts, 265; information, 216; instruments, 136; manual, 164, 194; 'evaluation of evaluation', 134; officer, 30, 239–41; programme, 87, 100, 123, 160, 228, 258; project, 112; resources, 265; staff, 56, 178, 212, 217, 248; strategy, 172; various forms of, 172; terminology, 77; evaluation-training sessions, 265; evolvement of, in the US, 51; *ex ante* evaluation, 132–3, 212; *ex-inter* evaluation, 132; *ex-post* evaluation, 9, 103, 115, 133, 212, 217; external, 2, 26, 28–9, 55, 63, 152–3, 156, 197; financing of, 212, 216; follow-up, 139; for women, 180; formalised (declared) Norwegian, policy, 164; global, of support to onshore fishery activities, 117; highlights, summary of, 271; 'immanent', 221–2; impact evaluation, 51; independent, 29, 155, 233–4, 245; independent and critical, 201; in the SIDA, 211; in-depth, 30, 40, 84, 87, 90; in-depth nature of the current independent, 232; in-depth probing, 174; institutional activities on, in India, 150; institutionalisation of, 8; instructions for, 164; internal ('built-in'), 2, 7, 26, 28–30, 33, 40, 49, 63, 77, 150–3, 155, 157–8, 160–1, 231, 233–4; quality of the, 154; joint Nordic, 68, 192, 205; legitimating function of, 47; locally conducted, 223; main purpose of, in Denmark, 25; management function of, 195; methodological issues of, 69; mid-term, 116, 152; milieux for, 174; new, 57; number of, 242; (motives and) objectives and policies of, 102, 106, 130; objectives and priorities of, 175; of aid within certain sectors, 108; of cross-cutting issues, 116; of development efforts, 125; of foreign aid, changes in the functions and organisational set-up of, 162; of multilateral assistance/aid, 67, 202; of past projects, 261; of people-centred projects, 92; of policy, 26, 257; of project impact and effectiveness, 93; of project operation and sustainability, 24; of projects, 11; cross-sectoral, of projects, 25; of support to the dairy sector in India, 117; of the effects of aid, 28; of the implementation of aid, 13; of the multilateral system, 197; on country programmes, 44, 102, 111, 155; open (*see also* openness), 30, 175, 197; operations-focused, 42; orientation of the, 47, 50, 197; overall, process, 159; performance of, vi, vii, viii, 1–2, 8, 22, 71, 110, 113; planning and use of, 244; planning and implementation of the, 263; planning of certain types of, 42; policy on, vi, vii, viii, 1–2, 8, 22, 102; potential users of, 47; preparation and implementation of the, 176; primary function of, 25; principal constraint on, 219; professional, 114; programme evaluations, 212; project evaluation, 28, 212; bilateral-grant, 115; project-oriented, 155; publications on, 61; purpose and use of, 104; (overall) quality of, 221–2; quantitative and qualitative dimensions of, 134; rate-of-return evaluation, 84; results, 74–5, 96,

INDEX

102–3, 107, 117–18, 121–4, 133, 158, 162, 213–16, 222–4, 231–2, 240–2, 244, 262–3; access to the, 78; dissemination and use of, 245; use of, 228, 231, 237, 241; role of, 131; role and methodology of, 54; role of, in decision-making, 132; role of, in development policy, 128; role of, in the administrative process, 127; role of, in the UNFPA, 228; scope and orientation/objective of, 21, 107; Scriven's goal-free evaluation, 51; sectoral, 109, 111; 'series' evaluations, 134; single-project, 110; specialist on, 154; state of the art of, 3, 60; status of, 214; techniques of, 257, 267; thematic, 109, 111; theory on, 149; development of the, 149; total, 183, 187; training in, 52; transcendent, 221; type of, 244; mix of types of, 244; utilisation-focused, 55–6; value of, 122; World Bank, 42
evaluation exercises, 158, 216, 234, 241; internal, 234, 237
evaluation findings, 3, 32, 43, 56, 81, 97, 139, 250, 252–4, 256, 261, 263–5, 267–8, 271; key findings, 94, 263, 265
evaluation function, 8–10, 12–13, 21–2, 30, 45–7, 50, 133, 151, 177–8, 189, 200, 228, 231; decision-related, 133; institutional split of the, 197; institutionalisation of the, 12, 50; internal structuring of the, 48
evaluation guidelines (*see also* guidelines), 10, 108, 110
evaluation methodology (*see* methodology)
evaluation methods, vi, 51, 73, 103, 110, 136, 138, 147
evaluation mission, 20, 109, 154, 159, 198, 238–41, 245; mission members, 240; practical arrangements for the, 241
evaluation performance, 60, 114, 177, 210
evaluation plan/planning, 23, 42, 68, 237
evaluation policy, 8, 20, 22–3, 26, 60, 100, 104, 106–7, 164, 170, 176, 181, 197, 210, 228, 230; declared (stated), 169–70, 195; formulation of, 123; Norwegian, 27, 169; of Denmark, 100
evaluation practice, 61, 186, 214; definition and purpose of, 106
evaluation reports (*see also* monitoring),
2, 24–5, 31–3, 3640, 42, 52, 54–5, 69, 75, 77, 79, 81–2, 91, 93–6, 113–4, 117, 119–22, 124, 134–5, 139–40, 142, 158, 170, 174–5, 178, 181–2, 189–91, 194, 198, 201–4, 212, 214, 216, 218, 242, 250, 252–6, 260–3, 265–8; best way of disseminating, 245; circulation of, 121; Danish, 29; distribution of, 187; formulation (findings) of the individual, 121, 260; independent, 242; internal evaluation reports (IER), 155, 157, 235, 242; recipients of the, 120
evaluation research, 55, 65, 128, 138; criteria and methods of, 138; definitions of, 51
evaluation studies, 10, 42, 44, 52, 82, 96–7, 102, 108, 134–6, 140, 146, 149, 152–4, 157–62, 194, 210, 214–17, 219, 223–4, 232, 252, 261, 264; Dutch, 153, 159; joint, 44, 136; ODA–sponsored, 79; sectoral distribution of, 135; selection process of, 83
evaluation systems, vii, 3, 11–12, 25–6, 28–9, 36, 47, 67, 74, 78, 128, 197, 202, 211, 220–4, 233, 241, 244, 249; British/UK, 25–6, 79; co-ordination of the overall, 246; co-ordination with other, 246; Danish, 25; dual (compartmentalised), 11, 26, 196–7; Dutch, 25–6; European, 27, 31; experimental, 79; German, 25; integrated, 197; main objective of the, 107; Norwegian, 25; 'official', 211; open, 39; performance of the, 39; quality of an, 221–2; structure of the, 225; Swedish, 210, 225
evaluation teams, 29, 33, 37, 44–5, 49, 66–7, 95, 108–11, 1201, 125–6, 136, 152, 160, 175–6, 192–3, 196, 198, 204, 214, 251, 256, 260, 266–7; composition of the, 175; external, 177, 193; inter-disciplinary, 174; joint(-venture), 125, 160; mixed, 136; mixed external/internal, 193; representatives from the, 190
evaluation unit/department, 1, 3, 5, 8–13, 22–4, 26–7, 29–30, 32, 38, 41, 46, 49–50, 55, 61–3, 66–9, 72, 78, 89, 102, 104, 106–8, 112, 115, 119–24, 156, 162, 174, 177–8, 190, 194, 215, 222–3, 230–4, 236–8, 240–2, 244, 248–9, 253–4, 257–60, 266, 268; central, 10, 131; constraints on, 248, 257; degree of independence

of the, 13; feedback from a, 248; functions of a, 248; institutional setting of, 45; internal, 161; of the OECD countries, 64; performance of, 45; Scandinavian, 29; staffing, structure and status of a, 248; the role of an, 248, 254
evaluation work, 49–50, 63, 67–9, 71, 74–6, 78, 82–3, 88, 92, 97, 104–9, 112, 120–4, 126, 130, 132, 136, 149, 153–4, 161, 168, 174–7, 186, 201, 225, 251, 257, 259–61, 267; commissioned, 45; donor agencies' evaluation work, 66; equal participation in, 66; independent, in-depth, 232; independent status of the, 123; recipient countries' evaluation work, 66; related to aid, 47
evaluators, 16–17, 20, 27–9, 32, 41–4, 47–8, 51–2, 56–7, 61–6, 69, 80–1, 85, 87, 92, 95, 125, 131, 134, 137–40, 145, 151, 153, 155, 159, 161, 176, 178–80, 194, 196, 199, 209, 214, 221, 250, 253, 255, 257–9, 261, 266; combination of external and internal, 7; external (outside), 2, 7, 26, 29–30, 44, 55, 77, 81, 139, 221, 223; fourth-generation, 57; from developing countries, 41; guidelines for, 85–6, 91; independent, 138, 194; in-house, 260; internal, 2, 28; local, 154; mixed teams of, 85; new, 57; Norwegian (or Nordic), 204; qualified, 214; recipient-country, 125; selection of, 20, 193; suitability of the proposed, 256; Third World, 45
EVSUMs (Evaluation Summaries), 94, 263–4, 266, 271; EVSUM system, 264–5; evaluation of the, 263
experts/expertise, 130–1, 139, 153, 174, 189, 192; evaluation experts, 265; external (outside), 67, 85, 130, 198, 212; independent, 134; in the technical area, 239; local, 111; short-term assignment of, 134; technical-assistance, 116–17
ex-ante: evaluation, 132–3, 212, 215; evaluation studies, 210, 215; expectations, 118; 'mapping' of project effects, 104
ex-post evaluations/investigations/studies, 7, 25, 29, 93, 103–4, 115–17, 132–3, 164, 213–15, 223, 255–6; systematic, 244

failure, 89, 92, 114, 118–19, 131–2, 137, 142, 251, 258, 262, 265, 267
family-planning, 168, 187–90, 228–9; service staff, 237
feedback, 4, 23, 28, 31–5, 37–40, 71, 87, 94–5, 103, 105, 117, 119–20, 123, 157, 173–5, 189–91, 197, 199, 211, 214, 219, 224, 228, 232–3, 237, 241, 250–3, 256, 261–2, 266–8; at the operational level, 263; at the policy level, 262; development and institutionalisation of procedures for, 231; effective, 261–2, 267; need for, 262; external, 262; from evaluation, 33, 35; function, 171; instant, 261; internal, 232, 262, 265; procedures, 124; mechanisms, 232, 262; of evaluation findings, 3; positive, 144, 241; effects, 144; procedures, 120; reception and utilisation of, 186; specialised, 37; system, controlled, 211; (existing) systems, general, 121–3, 262; techniques and procedures for, 32; through internal staff seminars, 264; to institutions in the donor country, 266; to the decision-makers, 38; to the developing countries, 267; to the general public, 35, 262; to the mass media, 35; to the outside, 38; to the political level and to the development community, 38; to the (potential) recipients of, 33–4, 39
field/fieldwork, 37, 154, 159, 174, 196, 204; field mission, 238–40; Field Monitoring Visits, 235; period, 159; staff, 237; surveys, 260
follow-up, 20, 27–8, 30, 37, 169, 175, 177, 184, 189, 199, 204, 232, 237–41; administrative, 7; follow-up action, 10; activities, 214; assessment, 38; commissions, 139; costs, 141; evaluations, 139; guidelines set for evaluation, 177; of the stated objectives, 177; reports, 214; strategy, 177
food aid, 82, 135, 181; economic impact of, vi; performance of, problems of, 75
Forss, Kim, ix, 32, 44, 114, 192, 208
functions, 216, 220

Germany, Federal Republic of (FRG), 2, 11, 23, 25, 27, 29, 31, 38–9, 44–5, 127–8, 131, 135–6; Agency of

INDEX

Technical Co-operation (GTZ), 129–30; Bensheimer Kreis, 130; Budget Committee of the *Bundestag*, 128; Carl Duisberg Society (CDG), 129–30; Federal Chancellor, 128 **Federal Ministry of Economic Co-operation (BMZ)**, 12, 128–9, 131, 134, 138, 146–7; central unit for evaluation and supervision, 131, 134, 136–7, 139; own evaluations, 136; policy-making levels of the, 12 German aid to Senegal, 135; German development policy, structure and organisation of, 128; German Foundation for International Development (DSE), 129–30; German Volunteers' Service (DED), 129–30; government of the, 142; development policy of the, 127; Kreditanstalt für Wiederaufbau (KfW) (Bank for Reconstruction), 129–30; West German ODA, 128

growth, 143, 179, 200; economic, 15, 22, 86, 101, 165, 179, 208; economic, social and cultural, 179; effects (of aid) on economic, 180; self-sustaining, 80; social and economic, 171, 179; stagnation in, vii

guidelines, 9, 14–15, 21, 24, 34, 45, 67, 106, 109–10, 121, 123–4, 128, 137, 164, 166–8, 170–3, 175–7, 180, 184–5, 192, 194–5, 198–200, 204, 230, 233–4, 236, 241, 264; basic, 129; evaluation, 10, 24, 119, 241; for consultants, formulation of, 157; for project formulation, 233; Guidelines for the Preparation of Evaluation Studies, 95; on institutional development, 88; on the role of manpower aid, 88; Project Guidelines, Evaluation, 126; technical, basis for, 132

health, 153, 188, 200, 203; health projects, 136; primary health services, 200
human rights, 15, 22, 165–6, 178–81; human-rights situation, research related to, 203; UN Declaration and Convention on, 166

identification, 93, 107; of external factors, 138
impact, 17, 24–5, 62, 77, 87, 90, 94, 96, 103, 107, 110, 118–19, 121, 131, 154, 156–8, 195, 222, 225, 227, 245–6, 259, 260; appropriate indicators of, 245; (overall) developmental, 135, 138, 141; direct, 210; environmental, 93; expected sociological, 252; immediate action, 55; (in-depth) impact evaluation, 51, 87, 106, 110, 244, 261; impact studies, 25, 27–8, 84, 159, 170–1, 215, 217; incremental, 55; measurement of, 110, 132, 245; of aid, 61, 64, 67, 81, 90, 179; of an aid intervention, 7; of British aid projects on low-income groups, 76; of evaluation on policy, 156; on policy development, 156; on projects, 156; of projects on local communities, 88; of the evaluations on the policy-making, 121; on development co-operation, 222; on policy-makers, 157; project impacts, 24, 85, 93, 215; sustainability, 102

implementation (*see also* aid implementation), 10, 13–14, 16, 18, 21, 23, 29, 31, 33, 37, 41, 43–4, 48, 51, 53–4, 57, 71, 79, 87–90, 93, 107, 115–16, 125, 128–30, 132–4, 137, 141, 145, 154, 164, 176–7, 195, 201–2, 224, 230, 234, 239, 243–4, 248, 254–6; efficient, 224; implementation function, 46; implementation/implementing level, 34, 170; implementation/implementing phase, 6–7, 33, 132, 164; (aid) implementing agency/authorities/set-up, 7, 12–13, 38, 43, 138, 140, 164, 175, 199–200; implementing evaluations, 83, 85; implementing unit of the aid administration (ODA), 12, 174; major constraint on, 243; of aid, 8, 35, 167, 172; institutions responsible for the, 9; of evaluation in foreign aid, 150; of the agreed recommendations, 240; operational units of the, 34; project implementation, 77; successful, 243

income: distribution, 165, 171; low-income countries (LICs), 166
independence, 10, 28–9, 55, 113, 174–5, 178, 193, 231, 248; degree of, of the evaluation unit, 13; economic and political, 208; independence variable, 204; political, 101
India, 5, 66, 149–150, 182–3, 194, 202,

204; community-development programme in, 149; complexity of the rural Indian situation, 103; dairy sector in, 117; Health Care and Family Welfare project, 111; Indian agriculture and rural sociology, 103; Indian government, 52; Mysore State Adult Education Council, 103; Young Farmers' Training Colleges managed by, 103
indicators, 13, 23, 25, 29, 31, 33, 36, 45, 73, 91–2, 117–18, 137–8, 222; appropriate, of impact, 245; indicators of progress, 233; means of verification of, 233; of achievement, 270; of success, 252; stated, 118
information, 2, 20–1, 25, 27–9, 31–7, 39–40, 47–8, 51, 53, 55, 62, 65, 75, 87, 106–7, 110, 113–14, 121, 123–4, 126–7, 132, 134–5, 140, 157–8, 160–2, 175, 201, 204, 208–9, 214–16, 218, 224, 229–30, 234, 237, 241–3, 253, 255, 263, 265; background, 228; baseline, 245; cross-agency, information-retrieval system, 64; direct exchange of, 65; discriminate information-sharing, 65; discrimination of, 65; exchange of, 64, 218; independent, 201; information banks, 40, 124; deficits, 132; management, 161; needs, 53, 56; on development issues, 202; on project effectiveness, 41; overload, 65; packages, 65; retrieval, 121; routines, 204; information system, 65, 145; computerised, 40–1, 65; evaluation, 124; management, 42, 95; (management), of the ODA, 40; organisation of, 46; storing and retrieving system, 107; technology, 124; unit, 198; users, needs of the, 47; restricted, 87; sources of, 219, 270; useful analytical, 227; written, 214, 216
input, 138, 151, 156, 158, 160, 163, 202, 218, 243–4, 251, 270; Dutch, 151; project, 138; resource, 173
inspection, 47, 138, 151, 154; inspectors, 48, 56, 151, 153
institutes/institutions (*see also* multilateral institutions), 43, 49, 88, 102, 128–30, 139, 143, 158, 174, 257, 261, 266; academic, 152; auditing, 113; independent auditing, 114;

institution-building, 45, 86-7, 242; institution-building projects, 243; commercial, 153; development-assistance, 130; development-finance, 168, 173, 181–2, 185; development-research, 112, 266; donor, 136; evaluation, 152–3; higher-education, 51; independent, 50, 110; international, 50; international financial, 60; Norwegian, 189; Institute of Development Studies, University of Sussex, 254, 267; outside, 111; parastatal, 128; political, 49, private-sector, 139, 193; public-sector, 139, 193; institutional activities on evaluation in India, 150; approach, 125; arrangements for oral communication, 158; challenges, 48; development, 28, 88; rivalry, 197; setting, 46; institutionalisation, 69, 150, 158; in the Netherlands, 150
International Bank for Reconstruction and Development (IBRD) (*see* World Bank)
International Development Association (IDA), 18, 181
International Labour Office (ILO), 15, 136, 204, 229
International Monetary Fund (IMF), vii, 24, 50, 69
intervention, isolated, 138; technical, 145; techniques, 145
investment, 143; private, 80; projects, 130
issues, 186–7, 189, 198, 218, 221, 228, 237–8, 242, 244–6, 252, 258, 266; aid, 79, 169, 187, 195, 202; commercialisation, 158; contextual, 24; core, 50; cross-cutting, 24–5, 87, 116; evaluation of, 116; development/developmental, 63, 117, 216; evaluation, 67, 245; macro-economic, 24; managerial, 243; North–South political, 169; overall, 186; policy, 224; sectoral and programming, 125; selection of, 42, 50; strategic, 24; substantive, 243; technical or institutional, 212, 244; thematic, 116, unresolved, 257

Kenya, 182–3, 202; Kenya Railways, 88
Kjekshus, Helge, ix, 3, 24, 60, 186

learning, 90, 211, 215, 224, 247; internal,

INDEX

28–9; learning aspect, 33, 40; lessons, 78, 249; process, 127, 132, 134, 142, 190; decision-oriented, participative, 227; learning-process approach, 89; on development policy, 131; organisation, 210; organisational learning, 210; system, 190, 223
lessons, 237, 242–4, 246, 248, 253–6, 259, 271; collection, analysis and feedback of, 237; computerised system for, learned from evaluation, 242; lessons from evaluations, 242; potential, 242; syntheses of, learned, 246
loan, 130; agreements, 115; non-project-tied loans, 130; refinancing, 130; tied-aid, 118
'logical-framework' system/method approach, 46, 52, 63, 77, 91, 136, 138, 150, 154, 197, 199, 230, 267

management, 7, 9, 23, 41, 43, 46–7, 72, 90, 92, 152, 270; administrative, 102; aid-management, operative units/part of, 21, 63; Coverdale system of, 72; development, 56; development-aid, 60; donor's, 42; higher, levels, 196; line, 250; management approval, 252; board, 100; consulting firms, 105; control of procedures and accounting, 200; (policy), decisions, 23, 219, 233; studies to support, 210, 213; efficiency, 72; flexible, 92; function, 2, 47, 196; function of evaluation, 195–6; information systems, 42, 95, 242; methods, 96; needs, 26, 47, 196; of aid, 196; of aid-programming and implementation, 125; of people-centred projects, 89; 'management' of Swedish aid, 218; of the programme, 249; of the single project, 122; management-oriented (unit), 162; performance, 7; perspective/point of view, 48, 160; (basic) (integrated), process, 53, 102, 219; techniques, 72; tool, 45, 104–5, 107, 125, 150, 156, 227, 236, 244; of projects and programmes, 72; middle and lower, grades, 73; project, 110, 198, 214; managerial concerns/problems, 25–6, 28, 46, 49–50, 63, 162; senior, 27, 82, 84, 92, 94, 249, 257; top, vii, 10–11, 31,

73, 81, 123, 178, 232, 248
managers (*see also* aid managers); Guide for, 92; host-country, 107; (project) managers, 32, 53, 92; policy, 124; programme, 124; project, 132
manpower, 112, 122, 151, 254–5; team, 136
media, news, mass, 31, 34–6, 135, 189, 191, 214; media people, 174, 189; negative, mass-media coverage, 114
methods, 163, 211; better, of dissemination, 242
methodology, 62, 64, 128, 136, 138, 150, 152–4, 211, 231, 238–9, 241, 268; evaluation methodology, 62, 77, 89, 154, 239; development of, 237; planning, 63, 69; technical-assistance, 87; methodological deficiencies, 69; issues, 214; issues of evaluation, 69; problems, 62
missionary organisations, 185, 202
mixed teams, 28–30, 198–9, 260; of evaluators, 85
monitoring, 1, 7–9, 11–12, 33, 44, 46–50, 53, 63, 71, 84, 90, 93–4, 97, 107, 117, 120, 122, 129, 131–3, 141, 145, 163–4, 194, 196–9, 216, 232–3, 254–5; central system for monitoring and evaluation, 24; costs involved in, 178; external, 30; financial (audit-type), 255; internal, 30; monitoring against objectives, 255; effectiveness, 255; missions, 255, 264; results, 265; monitoring and evaluation, 229–30; close relationship between, 233; complete system of, 233; components, adequacy of the, 238; co-ordinated system for, 233; plan for, 233; requirements for programmes, 236; for projects, 235; type of, 235–6; monitoring and evaluation reports, 25, 37, 236; system, 11, 228, 233; resources for, 12; monitoring function, 197; plan, 93, 254; procedures, 93; process, 137, 254–5; reports, 24, 93, 199, 212; system, 3, 46, 162, 196, 219, 254; monitoring and evaluation capacity, 107; processes, 92; stages, 80; 'monitoring systems', 214; unit, 159; of benefit flows, 77; of (project) implementation, 24, 255; of projects, 203, 212; project monitoring, 73; Project Benefit Monitoring, 77

285

Mosley, Paul, 76, 84, 86, 91
multi-bi aid (*see also* aid, multi-bi), 116, 166, 169, 181–2, 200, 202; evaluations, 117; programmes, 116; projects, 102, 116–17, 197; project evaluations, 117
multilateral agencies, 195, 246; evaluation by, 77; evaluation systems of some of the, 78; evaluation work of the, 77
multilateral aid/assistance (*see also* aid *and* organisation), 27, 34, 67–8, 108, 169, 171–3, 177, 181–2, 186, 200, 202; channels, 166; component, 26, 166; control of, 186; evaluation of, 67, 202; multilateral and bilateral aid, distribution between, 168; organisations/agencies, 101, 136, 177, 210
multilateral system, 17, 67, 181, 185–6, 195; evaluations of the, 197

Netherlands, The, 3, 11, 27, 31, 37, 39, 44–5, 149, 151, 153–5, 157, 161; aid evaluation in, 149; Directorate-General for Development Co-operation (DGIS), 150; dual evaluation system, 26, 29, 37; Dutch foreign aid, 155; Dutch Ministry of Foreign Affairs, 159; Dutch Organisation for International Co-operation (NOVIB), 155; Dutch organisations ... involved in foreign aid, 154; Dutch Volunteers Programme (SNV), 155, 158; Council of the, 159
Inspection Unit (Inspectorate), Ministry of Development Co-operation (Inspectie Ontwikkelingssamenwerking te Velde (IOV)), 11, 13, 26, 29, 31, 37, 68, 151–4, 156–62; development of the, 161; evaluations, 157; evaluation reports, 37; existing functions of the, 162; external evaluation, 156; impact of the, 158; inspection function of the IOV (*see also* inspection *and* evaluation inspection), 151, 153; objectives of the, 151, 153; results, 158; studies, 154, 158
National Advisory Council for Foreign Aid, 38, 157–8, 160, 162; Office of the Auditor-General, 151
non-governmental organisations (NGOs), 10–11, 14, 17–18, 26, 30–1, 35, 65, 71, 78–9, 103, 106, 129–30, 154–6, 158, 168, 171, 181–2, 185, 200; aid channelled through, 182; councils of, 158; evaluation by the NGOs, 155; government-sponsored NGOs, 150; international NGOs, 229; main champions of aid in Norwegian society, 185; NGO aid activities, 116; Norwegian, 201–2
Nordic countries (*see also* countries), 173; consultants, 192; experts, 192; Norwegian co-operation with the other, 174; research institutes, 192; universities, 192
Norway, 3, 13, 15, 17–18, 23, 26–7, 29, 31, 37, 44–6, 68, 163, 186, 201–3; aid, 166, 168–9, 171–3, 177, 181, 185; (overriding) aims/objectives set for, 26, 165, 171, 178, 181, 183–5, 197–8, 202; areas (sectors) of, 172; main objectives and principles of, 179; (predominant) objectives and guidelines of, 165, 167–8, 171, 176, 202; should be poverty-oriented, 166; should be recipient-oriented, 167, 180; should be untied, 167; total, 185, 188; whole spectrum of Norwegian, activities, 177; aid authorities, 176, 191; aid evaluation, 198; aid policy, 164, 173, 176, 180, 189, 200, 202; aid programme, 184; inclusion of Norwegian commodities in the, 167; business schemes, 188; Chr. Michelsen Institute in Bergen, 191; Church Aid, Sudan Programme, 202; consultants, 192; country programme, 180; development assistance, 200, 202; evaluation of the effects of, 176; development co-operation, Norwegian objectives and principles for, 210; development research, 203; (development) research institutes, 192–3; experts, 192; firms, 185–6; Norges Godtemplar Ungdomsforbund, 202
Norwegian Agency for International Development (NORAD), 11, 31, 37, 44, 46, 164, 167–9, 172, 174, 177–8, 181–2, 185–6, 189, 195–200, 203–4; administrative set–up within the, 175; aid implementation of the, 172; Board of the, 190; Director-

INDEX

General of the, 199, 203–4; evaluation office of the, 164; evaluation of the, activities, 201; framework agreement, 202; Handbook for Evaluation, 199; Information and Documentation Unit, 199; own administration of aid, 175; support to Norwegian NGOs, 201

Norwegian Institute of International Affairs, vi, viii; Norwegian Ministry of Development Co-operation, vii, 11, 169, 173–5, 177, 181, 185, 189–90, 197, 199, 203–4; evaluation division/unit/office of the, 189, 192–3, 197, 199, 203; officials of the evaluation division, 193; evaluation performance of the, 163; policy of the, 163, 168, 176; information unit of the, 189–90; Norwegian Ministry of Foreign Affairs, 11, 168–9, 177, 203; Norwegian Santal Mission, 202; Norwegian Shipping Academy, 202; Norwegian Trade Union Federation (LO), 185, 202, 204; Norwegian Volunteer Service ('Peace Corps'), 185, 188, 203; ODA budget, 180, 191; Pentecostal Mission of Norway, 202; Redd Barna (Save the Children) development activities, 202; research milieux, 191; universities, 192

objectives (*see also* aid *and* development), 6–7, 9, 13–22, 24, 33, 52–4, 57, 62–3, 71–2, 75–7, 79–80, 82, 85–6, 88–9, 91, 96, 106–8, 113, 116, 118–19, 125, 133, 137–8, 141, 150, 163–6, 168, 170–2, 175, 177–8, 180, 184–7, 189, 196, 198, 201–2, 204, 208, 214, 221–2, 227, 230–1, 233, 238, 243, 245, 248, 252, 255, 259, 261, 270; achievement of (pre-set), 89, 110, 238; clear statement of, 92; commercial, 82; commercial and political, 80; compartmentalisation of, 15, 17–18; conflicts in, between donor and recipient, 203; (seriously) conflicting/competing, 258; declared, 56; (basic) (core) developmental, 80, 198; Norwegian developmental, 173; fixed, 145; guidance for formulation of, 233; hierarchy of, 28, 91; implementation of project-related, 7; isolated, 138; multiple levels of, 8; national-development, 222; Norwegian foreign-policy, 173; objective clarification, 57; objectives set for aid (intervention), 45, 47–48, 134, 165, 171, 173, 180; changes in the, 163; of Danish aid, 101–2; (double), of evaluations, 102, 108, 155, 171–2, 195, 257; definition of, 107; of foreign aid, 162; operational/ operationalised, 16–17; overall, for aid, 170; overall (long-term), 26, 28, 118; overall system of, 141; policy, 21, 96; political, 74; programme, 243; project, 18, 25, 91, 234, 243; project-related, 18; relevance of, 107; stated, 16, 21, 91, 110, 118, 180; framework of, 114; unstated, 19–20

openness, 2, 30–2, 45, 68, 160, 175, 197

operative/operating/operational units divisions/activities, 7, 9–10, 12, 26, 33–4, 38, 106, 108–9, 120, 123, 190, 234; feedback to the, 28; level, 196–7; of aid management, 21; of the aid administration, 13; of the aid agency, 13; of the aid-delivery system, 63; plans, 141; (decentralised), units, 10, 46

organisation (*see also* multilateral aid), 7, 46, 56, 62, 155, 175, 202, 210–18, 220, 222–4, 227, 228–31, 234, 237, 244, 248, 256; aid organisation, 61–2, 69, 106, 219, 223–3; DAC, 64; European countries', 60; major, in Europe, 63; Swedish, 208; development-co-operation, 130; Dutch organisations ... involved in foreign aid, 154; effective, 209; external, 218; field effectiveness of the, 108; general assessment of field effectiveness of multilateral, 117; international, 67, 108, 117, 136, 149, 182; evaluation units of the, 108; knowledge bank of the home organisation, 65; local counterpart, 154; missionary organisation, 185; multilateral (aid) organisations, 64, 101, 116–17, 136, 169, 172–3, 202; evaluation units of the, 174; organisational complexity, 220; organisational set-up, 249; independent, 249; integrated, 249; private, 130, 172; professional evaluation organisation, 153;

Programme Evaluation Organisation, 149; quality consciousness and results of the international, 108; self-evaluating, 46; self-help, 135
Organisation for Economic Development and Co-operation (OECD), 3, 6, 15, 50, 52, 61, 68, 136; Correspondents' Group on Aid Effectiveness, 61; Expert Group on Aid Evaluation, 61; 'Methods and Procedures of Aid Evaluation', 255; OECD countries, 61, 68; evaluation officers of the, 61; evaluation units of the, 61, 64; OECD/DAC initiative on information, 161; OECD's terminology, 125
orientation of aid, 18, 49
output, 114, 131, 138, 234, 270; project output, 138
outsiders, 6, 28, 55, 124, 151–4, 158, 259–60

Pakistan, 88, 183, 202
participation, 28, 36, 42–3, 48, 67, 125, 136, 155, 159, 176, 179; external, 199; in the governing bodies of the multilateral aid agencies, 186; local, in decision-making, 180; Norwegian, in evaluation efforts carried out by multilateral-aid agencies, 177; of Third World partners and evaluators, 41; participants, recipient-country, 29; Third World, 44
partner, 67; countries, 44, 139; German, 126; international, 50
plan, 163, 243; for evaluation, 237; of operation, 214; rolling, two-year, for evaluation, 203
planning (*see also* aid activity, aid planning, family-planning *and* planning), 23, 34–5, 38, 42, 44, 53, 88, 124, 128–9, 132, 134–5, 137, 145, 150, 169, 175–7, 199, 201–2, 218–9, 224, 227; bad, 200; directives for, 24; economic, 142; evaluation, 42, 44, 83; programme, 24; strategic, 105; technical, 130; planning activities, 56; cycle, 43; department, 34, 184, 190; function, 190; horizon, 23; methodology, 63; of future aid, 172; operation, 138; process, 190; systems, 211; for evaluation assignments, 23; units,

33, 174; project-planning, 96, 137, 140–1; stage/phase, 63, 138; 'target-group-oriented project-planning' (ZOPP), 138
pluralism, 36; social, 130; value-pluralism, 52
polarisation, 144; economic, social and regional, 143; polarisation effect of large-scale projects, 144; social, 142
policy (*see also* aid policy), 23, 29, 54, 74, 102, 150, 156, 178, 181, 195–6, 237, 257, 259; country policy, 159; country-policy papers, 157; decisions on, 196, 224, 237; declared 171, 177–8, 189; development of technical, 241; donor's policy, 42, 144; evaluation of, 26; formalised (declared), Norwegian evaluation policy, 164; future, 241; implementation of the, 224; (policy) management decisions, 23; policy concerns, 189; conformity, 154; constraints, 21; declarations, 184; development, 26, 153, 156, 237; directives, 17; formulation and decisions/development, 106, 108; general policy-formulation level, 121; policy-generating, 152; generation, 151; processes, 158; Policy Guidance Notes (PGN), 94, 264; impact, 154; issues, 23, 25–7, 118, 224, 257; level, 33, 151, 156, 262; concerns, 25, 31; senior, 262; needs, 26; policy-makers, 9, 47, 49, 54, 156–7, 161, 181, 189, 195, 224; senior, 262; policy-making, 26, 61, 121, 124, 157, 160, 257; authority, 131; committees, 157; level, 170, 262; units, 162; policy managers, 73; policy-planning, 19, 123; observations, 162; orientation, 26; policy-oriented, 162; reviews, 165; systems, 36; unit, 157; poverty-focused, 80; project, 142
poor, poorer, poorest people/strata/sections/groups of the population, help for the, 4, 19, 75–6, 79–80, 86–7, 89–90, 101, 108, 119, 165, 178–9, 200, 203, 258; distribution of benefits to the, 259; effects of aid on the, 179; improvement of the conditions of the, 165; poor social strata, 171; worst-off, 166
population, 228–9; activities, 229; dynamics, 229; education, 229;

INDEX

integration of, in development planning, 238; policies, formulation, implementation and evaluation of, 229; programmes, 228; sector, 243

poverty, 61, 80, 86, 200; elimination of, 62; focus, 119; impact and effectiveness of aid on, 63; target groups, 100; the ODA's poverty-focus policy, 76, 82

poverty alleviation, 15, 18–19, 22, 25, 80, 150, 155, 168, 178–9; effect of aid on, 28, 179; impact of aid on, 27

poverty orientation (of aid), 165–7, 200; efforts to make the Danish aid programme genuinely poverty-oriented, 100–1; general, of Danish aid, 119; lack of, 118; Norwegian aid should be poverty-oriented, 166

priorities (*see also* country), 22, 175, 177, 259–60; priority countries, 169, 173, 180–4, 194, 203, 229; aid to the, 182; criteria set for the selection of, 184; economic and demographic, 229; distribution of aid between the, 184; total aid programme to each of the nine, 182

private enterprises, 168, 171; Norwegian, 204

problems, 66, 141–2, 144–5, 155, 195, 218, 231, 234, 270; aid implementation, 123; co-operation, 203; development, 113, 150, 215, 218; Swedish research on, 218; environmental, 92; evaluation, 268; management, 162; methodological, 62; of aid, 142; of food aid, 75; operational, 227; 'pipeline problems', 143; population, 228; problem areas, 203, 218; projects, 142; sectors, 75; problem-solving, 48; procedural, 125
(aid) procedure, 123–4, 127, 175, 200, 211, 220, 231, 241, 246, 259; administrative, 253; Basic Principles, 262; cover-note, 252; formulation of evaluation, 123; harmonisation and simplification of, 246; harmonisation of, for operational activities, 234; internal feedback, 124; internal ODA, 95; office, 95, 253, 264; procedural problems, 125; step-by-step, 241

process, 142–3, 221, 223, 227, 232, 256; development, 146, 268; dynamic, self-reinforcing (or self-destroying), 142; fluid, overlapping and ambiguous, 224; of co-operation, 215; of preparation, 238; planning, 190; policy-generation, 158; 'process' approach, 89; project-design, 232; structural change, historical dimension of, 145; unnecessary interventions in self-regulating, 134

programme (*see also* aid programmes *and* country programmes), 7, 16–17, 19, 24, 26, 43, 54–5, 71, 74, 80–1, 87, 93–7, 107, 116, 128, 131, 150, 153–4, 157, 159, 171, 186–7, 189–90, 196, 199–200, 203, 208, 210–14, 219, 221, 229–30, 233–4, 236–8, 242–5, 248, 251–3, 256–9, 264; bilateral, 116; cross-sectoral, 27; design and implementation of, 106; development-assistance, 17; donor's 42; effects of, 127; employment, 136; evaluation of, 87; improvement in the quality of the, 246; management of the 249; multi-bi, 116; preparation of, 241; operational, in developing countries, 229; population, 228; programme aid, 18, 74, 82, 167, 187; areas requiring external assistance, 203, 230; countries of the SIDA, 210; cycle, 7, 233; programme-delivery staff, 56; morale, 56; development, 229; evaluations, 52, 55–6, 212, 237–8; evaluation model, 56; Programme Evaluation Organisation (The Netherlands), 149; implementation, 236; officers, 32, 212, 220, 222, 239; performance, 107; personnel/staff, 57, 233, 237–8, 245; planning, 24; success, 42; unit of the UNFPA, 236–7; independence of the, 237; programming, 63, 102, 125, 146, 227; cycle, 229; system, 228–9; research and evaluation, 160; sector, 18, 27; sectoral or area-oriented, 18; selection of, for evaluation, 259; UNFPA-assisted, 241

progress, 234; control, 145; project-progress reports, 234; reports, 212, 215–17, 238; unit, 231

projects (*see also* multi-bi aid *and* planning), 6–7, 17, 19, 24, 26–7, 41, 49, 55, 71, 74, 79–81, 84–97, 103–4, 106–10, 113, 115–19, 121–2, 128,

289

131–2, 134, 136–7, 140–1, 143–5, 151–5, 157, 159, 164, 171, 173, 186–7, 189–90, 192, 195–6, 198–200, 202–3, 210–17, 219–22, 228–30, 233–9, 241–5, 248–9, 251–61, 263–5, 270–1; agricultural, 136; assessment of the efficiency, effectiveness, impact and sustainability of, 25; basic selection of, 256; British aid project, 76; capital phase of the, 90; country, 229, 233; decision on, 199; design and implementation of, 106; development, 5, 16; Dutch (-financed), 151–2; field staff, officers, 122, 152; formulation, implementation and administration of, 115; future operation and development of the, 110; health, 136; inception of, 270; industrial-development, 100, 221; Integrated Rural Development Project, Mpika, Zambia, 89; inter-country, 229, 233; internal rate of return of, 118; investment, 130; polarisation effect of, 144; local, authorities, 39, 122; long-gestation, multi-component, 94; medium-to-large-scale, 84; micro-level of the, 142, 144; 'model', 132; (project) monitoring of, 203, 212; multi-bi, 116, 197; multi-purpose, 135; national, sponsor, 137, 139; performance potential of the, 137; new, 28, 143, 242, 263; NORAD-financed, 199; ongoing, 241; evaluation of, 82, 85, 87, 114–15, 117, 153, 156, 231, 242, 246, 255; over-dimensioned, endowment, 141; overlapping, 219; past evaluations of, 262; performance and effectiveness of UNFPA-assisted, 230; problems, 142; project accounts, 113; activities, 42, 118, 140, 214–15, 220, 222; (traditional), aid, 18, 27, 159, 167, 187, 257; applications, 130; appraisal, 92, 108, 253–4; number of, 215; ODA Manual of, 93; technical, economic and social, 251; techniques, 92–3, 251; approval, 12, 244; area, 270; authorities, 270; project-beneficiary aspects, 63; benefits, 134; completion, 255; project-completion reports (PCRs), 12, 84, 90–1, 93–4, 254–6, 261;

cycle, 6–7, 91, 118–19, 132–3, 136, 163, 196, 212, 253; project-cycle approach, 154; design, 232–4, 243; needs for the revision of the, 234; description, 110; effectiveness, 41, 93, 255; effects, 104, 110; environment, 141, 220; evaluations: internal, 237; multi-bi, 117; (individual) one-off, 78, 119, 261; framework/system/approach/matrix, 72, 74, 88–9, 91–2, 252, 255, 259, 264, 267, 270; formulation, 229, 233, 243, 246, 253–4; formulation and appraisal system/stages, 91, 93, 123, 254; funds, 130; Project Guidelines, Evaluation, 126; implementation, 77, 110, 137, 141, 234, 243, 254; delays, 119; procedures for, 117; responsibility for, 243; schedules, 119; in developing countries, evaluations of, 152; in one and the same sector, 134; in the medical or technical field, 155; inputs, definition of, 138; level, 27, 62, 93, 151–2, 156, 258; project's life, beginning of the, 256; project's (ultimate) impact, 94, 106, 110, 137; management, 23, 53, 71, 86, 117, 170, 198, 213, 234–5, 244; financial and manpower capacity of the national, 141; definition of, 235; usefulness of evaluation for the, 231; managers, 92, 132, 234, 245; objectives, 18, 170, 222; of the same type, 134; outcome and impact, 85; outputs, 111, 118; definition of, 138; planning, 96, 137, 141; planners, 92; stage, 63; 'target-group-oriented project-planning' (ZOPP), 138; policy, 142; performance, 62, 106–7, 110, 115, 132, 222; interpretation of the, 119; planned, of the, 238; quality of the, 140; preparation, 110, 116; project-selection process, 92; proposal, 133, 230; purpose, 270; reports, 140; progress reports (PPRs), 234–6; reviews, 104, 114–16, 198; Tripartite Project Reviews (TPRs), 235–6; Final TPRs, 235; sites, 240; specifications, 141; staff/personnel, 32, 71, 160, 163, 212, 245; qualifications of the German, 141; qualification level of the, 137; submission, 252, 254, 264; success,

290

INDEX

42; supervision, 93; with measurable outputs, 86; relevance of the objectives of, 25; repeated, extensions, 132; research, 160; results of the, 104, 138, 214; negative results, 140; road, 248, 265; rural-development, 258; selection of, to be evaluated, 30, 75, 94, 259; sustainability of, 91; tied-aid, 115; tied loan/grant (investment), 115; trade-promotion, 136; turnkey, solutions, 118; type of, 243; untied-aid, 115; untied-grant (technical assistance, 115

quality, 220, 225, 244, 246, 256, 261; assessment of, 221; of aid, 262; of an evaluation system, 220

rate of return, 86; acceptable, 118; internal, 101, 118; rate of return evaluation, 84; realised, 86; realised, *ex post*, social, 86; realised, internal, 270
recipients/recipient countries (*see also* developing countries), 2, 10, 14, 16, 19, 21–3, 26–7, 31–2, 35–6, 39, 41–50, 53–4, 56, 62, 65–7, 87–8, 110–11, 120–2, 125, 144–5, 166–7, 169, 172–6, 178, 180–5, 188–9, 191–6, 198–201, 203–4, 212, 220, 223, 263, 266, 268, 270; administrative planning and aid-implementing set-up of the, 175; administrative set-up and research milieux of the, 176; administrative system of the, 184; (political) authorities of the, 19, 32, 37, 42, 44, 47, 120–1, 163, 173, 175, 191, 194, 196, 215, 223, 225; managerial capacity of the, 224; civil service(s) of the, 44, 49, 176; consultants, 192, 204; development of the, 204; development plans and priorities of the, 167; development policy of the, 173; development policy and performance of the, 102; experts, 192; inefficient administration in the, 200; integration in recipients' development plans or policies, 179–80; involvement of the public administrations of the, 45; involvement of the, in evaluation work, 89, 176; monitoring and evaluation capacity of the, 107; nationals of the, 195; new, 167; (main), of bilateral aid, 26, 102; of Dutch bilateral aid, 157; of Norwegian aid, 166; of Norwegian multilateral ODA, 173; recipient conditions of culture and politics, 63; recipient countries' academics, 45; capacity in evaluation, 51, 125, 176; competence in evaluation, 51, 176; consultancy firms, 45; participants (in evaluation teams), 29; representatives, 125; self-reliance, 229; recipient governments/administrations, 41–2, 115, 120, 167, 194, 204, 219, 223, 246; own evaluation units, 122; recipient orientation, 194; systems, 17, 39, 48, 184; research institutes, 192; research milieux, consultancy firms and administrators of the, 191; role of, 223; staff of the Dutch embassies in the, 152; total aid engagement to a, 173; universities, 192
redundancy, 220; built-in, 220; 'redundancy of functions', 220, 225; 'redundancy of parts', 220
reporting, 4, 7, 56, 141, 145, 159–60, 163–4, 236, 245; annual reporting, 120; effort, magnitude of, 215; evaluation reporting, 231; local, 160; of evaluation units, 108; (standardised), procedure, 214; project reporting, 255; simple, standardised, sheets, 65; systems, 93, 233; systematic, 214; two-track, system, 199
reports (*see also* evaluation reports *and* projects), 24, 152–3, 156–8, 160, 162, 176, 197, 203, 215, 218, 233, 240, 245, 259, 262–3, 266; by the NGOs, 155; DANIDA's annual, 120; draft, on programmes or projects, 245; draft outline of the final, 239; follow-up, 214; monitoring and evaluation, 25; monitoring, on project status, 24; periodical (bi-annual), on evaluation results, 231; project-completion reports (PCRs), 12; regional, 240; report-writing, 240; research, 218; true joint, 240; World Bank, 157
research (*see also* co-operation), 11, 51, 103, 112, 134, 159–61, 163, 174, 177–8, 198, 200, 218, 229; capacity,

291

223; growth of, 210; commissioned, 191; community, 162; competence, 174; co-operation, 209; criteria of scientific, 127; evaluation, 55, 128; evaluation and research unit, 186; funds, administration of, 105; in developing countries, 203; institutes, 6, 35–6, 51, 150, 191–2; independent, 191; Norwegian, 184; 191–3; milieux, 31, 51, 174, 180–1, 191; liaison with Norwegian, 174; national, 194; multi-disciplinary and inter-disciplinary, efforts, 51; operations, 51; product and development, 106; programme on women in development, 181; programmes, targeted, 191; projects, 160; related to human rights, 203; reports, 218; research and consultancy communities, 68–9; research and evaluation programme, 160; research side, 164; results, 210; scientific, 176; social-science development, 103; studies, 243; support, 203; value-neutral, 54; work, 267; workers, 265
researchers, vii, 54, 69, 126, 131, 139, 159, 174, 189, 198, 211, 216, 218, 223; academic, 160; external, independent, 29; from the recipient country, 44; Third World, 203
resident representatives, 10, 23, 35, 37, 169, 184, 190–1, 193, 199, 203
resource persons, 29, 44, 110, 125, 152
resources, 51, 87, 93, 97, 104, 111, 117, 122, 164, 175, 177–8, 197–8, 249, 259–60; allocation of, 34, 54, 114, 127; control of the use of, 133; distribution of, to the various recipients and sectors, 34; distribution of the additional, 144; evaluation, 75, 265; financial, 174, 177; internal competition for, 217; local, 141; natural, 208; need to optimise scarce, 259; overall, availability, 143; over-supply of, 143; resource input, 173; responsible administration of natural, 165; scarcity of, 260; constraints related to, 260; sectors, 34; UNFPA's allocation of, 229; Western-oriented, 258
review, 3, 6–7, 27, 44, 63, 93, 104, 115, 194, 199, 202, 217, 221–2, 225, 249, 255; activity, 197; annual, 33, 198,
219, 224; country review (CR), 236; donor-imposed, 56; external, unit, 151; internal, 197–8; major, 198; meeting, 236; mid-term, 7, 33, 93; minor, 219; Norwegian aid, 202; of effective aid organisation, 209; of Swedish aid, 209; policy, 165; project, 104, 197; review needs, 24; review reports, 94, 113; sector, 219; systematic, 24
Riddell, Roger, 24, 86, 89–90, 267
roads, 265, 270; gravel-top, 265

Scandinavians, 258; countries, 11, 31, 37, 39, 45
scoring, 90; process, 89, systems, 89, 96; techniques, 79
sector, 17, 24, 30, 34, 38, 40, 84, 88, 94, 132, 134–5, 172, 187–8, 201–3, 216, 230, 253–4, 260, 263–4, 268; assessment of the projects by, 142; bureau, 217; capitalised, 143; education and training, 88; evaluations, 115, 117, 203; of aid within certain, 108; of land-based, fishery-support activities, 116; multi-sector aid, 188; non-capitalised, 143; population, 243; population-related, 238; population-related, of the country, 44; private, 10, 14, 87, 139, 202–3; private-sector economic interests, 20; problem, 75; programmes, 18, 27, 160, 219; public, 50, 139, 202; reference, 263; reviews, 219; sector/sectoral: aid, 26, 74, 87; composition, 119; division, 199, 215; Sector Manuals, 94, 266; Sector Planning Manual, 264; syntheses, 78, 82, 84; sectoral and planning issues, 125; synthesis by, 264; voluntary, 79
security, 30; sectoral offices, 37, 190; 'security/safety clause', 193, 204
self-evaluation, 27, 30, 63, 233–4, 244; built-in, 232; system, 232; continuous, 74
self-regulation, 144–6; improvement of, 146; mechanisms of, 142, 145–6
social justice, 15, 171, 178, 181; effects of aid on, 179
spending: aid, 1, 35, 113, 170; department, 249; government, 112
Sri Lanka, 183, 202; Ceynor Development Project, 202
staff/staffing, 244, 248, 259, 263; family-

INDEX

planning service, 238; field, 237; in-house, 249, 260; internal, 120; internal, seminars, 264; limited availability of local, 243; need for and availability of local, 243; operational-agency, 265; out-house, 249; programme, 232, 238; staff-resource constraints, 232; staff-training courses/sessions/ programme, 37, 40, 95, 245; technical, 237
stakeholders, 2, 14, 20, 22, 32, 35–7, 39, 46, 48–50, 52–7; host-country, 41; outside, 49; potential, on the donor side, 35; stakeholder group, 57; Third World, 51
State Auditor, 6, 13, 50, 109, 118–20, 124, 164, 199–200; State Auditor's Office, 113–14, 126
strategy, 14–15, 21, 24, 49, 164–5, 172, 177, 181, 186–7, 191, 197, 200, 243; adequacy of the, 238; basic-needs, 15; development, 138; development of technical, 241; for evaluation, 172, 181, 192; industrialisation and trade, 165; international, 229; possible, for dealing with population problems, 228; strategic considerations on aid to specific countries and regions, 105; decisions, 225; plan for DANIDA, 121; planning, 105; welfare, 165
structure, 249; administrative, 164; structural adjustment, 15, 157, 159; imbalances, 143; loans, 21; programme, 18
success, 27, 44, 72, 85–6, 88–9, 91–2, 114, 118, 131–2, 134, 137–8, 239, 251–2, 258, 262, 265, 267, 270; global, 138; project and programme, 42, 73; success stories, 258
supervision, 53, 129–30; supervising process, 102
sustainability, 24–5, 28, 82, 85, 87, 90–1, 94, 107, 117, 159, 179, 244, 251; impact, 102
Sweden, 3, 12–13, 15, 23, 25, 27, 31–2, 37, 66, 199, 208–9; evaluation policy and performance of, 208; Import Promotion Office for Products from Developing Countries (IMPOD), 209; Ministry of Foreign Affairs, 12, 192, 209–10, 224–5; National Audit Board, 26, 210, 224; Public Enquiry on Development Co-operation, 206; Swedish Agency for International Technical and Economic Co-operation (BITS), 209–10; Swedish Agency for Research Co-operation with Developing Countries (SAREC), Swedish aid, 209–10; agencies' use of consultants, 26; effectiveness of, 56; major recipients of, 26; 'management' of, 218; organisations, 208; Swedish development aid/assistance, 208; organisation of, 225; Swedish Fund for Industrial Co-operation with Developing Countries (SWEDFUND), 209–10; review of the objectives and organisation of the, 209

Swedish International Development Authority (SIDA), 12, 26, 37, 40, 44, 66, 208–15, 218–19, 221, 223–4, 256; assistance programme, 219; board, 215; budget, 217; budget for bilateral assistance, 217; delivery system of the, 26; diversity of the SIDA's activities, 216; evaluation, 221, 223; activities, 214, 222, 224; policies of the, 210; Evaluation Reports, 215–16, 218; system of the, 212, 220; chaotic nature of the, 217; (special) unit of the, 26, 212–15, 217, 224; unit's plan of operation, 213, 215; Guidelines for Project Support, 212; interactions with external organisations, 218; job descriptions in the, 213; overall evaluation effort in the, 224; policies, 223; present and future co-operation, 213; programme officers, 212–16; daily workload of, 213; projects and programmes, 213, 218, 221; industrial-development projects in Tanzania, 221–2; 'Project and Programme Follow-up', 214; project staff, 215; role of, 224; staff/personnel in the, 213, 224; administrative, 213; state of the SIDA's programme in each country, 215; successive re-organisations of the, 224
system (*see also* aid systems), 220–1, 230, 242, 259, 263; adaptive, self-regulating, 219; components of the, 234; donor-imposed, 246; open, 219; simple, 246; system design, 219, 224; development, 246; the system's adaptiveness, 219;

293

properties, 220; synthesised computer, 265

Tanzania, 87, 182–3, 202, 204, 221–2; ODA-funded Songea–Makambako road in, 90; Tanzania Institute of Development Management, 204; UNFPA-supported programme in, 237
targets, 72, 168; for (Danish) evaluations, 115; target groups, 4, 39, 105, 108, 117, 119, 137, 141, 167, 179, 189, 270; definition of, 119; effects of aid on, 179; for Norwegian aid, 171, 179; living conditions of the, 141; poor, 166; target 'value', 215; volume targets, 168
Task Force on Concessional Flows, vii, 24, 69, 77, 96
technical assistance, 64, 103, 187–8, 192; advice, 94; advisors, 248, 255, 263, 265, 268; equipment, 130, 137, 141; experts/specialists (see also experts), 243; officer, 30, 92, 239, 260; projects, 138; skills, 260; staff, 233, 237; units, 236
technology, 137, 209, 221; appropriate, 155; choice of, 203; technology transfers, 203; measures, 130; traditional, 80, 258; western-type, 80
terms of reference (TOR), 20, 25, 30, 42, 44, 102, 108–10, 113, 119, 139, 152–3, 160–2, 164, 178–9, 184, 193–5, 199, 201–2, 204, 214, 221, 223–4, 238–9, 241, 256; formulation of evaluation mandates (terms of reference), 175, 239; TOR manual, 180
themes, 24, 117; evaluation theme, 173; thematic evaluations, issues, 116
Third World, 36, 52–3, 66, 131, 144, 165, 171, 181, 191, 193; authorities, 43; consultants, 45, 192; countries, 155; development, 201; development problems, 154; experts, 192; genuine, consultancy firms, 197; governments, 40–1, 43, 45, 56, 199; Norwegian exports to the, 181; Norwegian investments in the, 181; participation in evaluations, 44; partners, 31, 41; people from the, 267; relations with the, 35; research milieux, 196–7; researchers, 197; trade with and investments in the, 185, 188, 196, 203–4

tied aid, 20, 115–16, 258; bilateral, 116; Danish, 100, 102, 105; evaluation of, 115; to Egypt, 104; projects, 115
timing, 4, 6, 8, 53
trade, 80, 258; trade-promotion projects, 136
training, 88, 92, 95, 118, 1345, 209, 229, 232, 243, 245, 264, 266; briefing/training sessions, 245; evaluation of, 88; evaluation, sessions, 265; in design and evaluation of programmes and projects, 242, 245; international, programmes, 209; needs, 243; of family-planning service staff, 237; regional, activities, 232; seminars, 266; workshops, 254, 267
transparency, 131
Trone, Kerstin, x, 17, 39, 227
Tunisia, 210; programme country of the SIDA, 210; recipient of Swedish aid, 210

United Kingdom (UK), 2, 11–13, 20, 23, 27, 30–1, 38, 71–2, 74–5, 76–8, 112, 199, 254, 266; Aid and Trade Provision (ATP), 75, 80, 82, 93–4; aid policy, objectives of, 79; Cabinet Office/Treasury Financial Unit (FMU), 72–3; Department of Trade, 258; Financial Management Initiative (FMI), 72–3; Foreign Office, 258; government, 73; House of Commons Committee of Public Accounts, 74–5, 82–3, 85; House of Commons Foreign Affairs Committee, 76, 84, 88, 91, 93, 267; Independent Group on British Aid (IGBA), 76, 82–4, 91, 93, 266; Institute of Development Studies, University of Sussex, 79; Joint Management Unit (JMU), 73
Overseas Development Administration (ODA), 3, 25–7, 30–1, 35, 38, 40, 44–5, 72–9, 81–97, 249, 251–7, 260–8, 270; activities, 74, 76, 81, 255; aid to improve the prospects of success, 270; aid policy, 79–81; aid programme, 88; coverage, 263; Development Divisions, 260, 268; Economic Department, 251; effectiveness of the ODA's aid operations, 75, 80; evaluations, 97, 261, 266; evaluation activity, 74, 76, 81; Evaluation Department of the, 3, 11–13, 30–1, 38, 67, 75–6,

294

INDEX

81–5, 93, 249–55, 259–61, 263–6, 271; constraints on the, 260; functional departments/divisions, 12, 83–4, 250, 253, 258; geographical departments, 83–4, 250, 253, 256; evaluation of the ODA's poverty-focus policy, 76; evaluation procedures, 76, 91; reports, 75–7; ODA's (own growing stock of), 91, 263, 266–7; results, 74–5, 96; system, 97, 251, 266; teams, 266; evaluation-training sessions, 74; work/activity, 76–8, 88–9, 267; evaluators, 92; Geographical Department of the, 254; geographical desks, 260; geographical-desk officers, 263, 265; Guidelines to Evaluators, 85–6, 91; Internal Audit Unit, 82; Joint Funding Scheme, 79; management-information system (MIS) of the, 40, 265; Manual of Project Appraisal, 93; monitoring system in the, 90, 225; organisation of evaluation in the, 81; objectives, 82; own evaluation, 77, 85–6; performance as an aid donor, 96–7; project-completion reports (PCR), 12, 84, 90–1, 93–4, 254–6; project-framework matrix, 270; Projects and Evaluation Committee (PEC), 12, 38, 81–4, 93–5, 249–53, 260–2, 264, 267; absorptive capacity of the, 260; PEC system, 262; procedure of focusing on action-oriented recommendations, 262; Sector Planning Manual, 264; staff, 263; structure, 249; (chief) technical advisers, 84, 95, 225–6, 263; Training Division, 264–5
Overseas Development Institute (ODI), 76, 267; Parliamentary Select Committee on Aid, 75; Treasury, 267
United Nations, 17, 68, 228; agencies, 40, 67, 71, 185, 202, 242; assistance, 228; evaluation system, 77; evaluation systems used by, 77; General Assembly, 228, 232; Glossary, 53; organisations, 60; effectiveness of, 77, 117; Secretary-General, 42; UN system, 5, 17, 40, 42, 45, 52, 136, 173, 181–2, 186, 202, 228, 230–1, 234, 246; development efforts of the, 192; Joint Inspection Unit (JIU), 42–3, 52–3, 56, 77, 186, 202, 227–8, 231–2; overall evaluation of the, 227
United Nations Development Programme (UNDP), 61, 181, 229, 234
United Nations Educational, Cultural and Scientific Organisation (UNESCO), 5, 68, 149–50, 229
United Nations Food and Agriculture Organisation (FAO), 68, 77, 229, 237
United Nations (Fund for) Population (Activities) Fund (UNFPA), 3, 17, 30, 38–40, 44–6, 181, 227–33, 235–6, 239–41, 243–5; budget, 236; Central Evaluation Branch, 232, 235–6; development of evaluation in the, 246; evaluation policy, 227; unit, 236; role of the, in the, 236; field offices/staff, 239–40, 242; Governing Council of the, 230–2, 241–2, 245; Internal Evaluation Report form (IER), 234; performance of the, 227; Policy and Evaluation Division, 236; programme and technical people/staff at the, 240, 242; Programme Committee (PC), 240; programme, technical and field staff of the, 241; staff from the, 245; Technical and Evaluation Division, 236; UNFPA's evaluation system, 244; programme, 229; programming system, 229, 232; quality aspects of the programme, 236; staff, 240
United States Agency for International Development (USAID), 5, 26, 40, 53, 60, 65, 77, 95, 136, 150, 257, 262, 265; evaluation division in the, 254
universities, 36, 112, 139, 193, 198, 218; students at, 218; teaching and research programmes, 198; University of East Anglia, Overseas Development Group, 267; University of Sussex, Institute of Development Studies, 267; university research institutes, 54, 191–2
untied (grant) aid, 115, 167; bilateral, 119; grants, 100, 118; projects, 115

values, 49–50, 54, 57, 211; judgements, 127, 134, 143; policy-type, 27, 258; Net Present Value, 252; social values, 54; target 'value', 215; value-pluralism, 52; value

295

statements, 216

water (*see also* drinking water), 188, 200, 264; water project, 216; water-supply programmes, 188
women, 4, 18, 24, 87, 117, 165–6, 171, 179–80, 203, 239; as a target group, 167; as active participants in development, 119; concern for, 178; effects on, 234; evaluations of the effects of aid for, 180; impact (of aid) on, 85; improvement in the position of, 155; participation of, 80; research programme on, in development, 181; role of, 25, 82, 159, 241, 251; in aid projects, 117; situation/position of, 28, 159; vocational-training programme for, 18; women's concerns, 238; integration of, in the programmes, 229; women's dimension in UNFPA-assisted programmes, 241; women in development, 188, 203–4; women's main interest in development, 119; women projects, 188

work (*see also* evaluations): programme for independent, in-depth evaluations, 237; work flow, 250

World Bank, vii, 5, 17–18, 24, 27, 40, 50, 53, 61, 65, 69, 77, 83–4, 86, 89, 95, 136, 157, 181, 249, 263, 265, 267; evaluations, 42; evaluation system of the, 77; IRDP project in Noakhali (Bangladesh), 159; Operations Evaluation Department, 249, 268

World Health Organisation (WHO), 136, 229, 237

Zambia, 87, 182–3, 202, 204, 216
Zimbabwe, 180, 183–4, 202; Commodity Import Programme (CIP), 204

Notes on Contributors

Basil E. Cracknell is an Evaluation Consultant, formerly the Head of the Evaluation Department of the Overseas Development Administration, London. He was, for several years, the Chairman of the OECD DAC Expert Group on Evaluation. His publications include *The Evaluation of Aid Projects and Programmes* (ed.), ODA, London 1984.

Kim Forss is a Development Consultant. His main publication is *Planning and Evaluation in Aid Organizations* (PhD thesis, the Commercial University, Stockholm 1985).

Enno W. Hommes is Professor, Technology Development Group, University of Twente (University for Technical and Social Sciences), Enschede, the Netherlands.

Helge Kjekshus is Special Adviser for Research and Evaluation with the Ministry of Foreign Affairs, Oslo, Norway. He was for several years Head of the Division for Evaluation and Research in NORAD and, later, in the Ministry of Development Cooperation and a member of the OECD DAC Expert Group on Evaluation from its inception. Among his publications are *Aid and Development. Some Tanzanian Experiences* (with Samuel S. Mushi) (NUPI 1982) and *Ecology Control and Economic Development in East African History* (Heinemann 1977).

Stefan A. Musto is Director, Department for European Studies, German Development Institute, Berlin. He was the Convenor of the EADI Working Group on European Development, and a member of the EADI Executive Committee. He has published several books, including *Endogenous Development: A Myth or a Path?* (ed.) (EADI, 1985).

Henrik Schaumburg-Müller is an Associate Professor, Institute of International Economics and Management, Copenhagen School of Economics and Business Administration, Copenhagen.

Olav Stokke is Senior Research Fellow at the Norwegian Institute of International Affairs. He is the Convenor of the EADI Working Group on Aid, and was for several periods a member of the EADI Executive Committee. His more than a dozen books include volumes on Norwegian and Swedish aid and Third World policies. His recent publications include two volumes on *European Development Assistance* (ed.) (EADI 1984), *Trade and Development* (ed.) (EADI 1988) and *Western Middle Powers and Global Poverty* (ed.) (Scandinavian Institute of African Studies 1989).

Kerstin Trone is Deputy Chief, Technical and Evaluation Division, and Chief, Evaluation Branch, UNFPA.